AMERICAN INDIANS IN THE MARKETPLACE

DEVELOPMENT OF WESTERN RESOURCES

The Development of Western Resources is an interdisciplinary series focusing on the use and misuse of resources in the American West. Written for a broad readership of humanists, social scientists, and resource specialists, the books in this series emphasize both historical and contemporary perspectives as they explore the interplay between resource exploitation and economic, social, and political experiences.

John G. Clark, University of Kansas, Founding Editor
Hal K. Rothman, University of Nevada, Las Vegas, Series Editor

AMERICAN INDIANS IN THE MARKETPLACE

Persistence and Innovation
Among the Menominees and
Metlakatlans, 1870–1920

Brian C. Hosmer

 University Press of Kansas

Published by the University Press of Kansas (Lawrence, Kansas 66049), which was
organized by the Kansas Board of Regents and is operated and funded by Emporia State
University, Fort Hays State University, Kansas State University, Pittsburg State University,
the University of Kansas, and Wichita State University.

Library of Congress Cataloging-in-Publication Data

Hosmer, Brian C., 1960–
    American Indians in the marketplace : persistence and innovation
among the Menominees and Metlakatlans, 1870–1920 / Brian C.
Hosmer.
        p.   cm. — (Development of western resources)
        Includes bibliographical references and index.
        ISBN 0-7006-0983-0 (alk. paper)
        1. Menominee Indians—Economic conditions. 2. Menominee Indians—
Cultural assimilation. 3. Tsimshian Indians—Economic conditions.
4. Tsimshian Indians—Cultural assimilation. 5. Metlakatla
(Alaska)—Economic conditions. I. Title. II. Series.
E99.M44H64   1999
330'.089'973—dc21   99-16179

British Library Cataloguing in Publication Data is available.

Printed in the United States of America
10 9 8 7 6 5 4 3 2 1

The paper used in this publication meets the minimum requirements of the American
National Standard for Permanence of Paper for Printed Library Materials Z39.48-1984.

To my parents, who showed me the way,
and to my wife and daughter, who remind me
that the journey itself is what is important.

Contents

Illustrations

Preface

This book explores intersections between cultural identity and economic change. It advances what seems to me to be the rather commonsensical proposition that Indian people could understand the workings of the capitalist market system and at least attempt some constructive adaptations. In exploring this subject over the past decade, it has gradually occurred to me that Indians' "problem" with the market was not so much that they were somehow mystified by this economic and cultural phenomenon as understandably concerned about its implications. They understood that market capitalism encouraged and rewarded individualistic, entrepreneurial values, along with modes of behavior that tended to separate persons from their community. Perceiving these influences as corrosive to fundamental values that preserved, sometimes even renewed, community and identity, some Indians, Menominees and Tsimshians in this study, explored means to conform economic change to their needs. In the process, influences proved "reciprocal" in the sense that economic change effected cultural values while the latter informed a people's adjustment to the former.

My argument, that market capitalism presented Indian communities with tremendous challenges, often proving destructive to political, economic, and cultural independence, is scarcely novel. I hope that it contributes to an ongoing conversation that owes much to the work of Richard White. Like many ethnohistorians who labored in graduate school during the 1980s and 1990s, I was captivated by *The Roots of Dependency* and its adaptation of world-systems theories to American Indian history. White's book, and others well known and not so well known, guided me down that path of wondering about the influence of market capitalism on so-called pre-market peoples. Like many, I have come to the conclusion that while economics certainly is not everything, or does not explain everything, it is a lot, or explains much. I am persuaded by, among others, Immanuel Wallerstein, who argues that from its origins in western Europe of the fifteenth and sixteenth centuries, market capitalism has proven an extraordinarily powerful, and remarkably adaptive, phenomenon. For those peoples across the globe who organized their societies and economies differently, the introduction of capitalist modes of thinking and behavior—often through the "vector" of trade goods—constituted a crisis in meaning with the broadest of cultural implications.

Indians certainly recognized this peril and fought a losing battle, so White argued years ago, to forestall its most serious consequences. This is the familiar dependency paradigm, refined and amplified as it has been.

While acknowledging considerable debts to more creative scholars, my study nevertheless attempts a somewhat different construction. I suggest that as Indian peoples gravitated toward the market, some attempted to reshape its operations so as to be less destructive to cultural values on the one hand and productive of political and economic independence on the other. Some Menominees and Metlakatla Tsimshians apparently recognized that "the market" was not going anywhere, that this was the way the wider world had come to operate. This mandated accommodations with the market, for isolation surely meant poverty and lay their peoples and communities open to the forces of assimilation. The struggle, of course, was how to generate jobs and profits without dividing individuals from one another, thereby accelerating the very process they hoped to avoid. In what was a delicate balancing act, Menominees and Metlakatlans engaged the market in a complex dialogue, as it were, and attempted to forge accommodations with it. Difficult certainly, not successful according to all measures, but as a process it illustrates the ability of Indians to rationally perceive changing realities and attempt adaptations that protected their homes and values. To my thinking, what emerges from this study is less a story of assimilation versus resistance than a presentation of Indians as thinking human beings who, while they lacked the means to shape policies or the broad operations of the economic market, nevertheless could, and did, make any number of "local" decisions that affected their own lives.

As with any such project, mine demonstrates the power of collaboration, and I certainly owe debts beyond my ability to repay. During my protracted stay at the University of Texas, Austin, Jack Sunder served not only as dissertation adviser but as mentor and friend as well. I have benefited, certainly, from his exhaustive knowledge of literature on American Indian history but perhaps more from his good humor, gentle guidance, and willingness to allow me to chart my own course. I was his final doctoral graduate in what was a long career and can only hope that my presence rewarded his patience—and did not drive him into retirement.

Others at UT also played important roles in the germination of this project, and in my slow maturation as a scholar. To George Wright, now vice president at the University of Texas at Arlington, I say "thanks, friend," for your sage advice, timely encouragement, and friendship. John Lamphear lent his support and advice as well, and my exposure, through him, to African history added considerable methodological depth to this study. My wife and I also have fond memories of evenings spent on the

Lamphears' beautiful property in Leander, Texas. I am particularly proud of my association with Lewis L. Gould, among the most distinguished historians in UT's long line of such notables. Although I performed poorly in Dr. Gould's historiography seminar during my initial semester in graduate school, he still was willing to help with my dissertation, and I benefited from his legendary energy and commitment to training graduate students. Barbara Brower, a cultural geographer now at Portland State University, joined the team comparatively late, following another committee member's illness. I deeply appreciate her willingness to help me out of a bind; more important, the project was tremendously improved by the inclusion of her scholarly perspectives. Thanks also to graduate school colleagues Jim Marten, now of Marquette University; Debbie and Alan Cottrell; and Pat Goines. Finally, I would like to express my deep appreciation to numerous friends and colleagues at UT and in Austin, that gem of the Hill Country and among my favorite places on earth.

As important as graduate school was to the germination of this project, people and experiences away from UT deserve considerable credit for assisting its transformation into the book presented here. From its earliest stages, David Rich Lewis of Utah State University and Fred Hoxie, now history chair at the University of Illinois–Champagne-Urbana, generously offered their time and advice. Their comments proved particularly helpful, as did those offered by R. David Edmunds of the University of Texas, Dallas. Very special thanks go to my close friend David LaVere, whose ability to pare down complex concepts to their essence always impresses me, and to Theda Perdue, Michael D. Green, Denny Smith, Carolyn Johnston, and the rest of my colleagues at Perdue and Green's 1995 NEH Summer Seminar. I think I learned more about ethnohistory methods in the space of those six weeks than in all my years in graduate school. Jay Miller lent me his time and expertise when I asked, as did Peter Iverson and Richard White. Michael Harkin of the University of Wyoming's Department of Anthropology offered advice and clarification regarding Northwest Coast cultures, and David Beck of NAES College in Chicago helped me with Menominee concepts and reservation contacts. Colleen O'Neill flattered me by ordering, and actually reading, my dissertation and still asked me to participate in a terrific session at a meeting of the Western History Association. Other thanks go to Jim Ducker of the Alaska Historical Society, Steve Haycox from the University of Alaska, and Markku Henriksson of Tampere University in Finland. To those I have forgotten to mention, I am truly sorry.

This book would not have been possible without the generous help of native peoples in various communities, and I hope they find the final product useful, or at least interesting. On the Menominee reservation, a special thanks to Larry Waukau, Marshall Pecore, David Grignon, Jerilynn

Grignon, Verna Fowler, and tribal chairman Apesanahkwat. Larry was particularly patient as I repeatedly bothered him with questions, in person and over the phone. As President of Menominee Tribal Enterprises, he has a business to run, and I certainly interrupted several of his days. David Grignon, the tribe's Director of Historic Preservation, was equally generous with his time and particularly helpful in securing copies of photographs.

In Metlakatla, Alaska, my most profound gratitude goes out to the family of the late Russell Hayward. Mr. Hayward was a wealth of information on the history of Metlakatla, and I am particularly proud to have had the opportunity to spend a few wonderful days listening to him. To his wife, Cecilia, and his many children and grandchildren, my deepest appreciation. LaVerne Welcome took me on a wonderful tour of William Duncan's residence, now a museum. Arnold Booth spoke with me about Metlakatla history, as did Beverly Guthrie, Secretary of the Annette Island Reserve Council. My visit to Metlakatla was wonderful indeed.

Members of the community of Metlakatla, British Columbia, were at least as kind and hospitable. On a cloudy day during the summer of 1995 I had a delicious meal of freshly smoked salmon, dried seaweed, and rice topped with *oolichan* grease and felt transformed in place and time. Later that afternoon, Joyce and Elvin Leask offered their time and experiences. To band manager Frances Reese, councillors Sharon Morvin and Carol Beynon, and youth coordinator David Nelson, my deepest appreciation for a wonderful experience.

While I was in Prince Rupert, British Columbia, Susan Marsden of the Museum of Northern British Columbia offered her time and expertise and facilitated contacts. I consider her a valued colleague and friend. Paula Lawson of the Tsimshian Tribal Council guided me through the Clah Papers and produced photocopies. Jennifer Davies and Cliff Armstrong of the Anglican Diocese of Caledonia guided me through their archives, and I enjoyed sharing hot tea and conversation with them. My thanks as well to Helen Clifton of Hartley Bay, British Columbia, and Irene Shields, Dorothy M. Denny Utterberg, Pat Williams, and Sharon Seierup of the Saxman (Alaska) Tlingit community.

Archivists and librarians, of course, are essential to the completion of any scholarly project. Like many, I owe a debt of gratitude to John Aubrey, who showed me around the Newberry Library's wonderful collections, and to his associates, who cheerfully met my requests for materials and photocopies. While in Chicago, I visited the local branch of the National Archives, where Kellee Green, Archivist at that time, made my visit productive and enjoyable. Likewise, Mary Frances Morrow, Reference Librarian at the National Archives in Washington, D.C., guided me through the first of what turned out to be many excursions and at one point even allowed me to walk through restricted stacks in what was a successful quest for some particularly hard to find documents. Since that time, many archivists, librarians, and pages have facilitated my research in Washington. At the National Archives–Alaska Pacific Branch in Anchorage, Bruce Parham and Diana Kodiak were particularly helpful, both in 1995 when I spent a few weeks there and more recently when they tracked down photographs. I also benefited from the assistance of Richard Collins and his several associates at the National Archives of Canada in Ottawa, who filled several microfilm orders, as did Judith Hudson Beattie, Keeper of the Hudson's Bay Company Archives in Winnipeg. Andy Kraushaar, Reference Archivist with the State Historical Society of Wisconsin, found and delivered several Menominee photographs. Finally, my deepest thanks to librarians, archivists, and interlibrary loan assistants at the University of Texas, State University of New York–Oswego, the University of Delaware, and the University of Wyoming. Special thanks here to the University of Wyoming's Tamsen Hert.

My sincere gratitude to those institutions that financed portions of this project and, perhaps more important, offered me gainful employment. While in graduate school, I benefited from a Dora Bonham Research Grant and an award from the National Society of the Colonial Dames of America. I received two separate grants from the Newberry Library in Chicago which introduced me to that institution's wonderful holdings, pleasant surroundings, and helpful staff. The University of Delaware honored me with a substantial award from their General University Research Grant fund, which made possible my archival and field work in Alaska and northern British Columbia. The University of Helsinki, Finland, financed the initial presentation of what became my thesis. Finally, I received a Faculty Growth Award from the Alumni Association at the University of Wyoming, which financed a visit to the Menominee reservation, and my department and college permitted me to take a semester away from teaching in order to complete revisions. The College of Arts and Sciences also underwrote the reproduction of photographs.

I would be remiss if I failed to offer my appreciation to those who have hired me and guided my career thus far. Dave King and Doug Deal led the group that offered me my first academic job, and I owe a great debt to them and the entire faculty at the State University of New York, Oswego. David Allmendinger chaired the search committee that brought me to the University of Delaware. David remains among my most trusted advisers, and I feel a considerable attachment to him and to Delaware colleagues Guy and Suzanne Alchon, Ann Boylan, Peter Kolchin, George Basalla, Jim Curtis, John Montano, Arwen Mohun, and David Pong in the history department and Tom Rocek and Karen Rosenberg in anthropology. Colleagues at the University of Wyoming offered me my first tenure-track position and have been steadfastly supportive of my work. Thanks to colleagues Adrian Bantjes, Bruce Dain, Eric Kohler, William Howard (Bud) Moore, Dan Peris, Mark Potter, Phil Roberts, Ron Schultz, and Kris Utterback and secretaries Sharon Brown and Arlene Mascarenas.

One never fully appreciates how much work is involved in an undertaking like this, and how much you must rely upon the enthusiasm of others. Nancy Scott Jackson, Acquisitions Editor of the University Press of Kansas, believed in this project, and her support has meant a great deal to me. I thank Hal Rothman for forwarding my manuscript to Nancy and appreciate the hard work of Susan Schott and Rebecca Giusti for shepherding the production. My brother, Barry J. Hosmer, graciously offered to draw the maps, and my father, William A. Hosmer, produced the book jacket photo. This is rather appropriate, for in addition to his skills as a photographer, my dad is a very accomplished amateur historian. My thanks as well to graduate students Jurgita Saltanaviciute, who looked over footnote citations, and to Dan Cobb, who has challenged me to work harder. I also owe a tremendous debt to all my students, undergraduate and graduate, at every institution where I have had the pleasure of working. I do love teaching and find that I benefit tremendously from our association. Best of luck to you all.

As is customary in essays such as this, I reserve my most important expressions of gratitude for last. This is in part because I don't know how I can possibly express the depth of my appreciation to my family. My parents, William and Iris Hosmer, instilled in their children a love of learning and never wavered in their support for my chosen path in life—even as it has taken a lot longer than they anticipated. My dad, in particular, has frequently reminded me that doing what you love is everything. I cherish that advice and admire the man who offers it. To my sister, Jennifer, and my brother, Barry, thanks also for your consistent support and your willingness to offer the kinds of help that only family members can provide. I am blessed to have been born into such a loving family.

At the core of this growing family lie my wife, Victoria Murphy, and our daughter Megan Marie Hosmer. Victoria has suffered through my repeated absences—some physical, many psychological—our drifting from place to place in search of a secure academic appointment, missed and forgotten holidays, and hardships of all manner. She is the love of my life, and my most honest critic. A cliché certainly, but I could not have made it without her support and that of her parents, Ann and the greatly missed Colonel Meredith Murphy. Our daughter, Megan, has demonstrated to us both that work is not everything, that perspective matters, that the reason I do what I do is to have a positive effect on my tiny corner of the world, and that there is always time for Megan to play at daddy's "doop-doop" (computer).

Introduction

In the September 1912 edition of the *Red Man*, a periodical published by the Carlisle Indian School, there appeared an article entitled "The Menominee Indians Working Their Way." Its author was Angus S. Nicholson, superintendent of the Menominee Agency, a reservation located in northeastern Wisconsin, some fifty miles northwest of Green Bay. In the article, Nicholson made a rather remarkable claim. "To-day," he reported, the Menominees "are, as a whole, a busy and prosperous tribe—strong, healthy, vigorous, and hustling for their daily bread in other ways than that of the chase," their condition so improved that, in this instance, "the solution to the Indian problem . . . can be fairly said to be in sight."[1]

On its face, Nicholson's boast may seem less than startling—after all, for more than a century politicians, philanthropists, churchmen, and government officials had made a practice of boldly suggesting solutions to the Indian problem and equally bravely predicting that one program or another would achieve the desired end sooner rather than later. But the Menominee situation was different. On their reservation, far away from the tragic glory of the Plains battlefields and the failing experiment in allotment, improvement in the Indians' living condition was coming from an unlikely source: industrial labor. In 1908, and at a cost of just over $1 million (withdrawn from the Menominee tribal funds), the federal government constructed a modern sawmill and lumber finishing plant at a new settlement named Neopit. This project, so Nicholson reported, was intended to "insure to the tribe an additional profit in the sale of lumber . . . and at the same time . . . establish a school of industry which would become a source of steady employment."[2]

Nicholson contended that the mill exerted a profound effect on Menominee life. With both mill and town "humming with life," visitors could be treated to the sight of "modern houses constructed with proper regard to light and air conditions for health," and a large mill with a capacity of 50,000,000 feet of lumber yearly." Neopit also stood at the terminus of "a logging railroad in operation for the movement of logs to the mill" and boasted of electric lights, streets "laid out," and lots "platted." All of these improvements, as well as funding for schools, a reservation hospital, and aid to the destitute came from logging profits. So pronounced was the change that by 1912 just 100 of the 1,700 Menominees still drew federal rations.[3]

At the center of Menominee economic development stood the mill complex where, according to Nicholson's calculations, nearly 40 percent of able-bodied Menominee males found work. It was Indians, then, who participated in "all the many varied parts of the lumber industry," including furnishing "the major portion of the common labor that is necessary in every large work."[4] And, as laborers, they approached their work with unabashed gusto. Witness the description of a particularly dangerous phase of the work:

> In driving logs on the stream the Indian comes into his own, delighting in danger, skipping from log to log, tossing and tumbling in the turbulent waters as they slip downstream to the mill. Peavy and canthook his weapon, with horse and chain as an auxiliary reserve defense, he dislodges with a yell and a shout, cheer and cry, logs that have been grounded and threaten to jam; he races his fellow Indian, out-striving, out-doing each other in friendly rivalry, and when, in their work, one drops into the icy waters, they good-heartedly jibe each other on the mishap. But when the logs land, as they sometimes do, and a jam piles up, log upon log by hundreds, and the necessity arrives for one of them to go out on this shifting, restless mass to pry or cut the key logs loose, watch the careful yet apparently careless steps of everyone, yet in readiness to protect and save the man out on the jam, who has virtually taken his life in his hands.[5]

So adept were some of the workers that Nicholson proudly announced that the best could "command skilled workman's wages any place."[6]

For Nicholson, then, Menominee improvement was something to behold, especially when one considered how much the tribe had changed in the space of just two generations. "Sixty years ago a blanket Indian," he noted, but "to-day his children and grandchildren receiving education, taught manual work, and, in large measure, to be self-supporting. Is this not a record of which to be proud? Has not the Menominee reason to carry his head high among his fellow tribesmen?"[7]

Less than a decade earlier, a writer named George T. B. Davis offered another example of the beneficial effects of labor on Indians. In this case the inspiring story came from New Metlakahtla (now spelled "Metlakatla"), a model community located on Annette Island, Alaska, approximately 100 miles northwest of Fort Simpson, British Columbia, and 15 miles south of the logging and mining town of Ketchikan, Alaska. New Metlakatla was the brainchild of William Duncan, lay Anglican missionary to the Tsimshians.[8] From 1857 until his death in 1918, Duncan devoted his life to creating an independent and self-sustaining society among those who chose to follow him and his vision.

And what a vision it was. Arriving by sea, Davis observed "a quiet, peaceful village, set like a jewel between the blue sea and the purple mountains," a sight that filled him "with amazement and awe," causing him to exclaim, "Fifty years ago savages and today this!"[9] At New Metlakatla, the 800 Indians, under Duncan's direction, had constructed a modern town, with houses "on the average considerably finer than in an American village" of similar size, most being "mainly two stories in height, plentifully supplied with windows and usually a large veranda," and bordered with sidewalks, "wide and well built."[10] In addition to houses, New Metlakatla boasted a schoolhouse, a town hall, a boarding school, and a large church capable of seating 800 worshipers. This church, complete with "handsome pews," "ornamental pulpit," and a painting of the "Angels of Bethlehem above the pulpit," was entirely the handiwork of the Indians and, as the largest in Alaska, "has fitly been called 'The Westminster of the Indians.'"[11]

As impressive as these accomplishments no doubt were, even more significant was the town's commitment to labor and industry. Indeed, it was the success of Metlakatla's enterprises, chiefly salmon canning and lumber manufacturing, that made other improvements possible. As to the former, Davis reported that, over the course of the previous season, the operation produced some 800,000 cans of salmon of such high quality that, he suggested, "if any of our readers wish a good can of salmon and at the same time a souvenir from Metlakahtla let them ask their grocer for salmon put up by 'The Metlakahtla Industrial Company.'" Most impressively, all the work, from catching the fish to shipping the finished product, was accomplished by Indians. The sawmill likewise employed a goodly number of able-bodied males, and income generated from these businesses helped support several mercantile establishments, all but one operated by Indians. Together, the cannery, mill, store, and homes presented a picture of a prosperous community on a par with any new town of like size.[12]

Overseeing all of this was Duncan. As schoolteacher, pastor of the church, "advisor and counselor of his people," and manager of the cannery, sawmill, and store, as well as "the natural resort of anyone in trouble or difficulty," Duncan was truly the dominant figure in the community, the architect of the remarkable success story. Yet he did not accomplish this alone. The Indians, who displayed "energy and natural talents" that were nothing short of "amazing," provided the backbone for change, often working two jobs to earn extra money. As Davis observed:

Going to the native stores on several occasions I found them locked, until I discovered that the proprietors worked at the cannery or saw-mill during the day and opened their shops after a hasty supper in the evening. [T]he village photographer, Benjamin A. Haldene [*sic*], does not hesitate to work in the cannery when it is running and looks after his picture-making and developing after or before working hours.[13]

In addition to his other interests, Haldane was an accomplished pianist, organist (he played the pipe organ in the church), and leader of the celebrated Metlakatla brass band. His impressive achievements were matched by those of other Metlakatlans who demonstrated skill in, among other things, blacksmithing, silversmithing, wood carving, and basket weaving. All of these products were either used in the community or sold abroad. With these accomplishments in mind, no wonder that earlier one writer acclaimed Duncan as "the Alaskan Pearl Seeker" and praised the community as a success "with no parallel in the world."[14]

What was happening at the Menominee Reservation and New Metlakatla? At the very least, it seems fair to say that, during a period when most Indians were facing the prospects of deepening poverty, some enjoyed comparative prosperity, perhaps even independence, through what might be considered "economic development." The question is, How did this come about, and at what cost? One answer, of course, is to conclude that these were cases of cultural "assimilation" pure and simple. That, faced with the demands of a rapidly changing world and prodded along by particularly forceful "outsiders," certain Menominees and Tsimshians parted ways with so-called traditional ways to cast their lot with the white man and capitalism. The resulting prosperity, then, can be considered as evidence for the superiority of Anglo culture and maybe even for the essential incompatibility of native and Western concepts of resource use, labor, and socioeconomic arrangements.

But was it as simple as all that? If so, what does this say about prevailing conceptualizations of cultural change—formulations which, in general, suggest that cultural change is an exceedingly complex process and one usually accompanied by a substantial, often fatal, disintegration of social, political, and economic structures? Moreover, can anecdotal evidence of apparently successful adjustment to Western economic patterns truly be interpreted, at face value, as proof of attenuation of cultural values and a concomitant alteration in cultural identity? Perhaps, but there also is considerable evidence to suggest something more complex and varied, where change and persistence engaged in a dialogue that proved transforming in and of itself. If so, can the resulting mix inform our understanding of processes of cultural change, and in this case the impact of Western economic structures on supposedly "traditional" societies?

This study seeks to examine economic development among the Menominees and Metlakatlans from the last decades of the nineteenth century through the first twenty years of the new century. It has as its focus efforts by these two groups to incorporate new elements, in particular market capitalism, into their cultural lives. My approach is broadly ethnohistorical in that I seek to combine the historian's interest in narrative over time with the social scientist's emphasis on analytical theory. More the former than the latter, more historical than theoretical, this work proceeds from a simple question, namely, can so-called traditional societies make significant adjustments in one sphere of cultural life (in this case economics) while still maintaining a sense of discrete identity? In considering this question, it also will be a goal of this study to situate Indians at the center of the narrative, understanding Menominees and Tsimshians as "actors" in their own affairs, even if the documentary evidence does not always present them as such. Phrased more directly, did Menominees "choose" to become loggers and mill workers? If so, why? Why did certain Tsimshians decide to accompany William Duncan to Metlakatla and agree to take on salmon packing and other industrial tasks? What was in it for them? More ambitiously, can we proceed so far as to suggest that those Menominees and Metlakatlans who embraced these new economic relationships did so in order to maintain a degree of independence through economic modernization? If so, what can that tell us about Menominee and Tsimshian cultures, or about that complex dance between change and continuity that all peoples undertake but that is, seemingly, beyond the grasp of historical American Indians?

As students of recent ethnohistory will know, this study builds on the works of others who have labored to understand the nature and consequences of contact between European and Native American societies. During the period covered in this study, the prevailing idea, indeed, the virtual engine that drove policy making, was the notion that the assimilation of Indians into white society was inevitable and ultimately desirable; that Indians had to either become like whites or disappear altogether.[15] In essence, either choice involved "demise" of one sort or another. Resistance meant physical death; assimilation meant the end of distinctive Indian cultures.

What is remarkable, of course, is the consistency in thinking among policy makers regarding the inevitable end of distinctive Indian cultural identities, even as individuals could hold differing opinions on the morality of any particular course of action. Some, it is true, were honestly dismayed by the notion of the "vanishing Indian," while others believed that Indian cultures were essentially valueless relics of an earlier stage in human development. These views proceeded from, and in turn provided a foundation for, the belief in the superiority of western European cultures and their inevitable spread across the globe.[16]

Victorian era anthropologists articulated these ideas in an especially forceful manner. For E. B. Tylor, Lewis Henry Morgan, and most of their contemporaries, human culture was an organic entity that, over time, "evolved" through various stages, eventually reaching its most exalted expression—western European culture. "Cultural evolutionists," therefore, favored a hierarchical ranking of peoples, with "savagery" occupying the lowest stage, followed by "barbarism" and then "civilization." Understanding history as progress, they concluded that all cultures evolved in a universal, "unilinear" fashion. Hence, while Morgan in particular was dismayed by the passing of Indian lifeways, he remained convinced that cultural change was inevitable, that it resulted from the natural operations of history and environment.[17]

Despite the advances in the understanding of cultures that followed the extensive fieldwork of Franz Boas and his students, unilinear models of cultural change persisted until well into the twentieth century. In part this was the result of "salvage" anthropologists' overriding interest in documenting or, if necessary, reconstructing what they believed were "traditional" lifeways before they disappeared. Even so, Boasian cultural pluralism did have the effect of undermining both evolutionary history and older manifestations of the comparative method, and in doing so it paved the way for subsequent efforts at constructing a theory of cultural change. These efforts bore fruit in the 1930s with development of what commonly has been known as "acculturation" or "cultural diffusion" theory.[18]

Acculturation theory, most closely associated with the works of Ralph Linton, Robert Redfield, and Edward Spicer, seeks to understand the consequences of cultural contact by measuring the degree to which one or both societies adopt elements from the other. Acculturation theorists also attempted to sketch models of what Linton called the "process of culture transfer," by which they hoped to account for the great variability observed in contact situations. While proponents of this formulation offered somewhat different interpretations, acculturation theories generally posit an asymmetrical relationship between Western and non-Western cultures whereby prolonged contact inevitably resulted in a blurring of distinctions between human societies. In this sense, acculturation amounts to a documentation of the process by which non-Western peoples, and cultures, lose their distinctive identities and are assimilated into the mainstream.[19]

While acculturation theory marked a significant advance beyond the unilinear constructs, it too suffers from some rather persistent weaknesses. First of all, like nineteenth-century evolutionary theories, it is ethnocentric. By suggesting that contact between Western and non-Western cultures invariably leads to the disappearance of the latter—the "less-developed"—acculturation theory, like unilinear theories, implicitly places non-Western cultures at a lower "stage" in the worldwide evolution of cultures. This overtly deterministic reading of culture change also tends to discount the long-term viability of cultural adaptation short of assimilation or of wholesale resistance to change. In either case, acculturation theory suggests that alternative responses are ultimately unsuccessful, and often no more than way stations on the way to more thorough assimilation.[20]

Acculturation theory suffers as well from a tendency to ignore the complexity of culture and the role of individuals in shaping their cultural lives. As the anthropologist Loretta Fowler has pointed out, advocates of this formulation tend to assign "degrees of acculturation (that is, the extent to which people have lost Indian culture and accepted a white-oriented way of life) . . . according to arbitrarily selected cultural traits." In this process, "the meaning of particular behaviors may be interpreted from the ethnographer's perspective—he or she assigns the meaning, not native peoples themselves." In this formula, then, "individuals also are assigned arbitrarily to a place on the acculturation continuum; for example, an individual's participation in a native ceremony may be ignored in favor of his participation in Christian rites, and, on this basis, the individual is assigned to a transitional or white-oriented category." As a consequence of concentrating on certain "traits," outside of the overall cultural context, Fowler argues that these "'culture' traits are inappropriate measures of change or of assimilation." It may be, as she suggests, that "people change their behavior and develop new interests and concerns in response to new opportunities and challenges," and that "culturally appropriate roles" may in fact be related to a whole variety of social and cultural processes unseen or ignored by observers.[21] Phrased differently, critics of acculturation theory argue that it discounts the natives' role as "actors" in their own lives, too often describing native peoples as passive, as acted upon, as little more than pawns in the unfolding of larger historical forces.[22] In this sense, acculturation theory largely documents what whites "did" to Indians, not how Indians responded.

Nevertheless, acculturation theory has proven highly influential over the long term, and not just among anthropologists, sociologists, and historians. In economics, acculturation theory has a "cousin" in modernization, or convergence, theory. Closely associated with Walt W. Rostow,[23] modernization theory initially was advanced to explain the impact of the Western capitalist nation-state system on the underdeveloped world, particularly as it related to problems associated with Third World development. As explained in a recent article, modernization theory "postulates a growing similarity between developing and developed nations as an inevitable outcome of economic advancement." Consequently, "as lesser developed societies expand and diversify their economies, they will increasingly resemble more highly industrialized nations in other facets of their social organization—the 'melting pot' on a global scale."[24] Like acculturation theory, then, modernization theory argues for the inevitability of assimilation, its only real difference being that it isolates economics as the central mechanism for promoting culture change—or culture loss as the case may be.

During the twentieth century, the combination of acculturation and modernization theories often has provided the basis for formulating federal Indian policies—termination certainly, but even the Indian New Deal and more recent efforts at stimulating reservation economic development. By suggesting that prior to white contact Indian cultures were backward and poverty-stricken, policy makers, humanitarians, and scholars press for modernization by concluding that the tribes' condition will improve only as they become more closely incorporated into the larger social and economic mainstream. Conversely, poverty and underdevelopment among Indians is blamed on the persistence of so-called traditional social and economic structures. These archaic and outdated structures, it is argued, inhibit development and condemn Indians to a marginal existence.[25]

Yet for all its influence, modernization theory has been roundly criticized, often on the same basic grounds as acculturation. For instance, by "ranking" societies according to Western values, with Western capitalist nation-states occupying the top position, modernization theory, like the acculturation paradigm, is profoundly ethnocentric and highly deterministic. Consequently, it tends to discount the possibility that some societies might choose to combine aspects of traditional and modern economic practices. In a related sense, modernization, again like acculturation theory, consigns Indians and other non-Western peoples to an essentially passive role. It is the developed world, especially the powerful capitalist "world system," that provides the initiative for change; the developing world, and Indian tribes, are, in a sense, "acted upon."[26]

Beyond these theoretical weaknesses, both acculturation and modernization theories have faltered in predicting the varied outcomes of cultural contact. Throughout the Third World, efforts at modernization/acculturation often have failed to produce Western-oriented economic and social structures. As even a cursory examination reveals, peoples across the globe routinely reject Western modes of behavior, even after prolonged pressure to change. In North America, Indians have not disappeared but have steadfastly resisted assimilation, often against staggering odds. The United States experience strongly suggests that, despite the application of "modernizing" programs, Indian poverty and underdevelopment have persisted, even worsened. Ample evidence supports similar conclusions for Canada, the Third World, and other modern nation-states.[27] These problems, in the words of one writer, "instigated a theoretical crisis, causing one anthropologist to question 'our earlier expectations concerning the rate of American Indian acculturation and why full acculturation to White American ways of life is not occurring on the contemporary American scene.'"[28]

Out of a general frustration with modernization/acculturation formulations, then, scholars of the late 1950s and into the 1960s attempted to devise new models for explaining culture change. These new constructs sought to come to grips with the persistence, and deepening, of poverty across much of the underdeveloped world. They also sought to rectify the earlier theories' tendency to neglect the role of social and political conflict, including patterns of domination and subjugation, in defining the relationship between modern and traditional societies. What resulted were a series of models emphasizing "uneven development," constructs more commonly identified as "dependency" or "world-systems" theories.[29]

Influenced by Marxian interest in modes of production as a key analytical construct, theorists such as André Gunder Frank and Immanuel Wallerstein[30] seek to explain uneven development as the consequence of an essentially asymmetrical relationship among developed nation-states and less developed regions.[31] Proponents argue that the unequal relationship is the direct result of the dominance of the system of world capitalism whose main feature is the drive to expand and accumulate capital. As the developed nation-states expand, they lay claim to resources taken from less developed regions, resources that not only fuel their continued development but also set the stage for more entrenched patterns of domination and subordination. This is partly so because, either through overt conquest of territory or through unequal trade relationships, lesser developed regions tend to realize few benefits from the export of these vital resources. Ultimately, this all works to the advantage of the developed "poles" and leads to the subordination of the underdeveloped "peripheries." As the sociologist Thomas Hall explains, "the extraction of resources from these [peripheral] regions not only blocks development, but causes changes which retard development."[32] Among these changes is increasing poverty on the periphery, itself the consequence of resource extraction and the decline of old methods of self-sufficiency as fringe regions become economically dependent on both the extraction of resources and the labor provided by those industries.[33] Poverty works to deepen the uneven relationship between periphery and core to the point where peripheral regions become, in effect, economic "satellites" of the developed "metropoles" of western Europe and North America. This system, in turn, has led to what Frank termed the "development of underdevelopment" in Latin America and elsewhere in the less developed world.[34] As explained by sociologist C. Matthew Snipp, "the satellite-metropolis relationship not only fosters underdevelopment in the satellite; the growing impoverishment of the satellite also forces it to become increasingly *dependent* upon the metropolis, especially for economic assistance."[35] In this sense, then, underdevelopment is less the lack of development than the result of an inherently unequal economic relationship.[36]

Inquiries based on this premise have proliferated, spawning even more subtle analytical structures and such useful additions as "regions of refuge" and "internal colonies." In the former, isolating factors, like geography or the absence of marketable resources, may provide temporal and psychic "space" where subject groups may effect significant adjustments, holding off incorporation for a time. The concept of "internal colony" suggests that the mechanics of uneven development also apply to less developed regions located within particular nation-states. According to Snipp, "internal colonies . . . are created when one area dominates another to the extent that it channels the flow of resources from the periphery to the dominant core area." Hence, the same patterns of domination and subjugation found between developed and underdeveloped nation-states are created when one region, the internal colony, is exploited for the benefit of another.[37]

While we associate theories of uneven development with the effort to analyze the conditions in the Third World,[38] they also have attracted scholars seeking alternative models to account for the continuing plight of North American minorities. Here the internal colony model has proven enticing, particularly for those seeking an explanation for enduring poverty on Indian reservations. Joseph Jorgensen, for instance, contends that the history of Indian-white federal relations has been a series of administrative attempts to civilize reservation Indians by integrating their economies into the mainstream capitalist structure.[39] The result, however, has been not modernization but the deepening, indeed institutionalization, of underdevelopment, where policies invite further exploitation while providing few opportunities for Indians to exercise control over their economic lives. The end result is a state of "domestic dependency," a special form of internal colonization found in the United States. He argues further that, since the 1880s, dependency has worsened as the federal government, particularly the Bureau of Indian Affairs (BIA), perpetuated the tribes' subordinate status by enforcing a maze of restrictive regulations while actively promoting the alienation of Indian land and resources. In a similar fashion, programs (such as boarding schools) that were created on the assumption that traditional tribal life was the cause of Indian poverty succeeded only in damaging Indian families and societies while failing to dismantle the "so-called restrictive backward influence of tribal life." This argument considers the BIA, as an agent of the interests of the larger economic and political mainstream, to be responsible for domestic Indian dependency.[40]

Jorgensen's analysis has proven influential, but it is not immune from several nagging problems. As applied to the North American experience, world-systems theories generally lack evidence to support the contention that Indian labor, either on farms or in factories, was a significant factor in the development of American capitalism. Here the constructs' historical and regional specificity creates a mismatch when applied to circumstances in North America. Rather, it is the Indians' land that interested whites. According to Cardell Jacobson, Indians historically have been relegated to "an economics of uselessness," not prized as a source of cheap labor. This evaluation is supported by H. Craig Miner's thesis that in Indian Territory it was the Indians' land and resources, not their labor, that were prized by American corporations.[41]

More generally, this theoretical model seems unable to account for the great variation in impacts of the developed world system on underdeveloped regions. Most formulations simply posit that sustained contact results in core, periphery, and the intermediate stage of "semiperiphery," the last being an important, but not so well outlined, concept. Yet evidence suggests a whole range of outcomes. While some societies are destroyed, others are absorbed (or assimilated), and still others are "frozen" at a certain level of development or transformed into different types of social and economic units (such as "peasant" societies), to name just a few of the conceivable responses. This weakness, it is argued, derives from two main sources. First, as an attempt to create an overarching theory of historical forces, dependency too often pays scant attention to local circumstances such as indigenous forms of social organization and related cultural factors. Second, by emphasizing the centrality of this dichotomous relationship between periphery and core, dependency often becomes an overly static, perhaps even "deterministic," model that is insufficiently flexible to account for a whole variety of possible end points. Together, these deficiencies tend to discount the role of indigenous peoples as actors in their own affairs. In this sense, the discourse resembles the acculturation/modernization approach, but as its reverse image. Just as older theories of cultural change posit the inevitable assimilation of indigenous peoples into the mainstream society, dependency suggests that contact between discrete groups invariably results in the "development of underdevelopment."[42] Therefore, dependency, while ostensibly an effort at considering the "other side" of the contact equation, often amounts to an analysis of white domination of Indians, not of how Indians reacted to challenging situations.

In a related sense, dependency (like earlier theories) also has been criticized for implying that, prior to white contact, indigenous societies existed in a state of equilibrium, that somewhere in the distant past traditional societies functioned in an environment of near stasis. Nothing can be further from the truth. As a number of scholars have pointed out, so-called traditional societies are themselves the result of generations of development and change as new circumstances mandated adjustments. For example, many, if not most, "tribes" familiar to us today are the consequence of smaller societal units coming together as dictated by choice or necessity.[43] Again, by emphasizing the degree to which white contact disrupted traditional societies, dependency theorists discount the historical fact that non-Western peoples, like peoples everywhere, have always adapted to the world around them.

Despite these problems, world-systems theories remain vital constructs. At the very least, they focus attention on the global expansion of the capitalist world system and offer a systematic description of the ways in which these interactions shape development and underdevelopment. Furthermore, by promoting a stable framework to facilitate comparison between societies and contact situations, world-systems theories recommend a coherent, although admittedly controversial, explanation for the persistence of poverty and underdevelopment among many of the world's indigenous populations. Finally, and particularly relevant to this study, this model has stimulated a real interest in studying the economic aspects of Indian life, focusing attention on aboriginal economic behavior as well as the impact of capitalism on Indian life. Here we dismantle the notion that Indian economic activity was limited to the fur trade and occasional wage labor, thereby opening our minds and eyes to new avenues for inquiry.[44]

Perhaps the most celebrated application of these concepts to the American Indian situation is Richard White's book *The Roots of Dependency: Subsistence, Environment, and Social Change Among the Choctaws, Pawnees, and Navajos*. Published in 1983, White's study remains a testament to the utility of dependency formulations and has spawned a growing body of related inquiries, which this study aspires to join. Throughout *Roots of Dependency,* White demonstrates that the breakdown of traditional means of subsistence was at least partially related to the drive to bring Indian resources and labor into the market. Economic change is recognized as a critical factor in producing dependency, but it is not the only factor. Indians, so White argues, found market relations so "threatening" that they "resisted them, with temporary success for generations." By suggesting as well that "culture here controlled economics," White calls upon scholars to understand cultural change as the consequence not solely of economics but of the "reciprocal influences of culture, politics, economics, and environment." If the result was dependency, then, the causes were rather complex.[45]

Other ethnohistorians have employed similar formulations with notable success. Daniel Boxberger and Arthur McEvoy trace the decline of Indian fishing and self-sufficiency in the Pacific Northwest to the intrusion of white commercial fishing. David Rich Lewis has produced an original discussion of the role played by agrarian policies in driving three western groups into dependency, and William Cronon argues that dependence on goods obtained through the fur trade worked to the disadvantage of New England Indians by making them a party to the ecological degradation that eventually stripped them of the ability to meet their subsistence needs. Also, while he is critical of some of the shortcomings of dependency, most notably its failure to consider indigenous forms of social organization, Eric Wolf has offered a compelling analysis of the impact of Euro-American social, political, and economic institutions on non-Western peoples, Africans as well as Indians.[46]

Besides these full-length studies, other scholars have worked to address the shortcomings of dependency by offering important refinements. Thomas Hall, Duane Champagne, and C. Matthew Snipp have endeavored to modify earlier formulations by suggesting new ways to account for the variability of contact experiences. Taken together, these newer formulations place more emphasis on indigenous social, cultural, and economic institutions and seek to link certain "types" of reactions with specific societal characteristics.[47] More recently, Hall and Christopher Chase-Dunn have pursued a useful collaboration in which they seek to broaden, and indeed vitalize, the discussion. By investigating the spatial dimensions of world systems, considering whether and how such systems "transform" themselves, or are "transformed" by circumstances, and inquiring into the relationship between modes of accumulation and the rise, fall, and "pulsations" of world systems, they have added much to the ongoing conversation.[48] While it may be argued that these studies often have the collateral effect of weakening the comprehensive nature of the original dependency formulations, they do offer substantial promise for greater understanding of the mechanics of social change as future empirical studies add to the storehouse of information.

At one level, the present study is designed to add to this storehouse. Like the contributors to *Native Americans and Wage Labor: Ethnohistorical Perspectives*, edited by Alice Littlefield and Martha C. Knack,[49] I am interested in offering insights into the linkage between economic "modernization" and cultural change. To do so, I intend to draw upon basic dependency constructs as well as revisions to that theory that are most applicable to my work. One of the principal aims throughout this study will be to suggest that, in these two cases, the introduction of market capitalism did not produce wholesale "assimilation" in the sense that old modes of social and cultural life were forever abandoned. Rather, this work seeks to provide evidence to support the notion that Indian cultures had and have the power, indeed the flexibility, to adapt to market capitalism, and in a way that stops short of outright disintegration or loss of a sense of cultural distinctiveness. In effect, I intend to suggest that certain Menominees and Tsimshians of Metlakatla found ways to "redefine" aspects of their cultural life to incorporate nontraditional elements.

In presenting "redefinition" as a useful concept, this book also draws upon the work of Loretta Fowler, who, in her studies of the Northern Arapahoes and Gros Ventres, asks the question, "Did progress, in the officials' sense, inevitably lead to culture loss?" Influenced by groundbreaking studies of Marshall Sahlins and Clifford Geertz, Fowler seeks to emphasize the role of Indians as significant actors in the processes of cultural adaptation.[50] In the process of confronting new situations, Fowler argues, "[m]eanings [of traditions, culture, etc.] are altered in the light of new concerns and new aspirations drawn from new events, relationships, and circumstances. These symbols are invented, discarded, and reinterpreted as they are adapted to new social realities. A community's view of itself and its past is reconstructed and new symbols of identity emerge in the light of new social, ecological, and psychological conditions."[51]

If, as Richard White wrote at a later date, "life was not all a business,"[52] Fowler's approach helps us recognize the importance of that interplay between internal cultural institutions and the larger context of relations between whites and Indians. Just as significantly, it highlights the central role of Indians in analyzing changed circumstances and constructing satisfying responses that have their basis in familiar modes of behavior. Ethnohistorians Morris W. Foster, Melissa L. Meyer, and Daniel K. Richter guide us further down this path by emphasizing the centrality of cultural identity to behavior, even as we recognize that modes of reckoning "identity" can change over time.[53] This is an important point, for as we come to accept the notion that cultural identity can be fluid, we also must guard against the assumption that what is happening is nothing more than stubborn resistance to change, or "cultural persistence," as it is sometimes termed. Fowler herself addresses this issue and suggests that studies which focus on resistance to change "may, in the end, promote stereotypes about 'real' Indians," while obscuring the historical fact that cultures constantly adapt to new situations. In her words, such studies that emphasize cultural persistence tend to "characterize 'real' Indians as unable to adapt in constructive ways to their changing circumstances." As a consequence, "success and survival become un-Indian."[54] More recently, one Navajo man made a similar point. "Traditional Navajo values," he told an interviewer, "do not include poverty."[55]

The danger of an overly "romantic" view of the continuity between past and present is emphasized by Rolfe Knight. In his groundbreaking study of Indian labor in British Columbia, Knight contends that:

> there were a number of businesses in which Indians worked, as wage workers or as contract laborers, which only the most unregenerate romantic can dismiss as traditional. Some may wish to see Indian labor in logging as akin to stalking the forest primeval, and may find no major difference between the occasional tree falling in aboriginal times and the mass of horses, skids, spring boards, steam donkeys, cable, bull blocks, etc., used in commercial logging. In fact, there was very little similarity between indigenous woodworking and the demands and skills of commercial logging.[56]

So, instead of interpreting cultural adaptation as a "damning comment on the 'depths' to which native peoples have been forced," Knight advocates giving "those earlier generations [of Indians] credit for being something more than mere pawns responding to the acculturation pressures of Euro-Canadian society. They recognized, better than many romantics today, that no solution existed in a return to a mythical golden age, even if that were possible."[57] Adaptation to market forces, then, was no easy task. It involved significant dislocations and sacrifices, challenges not all were equipped to meet. But the fact that some did represents a significant, if seldom studied, aspect of the history of the native peoples of North America. And, to repeat, it will constitute a major theme developed by this study.

A last point needs to be made, and it involves choices. Why concentrate on these two examples? At the outset it is important to note that the situations on the Menominee Reservation and at New Metlakatla are different in some important ways. First of all, unlike Menominee, the operation at Metlakatla often was dominated by William Duncan. Moreover, while economic self-sufficiency was an integral part of Duncan's operation, the Metlakatla "system" was an all-encompassing project that sought to create a Christian community resembling the small, self-contained villages of Duncan's home in Victorian England. By contrast, while governmental regulations, programs, and BIA administrators dominated much of social, political, and economic life on the Menominee reservation, the program of assimilation was not so all-encompassing, at least on the surface.

Also unlike the Menominee agency, Metlakatla was not a "reservation" as we generally understand the term. Rather, it was a community of Tsimshians, along with a few individuals from other Northwest Coast groups, who chose to follow Duncan and his dream of creating a godly, and economically self-sustaining, society. Furthermore, Alaska was the Metlakatlans' second home. Their first, "old" Metlakatla dates from 1862 and was located in coastal British Columbia. Following a series of conflicts with religious and political authorities in Canada, Duncan and his charges fled British Columbia for Alaska, where they re-created their community under the protection of the United States government.

This difference, of course, complicates comparison by adding into the equation administrative institutions other than the United States Bureau of Indian Affairs. This is indeed a significant distinction, which this study will seek to address. Even so, my argument will be that, insofar as economic modernization and assimilative goals are concerned, the differences between Canadian and American administration were relatively few, and the distinctions between white-Indian relations in British Columbia versus those in the United States were even less significant.

Despite these differences, in terms of general aims, underlying philosophy, and results (at least as reported by its proponents), Metlakatla and the Menominee Reservation were strikingly similar. From the perspective of non-Indians, both sought to further Indian "improvement" by promoting the growth of industries. Moreover, "economic development" in each case was designed to achieve certain fundamental objectives. First, both were united by a desire to provide a means whereby Indians could earn a living, thereby relieving governmental or philanthropic agencies of a significant financial burden. Second was the commitment to teaching Indians the "habits" of labor, thrift, and other skills deemed necessary for survival in the Anglo-American or Anglo-Canadian world. In other words, enterprises were intended to serve as "schools of industry" for the Indians. Finally, both were designed to provide the community with a measure of economic independence by exploiting nearby resources to manufacture products that then could be sold at a profit. This last aim is significant because it indicates that both of these projects were meant to operate over the long term, that in each case the design was to create local economies which would be, in a sense, self-perpetuating, and that Indian communities were supposed to remain integrated, functioning units. This difference distinguished Menominee lumbering and the Metlakatla system from other labor-oriented programs, such as those involving independent farmers and off-reservation wage labor, which were intended to break apart the tribal community and force Indians into the economic mainstream as soon as possible.

As this study progresses, other similarities should come to light, a few of which may be suggested here. From the Indians' perspective, natives came to view economic modernization less as a threat to their tribal life than as a means for maintaining a certain degree of independence. In a related manner, it may be possible to suggest that Menominees and

Tsimshians had similar reasons for embracing wage labor and that the experience affected their societies in similar ways. Many Indians confronted their changed world and responded by making what they felt were reasoned choices. Finally, and perhaps most important, both situations contributed to revisions in natives' sense of cultural identity. By the early decades of the twentieth century, the meaning of "being Menominee" was both similar to and distinct from what it had been in earlier times, and "Metlakatlan" came to mean more than place or association with a particular missionary, even though, in both places, the combination of new and old was complex and varied.

From here, then, begins the process of documenting the economic and cultural change as it unfolded in these two areas. One final note, though. As a historian and not a theoretician, I do not intend to use this study to prove or disprove any one of the formulations presented in this chapter. Rather, I have used the ideas of others only as a starting point and intend to pick and choose from the literature as suits my needs. What results, I hope, will be an interpretive study that does not sacrifice descriptive detail or the narrative tradition in the interests of supporting or deflating some abstract theoretical construct.

CHAPTER ONE

The Menominees

When Superintendent Angus Nicholson wrote of the Menominees' transformation into "self-supporting" lumbermen who "could command skilled workman's wages any place," he, of course, was limiting his discussion to that segment of the population that participated in the logging industry.[1] But not all Menominees lived in Neopit. Not all lived in clapboard houses or worked in the lumberyards or on logging crews. Some lived away from the new town, where they hunted, gathered wild rice, speared sturgeon, and honored traditional ceremonies. But peyotist or Christian, logger or craftsperson, schoolteacher or shaman, all could claim to be truly "Menominee." And identity was important. It distinguished one from neighbors—white, Oneida, Winnebago, and Stockbridge—while uniting Menominees through shared heritage.

According to the Menominees, this past began when Mätc Hätwätuk, creator of the world and all its inhabitants, caused a great bear to come forth from under the earth at a place near where the Menominee River enters Lake Michigan. Upon reaching the surface, this underground bear, whose earthly representative was the turtle, became a man, Sekätcokémau, also "chief of chiefs." Sekätcokémau was soon joined by a woman who also sprang from the great underground bear, and together they set about the business of creating a home. While the man constructed the first mat wigwam, built a canoe, and fished for sturgeon, his mate awaited his return. Afterward she cleaned and dried the catch, then sacrificed some to the great powers. After a time, the first man and woman were visited by three thunderbirds (Inä'mäki), which also had taken the form of men. Understanding the Inä'mäki to be representatives of Mätc Hätwätuk, Sekätcokémau and his mate invited them into their home. Following a meal of sturgeon, the host announced that he intended to "ask all living beings to meet me here in council . . . so that they can assist me and form a league with me." He informed the visitors that his servant, a naked bear, would go forth among the living creatures and invite them to the council. To this the Inä'mäki gave their approval, thanked the host for his hospitality, and departed.[2]

Setting about on his rounds, the naked bear offered invitations to wolf (Múhawäo), beaver (Nomä), and crane (Kwutä'tcia); then to Awä'se the black bear and Pinäsiu the bald eagle. Most made their way to the council site without incident, but wolf found his way blocked by Lake

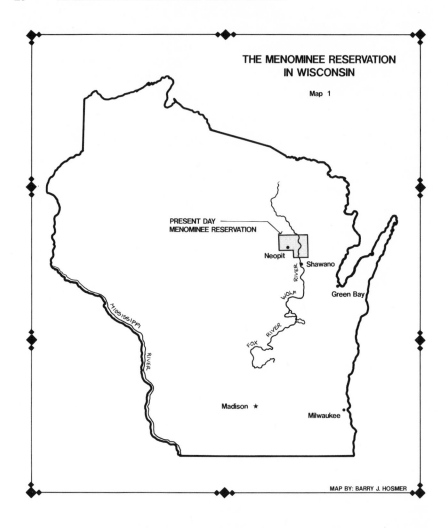

THE MENOMINEE RESERVATION
IN WISCONSIN

Map 1

PRESENT DAY
MENOMINEE RESERVATION

Neopit

Shawano

WOLF RIVER

Green Bay

MISSISSIPPI RIVER

FOX RIVER

Madison ★

Milwaukee

MAP BY: BARRY J. HOSMER

Michigan at Green Bay. As he contemplated his predicament, the water suddenly spoke to him, offering to carry him to the other side. Initially wolf hesitated, but when a wave called on him to "jump on my back," he did so, and the wave carried him safely to the other side. "Thank you, my friend," the grateful wolf replied, and promised that "henceforth you and I shall be partners, our totems shall be the same, and my descendants shall bear your name." This is how the wolf and wave came to be linked and why some of that clan take the name "Teko," or wave. A similar story explains the association of black bear with bald eagle, as the latter lent the former one of his wings to fly over a body of water.

At last all gathered in council, where Sekätcokémau addressed them.

"My friends," he said, "I have called on you to meet here for this purpose. We are of animal nature, but I propose that we change our forms and commence to exist as human beings." All agreed, set forth to gather their families, and returned to that place to set up homes. They became human beings, ancestors of the Omä'nomänéo.[3]

By the time ethnographers began compiling information on the Menominees, centuries of contact hampered efforts to reconstruct the distant past. Changing times even rendered obscure the original meaning of their term for themselves, rendered variously as Omä'nomänéo and Mamaceqtaw, although recent research translates it as "The People Who Live with the Seasons." "Menominee" derives from the Ojibwa *mano'mini*, or "wild rice people," a term equivalent to the French *nation de la folle avoine* (nation of the wild rice, literally "crazy oats") or, more commonly, Folles Avoines.[4] More certain is their linguistic and cultural relationship with other Central Algonkian peoples, particularly the Potawatomi, Sauk, Fox, and Ojibwa. Menominees also share certain cultural traits with their neighbors to the south, the Siouan-speaking Winnebagoes (Ho-Chunk). The archaeological record suggests that, unlike these more recent arrivals to the region, ancestors of the Menominees have inhabited northeastern Wisconsin for centuries, perhaps even millennia. Today's 7,100 Menominees occupy a 230,000-acre reservation northwest of Green Bay and of their earliest known homeland.[5]

As near as can be determined, the precontact Menominee occupied a single village at the mouth of the Menominee River, from which they exploited the region's abundant flora and fauna. Away from the riverbed and lakeshore rose a mixed coniferous and deciduous forest that gave way to an oak savanna interspersed with wetlands and tallgrass prairie as one moved to the south and west. Men used the resources to construct timber and bark wigwams, canoes, and various tools, while women fashioned cooking utensils and wove bags, blankets, and mats. The environment also supported populations of white-tailed deer, black bear, fine furbearers like the beaver, muskrat, otter, marten, fisher, and mink, along with smaller numbers of elk, red fox, lynx, bobcat, timber wolf, badger, and, at least until the 1820s, the occasional bison herd. Although the Menominees organized hunting parties and relied on deer for animal protein, fish, waterfowl, and plant foods constituted the bulk of their diet. During March and April lake sturgeon in great numbers migrated up the Menominee River to spawn, and in autumn whitefish and Great Lakes herring (cisco) repeated the cycle. From canoes and riverbanks, Menominee men used spears or fish traps and brought their catch home to be prepared and dried by women. Seventeenth-century Europeans noted intensive fishing and drying activities "sufficient to maintain large villages," along with the use of nets to capture ducks, geese, and pigeons as they fed on ripening wild rice.[6]

If the annual fish runs made it possible for the Menominees to maintain a sedentary existence from early spring through late fall, wild rice harvesting enhanced that pattern, particularly since Menominee horticulture was limited to small gardens. An annual grass characterized by five- to ten-foot stems, abundant broad leaves, and scores of husks surrounding slender cylindrical kernels, wild rice (*Zizania aquatica*) flourished in the slow-moving streams and quiet lakes of northeastern Wisconsin. Menominee traditions describe wild rice (*meno'mä*) as one of the foods, along with fish and sugar maples, given to Sekätcokémau by the culture hero Mänä'bus, who promised abundant harvests in exchange for ritual purity. As an ingredient in stews and soups, or a dish in and of itself, sometimes topped with maple sugar, wild rice became a staple in the Menominees' diet, not to mention an important component of their regional reputation. One nineteenth-century observer wrote that "the Canadians designate them Folls [*sic*] avoine . . . wild oats, or rice," as "this is one of the principal articles on which the Indians subsist in this quarter." He went on to remark of harvests so substantial "to support several thousand Indians for one year," something United States Indian agents noted as well.[7]

Wild rice harvesting demonstrated the plant's nutritional importance, the division of labor between men and women, and traditional concepts of property rights. As the rice began to ripen in late August, the month of Pohia-kun ka-zho (wild rice gathering moon), villagers established temporary lodging near the beds. At this time, men of the *mitewuk*, or warrior society, took charge of the camp to prevent premature harvesting and to manage gathering activities. Since Menominees subdivided rice beds into family-based units of production, the *mitewuk* also ensured respect for prior claims, which were indicated by tying standing stalks into bunches with strips of bark or rawhide. Once grain had ripened, women, and sometimes men, returned via canoe to their parcels, used a curved staff to bend the stalks over the gunwale, and, with a specially fashioned stick, or *powa'qikan*, knocked the rice, husks and all, onto mats laid in the hull of the craft. While men helped in gathering and storing for future use, Menominee women were responsible for curing, drying, and winnowing. Threshing, or separating grain from husk, was considered man's work, although evidence suggests that men and women shared this task.[8]

The gender-specific nature of wild rice production supports the notion that women in aboriginal societies realized a measure of autonomy through division of responsibilities. Menominee women not only controlled the fruits of their labor, the rice, but also probably held the right to a family's rice beds. A similar pattern obtained for maple sugar manufacturing. Usufruct rights to maple groves resided with women, and females controlled the resulting product. Even so, this division of labor should not be understood as rigid or static. Men sometimes aided in gathering wild foods or in producing maple sugar, and women could be hunters or canoe makers.[9]

Male and female, young and old, Menominees organized social relationships around a number of patrilineal, exogamous clans. These clans were grouped into seven phratries (*witisianum*, or "brotherhood"), one each for the animal-people attending Sekätcokémau's original council. There also is evidence for a dual, or moiety, division, although its structure remains unclear. While Menominee lineage groupings seem to have lacked unique ritual obligations or special ceremonial functions common among other Central Algonkians, they did play an important role in determining leadership. Representatives from each of the seven *witisianum* came together to constitute a village council, with the preferred arrangement elevating individuals from the "chiefly" clan within each phratry. Similarly, the head of this council always came from the current representative of the principal ("unworthy chief") clan within the Sekätcokémau *witisianum*. Yet Menominees also cherished personal autonomy, meaning that council members relied on persuasion and consensus building to exercise influence over civil matters.[10]

The dual values of clan allegiance and personal autonomy also guided military affairs. Where leadership in the *mitewuk*, or sacred war bundle holders, resided in the several bear clans, membership remained open to all men of demonstrated ability. At the same time, obligations to lineal relatives influenced one's participation in warfare. Since *mitewuk* duties included policing the camp, regulating the wild rice harvest, and mediating blood feuds, particularly those occasioned by murder, the arrangement rewarded particularly talented individuals, just as it respected personal autonomy. The *mikäo*, or head man of the *mítewuk*, represented the only exception to this pattern. Chosen from one of the bear clans, the *mikäo* held and protected the tribe's sacred war bundle and often acted as spokesman for the principal chief. Yet when individuals assembled their own caches of sacred objects, these bundles were personal property, not that of clan, lineage, or society.[11]

Menominee spirituality emphasized this same constellation of values. They placed great stock in the power of special visions as well as regular, or "night," dreams. Visions and dreams were the most important means for gaining, holding, and protecting spiritual "power." Known variously as *tata'hkesewen* (that which has energy), *maska'wesen* (that which has strength), and *adpe'htesewen* (that which is valuable), power was a substance of immense importance at once deemed essential for success in all life's endeavors and, when misused, a force capable of causing great harm. This notion of the two natures of power corresponded to the Menominee sense that the universe was divided between good (headed by Mäct Häwätuk) and evil (Ana'maqki'u, "powers below") and that these forces engaged in perpetual struggle for supremacy. Through prayer and sacrifice, mankind aided the forces of good; in return, benevolent spirits provided spiritual assistance in the form of medicine bundles and, through the workings of Mänä'bus, cures for sickness.[12]

Owing to its vital place in the Menominee worldview, virtually everyone sought to secure power. At the onset of puberty, boys and girls secluded themselves in an isolated location where they darkened their faces with charcoal, fasted, and awaited the onset of a vision, typically a visitation from one or more supernatural beings. These messengers offered protection, promised certain benefits, presented the faster with objects for his or her medicine bundle, and occasionally placed the essence of a small animal within the person, where it remained for life. Upon returning home, supplicants conferred with *wábano* (men of the dawn, or eastern men), ritual specialists who interpreted the vision, indicated the powers and responsibilities associated with the particular spirit, and helped the dreamer choose a name that properly represented that experience. Clairvoyant, endowed with the ability to change their outward form, and skilled fire handlers, *wábano* were individual practitioners who owed their powers to visions that formalized an association with either the morning star or the sun.[13]

Power also had a darker side, for Menominees understood that illness and misfortune resulted from broken taboos or the operations of witchcraft. In such cases, the afflicted might enlist the aid of the *cese'ko* (also *je'sako*, or "jugglers"). Healers, diviners, and medicine men, the *cese'ko* determined the cause of sickness and effected cures by applying medicines, sometimes "sucking" a bone fragment or other foreign object from the afflicted. They also found lost articles, caused rain to fall, aided hunters, and could even see inside an individual's medicine bundle. Their considerable powers identified *cese'ko* as persons to be feared and respected, for they could do evil as well as good. So while Menominees relied upon *cese'ko*, they also kept their distance, fearing the loss or corruption of their personal powers.[14]

While the quest for power and the importance of individual ritual practitioners illustrate Menominee values of personal autonomy and openness to spiritual forces, the Medicine Lodge Society (*mete'wen*, also *mitä'wit*) reveals their facility for absorbing and reshaping foreign influences. According to society members, *mete'* ceremonies and associated paraphernalia came to the Menominees through Mänä'bus, who offered a more effective form of worship. Ethnographers posit an Ojibwa origin and trace its introduction to the early postcontact period. In any case, the *mete'wen* became the Menominees' most important ceremonial organization, and its observances reinforced deeply held values. To fulfill the primary aim of prolonging the lives and health of the society's members, *mete'* observances directed their attention toward gaining, holding, and protecting spiritual power, which meant shielding members against evil forces. Rituals also linked past and present, featured a recitation of the Menominee genesis, incorporated familiar healing practices, and made room for *wábano* specialists. Yet unlike the individualistic and inclusive dream quest, Menominee men and women became *mete'* members only by invitation or through inheriting a particular kind of medicine bag. In its rituals and purposes, the *mete'wen* demonstrates an evolving Menominee identity, one grounded in fundamental values but sufficiently flexible to accommodate to changed circumstances.[15]

Menominees embraced the *mete'* at an important time in their history. For nearly 200 years following Jean Nicollet's 1634 arrival in the northern Great Lakes, the fur trade defined the relationship between the Menominees and outsiders, French and British, Americans and native. Reduced in numbers by early exposure to infectious pathogens, the Menominees also faced an influx of eastern refugees, driven westward by disease, warfare, and the seventeenth-century expansion of Iroquoian peoples into the Ohio Valley. Over time, "transitional" Ojibwa-Menominee bands developed north of Green Bay, while to the south, Menominees and Winnebagoes lived in close proximity. Others responded to this demographic "revolution" by forging relationships with fur traders and colonial authorities, a demonstration of which came with the creation of a new village near the French post of La Baye (Green Bay). The French, and later the British, found in the Menominees trusted allies and skilled intermediaries.[16]

Conforming to the general pattern, the fur trade initially enhanced Menominee prosperity and security, its subtle pressures on traditional ways becoming evident only later on. Trapping animals and preparing and trading hides competed with customary subsistence activities, and the steady depletion of local populations of fur-bearing species meant that Menominee hunters, and their family members, ranged farther afield. While a truncated version of the older fishing and gathering economy survived, other social structures did not. Villages fragmented, mobile, clan-based bands took their place, and, for a portion of the year, these bands acted independently of one another. Although Menominees continued to visit fishing and ricing territories, increased mobility elevated the importance of deer meat to their diet. In the long run, narrowing subsistence diversity also rendered the Menominee economy less secure.[17]

The fur trade changed Menominee life in other ways. A disrupted subsistence cycle influenced leadership patterns by placing a premium on one's ability to maintain ties with Europeans. Missionary activity opened fissures within and between bands, sometimes along gender lines, particularly as churchmen sought to impose patriarchal values upon Menominee society. Tracking and trapping probably undermined women's autonomy by binding them to activities of men at the same time that manufactured goods competed with clothing, mats, and utensils produced by women's hands. Even so, it would be a mistake to conclude that sustained contact resulted in the complete submission of women. No less than men, Menominee women found creative ways to protect cultural values. They traded foodstuffs and manufactures, exerted influence through the *mete'wen,* and rejected religious and cultural innovations that threatened their autonomy. Women also entered into unions with traders and were cultural "brokers" as well as wives, partners, and lovers.[18]

Interracial unions also produced children. Although statistics on racial admixture are inconclusive, available evidence indicates that by the mid–nineteenth century, one-half to two-thirds of the 1,700 Menominees were mixed bloods. Menominees integrated their "métis" brethren by creating two new phratries, prairie chicken and hog, an innovation that made sense culturally. This accommodation to changed circumstances also facilitated the rise of mixed bloods to positions of influence. The career of Thomas Carron and his descendants illustrates this latter point. Son of a French trader and a Micmac mother, Carron arrived among the Menominees sometime after 1710, fathered four children by a woman named Waupese- siu, and by midcentury had emerged as Chief Sheka'tshokewe'mau's principal spokesman. *Mikäo* in everything but title, Carron derived influence from his ability to negotiate effectively with whites, and he reportedly convinced the tribal council to remain aloof from Pontiac's multitribal alliance. When the elder Carron died in 1780, two of his sons, Konot (also Claude, or Glode) and Tomau, took over. Of the prairie chicken *(pä'kääqkiu)* phratry, the two sons were at least as influential as their father, probably more so given the increasing importance of trade and Sheka'tshokewe'mau's advancing age. Sometimes referred to as a "chief," Tomau followed his father's lead by preserving ties with Europeans, particularly the English, while rebuffing Tecumseh just as Thomas Carron had rejected Pontiac. Although no Carron ever became head chief, three generations served as influential advisers. After Sheka'tshokewe'mau's death in 1821, Tomau and then his sons Josette (Joseph Carron) and Ma'qkata'bi (Thomas Carron) advised Oshkosh (Bear Claw), the old chief's grandson and successor.[19]

Carron and his sons also played a prominent role in nineteenth-century diplomacy. As poverty, even starvation, accompanied the decline of the Great Lakes fur trade, Menominee leaders turned to traders and the

United States government for aid and could offer only land in return. Treaties concluded in 1821, 1832, 1848, 1854, and 1856 ultimately relinquished 9 million acres of land for cash, food, subsistence goods, an account administered by the United States Treasury, and a 230,000-acre reservation along the Wolf River. While two generations of Carrons signed on to these agreements, Oshkosh's name appears as well, even on the controversial 1848 treaty. That arrangement called on the tribe to exchange its remaining holdings in Wisconsin for $300,000 and title to 600,000 acres in Minnesota. This pact also provided a cash settlement to some 700 métis who chose to renounce their tribal affiliation, thereby escaping removal.[20]

But the Menominees never moved to Minnesota. After finding Crow Wing worse than "the poorest region in Wisconsin," Oshkosh demanded a temporary home along the Wolf River and a new set of negotiations. The Interior Department consented, and in 1854 the Menominees surrendered their claim to Crow Wing for 276,000 acres in northeastern Wisconsin. Two years later the tribe signed a final agreement in which it relinquished a 40,000-acre strip of land along the southern border of the reservation to Stockbridge and Munsee immigrants.[21]

Confinement to a reservation forced the Menominees to revise their social, political, and economic lives once again. Given the demise of the fur trade, they gradually returned to a semisettled lifeway, although new reservation settlements often approximated fur trade era bands and increasingly reflected religious and cultural distinctions. Reservation life, combined with a half century of treaty negotiations and Oshkosh's steady leadership, also enhanced the influence of the head chief. All this meant that while Menominee life retained some of its decentralized character, other forces promoted a return to a more sedentary, village-oriented pattern.[22]

The first twenty years following the 1856 agreement proved difficult. While poor land, inadequate supplies, and a general lack of interest hamstrung efforts to promote farming, the Menominees also suffered from a vacuum in leadership. Oshkosh died in 1858, and after a two-year struggle over succession, factions honored tradition and agreed to the elevation of the old chief's eldest son, Ahkonemi (Oshkosh). But Ahkonemi Oshkosh remained an unpopular choice among the métis population, some of whom authored an 1870 petition calling on Washington to remove him as chief. Before the department could act, Ahkonemi's tenure ended abruptly just the next year. Charged and convicted of killing a man in a drunken brawl, Ahkomeni found himself serving a three-year sentence in the state penitentiary, and leadership passed to his younger brother, Neo'pit.[23]

Neo'pit proved an able leader who did his best to unite an increasingly fractious group. In his early forties when he became chief, Neo'pit held the position by virtue of heritage and served as a prominent *mete'* official. He also had married wisely. Wa'benomitä'mu (Wabeno Woman) was one of Josette Carron's daughters, and their marriage symbolically bridged the rift between past and present, métis and full blood. Symbolism aside, the 1870s also witnessed deepening divisions as ethnic and clan distinctions began coalescing into geographic blocs. Where prominent métis like Sam Teko and Keshena settled at Little Oconto (later known as South Branch), in the northeastern section of the reservation, Neo'pit's followers congregated in and around "Kinebaway," four to six miles up the Wolf River from the agency headquarters at Keshena.[24]

Unsettled conditions notwithstanding, Menominee prospects were not altogether desperate. In 1871 alone, revenues from sales of maple sugar, wild rice, and furs surpassed $22,000. When combined with a $16,000 annuity payment and an additional $8,000 drawn from interest on tribal accounts, Menominee income exceeded $46,000, not including wages from off-reservation labor. More important, the reservation held 250 to 500 million feet of valuable timber. But while tribal members had operated a small sawmill for nearly twenty years, the Keshena mill remained strictly a noncommercial venture. Concern that a logging enterprise might distract Indians from farming, combined with probable opposition from commercial firms, meant that the Indian Office limited the mill's mission to supplying building materials and fuel. It also voided an 1861 agreement whereby lumberman Robert A. Jones agreed to supply one hundred barrels of flour in exchange for the right to exploit reservation forests. By 1871, however, conditions had changed. Commenting on the reservation's "extensive water-power and abundant facilities for removing timber to market," not to mention the chance to "furnish [Indians] work during the winter season," newly appointed agent William T. Richardson requested, and received, permission to hire Menominee lumberjacks. That winter, Indians cut and transported approximately 2 million feet of pine logs. Brought to market, these logs sold for $23,731, out of which loggers earned $3,000; another $12,000 went to the tribe, and the balance covered supplies and "scaling" (the method for determining the quantity and quality of cut timber). Richardson was so pleased with the results that he determined to expand operations. Arguing that "the Indian will work much like other men if he receives the same help and inducements," Richardson set out to demonstrate that, working "on their own lands, . . . cutting their own pine, for themselves," Menominee loggers would come to "have an interest in making the business go on successfully." Armed with this evidence, Richardson requested $12,000 to expand operations and construct a shingle mill. This, he claimed, "will pay for itself in two years, . . . furnish the tribe with cash labor," and insulate Indians "from the vices and temptations of the ordinary lumbering business."[25]

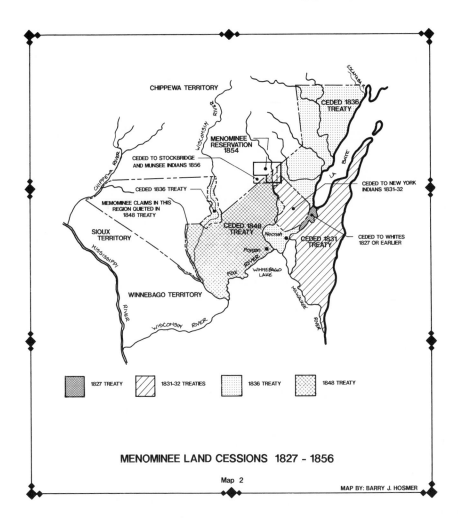

CHIPPEWA TERRITORY

CEDED 1836 TREATY

MENOMINEE RESERVATION 1854

CEDED TO STOCKBRIDGE AND MUNSEE INDIANS 1856

CEDED 1836 TREATY

MENOMINEE CLAIMS IN THIS REGION QUIETED IN 1848 TREATY

CEDED TO NEW YORK INDIANS 1831-32

SIOUX TERRITORY

CEDED 1848 TREATY

CEDED 1831 TREATY

CEDED TO WHITES 1827 OR EARLIER

Necnah

Poygan

WINNEBAGO LAKE

WINNEBAGO TERRITORY

FOX

WISCONSIN RIVER

1827 TREATY   1831-32 TREATIES   1836 TREATY   1848 TREATY

MENOMINEE LAND CESSIONS 1827 - 1856

Map 2

MAP BY: BARRY J. HOSMER

The Indian Office agreed, sanctioned logging for the next five years, and watched as production climbed. Between 1872 and 1876, Menominee loggers harvested over 24 million feet of timber, with more than half during the banner season of 1875–76. During that year, the tribe grossed nearly $78,000 on sales of just over 13 million feet, and 100 loggers each earned an average of $130 for ten to twelve weeks of work. The shingle mill also converted nonmarketable timber into salable building materials while generating employment for a handful of workers. Many converted their wages into new homes, while others took up farming, confounding predictions that wage labor would undercut such efforts. Richardson's successors also praised the project. In 1876, Agent Joseph C. Bridgeman reported that most

Menominees now "have permanent homes, . . . cultivate their patch of ground," and make "quite a good living." More striking was the tribe's determination to use profits to improve life across the reservation, for logger and nonlogger alike. In 1873 the tribal council voted to provide home builders with lumber, shingles, nails, and sash for three windows, all free of charge. This suggests that even as Bridgeman commended a developing "spirit of rivalry," Menominee leaders were attempting to balance novel individualistic ideas with older communal values. The council's actions demonstrated a recognition that enterprise could under-mine community, and they resolved to share profits derived from what was, after all, a *tribal* resource.[26]

Concerns over the market's impact proved well founded. Commer-cial firms dwarfed the Menominees' tiny lumbering operation, placing it at the mercy of forces they could not influence, threatened by corporations that coveted their timber. In the latter case, a loose combination of logging companies, mill operators, and lumber wholesalers popularly known as the "pine ring" lobbied Congress to open tribal lands, spread rumors that inexperienced Indian lumberjacks were destroying timber, and bankrolled ingenious ventures like the Keshena Improvement Company. This was a scheme to dredge shallow portions of the Wolf River (supposedly to ease transportation of logs) and charge tolls on logs floated downstream. Agent Thomas Chase denounced the plan as a blatant effort to drive the Menominees under and resigned, frustrated with the Interior Depart-ment's "futile efforts to punish certain pine-thieves and to prevent the extortions [*sic*] of the Keshena Improvement Company."[27]

Wisconsin lumber purchasers also conspired to drive down timber prices. Since the Menominees produced a comparatively small share of the logs brought to regional markets, they often faced the choice of accepting low prices or holding back their logs in the hope that the forces of supply and demand would work in their favor. Agent Chase tried both alternatives. In 1873 he sold logs at prevailing prices but soon found that revenues barely met expenses. The following year he banked 2 million board feet of timber. This also proved disastrous. Not only were Indian loggers unable to repay their creditors on time, but when Agent Bridge-man sold this timber in 1875, prices were lower still. "It is unfortunate that the logs cut in 1873 and 1874 by my immediate predecessor were not sold by him," Bridgeman reported, "as he was offered $2 per thousand [feet] more than they sold for this season. Like others, he held out for a rise, which, owing to the severe hard times all over the country, did not come with the opening of spring, but a heavy decline in lumber [prices] followed, from which it has not recovered."[28]

Bridgeman tried a different strategy. Acting under the assumption that increased production might afford the Menominees some influence over lumber markets, he determined to expand logging, and this approach accounted for the unusually heavy cut during the 1875–76 season. But Bridgeman's decision scarcely could have come at a less opportune time. In January 1876, the Interior Department abruptly suspended Menominee logging. Its action was prompted by *United States v. Cook* (1873), in which the United States Supreme Court declared reservation resources off-limits to commercial exploitation, absent specific congressional authorization. Congress withheld its permission, the Menominee enterprise shut down, and Bridgeman (more accurately the tribe) faced a mountain of new debt. The result was that while the truncated 1875-76 season produced a record yield, revenues barely covered expenses and failed to satisfy creditors. An effort to recoup losses by authorizing another harvest in 1876–77 blew up in Bridgeman's face when Congress took a dim view of the agent's initiative and ordered that the logs remain on the ground, unsold and deteriorating.[29]

When Ebenezar Stephens took over as agent in the fall of 1879, he found the Menominees attempting to make the best of their situation. His report noted "marked growth in all branches of industry in which the Indians are capable of taking part" and claimed that fully 90 percent of the 1,450 Menominees made their living through "civilized pursuits," resulting in "a fair harvest this season." He also called attention to the fact that the gristmill was "operated entirely by Indians, in a manner that would do credit to many settlements among the whites." As for the Menominee loggers, while only a few found work in the agency sawmill, others took their skills and muscles to "the pineries, the rivers, [and] the railroads."[30]

Yet closer examination of the agent's own statistics reveals a more sobering picture. In fact, farm output in 1880 stood at virtually the same levels as during the 1870s, despite a steady increase of lands in production. Nonfarm statistics showed similar stagnation, if not outright decline. Maple sugar production hovered at between 60,000 and 80,000 pounds per year during the early 1880s, down markedly from the previous decade; revenues from fur sales totaled just $500, barely one-tenth the levels recorded during the 1870s; and a similar rate of decline held for wild rice harvests. Given that 1880 marked the final installment of annuity payments derived from land cessions, it is no wonder that many Menominees began seeking outside employment. So, too, did efforts of a few "enterprising individuals" who introduced a small trade in machine-made beadwork. That these craftsmen were males offers suggestive evidence that, stripped of its most powerful economic enterprise, the local economy proved incapable of meeting the tribe's needs.[31]

Economic dislocation coincided with a new round of social instability. In January 1881 Stephens expressed his concern over the appearance of a "new dance" whose adherents, he wrote, "neglect all other duties in their enthusiasm for it." Although he admittedly was uncertain about the nature, origin, or message of the movement, the agent's response reflected that generalized fear of religious enthusiasm so common among Indian Office administrators. Stephens's remedy was as predictable as it was proscriptive. Where "it is evident that no good can be expected from this new demonstration of heathenism," he wrote, it was equally clear that "much evil may arrise [*sic*] if it is allowed to take root." Determined to "choke" the dance "in its infancy," Stephens recommended withholding the annuity payments of those attending its meetings.[32]

The subject of Stephens's concern was the *ni'mihe'twan,* or Dream Dance, and his account accurately portrays at least one of its characteristics: it was new, or at least seemed that way. Best evidence posits an introduction date of 1879 or 1880, probably via Potawatomi or Ojibwa converts. Scholars understand *ni'mihe'twan* as a "messianic" movement, an example of those periodic religious upheavals that appear among Native American societies undergoing acute political, material, and spiritual distress. There is much to recommend this interpretation. From the usual dramatic revelation, here granted to a Sioux girl as she hid from white soldiers during an attack on her village, there followed a promise to restore old ways upon proper fealty to new rituals. Equally common are the warning that hardships constituted spiritual retribution for abandoning cherished values, the introduction, again through the revelatory experience, of novel religious forms, as well as a commandment to spread the message of renewal among Indian peoples generally. Moreover, the central importance of the Sioux intermediary combined with the movement's place in time have led to obvious comparisons with the more famous Ghost Dance.[33]

But if the Dream Dance reflected just one example of a well-documented phenomenon, its roots held fast to the soil of traditional Menominee values. Like the Medicine Lodge Society, also an introduction from the outside, the Dream Dance was intimately associated with gaining, holding, protecting, and renewing spiritual power. The sacred drum *(te'we'hekan)* became the physical manifestation of power, its deep tones the utterings of the creator and other spirits who poured some of their power into the original instrument. The drum head, painted half in blue, half in red, the two sides bisected by a yellow line, represented the dualistic nature of the universe, as well as the necessity for individuals to steer a path between opposing forces. So great was the drum's accumulated force that its holder was considered particularly powerful, capable of inflicting misfortune upon transgressors. In this sense, the drum and associated ceremonies offered spiritual renewal by emphasizing the importance of living a "good life" according to Menominee principles.[34]

Just as the Dream Dance phenomenon demonstrated a longing for spiritual regeneration, its message suggests an effort to reach accommodation with uncertainty and through the medium of fundamental, although once again shifting, cultural values. For instance, while individuals paid a fee for membership in the Dream Dance Society, the amount was substantially less than the corresponding mechanism for acceptance into the Medicine Lodge. Considering also the absence of "hereditary" avenues for membership, such as existed in the *mete'wen*, the *ni'mihe'twan* was a far more inclusive organization, theoretically more responsive to the needs of a community suffering from fragmenting clan and lineage bonds. The fact that the Dream Dance incorporated Christian imagery, mandated sobriety, honored thrift and labor, and relegated women to supportive, and less prominent, roles illustrates as well its accommodationist message. One convert expressed the movement's appeal and, not incidentally, its adherents' efforts to interpret new realities through a traditional prism, when he argued, "If I thought that our dance was a step backward, I would have nothing to do with it; neither would Neopet [*sic*]."[35] He also defended the movement in words that should have resonated with Agent Stephens. "We do not take the young men from their work," he explained, but "try to help them to work better. If I had a flag of my own I should want to have painted on it a picture of a plow and over that my totem, the eagle. This flag I should like to see always waving over our dance. I want all my children to go to school to learn just what the white men know. . . . We are doing the best we can."[36]

All this strongly suggests that the timing of the Dream Dance phenomenon was important. As much a reaction to life's uncertainties as the desire for spiritual renewal, the dance sought to integrate increasingly "individualistic" values at that moment when both the benefits and pitfalls of the logging venture became especially apparent. Where early attempts to generate employment and income from logging showed some promise, they also exposed the Menominees to market and political forces over which they had little influence. At the same time, the on-again, off-again nature of the new enterprise heightened this sense of insecurity at the very time that it benefited individuals unevenly. Novel avenues for material advancement coincided with a weakening of older patterns of social organization, and out of this mix grew a movement to embrace new realities at the same time that it offered means for reinvigorating the Menominee sense of community. In this sense, the Dream Dance represented less an adjustment to a new "culture" than an effort to come to grips with a social and economic order that, while certainly promising, also failed to deliver material security.

Stephens viewed the situation otherwise, and his response probably contributed to another instance of social fragmentation. In two urgent communications to the commissioner's office dated August 1881, he expressed his intention to suppress a new round of ceremonies, by force if necessary. Claiming that "dreamers threaten war, and say whites have no business in this country," the agent called for federal soldiers "to arrest leaders among the Menominee" and expel some forty Potawatomi and Ojibwa adherents then on the reservation. This proved too much for the most culturally conservative among Menominees. Faced with unremitting, not to mention overheated, hostility from their agent (anticipating a "serious outbreak," Stephens also called for the immediate arrest of "six hundred" Sioux, Potawatomi, Ojibwa, and Winnebago "allies"), they retreated to Zoar, located in the remote northwestern corner of the reservation. Yet while migration provided freedom, isolation exacted its price. Detached from the body of the tribe, residents of Zoar found it increasingly difficult to influence decision making, centered as it was in and around Keshena. This same confluence of geographic and philosophical distance also impeded the efforts of Menominee leaders, like Chief Neo'pit, to forge consensus on divisive issues, particularly, as it turned out, the conduct of commercial logging.[37]

His overblown reaction to the Dream Dancers notwithstanding, Stephens also recognized the link between an unstable local economy and the potential for social unrest. In short, he called for an end to the logging moratorium. For Stephens, as for Richardson some ten years earlier, logging represented not only the best hope for "employment during the winter season" but also the means to transform the Menominees into hardworking, independent laborers, if not farmers. After all, it was "not money that elevates the Indian," so the agent concluded, but rather "employment in some kind of honest industry."[38]

Although probably less certain about the benefits of cultural transformation, Neo'pit could agree that the tribe now depended on logging, or at least its financial benefits. But this proved complicated. As a leading member of the Medicine Lodge Society, Neo'pit had responsibilities that certainly included respecting, indeed protecting, social and spiritual conventions. Yet he remained mindful of the uncomfortable truth that poverty bred dependence, that the Menominees had to come to terms with economic forces swirling in and around their homeland. His solution was to join Agent Stephens in requesting the resumption of logging. To do otherwise invited not only material hardship but also the prospect that fires, not to mention trespassers, might deprive the tribe of its only means to salvage some modicum of economic independence. This growing sense of urgency ultimately led Neo'pit to offer a dramatic proposal: the tribe would sell its timber to outside firms—minus any requirement to hire native laborers—and then accept allotments. This plan resembled logging agreements already in operation on the timber-rich Ojibwa (Anishinaabe) reservations of northern Wisconsin and Minnesota and carried the same risks. But Neo'pit was anxious. "We want to sell our timber for a fair price," he told a local newspaperman, "and we will give the purchasers four or five years to take it away in, and then we want our lands allotted to us." At the same time, however, the chief also made it clear that potential agreements covered timber, not land. "We accepted our present reservation when it was considered of no value by our white friends," he continued, "all we ask is to be permitted to keep it as our home," for "our children and grandchildren." Faced with the choice of holding out for everything, and perhaps gaining nothing, or cutting a less attractive but more certain deal, he chose the safer course. He would rather sell the timber than lose the homeland.[39]

Although the Indian Office declined to act on Neo'pit's proposal, the incident highlighted something about Menominee values, or at least those of their leader. Homeland was important. Old Oshkosh had recognized this when he fought removal, and Neo'pit now sought accommodation, but always with an eye toward maintaining land and community. Creative accommodation had always been a hallmark of Menominee adaptation to changed circumstances, and, given this context, Neo'pit's decision made sense. But there was more to it than this. While whites like Agent Stephens understood logging as a powerful engine for cultural change, the Menominee leader subtly reversed that equation. Logging meant security. It fed the hungry, housed the needy, and shielded the people from complete dependence on annuities. It also was his trump card. Neo'pit understood that white lumbermen coveted Menominee timber and would take it if given the chance. So he offered a trade. The next challenge would be to find a way to make new arrangements work. Here again, the Menominee facility for reinterpreting values, while maintaining a sense of community, would be put to the test.

CHAPTER TWO

Commercial Logging During the 1880s

When the Menominees set out to protect their nascent logging enterprise in the years around 1880, they were confronting perception as well as policy, expectations along with action. While the "official" dialogue emanating in and around policy-making circles concerned the relative benefits of logging and wage labor, compared with subsistence farming, as a means for promoting the government's agenda for cultural change, one subtext had Indians at odds both with decision makers and with private, commercial interests. Still another involved an ongoing discussion, among Menominees, over social and cultural "values." These several dialogues operated simultaneously throughout the 1880s, sometimes independently, more often intersecting at various points along the way, producing a creative tension that came to define Menominee life during the 1880s.[1]

At the nexus of these various dialogues lay Menominee commercial logging. While their historic participation in the fur trade had introduced Menominees to the implications of an exchange economy, and a decade of logging suggested a pathway—for some anyway—toward material security, the expanding enterprise nevertheless presented a series of complications. At a time when policy makers remained convinced that the true path toward Indian assimilation passed through the family farm, ambivalence characterized the official reaction to wage labor in general, Menominee logging in particular. Those who cared to consider "what was best" for Indians generally regarded wage labor as, at best, a temporary expedient and, at worst, corrosive to values of self-reliance they were trying so hard to impart. Images of the lazy, improvident Indian supported as well the notion that the discipline of wage labor might be beyond the capacity of "traditional" peoples.[2]

This ambivalence toward Indians as laborers is reflected as well in scholarly treatments of the past. Historians, anthropologists, sociologists, and economists have tended either to ignore Indian participation in the broader economy or to present it as evidence of near-complete "acculturation." Neither formulation accurately reflects the past. From the Great Lakes to Indian Territory, extending from fragmented holdings in the hills of North Carolina to Great Basin reservations and reserves along British Columbia's Northwest Coast, the late nineteenth century witnessed a steady expansion of Indian participation in North American economies. The full extent of this historical development, doubtless known to Indians even as it was bemoaned by some white observers, is just now coming to light. Although it is possible to argue that Indians selling their labor is an indicator of deepening economic dependency, discerning its impact within Indian communities remains a considerably more complicated task. Conceptually, wage labor is different from exchange, or trade, in that it involves the "commodification" of effort in ways that were foreign to most Indian societies—even in the late nineteenth century. This development also contained within it revolutionary social implications. For if individuals, Menominee loggers in this case, Tsimshian salmon fishermen in the next, came to demand control over the "fruits of their labor," could this have a withering effect on community values? And if there was this withering of collective bonds, what then for Indian identity? Does this take us, as students, back to where we equate certain behavioral changes with creeping assimilation, or acculturation?[3]

This is no mere academic exercise, for during the 1880s the Menominees faced just these kinds of dilemmas. With expanded logging came consequences. Interests, even values, diverged, fortunes rose and fell, and tribal politics exposed the depth, sometimes, of these disagreements. Increasingly as well, these conversations were expressed in the language of logging, attesting both to the growing importance of the enterprise and to the fact that commerce was the language of outsiders, both policy makers and "customers." The 1880s, then, were important times for the Menominees. Although this chapter does not suggest the development of a new Menominee "identity," one that reflected consensus on the relationship between logging, wage labor, and "Menominee-ness," it does argue for two related ideas. On the one hand, we see an elaboration of older habits of creative adaptation. At the same time, some Menominees, and for various reasons, began to advance a strategy of "purposeful modernization," a modern term for the notion that Menominee cultural survival and commercial development were intricately linked. Although a full elaboration of this second idea would come later, closer examination of preliminary "conversations" challenges us to reconsider concepts like "traditional" and "progressive."[4]

But the first order of business in 1881 was restarting logging, suspended as a consequence of fallout from the United States Supreme Court's decision in *United States v. Cook*.[5] While the Indian Office had rejected Neo'pit's bold proposal to sell off timber and institute allotment, Commissioner John D. C. Atkins personally authorized a resumption of logging in November 1881. The next month, 125 Indian loggers returned to the forests, and Agent Stephens prepared to market the anticipated 4 million to 6 million feet of logs. Although the commissioner's orders limited the harvest to damaged, or "dead and down," timber, it still seemed that after the long delay, logging might yet fulfill its considerable promise.[6]

The commissioner's orders were not all they seemed to be. Congress still had to authorize Menominee logging, and with it the power to conduct sales, an action it did not take until March 1882. In the meantime, native lumberjacks banked 5 million board feet of previously dead and down pine. As logs sat in streams, creditors clamored for their money (one shut off the flow of capital altogether), starvation threatened oxen used to transport logs to riverbanks, and local lumber merchants angled again to manipulate the market for Indian timber. When Ebenezar Stephens warned that conditions were "not very encouraging to the Indians who are willing to work when opportunity offers," he was, it turned out, describing what became a decade-long pattern of inconsistent and contradictory actions on the part of federal officials. Partly related to continuing ambivalence toward Menominee logging, but influenced as well by pressure from non-Indian logging interests, this exercise may be expected to have dampened Indian enthusiasm for the enterprise.[7] But it did not, and when Congress finally acted it released the energies of Menominee loggers. For the next five seasons, harvests averaged 5 million board feet, and the number of Indian lumberjacks jumped from 125 in 1881–82 to 260 in 1884–85. In 1882 alone, earnings approached $47,000, which, after covering $7,000 in expenses, left some $40,000 to be divided among the 125 loggers, or an average of $320 per man for roughly twelve weeks' work. This was particularly significant given that farming remained at a subsistence level, and income from activities such as maple sugar manufacturing, berry picking, and fur trading declined steadily.[8]

Under the 1882 legislation and associated regulations, logging proceeded under a rather simple set of rules, at least for the first half of the decade. Upon approval by their Indian agent, local traders advanced supplies to individual Menominees, who then hired workers and went into the forest to cut timber, but dead and down timber only. Logging camps worked independently over the course of the summer and by early spring delivered their logs to the banks of the Wolf and Little Oconto Rivers. At this point, lumber dealers purchased the logs and divided proceeds according to the quantity and quality cut by each team. Camp leaders then settled debts, paid their employees, and, if everything went well, had a little left over. Some used their profits to build homes, as evidenced by the fact that Indians constructed an average of twenty new houses per year throughout the 1880s. Others attempted to clear land for farms, while a few, so it was said, frittered away their money in frivolous pursuits. In any case, logging provided Menominee lumberjacks with a reliable source of income while leaving summers free for them to attend to other interests.[9]

It is, of course, quite likely that not all loggers, let alone all Menominees, benefited equally from the enterprise. A select few, most notably Joseph Gauthier, a mixed-blood trader and interpreter, and Mitchell Chickeney, son of band chief Mah Chickeney (Mä' tshikine'u), set themselves up as traders, advancing supplies to loggers in the hope of deriving greater profits at the end of the season. More properly considered "middlemen" between loggers and non-Indian merchants, Gauthier and Chickeney took advantage of the chronic shortage of investment capital on the reservation as well as the Menominees' mistrust of white traders by obtaining goods from outsiders on credit and then advancing those same supplies to Indian loggers. While a demonstration of considerable ingenuity, this arrangement also was fraught with peril. On at least two occasions, Gauthier and Chickeney had to petition the Indian Office to withdraw funds from tribal accounts to repay their own debts, and in 1883 an attorney representing local non-Indian merchants made a similar request, writing that "we cannot get our money" because of a delay in selling Menominee logs, a situation which left merchants "on the verge of ruin."[10]

Evidence strongly suggests a close link between family relationships and participation in logging. While data from the early 1880s are scanty, logging schedules from later in the decade indicate that Menominee loggers generally worked in family groups, pooling their resources and labor in order to realize greater return. A logical course of action, this practice was, however, in technical violation of a departmental directive prohibiting "contracting," or "speculation." Inserted at the behest of Stephens, who argued that granting Indians the latitude to hire laborers undermined the educational benefit of work (it was, he wrote, "not money that elevates the Indian," but rather "employment in some kind of honest industry"), this stipulation nevertheless was routinely ignored.[11]

It is difficult to overstate the importance of logging to the reservation economy. If we assume that roughly one-half of the 1,400 Menominees were males, and of that 700 about 150 were school-age boys (a figure supported by census figures), somewhat over 40 percent of Menominee adult men were loggers. This, of course, ignores those physically unable to undertake hard labor, but a reasonable estimate nevertheless suggests that one out of every two able-bodied men derived at least a portion of his annual income from logging.[12] Just as telling is evidence that men from a variety of backgrounds participated to one degree or another. In an 1883 record of loggers' accounts with a local creditor, men holding Menominee names appear with equal frequency as those with non-Indian appellations. While surnames are an inexact measure of age or cultural orientation, it is nevertheless instructive that Neo'pit, his brother Ahkomeni, and band leader Louis LaMotte show up as logging contractors. So, too, do Joseph F. Gauthier, son of the trader Gauthier, and

Mitchell Chickeney, thus demonstrating again that ambitious young men might parlay family connections into opportunity, and that logging was central to these dreams.[13]

Despite logging's apparent appeal to Menominees of varied backgrounds, it is clear as well that benefits, or profits, flowed through the community unequally. This concerned those Menominees who worried that economic stratification carried the potential for social discord. This issue also presents analysts with a complex problem in that the divergence of material interests reflected, and probably enhanced, deeper disagreements having as much to do with values as with money. Typically presented as the conflict between "progressives" on the one hand and "traditionalists" on the other, or "mixed bloods" versus "full bloods," this overly simplified picture of Indian social interaction has been rightly criticized for creating artificial dichotomies, and for implying the existence of stable parties, or "factions," when in fact life was more complex and shifting. Nevertheless, this old progressive-traditionalist arrangement remains useful if employed with caution. It does describe general behavioral distinctions that imply divergent constructions of identity, or cultural "orientation." If we understand as well that individuals made, and make, distinctive adjustments to the world around them, that these adjustments are anything but static, and sometimes include seemingly "contradictory" elements, we can, it seems, understand "progressive" and "traditional" to suggest extreme positions on a "continuum" of cultural values where most individuals occupied places in between.[14]

For the Menominees in the 1880s, this continuum of cultural values and behaviors was at once the product of a long history of creative adaptation and newer accommodations to the world of commercial logging. In general terms, the operative elements for understanding Menominee cultural orientation were the degree to which some embraced individualistic, even "entrepreneurial," values seemingly in conflict with an ethos that placed greater emphasis on maintaining group harmony. This is not to suggest that mixed parentage was unimportant or that Menominee society was so inflexible as to preclude the coexistence of different values. After all, earlier generations of Menominees had successfully integrated such individuals into the community through two new clans, and fundamental Menominee values, those of loyalty to the clan and individual autonomy, suggest cultural support for both sides of the new equation. This situation was rendered even more complex by the evident participation in logging of Christians and *mete'wen* practitioners along with men across successive generations. All this suggests that cultural orientation alone was not a deciding factor in predicting economic behavior.[15]

If Menominee society was sufficiently flexible to reconcile numerous combinations of values and behaviors, the expansion of logging sometimes placed individuals at cross-purposes. These occasions demanded creative leadership, and in 1882 Neo'pit responded by convincing the tribal council to deduct one dollar from each thousand feet of timber cut and sold by Indian loggers. Funds raised in this way were earmarked for a special account to support the poor, sick, and disabled. A recognition that while the number of loggers swelled, others were in danger of falling behind, the new fund held special importance for the approximately 400 "traditionalists" from Zoar. Although regarded by at least one Indian agent as "peaceful and temperate and the most law-abiding class in the tribe," the most culturally conservative Menominees largely eschewed logging and farming, and tended to eke out a meager existence in the declining activities of hunting, gathering, and trading. Physically distant from agency headquarters at Keshena, they also had different attitudes regarding enterprise and individuality that removed them as well from the center of decision making.[16]

It was at least partly for these people that Neo'pit acted. While he supported logging and even participated from time to time, the head chief's decision to assess a "tax" on loggers indicated concern over the fractious tendencies of individualistic values and behaviors even as he appreciated that to cripple entrepreneurial activity might undermine broader community interests. Facing a true dilemma, Neo'pit proposed a solution that recalls his earlier offer to sell off reservation timber in favor of allotments and larger per capita payments. Both times he attempted to strike a balance between the evident benefits of logging and the demand that all tribal members share equally in what was, after all, the Menominees' collective patrimony. In doing so, however, the chief also placed himself at odds with those loggers who resented any efforts to deprive them of the fruits of their labor. While his prestige probably shielded him from direct challenge, Neo'pit's action also revealed the increasingly complicated nature of Menominee politics.

It was not long before Agent Stephens found out just how complicated the politics of logging had become. In a letter dated 2 June 1882, four Menominees expressed their unease at the agent's plan to deduct a "stumpage fee" prior to distributing the proceeds of the timber sales. Signed by Ohopahsa, the headman of the Oconto River community, a distant relative of Chief Neo'pit named Louis Oshkenaniew, the chief's deposed brother Ahkonemi, and the trader Joseph Gauthier, this letter charged the agent with breaking faith with loggers. "At a council of our tribe," the Menominee lumbermen wrote, "our Agent told us we could go to work, and cut and manufacture into logs, dead and down timber, and that we would receive the full amount realized for the logs." After completing the "expensive and hard" work, loggers found that "our Agent, without telling us, went to Washington, and on his return told us that you had decided that we must pay stumpage."[17]

As this letter sat in the commissioner's office, a second challenge to Stephens materialized. On 29 June ninety-seven Menominees called for the agent's removal. Organized by Ohopahsa and three other band chiefs, Louis Keshena, Peter LaMotte, and John Keneabay, this group alleged that Stephens was "unfit to be in the Indian Service" because he was widely "believed to have been dishonest in his dealings with the tribe."[18] Neither Neo'pit nor his two principal associates signed this petition, however, and in January 1883 the three chiefs drafted a response in which they expressed "great confidence" in their agent. Writing that "during the past four years he has always been our true friend and protector," they steadfastly maintained that "by all his transactions for us," Stephens had proved his honesty.[19]

As it turned out, Stephens left the reservation in the fall of 1883, but it remains uncertain if resistance to his presence hastened his departure. In a sense, though, neither Stephens's fate nor that of Neo'pit's logging tax (which jumped to 10 percent of gross sales by 1884),[20] is as important as what this sequence of events tells us about Menominee political activity. Ostensibly a demonstration of opposition to perceived interference by an outsider, these three pieces of evidence indicate the growing influence of logging, and logging-related, issues and the continued potency of band-centered leadership patterns. Of those four who signed the first document, one, Ahkomeni Oshkosh, owed money to a Shawano trading concern and another, Joseph Gauthier, was related to an important merchant. In the second petition, Ohopahsa was again in the forefront, and we detect as well a high degree of correlation between Stephens's opponents and our "benchmark" 1888–89 schedule of loggers. Read in combination, the 1882 petition and 1888–89 logging schedule also reveal the continued importance of familial ties. Among those signing the 1882 petition were several members of such prominent families as Corn, Dodge, LaMotte, Mah-ke-metas (Mahquemetas), Oshkenaniew, Skesick, Waubano, and Waukecheon. Each family was represented in the list of loggers from later in the decade, and in many cases, the very same individuals show up in both accounts. Finally, it is also clear that, even considering the growing influence of Menominee logging interests, older forms of leadership still held sway. This was particularly evident in the letter supporting Agent Stephens. Not only did Neo'pit and the other prominent chiefs claim, with some justification, to be speaking for the entire community, but they also convinced Ohopahsa to "switch sides" and lend his name to their letter. What was developing, then, was an evolving Menominee politics, with the influence of loggers checked, at least for now, by respect for family, band, and clan.[21]

Logging contributed to political jockeying in other ways. With improving material prospects came a number of applications from individuals claiming Menominee heritage, all of whom now requested formal adoption into the tribe. The tribal council responded favorably to some petitions, notably one forwarded by Joseph Gauthier, the mixed-blood trader who also served as interpreter for some government functions and dealings with local whites.[22] Nevertheless, the enrollment question was exceedingly complicated and subject to differing interpretations. Nonloggers, for instance, concluded that enlarging tribal rolls threatened their very livelihood by subdividing already shrinking annuity payments. Frustrated, they fought back by forwarding a petition designed, as Agent Andrews maintained, "to exclude the half breeds from sharing in their annuity payment." Andrews responded by requesting from the Indian Office a clarification of the conditions under which "mixed bloods upon a reserve have a right to share [annuity payments] with full bloods."[23]

Although the total number of genetic "full bloods" was probably quite small by the 1880s, this request expressed the discomfort felt by nonloggers over the growing importance of logging, and they chose to vent their hostility in the direction of non-Menominee men who had married Menominee women. Tempted by bright prospects for financial gain, "squawmen" found it a relatively easy matter to skirt the rules that prohibited them from entering into logging contracts. They simply had their wives apply for "chances," as such contracts were called, and signed themselves on as "employees," which enabled them to hire teams, cut timber, and profit from logging in the same fashion as any regularly enrolled Menominee.[24] According to Agent D. P. Andrews, even those who had never lived on the reservation now returned "and wish to share in the spoils of that chance." Given the numbers of legitimately enrolled men and "large boys able to work," Andrews asked, "how many chances or shares should a squaw be allowed?"[25]

How many chances indeed. A difficult question in and of itself, the enrollment issue ranks as only one complication plaguing Menominee logging. Local lumbering concerns, as always coveting reservation timber, manipulated the log market, sending prices for Indian logs plummeting and driving Menominee contractors toward insolvency. Indian Office inspector Robert Gardiner noted the nefarious intentions of local lumbermen in his 1884 report, which concluded that Indian logs "sold very low," largely because "the Oshkosh Lumber and Mill men did not bid on these logs." The reason, so Gardiner discovered, was to "discourage the Indians from Logging in the future," with the aim being to "induce . . . the indians [sic] to ask the Government to sell their Pine Land to individuals, corporations or Syndicates."[26]

Gardiner's solution—sell the logs to the agency trader who had submitted a more reasonable offer—was one way to combat the pine ring, but by no means the tribe's only tactic. In 1883, Menominees voted to keep their 4.5 million feet of logs off the market. Ohopahsa, who emerged as the spokesman for this controversial decision, asserted in a letter to the Indian commissioner that while "the Menominee Indians wants [sic] to work, cut, and lumber," local timber concerns were thwarting their efforts. These "lumber Manufacturers and buyers," he continued, "have been trying to buy our Pine lumber" for between four and five dollars per thousand feet when the going rate was nearly four times as high. Fearing that "we are going to be robed [sic]," Ohopahsa called on the commissioner "to help me as my friends and my nation begs [sic] me to help them and as I can [not] do anything I therefore beg to *you* to help *us* with *your* Power in regard to us."[27]

This strategy recalled Agent Chase's efforts of a decade earlier and proved no more effective. Bids remained low in 1884, and the addition of previously cut timber to the market drove down prices still further, to a point where Agent Andrews reported "a clear lòss to the lumbermen of about $6,000."[28] The decision to withhold timber also made it difficult for contractors to settle debts, which damaged relations with merchants. In 1884 a group of Shawano businessmen lobbied for a lien on timber revenues, hoping to force the Indian Office to repay logging debts, out of the Menominee annuity fund if need be. Although officials in Washington apparently failed to satisfy the merchants' request, the incident was one of several where Indian loggers found it difficult to meet their financial obligations. Chronically short of capital, loggers struggled under an unwieldy system that, even under the best of circumstances, left them at the mercy of creditors who may have had ulterior motives. The combination of below-market offers for their logs and mounting debt left Menominees caught between defaulting on financial obligations, thereby jeopardizing future operations, and selling their timber at a clear loss. Neither option was particularly attractive.[29]

Frustrated by a system that left loggers chronically indebted, the Indian Office changed the rules in early 1884. From here on out, the agent used tribal accounts to provide credit directly to loggers. This represented a logical solution to the problem, and in 1884 alone loggers secured nearly $8,000 to finance their operations. But the new system suffered from some problems. It could be cumbersome, as the agent authorized orders for supplies and then had to await action from Washington to pay for them, and did nothing to prevent traders from overcharging Menominee customers. At the same time, it effectively reduced the independence of Indian loggers, placing them under the direction of the agent, who doled out money and supplies as he saw fit. While preferable in many ways to the prior method, the new system was heavily paternalistic, demonstrating that logging proceeded at the pleasure of the Indian Office.[30]

Just how capricious this support could be showed itself in several ways, from agents who proved less than committed to the logging operation to an Indian Office that responded harshly to any perceived problems. Even as he endorsed the construction of a sawmill at Keshena, Agent Andrews still decried logging as promising such "glittering prizes" that Indians "turned disgusted from the plow and field," denigrated the Indian tradesman for "liv[ing] his wages up as he goes along, if not faster," and ultimately advocated selling the rights to all reservation timber.[31] As for the Indian Office, it suspended logging in 1885 and again in 1886 after receiving reports that Indian lumberjacks were harvesting standing green timber. This clearly violated the dead and down limitations. But while officials viewed this as a question of law and order, it may be that Menominees were expressing "ownership" over their resource and chafing under regulations that prevented them from utilizing the most valuable timber. In any event, the Indian Office responded by ordering logging halted, leaving production at just 3 million feet during the two interrupted seasons.[32] It was only after the tribe's new agent, Thomas Jennings, responding to the "earnest solicitation of the Indians," pleaded with the Interior Department to reauthorize logging that Menominee lumberjacks enjoyed a full season's work.[33]

In Thomas Jennings, Menominee loggers found a consistent, sometimes aggressive, supporter who observed that the enterprise not only funded the agency hospital, poor relief, and new homes but also promoted "habits of industry and foresight" and a general improvement in material comfort. All these changes appealed to an agent who was, after all, promoting assimilation. At the same time, Jennings remained mindful of the Indian Office's preference for farming over industry; in 1887 he promised "to inculcate the idea" that "cultivating the soil . . . was the only way that an Indian could secure a comfortable living and the necessities and luxuries of life." Yet, even as he announced his intention "to induce the Indian to pay less attention to logging and to devote his attention to cultivating the soil," the agent also promoted an expansion of logging.[34] This effort bore fruit when Menominee loggers cut over 8 million feet of timber during the 1887–88 season, the highest total in more than ten years. Log sales surpassed $86,000, a new record, and Indian loggers earned just over $76,000, with 10 percent of the gross sales, or $8,600, set aside for poor relief and support for the agency hospital.[35]

Jenning's efforts notwithstanding, the Menominee logging venture remained secure for little more than a year. In the fall of 1888, Attorney General Augustus H. Garland issued an opinion that revived the question of title to natural resources on Indian reservations. Relying on *United States v. Cook,* Garland ruled that the "right of Indians on any Indian reservation is one of occupancy only." While this "carries with it the right to improve the land by clearing it," including "the right to sell or dispose of timber on the land cleared," he argued that it expressly denied Indians the authority to "cut or sever" any timber for the purposes of selling on the market. Significantly, this prohibition also included dead and down timber. In this instance, he wrote, "the right and title to the Timber is absolute in the United States," and may not be cut or sold for profit alone.[36]

Garland's pronouncement meant that timber cutting ground to a halt once again, highlighting the tangled legal and constitutional questions surrounding Indian exploitation of resources held in trust by the federal government. Given the now heavy Menominee reliance on timber revenues, this action could have proved disastrous had it not been for two events. On the national front, timely lobbying by C. C. Painter, corresponding secretary of the Indian Rights Association, yielded a temporary solution in the form of a 1889 congressional action permitting the president to authorize logging of dead and down timber on a year-to-year basis.[37] At the same time, Agent Jennings cleverly seized on a loophole in the attorney general's opinion—that Indians could cut and market logs as long as the harvest was a consequence of clearing lands for farms and homes—to restart the work. One hundred eighty-six Menominee loggers took to the woods and over that winter cut 18 million feet of timber, much of it green, which they sold for over $154,000.[38] Both of these totals were new records, as was the $139,000 paid to Indian contractors. While there was some suspicion that Jennings had abused the exemption by permitting cutting well beyond the total needed to clear land, an investigation turned up no wrongdoing.[39] When the new rules took effect the following year, production soared as Menominee loggers earned $196,000 on sales of just over 25 million feet of mainly dead and down timber.[40]

Stability proved elusive once again, as Congress considered the status of the tribe's valuable green timber, estimated at more than 400 million board feet and worth as much as $40 million.[41] The debate over Menominee standing pine, long coveted by Wisconsin lumbering interests, dated from late 1887, when Philetus Sawyer, a United States senator and a wealthy lumberman from Oconto, Wisconsin, introduced a bill to permit the outright sale of reservation timber. Sawyer's ally Myron McCord, the House member representing the Oconto area, sponsored a similar bill and promised to steer it through the lower chamber. Like Sawyer, McCord also had close ties with lumbermen, but the obvious conflict of interest proved no impediment, as a number of prominent lawmakers, including the chairman of the Senate Committee on Indian Affairs, Senator Henry L. Dawes, openly supported the Sawyer-McCord efforts.[42]

On the Menominee Reservation, however, the reaction was much different. Agent Jennings denounced the bill as the work of lumbering interests who "have left nothing undone to convince Authorities in

Washington that the Indians can not lumber successfully." He also predicted that, should the Sawyer-McCord proposal prevail in Congress, Menominees would "in a few years of riotous living have nothing left but a sandy land covered with pine stumps."[43] Indian reaction was stronger still. In an 1888 petition addressed to Senator Dawes, the 187 signators expressed two main concerns and offered an alternative plan. On the one hand, the petitioners feared that it "would be demoralizing to our tribe to have a large number of white men on our reservation for a number of years," as "our people would be to a great extent corrupted." Their second objection highlighted ongoing, and well-placed, mistrust of local lumber operators. Reminding Senator Dawes that "out of a vast extent of territory owned formally by our tribe the timber on our reservation is all we have left that is of value," the petitioners predicted that the proposed legislation would encourage the powerful to form "rings" and to purchase "our timber . . . at a price very much under its value." Affirming their determination "to cut and haul the logs to the rivers at a fair and reasonable compensation," the Menominees asked Indian Office personnel to oversee the log sales and place the balance of the proceeds, less moneys due Indian contractors, in a special account "to be invested or paid to our tribe in such a manner as shall be deemed equitable and just."[44]

These communications proved just opening salvos in a two-year political struggle. At one level, the acrimonious contest pitted Agent Jennings against Wisconsin lumber interests and their congressional supporters. Viewed from this perspective, Jennings emerges as a champion of Menominee entrepreneurs and is rewarded with their loyalty as he fights to retain his position. This remains an accurate picture of the struggle, as far as it goes. Equally significant, however, is the evidence that it was during this struggle that Menominee entrepreneurs found their voice. A change that was less revolutionary than evolutionary, this habit of political activity on the part of Menominee loggers demonstrates that entrepreneurs possessed a clear understanding of the issues being debated before Congress, that they were determined to add their perspectives, and finally that their opinions carried some weight.

For Congress and the local media, Representative McCord combined a passionate defense of his proposal with a vicious attack on Jennings and on the Menominee logging venture generally. Claiming support from Wisconsin's entire congressional delegation, "editors of most local newspapers," and indeed all "who have studied the question," McCord calculated that the timber sale would generate $2 million, or "an annual annuity . . . of $75,000, or to each head about $50, or say, $200 to each family of four persons." This, he wrote, was preferable to current arrangements, which promised a dismal future of denuded forests, not to mention profits "squandered by a few favored ones of the tribe, while the bulk of the tribe will be destitute."[45] Standing in the way, however, was the Indian Office, and particularly Agent Jennings. In a virtual laundry list of accusations, McCord charged that the agent had allowed schools, roads, and agency property to deteriorate; had, in contravention of departmental regulations, permitted white men to be employed as loggers; was guilty of nepotism in filling agency posts; had solicited and accepted bribes; and had encouraged Indians to default on repaying debts to all traders save Garrett Sullivan, who just happened to be Jennings's brother-in-law. Equally damaging were the congressman's charges that, contrary to the agent's official reports, logging operated at a deficit, and Indian contractors still owed creditors nearly $25,000 on the previous year's work.[46] He then added the explosive charge that Jennings was guilty of selling liquor to Menominees, an activity he linked with the agent's Catholicism and Democratic Party affiliation.[47]

Jennings denounced the intentions of lumbermen and their allies, offering statistics to prove that logging was financially profitable and predicting a loss of at least "one million, three hundred thousand dollars," should the Sawyer-McCord measure prevail. In just the previous season, he noted, the tribe converted nearly $60,000 in logging profits to agricultural and domestic "improvements," and construction of homes and stables. This, Jennings concluded, explained "why the Menominees are almost unanimously opposed to selling their pine timber on the stump." He concluded as well that, since "I dare to defend the Indians and stand up for their rights," his opponents threatened to expel him from the reservation unless he used his "influence with the Indians and others, for the purpose of securing passage of the Pine Bill." Casting his actions as a simple matter of conscience, the agent stood firm.[48]

Conscience or not, it is clear that Jennings's position reflected the sentiments of a substantial segment of the Menominee population. In March 1888 the tribe financed a delegation to Washington. Led by Chiefs Neo'pit and Chickeney, this contingent expressed the Menominees' opposition to the Sawyer-McCord bill and reiterated their long-standing hostility toward any measure promoting the sale of standing pine to outside concerns.[49] In October came a second anti–timber sale petition, this time signed by 139 Menominees, and in January 1890 the tribe again dispatched Chiefs Neo'pit, Mah Chickeney, and Neahtahwapony, along with logger Joseph Oshkenaniew and interpreter Joseph Gauthier, to Washington, D.C. This delegation carried a document, signed by 162 Menominees, investing them with power of attorney "to take such means as they may find necessary" to, among other tasks, have Agent Jennings reappointed and prevent the passage of any bill "providing for the sale of our Pine Stumpage or lands." The three chiefs, along with Gauthier and

Oshkenaniew, also were encouraged to hire a lawyer and, perhaps surprisingly, to request the allotment of reservation lands in severalty.[50]

Spread over nearly two years, these communications demonstrate at the very least that opposition to blanket timber sales was widespread and seemingly linked with positive feelings toward Jennings. Even closer analysis reveals intriguing connections between logging and political activity, promising insights into the evolution of tribal politics during the last decades of the nineteenth century. This analysis begins with the correlation between petition signators and loggers, as recorded in the 1888–89 logging schedule and another survey conducted for the 1889–90 season. Of the 187 names attached to the 1888 petition, 70 were loggers themselves, with many more probably related to loggers, judging by the appearance on petitions of several individuals with the same surnames. Similar percentages appear for the second petition, with 68 of the 139 names matching directly, and for the third, with exact correlations for 74 out of 162 signatures. Again, even higher percentages are likely if we include relatives and consider possible variations in the spelling of Menominee surnames. This confirms what might be an obvious conclusion: that Menominee lumberjacks interpreted the Sawyer-McCord bill as detrimental to their livelihoods, recognized that the national legislature held authority over their business, and, consequently, sought to influence decision makers accordingly.[51]

Of course, numerous individuals who cannot be directly linked with logging also signed the petitions. This suggests at the least that nonloggers endorsed logging, perhaps because it was a *tribal* operation that provided employment, distributed benefits throughout the community, and confirmed notions of collective ownership over reservation resources. The conclusion that logging corresponded with accepted patterns of Menominee social organization is supported as well by data indicating that actual logging operations were carried out by families, acting collectively. Not only did relatives pool their resources, sometimes forming "companies" such as those run by the Corn, Dodge, Gauthier, Grignon, Law, Peters, Wapoose (Waupoose), and Wiscoby (Wisecoby) families, but band, clan, and family leaders appear to have been nominally in charge of the various camps. This accounts for the large disparity observed between logs produced by scions of prominent families and the average log production, per individual contractor, per year. During the 1888–89 season, for instance, Reginald Oshkosh and his aged father, Neo'pit, delivered more than 2,000 logs to the banks of the Wolf River; the average was fewer than 500. Leaders of other important families, like Chickeney, Gauthier, Grignon, LaMotte, Law, Mahkimetas, Waukecheon, Laframboise, and Waupoose, also rank among the largest producers, and most of these individuals, or their relatives, appear on each of the three petitions regarding the Sawyer proposal. Perhaps not surprising given the Menominee emphasis on clan and band loyalty, this pattern may have been particularly instrumental in securing widespread support for logging by, in a sense, adapting logging to fit societal values, rather than the other way around.[52]

Yet logging also exerted pressure on the Menominee social and political order. Conspicuously absent from any petition or schedule of loggers is Wieskesit, leader of the Zoar community. This indicates that distance from Keshena probably meant isolation from logging work. It may mean as well that the most culturally conservative Menominees, those who deliberately gathered in that remote region in the first place, avoided logging for reasons other than proximity to markets. It suggests also that these "conservatives" tended not to participate in the great changes overtaking their society, at least not overtly.

At the other end of the social spectrum lay the Oconto, or South Branch, community. Located some fifteen miles northeast of Keshena, Oconto was home and workplace to many loggers, whose total production nearly equaled that of the Wolf River camps. But while logging provided Oconto families with avenues toward material gain, the community lacked some of the amenities found at agency headquarters. Physical isolation also may have encouraged independent entrepreneurial and political activity. John Corn, a successful Oconto logger, requested authority to operate a local sawmill, to take logs as "payment" for services rendered to Indian loggers, and to sell his own lumber to off-reservation whites, independent of tribal transactions. The department evidently denied his request even though the only reservation sawmill was located in Keshena. In 1887, thirty-two men, all loggers and all signators to that series of petitions discussed previously, called upon Indian Commissioner J. D. C. Atkins to open a branch store in Oconto. Authored by Mitchell Oshkenaniew, Joseph's son, this communication stands as evidence of the rising prominence of logging interests in Oconto, as well as for members of that particular family. Joseph, after all, accompanied the three chiefs on their 1890 journey to Washington, presumably as Oconto's representative, and in 1889 the obviously literate Mitchell served as one of four "witnesses" overseeing signatures to the 1889 petition. Given the apparent demise of Oconto headman Ohopahsa, the Oshkenaniews, members of the bear clan and not so distantly related to Chief Neo'pit, gradually assumed positions of leadership in that community. Oconto logging and political activity stand out in other ways as well. Oconto petitioners consistently outnumbered their compatriots from the wolf, and women were more likely to hold logging "chances" there than in the Keshena area. The latter produced the interesting situation in which wives held the right to log, but husbands, presumably non-Menominees, signed petitions. Taken together, this evidence strongly suggests that distance from agency head-quarters produced independence, and in Oconto, more overtly than else-where, political objectives came to be expressed through logging.[53]

Political activism coincided with a reduction in the formal authority of chiefs. While Menominees deferred to Neo'pit and his two associates on official matters, it is clear that loggers, and the Indian Office, gradu-ally came to dominate the dialogue. On the occasion of Neo'pit's 1890 delegation, Agent Jennings observed that while "the old chiefs are now in Washington," it was only "through custom [that] the younger and more enlightened ones allowed them the honor of representing the tribe." Jen-nings himself had influenced this emerging divergence in influence when, in 1889, he supported the creation of a Court of Indian Offenses. Headed by the three old chiefs, now designated "judges," this body held authority over "minor offenses," most having to do with crimes associ-ated with alcohol use. In exchange, Neo'pit and his two associates relin-quished their hereditary claim to political leadership as important decision-making authority, including the right to call meetings of the tribal council, now passed to the agent and the Indian Office.[54]

Support for established leadership did not equal confidence, how-ever, and in 1889 the emerging political and entrepreneurial "activists" enlisted the aid of Colonel Fred T. Ledergerber, an attorney based in St. Louis. The decision to hire Ledergerber marks an important moment in Menominee history. No longer convinced that petitions, delegations, and the good intentions of their agent were sufficient to head off the designs of the pine ring and its congressional allies, certain Menominees chose to confront their antagonists in a novel manner. Promised a $50,000 retainer drawn from tribal funds, Ledergerber intended primarily to combat the proposed timber sale and also was instructed to seek a special allotment bill; both items represented the loggers' agenda. The Sawyer-McCord bill, of course, threatened their principal source of income. Allotment, on the other hand, may be understood both as an expression of loggers' conclu-sions that, absent individual title, all timber could be lost and, perhaps more significantly, as evidence that some loggers had internalized an individualistic, entrepreneurial ethos that held personal property, and profit, in higher regard than communal, or "tribal," values. In both respects, the Menominees resemble the situation Melissa Meyer has observed for White Earth Anishinaabe timberlands, and those forces may explain why the allotment request accompanied every petition for-warded during the 1880s.[55]

In Washington, the Menominees' decision to move outside recog-nized channels and hire a lawyer-lobbyist provoked considerable contro-versy. Although Interior Secretary Noble endorsed Ledergerber's contract, others, including Representative McCord, found it a dangerous proposition. Oblivious to developments within Menominee society, McCord denounced the "fifty thousand dollars for one year's service and no limit to the expenses he may incur!" and blamed Agent Jennings. He argued that the Indians "were induced to sign such a contract by false representations, and by other corrupt means," and claimed that "the very men who signed this contract" had now changed their minds. He further called upon the commissioner to void Ledergerber's contract, which was, he wrote "a great injustice and outrage on an ignorant people, whose rights it is *our* duty to protect."[56]

McCord's opposition seems to have thrown the tribe into a state of turmoil. Some Menominees, including Joseph Oshkenaniew and Joseph Gauthier, did in fact disavow Ledergerber.[57] Defending himself, Ledergerber fired off a note to the commissioner that included a statement by the three old chiefs, then in Washington, recanting their decision to cancel his contract and recounting a tale of deception. "After waiting in Washington for a week after the appointed time for Col. Ledergerber to call on us," they began, "we were told that he was in the city and was doing our business and ignored our presence entirely (which we found afterwards to be False)." Only later, wrote Neo'pit and his associates, did they learn that pressure to disavow the lawyer constituted "a trap set by men who wanted to secure the passage of the Sawyer and McCord Bills," and they now regretted their previous move, just as "our people" are "very angry with us for our action in this matter."[58]

Other Menominees were not so forgiving. In an open letter to the Milwaukee *Sentinal,* an unnamed Menominee wrote that "it was with a full consent of the whole Menominee tribe that said contract was made without the advice of any white man." The tribe, he maintained, "deemed the move prudent, . . . to secure a lawyer who would defend our interests, than to let the pine land ring steal several millions from us." Asserting the Menominees' intention not "to be dictated too [sic] by an agent or anyone else,"[59] the correspondent concluded on this forceful note:

> If we dare to assert our rights, we are . . . branded as rebels and defying the government. No, we do not defy the government but we mean to continue until we make it plain to our Great Fathers in Washington that we are victims of unscrupulous men who want our property and that we are now, as in all our history, loyal to the government and we think we deserve its protection against organized persecutions.[60]

It is not clear whether Ledergerber ever conducted any legal work on behalf of the Menominees, or if he collected his retainer. In 1890, though, the Menominee delegation in Washington hired a second attorney, Philip

B. Thompson of Washington, D.C., and promised him $10,000 in May 1890 and $5,000 in May 1891.[61] His efforts remain obscure as well, but in a sense the actual legal work performed is less important than the act of seeking outside counsel. This action indicated the loggers' determination to protect their interests, not to mention their growing influence over decision making and access to tribal funds.

Some Menominees, however, were not at all satisfied with this turn of events. In early 1888 Jennings received word from the commissioner that "half-breeds not Menominees are cutting green timber" on the reservation. His reply was to deny the accusation vehemently and lay blame on certain disaffected Indians. "The whole matter," he wrote, "arises from one or two men who are jealous of Joseph Gauthier the Interpreter because, in a full council, called by themselves, he opposed the sale of their pine." To make matters worse, this council also appointed Gauthier as interpreter for the Menominee delegation sent to Washington to protest the Sawyer-McCord measures. At the head of this splinter faction, Jennings claimed, was none other than Ahkonemi Oshkosh, the deposed chief and elder brother of Neo'pit. According to Jennings, the senior Oshkosh "wanted to visit Washington in order to lay his case before you thinking that he could get you to reinstate him and depose his brother who is chief." As for the rest of the tribe, Jennings remained confident that they had "followed my instructions to the letter about not cutting standing green timber," even in spite of "advice of certain white men in Shawano who are doing all they can to demoralize the Indians so as to make political capital out of it."[62]

Not to be denied, Ahkonemi Oshkosh and two Menominee allies drafted a petition of their own, which they forwarded to the commissioner's office in March 1888. Its substance undercut the authority of the tribal delegation in Washington and suggested that most Menominees in fact favored selling their timber on the stump. Asserting that "the majority of lumbermen that are now lumbering on our reservation are half breeds and are not members of the Menominee tribe," the former chief and his associates charged that the delegation in Washington was "sent by Indians called lumbermen" and did not represent "the interest of the tribe by opposing the sale of our Pine timber." The best solution, he concluded, was for "our tribe [to] share equally in the money's [sic] derived from our pine forest," in other words, a massive timber sale. He also asked that this action be taken immediately, "before the great bulk of it is lumbered through, wasted, and destroyed by Indians and half breeds."[63]

While there is no evidence that the commissioner was inclined to take the word of three Indians at face value, it is clear that turmoil surrounding the status of reservation timber caused the department to reexamine the situation. In March 1890 Commissioner Morgan dispatched a special agent to Wisconsin with the responsibility of investigating and evaluating all aspects of the Menominee logging operation. After two months on the reservation, Agent Frank Lewis submitted a lengthy report, which conceded that logging had brought to the reservation certain "material improvements" but nevertheless concluded that very few Menominees profited substantially from logging. This he blamed on exorbitant rates charged by traders for supplies and the Indians' tendency to fritter away their earnings. He also charged Indian loggers with defaulting on their debts, while defiantly cutting green standing timber. Finally, the special agent also condemned Thomas Jennings. Writing that "I can not find in what way he has advanced their interests," Lewis went on to assert, with what seems to have been unintended irony, that the agent "has done nothing but try to cater to their wishes, and let them do as they pleased." At the same time, however, Lewis accused Jennings of seeking to convince his charges "that every body in the country was in a ring to rob the Menominees of their pine," while "assiduously [holding] himself up to them as a model man and agent."[64]

Although Lewis's conclusions regarding profits were open to debate,[65] he was on the mark in highlighting the depth of the Menominees' loyalty to Jennings and their deep mistrust of lumbermen, political officials, and the Indian Office. This became clear when the inspector brought word that the Harrison administration had decided to replace Jennings with a Republican, Charles S. Kelsey. Many Menominees greeted the news by venting their dissatisfaction, and in no uncertain terms. "We object to his appointment," said one Menominee, "because we know by whom he was appointed, the people that have always wanted our handful of pine." Another Indian, the mixed-blood logger Tom LaBelle, echoed these sentiments when he protested, "I don't believe that the government appointed Mr. Kelsey for our agency." Rather, it was "our enemies who have appointed him," and by enemies he meant "Sawyer and McCord." These congressmen, continued LaBelle, "are the men that we call in our language 'pine sharks,' for they want to swallow our pine and property." Jennings, by contrast, had fostered improvements, from "farms" to "teams, wagons, pumps, etc."; more important, so LaBelle continued, he had "given us our rights, . . . told us the truth, and is the first man working for our benefit." Still another suggested paying Kelsey to stay off the reservation if that would secure Jennings's reappointment for another term.[66]

By early May, Lewis, now joined by Kelsey, was growing increasingly impatient with Menominee resistance. Menominees likewise stood firm, and at one point Chief Neo'pit turned to Jennings and said: "I command you not to turn over my property, that is under this roof [agency headquarters] to any man. I take you as a prisoner, in the name of the

Menominee tribe." Lewis countered that the "law now compels Mr. Jennings to turn over the property to Mr. Kelsey," and added that some Menominees, in particular Ahkomeni Oshkosh and his associates, had offered their support for the new agent. These assertions had the effect of ratcheting up the pressure. One mixed-blood logger, for instance, questioned whether the special agent was not really acting in the interests of "the Shawano people," meaning local non-Indian lumbering concerns. Joseph Oshkenaniew adopted a different tactic and accused Ahkonemi Oshkosh of having "stained the ground under heaven with blood," and his followers of "dancing day and night" and holding their children out of school. "If you say they [Ahkomeni and his followers] obey the law of the government," concluded Oshkenaniew, "then we will all go and dance."[67]

From here the situation deteriorated to a point where violence threatened. On 31 May, Lewis installed Kelsey and ordered Jennings to turn over control of agency headquarters and all official papers. This Jennings refused to do until a formal inventory could be completed, and an increasingly agitated group of Menominees backed him by gathering on the grounds of the agent's residence. Lewis then ordered the locks changed on the agency buildings. But later that afternoon, Indians simply broke into the office and placed a lock of their own on the door. This infuriated Lewis, who then threatened to arrest those Indians guilty of "house breaking" and smashed the new lock. By this time the Indians "were wrought up to the highest pitch of excitement." Father Odoric, headmaster of the reservation's Catholic school, advised Kelsey to leave the reservation until the situation calmed down, and after similar warnings by the chief clerk and agency farmer, the prospective agent moved to Shawano. Jennings finally left in early June, and Kelsey took control of the agency, but not before he received a stern warning from Washington. "If you cannot take possession of the agency and settle the matter in peace," wrote Interior Secretary Noble, the department promised "to appoint one who will do so."[68]

The Menominees had failed in their effort to retain Jennings, and this failure was to leave deep wounds and bitter memories that impeded Kelsey's effectiveness as agent. But while the tribe was understandably frustrated by this turn of events, the experiences surrounding the fight over the Sawyer bill and the question of Jennings's retention as agent proved to have important consequences for its sociopolitical "culture." The year 1890 also brought a new law regulating logging on the Menominee Reservation. This law, however, ignored the Sawyer proposal as Congress formulated a plan that recognized the tribe's right to cut and market reservation timber, including green standing timber. A landmark in the development of Menominee logging, the legislation also established a mechanism for funding the tribal enterprise, managing the yearly harvest, and distributing earnings among tribal members. In October a tribal vote approved the proposal, and Menominee logging prepared to enter a new, and ultimately more prosperous, era.[69]

But passage of the 1890 measure remained just a single act in a long play. Only a bare majority offered their endorsement, and it took two ballots. This process, as we will discover in the next chapter, was complicated, another step in which the evolution of Menominee politics was intimately related to logging and the changing status of loggers. Left unresolved, however, was the issue of allotment. Despite repeated requests for a special allotment bill, Congress declined to place the Menominees in compliance with Dawes Act priorities. This decision was to have important consequences during the next decade and well beyond. At the very least marking the Menominees as rather unusual among those tribes holding significant, and easily obtainable, natural resources, the absence of allotment also affected the now intertwined fates of logging, tribal politics, and ethnic identity. Just how these intersected became ever more clear during the 1890s.

During the 1880s, the principal developments revolved around this triad of logging, political activity, and cultural values. The expansion of logging had, on the one hand, encouraged a nascent entrepreneurial spirit among those most closely associated with the business. These new values could be interpreted as being in direct conflict with a communalism that had characterized Menominee life in former times. Some Menominees discerned this conflict and responded in a variety of ways, from isolation in the case of the Zoar community to Neo'pit's efforts to reach some sort of accommodation between old and new. The struggle over the Sawyer-McCord bill and other challenges to logging placed the question of values in stark relief, demonstrating to loggers, anyway, that the stakes were high. This struggle also "politicized" loggers, convincing them of the need to act while simultaneously reinforcing their sense of power and even entitlement. Already apparent during the 1880s and more so in the following decades, the expansion of logging served to enhance the influence of loggers, and vice versa.

But discovering a divergence of values and documenting the rising influence of a particular segment of Menominee society tells only part of the story. In many respects the most important component of this segment in Menominee history was that loggers' political activism did not create substantial rifts in the social fabric. That loggers respected established leadership, operated according to clan and band ties, and accepted the idea that some profits must filter down to the collective community demonstrated that Menominee values were remarkably flexible, sufficiently so that we might argue that culture, in this sense, "managed" economic and social change. The next decades would test this arrangement as this new cadre of loggers/political activists/economic "modernizers" prodded their brothers toward accepting novel economic and social relationships. Operating at the same time were countervailing forces that asked loggers to protect the tribe's sense of independence and right to chart its own course, to be modernizers, not assimilationists; Indian entrepreneurs, not white men with red skin.

CHAPTER THREE

Mitchell Oshkenaniew and Logging During the 1890s

The congressional act of 12 June 1890 opened a new era on the Menominee Reservation. Since green logs brought much higher prices than dead and damaged timber, broadening the logging mandate to include standing pine promised greater profits. The new legislation also offered at least the chance for some stability. By satisfying the demands set forth in the *Cook* decision, namely, specific legislation permitting Menominee logging, the 1890 measure sanctioned that enterprise in the name of the federal government. Just as important, it also ended the battle over the Sawyer bill, and with it the likelihood that Menominee timber would be sold "on the stump." No small accomplishment, this meant that the Menominees parted ways with other timber-rich tribes, most notably the Anishinaabeg of Wisconsin and Minnesota, who, absent similar legislation, saw their timberlands denuded, their people left virtually penniless. By contrast, the Menominee law not only endorsed Indian participation in logging but also underwrote the venture, provided for guiding regulations, and established mechanisms for saving, investing, and distributing profits. Logging flourished in this newly stable environment, and by the turn of the century, tribal coffers surpassed $2 million, above and beyond wages paid Indian contractors and their hired help.[1]

Logging's expansion also meant a further elaboration of ongoing social and political adaptations. A decade of fighting to retain the right to log had effectively "politicized" many Menominees, and some came to appreciate not only the necessity of organizing but also their ability to influence events. Logging, of course, had created new avenues toward material security, but it also educated some Menominees in the workings of the mainstream economic and political system. Comparative wealth and facility with the white man's world proved a powerful combination as the 1890s witnessed a rise in the fortunes of Menominee loggers. While these Menominee "entrepreneurs" did not displace either traditional leaders or the principles behind legitimate authority, they nevertheless offered a competing framework for leadership. Their mere presence in positions of some influence suggested that pathways toward leadership passed through, or at least near, logging camps. While it might be expected that the rise of the entrepreneurs engendered resentment, it is equally clear that, just as before, Menominee cultural values "managed" change. Consequently, while entrepreneurs, or "progressives," as they may have considered themselves, amassed considerable influence by 1900, their rise did not bring about crippling factionalism. As we will see, this pattern of "culture managing change" remained central to the Menominee experience with logging.

The act of 12 June 1890 (Public Law 153) delineated, in considerable detail, the parameters under which logging could proceed. Under P.L. 153, the Indian agent, acting through the secretary of the interior, could employ, "at a reasonable compensation," tribal members to cut timber on reservation lands and haul logs to riverbanks or to timber markets downstream, where they would be sold to the highest bidder. At the same time, Congress limited the annual cut to 20 million feet. Designed primarily to prevent the overextension, and accompanying indebtedness, of small-scale Indian lumbering operations, this provision also embraced conservation principles, promoting the idea of sustained-yield forestry. To guarantee that tribal lumberjacks abided by the regulations, their Indian agent was instructed to hire an assistant superintendent of logging and was empowered, but not required, to appoint someone to oversee the sale and delivery of Menominee logs. Timber sales were to fund both positions.[2]

Public Law 153 also dealt with financial issues. Each year, the interior secretary could withdraw a maximum of $75,000 from tribal accounts "for the payment of the expense of cutting, banking, scaling, running, advertising, and sale," a loan the tribe was required to repay out of the gross proceeds from each year's log sales. The 1890 act also broke with past practices regarding the distribution of profits. Unlike old rules that allowed individual contractors to keep money left over after meeting expenses and the 10 percent "stumpage" fee, Indian lumberjacks now were paid a fixed amount per thousand feet cut and banked.[3] This fee was based on the quality of timber harvested and the difficulty in bringing the logs to market. Any amount above and beyond these "wages" reverted to the tribe and fell under certain stipulations. After meeting expenses (including wages paid to employees, who were the responsibility of the individual contractors), repaying the government loan, and settling other outstanding debts, one-fifth of the remainder was earmarked for a "stumpage fund" devoted to supporting the tribal hospital and poor relief. The other four-fifths was to be deposited in a special account, administered by the United States Treasury and earning 5 percent interest annually. Tribal members could draw upon the accumulated interest in the "Menominee Log Fund" (or four-fifths fund) in the form of per capita payments or financing for building homes or roads, clearing farms, or other projects of this type. This last feature demonstrated that Congress now intended to use timber profits to foster economic development and, not incidentally, social change.[4]

Although a majority of men ultimately assented to the new arrangements, as required by law, the procedural details are interesting. On 8 and 9 July, Menominee men attended a council, called by Agent Kelsey, in which Interior Department officials and Kelsey explained the legislation and made a pitch for tribal approval. While no Indian accounts of this meeting seem to have survived, communications among the government principles paint a picture of a polite but ultimately skeptical audience. When, for instance, Menominees asked for an explanation on the method of paying loggers or the appointment, and source of salaries, of logging specialists, the representatives brushed off the questions, promising that problems would be settled at a later date. Such prevarication may explain the less than conclusive outcome. Of the 320 in attendance, 124 voted for the act, 89 registered their opposition, and the rest abstained. Secretary of the Interior John W. Noble ultimately concluded that since fewer than half of those Menominees present at the council actually registered their approval, the vote could not be considered binding. His solution was to have Indian Office representatives find Menominees willing to assent to the act and add their names to the 9 July roll call. This method, rather than a second council and a second vote, produced 211 votes in favor: more than enough.[5]

The close vote and unorthodox means for securing tribal approval indicate, at the very least, a distinct lack of enthusiasm for Congress's handiwork. Even more telling was the fact that Neo'pit, Mah Chickeney, and Neahwapuny cast negative votes, and the three chiefs were joined by band headman John Keshena, as well as Louis, Joseph, and Mitchell Oshkenaniew. The 9 June tally also indicates that loggers accounted for 66 of the 89 no votes, with 46 coming from Oconto loggers. While Wolf River loggers were twice as likely as Oconto men to favor the measure (46 to 20), it is at least as interesting that a clear majority of supporters cannot be identified as loggers at all. Most of these signatures also fail to appear on that series of petitions from the 1880s. Given the presence of Wieskesit, we can surmise that a healthy percentage of yes votes came from cultural conservatives, or at least Menominees living in the vicinity of Zoar. Other conspicuous supporters include Joseph and J. F. Gauthier, father and son, agency interpreter and logger-trader, respectively, and twenty-eight Menominees living off the reservation in Marinette County, Wisconsin. Marinette Menominees also made explicit their "claim" to "the right to share in the proceeds of sales of Timber." This suggests both the lure of logging profits and the conviction that reservation timber belonged to Menominees collectively, rather than to lumberjacks as a consequence of labor performed. This notion of a vested, inherited right to proceeds derived from exploiting *tribal* patrimony may have attracted cultural conservatives to the act, since they, so far as we can determine, chose not to participate in logging.[6]

If nonloggers appear to have been most likely to support the act, why did loggers, and particularly Oconto loggers, vote against it? Clear answers are difficult in the absence of direct testimony, but a credible conclusion seems to proceed from the proposed changes in the structure of logging. When considering the annual ceiling on timber harvest, payment of set "wages" to logging contractors, restrictions on the use of logging funds, and even the appointment of non-Indian supervisors, it is clear that the 1890 act transformed Menominee logging from a comparatively ad hoc enterprise into one virtually controlled by outsiders. The Indian Office, not Menominee entrepreneurs, now decided where and how much to cut. More troubling, at least from the perspective of Indian entrepreneurs, was the fact that under the act they became virtual "employees" of the Indian service in that they received predetermined sums and found themselves subject to oversight by logging inspectors. An appreciation that the act meant a loss of freedom may have bothered individuals like Mitchell Oshkenaniew, especially if we accept the conclusion that experiences during the 1880s had produced, and encouraged, individualistic, entrepreneurial values among some Menominees. This loss of freedom also may have been felt acutely by Neo'pit and his fellow chiefs, as it was contemporaneous with their own loss of autonomy. In a connected sense, what may have appealed to cultural conservatives, that the act recognized a collective right to the timber and logging profits, may have been just the element that most bothered entrepreneurs.

Absent vocal testimony the preceding is just speculation, and we must consider other factors accounting for the close vote in 1890. For instance, Menominee values that emphasized the suppression of public discord, or the avoidance of public confrontation, may explain the high number of abstentions on July 9. This supports the thesis of a growing psychological gap between entrepreneurs and others—conservative or not—as the embrace of individualistic values concerning economic behavior also may have translated into a willingness to engage in public confrontation. This may have pressured the more conservative Menominees, for whom direct confrontation was anathema, to keep quiet rather than vote for the act, which seems to have been their inclination. If so, supporters may have outnumbered opponents by a considerable margin.

Decisions on the act also may have been affected by one other factor, not mentioned directly in the legislation but an undercurrent in the discussion. That was allotment. Despite repeated requests for allotment, the 1890 act said nothing about conforming the Menominee Reservation to the dominant Indian policy initiative. In fact, by enshrining a collective right to timber profits, effectively endorsing communalism over individuality, it really accomplished just the opposite. This result also placed the tribe in direct contrast with Wisconsin and Minnesota Anishinaabe Reservations whose rich sources of timber render their situations most comparable to the Menominees'. The 1890 act also effectively ended serious consideration of Menominee allotment, in the halls of Congress and seemingly in Oconto, Keshena, and Zoar as far as we can see. But documenting the end of allotment discussions does not explain why the Menominees were spared when so many others were not. Some historians suggest that allotment failed because cultural conservatives opposed it, and ultimately prevailed.[7] This may in fact be accurate, but why, one asks, should the Indian Office have listened to those individuals when literate Menominees, and Chief Neo'pit himself, were on record as favoring the subdivision of tribal lands? Lack of documentation requires speculation, but an informed analysis suggests that the Menominees may have escaped allotment because of opposition from local timber interests. Wisconsin's representatives to the Congress, well connected with the timber industry, were conspicuously silent when it came time to act on Menominee requests to be allotted. Had the lumbermen wanted Menominee allotment, they surely would have pressed for it and placed that provision in the 1890 act. It may be that Wisconsin lumbermen saw an advantage in keeping the reservation timberlands intact, reasoning that it might be better to purchase the timber as a unit than deal with individual allottees, among whom were experienced logging contractors who might strike hard bargains. This behavior, of corporations endorsing Indian sovereignty out of self-interest, was unusual but not unique. H. Craig Miner documents similar activities on the part of railroad companies and cattle syndicates in Indian Territory. Seeking to maximize their own profits while preventing competition from other businessmen, some business entities actually promoted tribal sovereignty—so long as it suited their interests.[8]

None of this should suggest that Menominees played no important role in preventing the allotment of their homelands. It does, however, take into account the simple fact that Indians exercised very little influence over national policy, that differences in "power" are important even as we document the ways Indians resisted, adapted, and survived. Allotment was national policy, pursued with considerable vigor, especially in places where money was to be made. So, while Indian opposition no doubt played a role, it is quite likely that the Menominees escaped allotment quite by accident, as a consequence of business calculations by Wisconsin lumbermen and their congressional allies. It is important as well to recall that this decision against allotment probably disappointed a good number of Menominee entrepreneurs.

Entrepreneurs also found that the new act brought new restrictions, ones clearly evident when Agent George Ganz and Charles Montclair, superintendent and assistant superintendent of logging, respectively, drew up the season's logging plan. As the details of this plan became clear, Menominee loggers found that Agent Kelsey now ran most aspects of the enterprise. He hired experienced scalers and oversaw the distribution of wages to laborers, ensured that all debts were paid promptly, set prices paid to contractors (no more than five dollars per thousand feet), settled all accounts at the conclusion of each logging season, and advanced supplies to camp leaders at his own discretion. The agent's responsibilities also included requiring Indian contractors to submit monthly records detailing production, labor costs, and expenses. Other regulations had a rather different tone and intention. Reflecting the evident aim of inculcating a work ethic among supposed "full-blood" Indians (those who needed it the most), neither "squaw men" nor white men "of any class" were to head logging teams, nor were they supposed to work as general laborers unless specifically authorized by the agent. At the same time, the plan of operations required that "all Menominees who are able and desire to engage in logging, or as laborers in logging camps, be allowed to do so."[9] Kelsey also hoped to influence Menominee work habits by paying loggers by the piece rather than by the hour or day, and by withholding wages until the completion of work for the season. This method promised to increase production while combating, he wrote, the Indians' tendency "to be off on a drunk after every pay day." Finally, he advocated a "liberal policy" concerning the $75,000 set aside to finance Menominee logging, warning against forgetting the differences between Indians and "experienced white loggers." "Unless the contractor has some incentive," meaning the prospect of profits even if expenses proved excessive, "very little work would be done." A recipe for paternalistic management, Kelsey's words clearly reflected Congress's intention to use logging as an agent for cultural transformation.[10]

These regulations were not formally approved until January 1891, by which time a record number of Menominee lumberjacks had begun working. By late December, Kelsey had signed off on 138 contracts, a promising sign to be sure, but these agreements authorized a total cut in excess of 60 million feet, fully three times the maximum set by law. Kelsey then panicked, unilaterally altering the logging contracts and thereby reducing the totals allowed to each camp leader. This proved a highly unpopular decision, since Indian contractors already had incurred debts for supplies and hired laborers based on a projected harvest. A smaller take meant lower profits and, in turn, threatened the contractors with financial obligations beyond their limited means. It also demonstrated, clearly and convincingly, that the agent, not Indian entrepreneurs, controlled Menominee logging. Even so, Kelsey nearly succeeded in accomplishing his objective: The adjusted tally for the 1890–91 season stood at 22,769,560 feet.[11]

Menominee loggers responded to Kelsey's action with understandable anger, the tenor of which reflected disappointment with their agent's heavy-handed administration and lingering bitterness over the forced removal of the popular Thomas Jennings. Already inclined to believe that Kelsey's real loyalties lay with his congressional patrons, many complained that their agent was serving the interests of those who sought to discredit Indian logging. Leading the way was Mitchell Oshkenaniew, the Oconto logger. In May 1891, Oshkenaniew, charging that "I have been wronged," complained directly to Interior Secretary Noble. This letter and subsequent actions inaugurated Oshkenaniew's rise to prominence, but at this moment the Oconto man had a rather personal score to settle. His original contact called for delivery of 800,000 feet of logs at $3.00 per thousand feet, and to accomplish that task, so he related to the secretary, Oshkenaniew bought supplies on credit and by January had cut and banked 291,000 board feet. Only then did Kelsey inform him that his new limit was 250,000 and that he would be paid $2.75 per thousand feet. This meant that Oshkenaniew was to be held responsible not only for some 41,000 feet of timber he could not sell but also for financial obligations made prior to beginning the season's work. In an angry reply, Oshkenaniew charged that Kelsey "utterly disregarded the agreement made between myself and the asst. superintendent," claiming that "the officials are down on me for criticizing and making remarks concerning the management of our affairs and [for] standing up for my people."[12]

Oshkenaniew also presided over a meeting of disgruntled Menominees, mostly loggers, who then resolved to take their case to a higher authority. Complaining that Kelsey's unilateral decision to alter existing contracts had "left them without means to pay for the supplies," they contrasted their hardship with the fact that tribal accounts still paid full salaries to the non-Menominee superintendent, assistant superintendent, and scalers. The only conclusion to be drawn, so they noted sarcastically, was that the 1890 legislation "would be more properly named were it headed: 'An Act to provide places for a lot of white politicians and to provide good salaries for same to be paid from the money of the Indians.'"[13] To add fuel to these charges, the Menominees also contended that logging superintendent Ganz had forced Indians to build a road linking off-reservation lumber markets with a piece of land occupied by Henry Sherry, a local white man who claimed to have purchased the land from the state. When Indian loggers balked, Oshkenaniew said that Ganz "threatened . . . that if any Indian refused to obey orders he shall not be permitted to log." Intimidation succeeded, and a number of

Indians began the arduous task of constructing a road through dense forest.[14]

In this tense atmosphere, Menominee anger over Kelsey's decision quickly developed into fears of yet another conspiracy to deprive them of their timber. Echoing earlier complaints, the petitioners charged that "white officials" really intended "to show that we are improvident and incapable of transacting business" so that the 1890 law "may be repealed and the white man allowed to come upon our reservation and steal from us our little remaining timber." For that reason, the Menominees called on the Bureau of Catholic Indian Missions and the Indian Rights Association to investigate, and then "bring about a better state of things." What Oshkenaniew and his associates meant by a "better state of things" was, as it turned out, quite simple: replace Kelsey's management team with men "who will work for the interests of the Indians and not for the 'Lumber Kings,'" preferably "Indians when competent"; limit logging contracts to enrolled Menominees; and "reimburse" those Indians "who have incurred losses by reason of the above recited action of the officials."[15]

The Menominees got their inspection; in fact, they got two. But two investigations did not necessarily result in a satisfactory conclusion. In April, James I. Cisney, an experienced Indian Office functionary with prior ties to Kelsey, concluded that while the decision to reduce logging contracts was controversial, he found no evidence of duplicity on the agent's part. In fact, Cisney determined that Kelsey had given Indian contractors ample warning against overextending themselves. Moreover, since logging rules did not take effect until 7 January 1891, long after that season's work began, Cisney concluded that the initial contracts actually lacked firm legal standing. On another matter, the Indian Office inspector cleared Superintendent Ganz of wrongdoing, even as he found some evidence of a "scheme" to have roads cut to Henry Sherry's property. But concluding that operations had been conducted "as fair[ly] as could have been," Cisney suggested that "had the Indians obeyed the instructions of the Agent and Superintendent of logging they would not have sustained any loss."[16]

If Cisney's report treated Kelsey and Ganz with care and understanding, the same cannot be said for those Menominees who raised the complaint. Revealing the ambivalence with which Indian Office personnel regarded Indians whose praiseworthy initiative just as often proved inconvenient, Cisney reserved his harshest words for so-called Christian Indians. He charged, in fact, that as the new rules opened the door to broader participation, this "does not suit the Christian faction as they want it all," suggesting, although without evidence, that prominent loggers "hired . . . Onidas [sic] and Stockbridges" to labor for them and failed to honor financial obligations. Both characteristics contrasted with the behavior of "pagans," who, Cisney maintained, had "done the work themselves," and "paid their debts." Just as tellingly, Cisney charged that those behind the protests were "the same set that made the trouble when Agent Kelsey took charge."[17]

When the Reverend William J. Cleveland led the Indian Rights Association's inspection of the Menominee Reservation in the early summer of 1891, he also noticed a palpable suspicion, among loggers particularly, that "logging was purposely mismanaged to make it appear that the Indians are incompetent." This complaint was, so Cleveland concluded, related to an emerging conflict between Menominee entrepreneurs and their agent, or a "very bad state of things" generally. On the one hand, the reverend repeated Kelsey's claims that the tribe's abortive contract with the lawyer-lobbyist Fred T. Ledergerber was part of a scheme for some "to get control of the best timber lands for themselves as against other members of the tribe who had equal claim to it." At the same time, even Cleveland conceded that Menominees had a point in protesting some of Kelsey's actions. He had allowed Representative McCord's son-in-law to open a reservation store, even though the Indian Office had promised that such licenses were to be reserved for enrolled Menominees. Moreover, Cleveland also found that the agent had denied agency posts to qualified Menominees. One of those affected was Mitchell Oshkenaniew, who, despite being "fully competent," saw a white man installed as assistant agency clerk. All this led Cleveland to conclude that whereas Kelsey was "a well-meaning, honest old man," he nevertheless was "practically in the hands of the men who got him the appointment." In his cover letter transmitting the report to Commissioner Thomas J. Morgan, Herbert Welsh added the more urgent question, "Cannot something be done for these poor people?"[18]

Ill served by their agent perhaps, the Menominees hardly seemed poor. Gross revenues from sales of the 22,769,560 feet totaled $232,262.78. After deducting $77,174.05 to pay Indian contractors and meet expenses incurred in scaling and advertising, the net total deposited in tribal accounts exceeded $155,000. One-fifth of the net, or just over $31,000, went to the tribal poor fund, with the remaining $124,000 deposited in the newly created Menominee Log Fund.[19] Judged by statistics alone, 1890–91 ranked as the best season to date by far.

Yet figures tell only a portion of the story. In spite of the record revenues, tribal contractors ended the year heavily in debt. Partly the consequence of the decision to alter contracts midway through the season, loggers' financial problems worsened following an Indian Office ruling to withhold $27,000 garnered in the sale of the 2.7 million board feet cut in "excess" of the legislative limit. Dealing with the "overcut" proved complicated and contentious. Initially, the Interior Department determined that, since the legislation was quite specific in forbidding sales exceeding 20 million feet, it had no choice but to withhold the surplus. This proved impossible, however, for, by the time the department came to this decision, it had already authorized the sale of the entire 22.7 million feet. Pressured by Wisconsin merchants who had already agreed to purchase Menominee logs, Secretary Noble partially reversed himself; he allowed the delivery of the full cut but placed revenues in an escrow fund, satisfying purchasers, but at the expense of Indian contractors.[20] Kelsey argued that "if there was a right to sell surplus logs, there is an equal right and duty to pay the Indians for banking them," warning that the secretary's action would renew charges "that there is a purpose in the Department to defraud and oppress them."[21] After all, he continued, "the Indians were *employed* to bank these logs, and expect pay for such labor and services," just like any individual or company. Kelsey's argument seems to have been persuasive, for in 1892 the department released the $27,453.40 in question. Of that total, individual contractors received $8,968.53, with the balance deposited in the two tribal log funds.[22]

While the Indian Office wrestled with surplus logs, it simultaneously revised logging regulations, working toward preventing a recurrence of problems that had plagued the 1890–91 season. New rules provided that any contractor who cut more timber than allowed under his contract forfeited the surplus; that no Indians other than Menominees were to be employed without the agent's specific approval; and that neither the agent nor the Indian Office was to assume any responsibility for debts incurred by individual contractors. In an effort to bolster the financial standing of Menominee contractors, the Indian Office provided further that "when one half the logs contracted for by any Menominee shall be banked as required, . . . 50% of the price for banking such logs may be paid to the contractor," with the balance coming at the end of each logging season. Both Kelsey and Menominee leaders endorsed the change, deeming it an important step in improving loggers' credit with traders and storekeepers.[23]

Of all the measures proposed and adopted, perhaps the most interesting, and the most illustrative of the tenor of Menominee opinion, was one that failed. In the spring of 1891, Menominees requested that P.L. 153 be amended to allow a greater quantity of logs to be cut and sold in any one year. They made this request because, as Commissioner Morgan suggested in his annual report for 1891, the present limit "does not give them work enough for the season." Yet, despite every indication that the loggers could have handled as much as an additional 20 million feet at minimal additional expense, Washington denied the request. Morgan contended that "it is doubtful if authority to sell a greater quantity in one season would be beneficial [to the Menominees]," for it might induce them to turn their attention wholly to the lumber business, to the neglect of farming interests." His explanation illustrates the degree to which, once widely accepted, prevailing concepts regarding Indian cultural "progress" proved difficult to alter, even in the face of evidence suggesting other possibilities. For federal bureaucrats, then, Menominee logging still was viewed as a temporary activity, a way station on the road to farming.[24]

By contrast, many Menominees regarded logging as important in and of itself, perhaps their best chance to secure economic independence. Some also reasoned that if the tribe could realize economic self-sufficiency by exploiting their forests, they could conceivably exercise control over their destiny. Spurred on by the battles over contracts, disposal of "surplus" logs, and the divisive conflicts surrounding the installation of Kelsey, Menominee entrepreneurs became increasingly vocal in their quest to wrest control of the logging enterprise away from the Indian Office bureaucracy. For the rest of the 1890s, these self-styled "progressives" influenced political dialogue on the reservation, all the while pressing their agenda of economic modernization, political autonomy, and social change. This process also placed them at odds with federal officials and with members of their own tribe.

As the Menominee modernizers labored to find their political voice, they rallied around Mitchell Oshkenaniew. The Haskell Indian School–educated son of a prominent Oconto family, Oshkenaniew combined a lumberman's background with a combative personality and a keen understanding of the white man's political, legal, and economic institutions. In one sense, he was the prototypical "progressive" Indian, very much the type of native leader whites hoped the boarding school system would create. Articulate, ambitious, and seemingly convinced that the Indian's future lay in adapting to the white man's world, he captured everyone's attention at a time when old verities were being supplanted by a new order. Yet Oshkenaniew's abilities as an organizer were matched by a talent for inflaming passions and confronting his opponents at every turn. Even as these tactics drew many like-minded Menominees to his side, they also alienated some who recoiled at his undisguised ambition, fearing he sought personal gain at the expense of the tribe as a whole. Non-Indians also mistrusted Oshkehaniew, some dismissing him as a rabble-rouser who took advantage of unsettled social and economic conditions to turn the Menominees against federal authority.

The withering away of civil leadership among the Menominees facilitated Oshkenaniew's drive toward influence. By 1890 the Indian Office had persuaded Neo'pit and his associates Chickeney and Ne-ah-tah-puny to relinquish civil authority entirely, and this formalized the transfer of governmental responsibility to the agent and the Indian Office. The three chiefs, now quite elderly, continued to hand down judicial decisions but no longer exercised authority over civil matters. While they lived, they held some influence among their tribesmen, but their position was diminished by the recognition that it was the Indian Office, not the tribe, that would appoint their successors.[25]

Oshkenaniew and like-minded Menominees chafed under this paternalistic system and all it symbolized. It was just this sort of situation that drove many Menominees to demand the retention of the popular Agent Jennings and to protest Kelsey's handling of the logging enterprise. An important principal in these battles, Oshkenaniew seemed emboldened by confrontation, determined to air his suspicions that outsiders schemed to rob Menominees of their timber. He was particularly disappointed by the results of the 1891 investigations. In a letter to Herbert Welsh of the Indian Rights Association, Oshkenaniew charged that Reverend Cleveland had been deliberately misled by Kelsey and Ganz and therefore missed the central issue, namely, "that the[se] officials resorted to deception purposely to run us in debt." Ganz, so Oshkenaniew charged, set log prices so low as to make it impossible for Indian contractors to make any money, and Kelsey exacerbated this problem when he revised logging contracts halfway through the season. At the same time, the two men reportedly refused to advance money to logging contractors, as provided for by the law, with the result being that Menominee lumberjacks had to purchase supplies on credit and at inflated prices. But why would Ganz do this? To Oshkenaniew, the issue was simple: by paying Menominee contractors low prices for their logs, adjusting contracts in midstream, and withholding advance payments, the superintendent "nett[ed] a big sum for the Government." This also justified his salary, and that of his assistant, even when "one Indian could do all that work just as well." Demanding that Ganz, a man "bitterly hated by Indians," be removed from office, Oshkenaniew asked as well for payment of per capita annuities out of the log fund ("we have plenty of money in the Treasury at Washington," he wrote), timely advances from the $75,000 fund, and higher prices for logs. After all, so Oshkenaniew reminded Welsh, "the pine belongs to us," and Menominees, not government agents, deserved the benefits.[26]

All this was too much for Kelsey, who complained of Oshkenaniew's "gift for perversion of facts" and requested authority "to order such [a] persistent mischief-maker . . . to be removed from the reservation." For his part, Oshkenaniew appears to have been seeking confrontation, but carefully, choosing only those issues that would resonate across the reservation, among loggers and nonloggers alike. Such conflicts, he may have reasoned, would redound to his benefit by casting him, and his actions, as those of a Menominee "patriot," determined to protect the tribe's patrimony, and very sovereignty, from all manner of despoilers.

One likely issue was the old "squaw men" problem. In October 1891 the Menominee court prohibited women with enrolled husbands from entering into logging contracts. Kelsey counseled against reversing practices that allowed contracting by Menominee women married to non-Menominee Indians. He denied as well that white squaw men had engaged in any logging at all, arguing instead that since "half-breeds and Indians from the outside, married to Menominee women," claimed "equal rights with other Menominees," there was no reason to deny their requests.[27]

Oshkenaniew presented a different version of the dispute. In two separate letters from late 1891, he argued for denying tribal rights to all "mixed bloods who are not and were never members of the tribe" and asked, quite tellingly, whether "white people [can] own and hold property on the reservation." While current practices denied most Menominees the right to enter into contracts on behalf of their non-Menominee husbands, some individuals found ways around the law. By permitting this manner of contracting, "mixed bloods," even some "not on the rolls as members of the tribe," came, he said, to "enjoy the privileges to work and log on this reservation." This was "a violation of the rules," but, more important, it "crowded out" qualified Menominee workers. After all, since there were "enough Menominee laborers to handle the 20 millions of feet of logs," would it not "be a great deal better if the contractors are entirely prohibited from hiring outsiders"?[28]

Time added still more to the developing confrontation. Even as Kelsey again charged his tormentor with "creat[ing] dissatisfaction to the extent of his ability, by misrepresentation and prevarication," the young leader had, by late 1891, effectively isolated the agent. In the process, he also emerged as someone who could deal forcefully with whites, contrasting him with Neo'pit, whom Oshkenaniew now openly dismissed as "ignorant" and under Kelsey's control. This tactic further enhanced Oshkenaniew's reputation as one who would see to it that logging benefited all segments of the legitimate Menominee community. His argument, and certainly his activities, proved persuasive. In November 1894 the Menominee council limited participation in logging to enrolled adult males by prohibiting all Menominee women from taking out contracts. Kelsey's successor, Thomas H. Savage, then inflamed matters by threatening to defy the decision, an action that seems to have convinced loggers that self-determination, not just the enterprise, now was at stake. "Our agent," wrote Menominee logger Alex Peters, "reports [to the commissioner's office] that a faction of the tribe were [sic] clamoring against the half breeds." Countering what he considered a deliberate misrepresentation of the situation, Peters claimed that the "only persons who would suffer by reason of the action of our council" were "the men whose parentage are [sic] such as would not entitle them to membership in the tribe." He also suggested that Agent Savage was deliberately circumventing the council's rulings, since "his intimate friends have bought contracts from the women, and if the women were barred from taking contracts they would lose money."[29] All this led Peters to declare, "Our Indian Agent is getting so that he does not consult with the tribe upon matters which properly belong to the jurisdiction of our council, and when he consults with any of us, he does so with a few, perhaps two or three members of the tribe [who are] his chosen friends." He then asked, "Has our council no power whatever to regulate any of our own affairs, and is it right that our Agent should disregard our councils and do as he pleases?"[30]

Indian complaints against imperious agents hardly were unique to the Menominee Reservation. But now Oshkenaniew and the emerging generation of Menominees took an important step by transforming dissatisfaction into political influence. First, a special tribal council appointed a six-man delegation, led by Oshkenaniew, to lobby for distribution of the one-fifth portion of timber sales on a per capita basis, a position that reflected the wishes of nonloggers who had requested per capitas in a July 1891 petition. Of even greater significance was this council's second action, the creation of a new tribal constitution. A clear indication of frustration with the virtual absence of effective civil leadership—at least to the loggers' satisfaction—the new charter's most salient provision established a "business committee" and invested it with the authority to negotiate directly with the Indian Office and Congress. Within months, the new leadership had recalled Neo'pit and Chickeney from Washington, replaced them with Mitchell Mahkimetas and Louis (although not Mitchell) Oshkenaniew, and hired an attorney to work toward desired legislative changes.[31]

Agent Kelsey found the whole sequence of events alarming, detecting "the work of two young Indians: Mitchell Oshkenaniew and Peter LaMotte," who were "ambitious of taking the management of tribal affairs upon themselves." The agent also claimed, first, that the crucial council took place without his consent or knowledge, a violation of established procedure, and then suggested that the meeting never took place at all. Instead, he wrote, Oshkenaniew and LaMotte fraudulently "attached" to the constitution names and notary seals associated with an earlier vote. Oshkenaniew disputed the charges. In a letter to the commissioner he denied any underhanded tactics and affirmed that the constitution "was voted for unanimously in the presence of the Indian Agent." Sixty-eight Menominees added their support when they denounced Kelsey's plan "to mislead a portion of the ignorant members of our tribe," in order "to preserve the present existing law," which "has proved defective, and all in the interest of monopolists and to the detriment of our material progress."[32]

By 1894, Oshkenaniew was arguably the most influential member of the tribe. While not selected to serve as a member of the business committee, he was, it seemed, accorded the even higher honor of becoming the tribe's sole representative in Washington. Empowered to represent the Menominees "in any and all matters that may be pending in the Departments of the United States to or of the interest of our tribe," Oshkenaniew was responsible for resolving three outstanding claims. One involved recovering $40,000 in legal fees dating from the abortive 1848 removal treaty. A second had to do with the State of Wisconsin's claim to sixteenth-section lands, located on the reservation, under the 1862 Homestead Act. The third involved a disagreement with the Stockbridge and Munsee tribe over occupancy of reservation lands, a dispute that arose from the 1856 treaty which provided those tribes with a portion of Menominee property. Menominees had long argued that the deal proceeded without tribal approval, and logging only complicated the matter. According to Oshkenaniew's contract, the Stockbridge-Munsee lands included a valuable stand of timber, "a large portion or all of which . . . has been cut down and sold," for which the Menominees now asked to be reimbursed at fair market value, or $30,000. Altogether, Oshkenaniew was to recover some $215,000: $40,000 in legal fees, $30,000 for the Stockbridge-Munsee timber, and $145,000 for the lands claimed by the State of Wisconsin. In return, he had twelve years to complete his tasks and was promised "a sum equal to Twenty-five (25) per cent of the moneys or property that may be recovered." But payment was contingent upon success; failure to secure cash or property entitled Oshkenaniew to no compensation at all.[33]

New constitution, business committee, Oshkenaniew in Washington—taken together, they indicate that Menominee entrepreneurs had come to influence, if not dominate, tribal politics by the middle 1890s. And they did it essentially by creating a "civil government" more to their liking. Logging issues took center stage in tribal councils, not to mention in negotiations with Indian Office personnel, and the old leadership was asked to step aside. Evidence for the predominance of an entrepreneurial "agenda" shows up in the series of votes where those affirming change can be linked, individually or by family, with logging. But the most telling piece of evidence supporting this conclusion is the rise of Mitchell Oshkenaniew himself. His high-profile confrontations with Agent Kelsey and his practice of dealing directly with outsider power brokers—the Indian Office and Indian Rights Association, for example—established for him a reputation as one who acted as a leader is supposed to act. He also built coalitions, appealing to nonloggers by convincing Wieskesit, leader of the Zoar community, to take a seat on the 1894 business committee. Similarly, his efforts to secure per capita annuities from logging profits appealed as much to nonloggers as to loggers and made the powerful statement that reservation timber belonged to the community collectively, not just to loggers. Here again Oshkenaniew took on the role of Menominee chiefs, who were, after all, charged with the responsibility of looking out for everyone. The fact that Oshkenaniew was of the bear clan, a cousin to Neo'pit, did not hurt his position either, and this combination of behavior, heritage, and changed circumstances may have muted, for a time anyway, the always powerful undercurrent of mistrust of entrepreneurs.

Prosperity seemed to follow Oshkenaniew as well. During the 1891–92 and 1892–93 seasons, an average of eighty Menominees entered into logging contracts, meeting but not exceeding the 20-million-foot quota each year. Gross revenues for these two seasons neared $500,000, with loggers earning just over $136,000. Tribal accounts grew as well, with over $270,000 added to the four-fifths fund and another $68,000 set aside to aid the hospital, schools, and the poor. The commissioner reflected this new optimism, boasting in his 1892 report that "the workers [now] receive fair wages and a sum is accumulating in the United States Treasury to the credit of the whole tribe, which is only just, since all have an equal interest in the timber."[34]

But there were cracks in Menominee prosperity. Logging remained a sufficiently expensive business that many chose not to participate. Indeed, while adult male members of the tribe (and women married to non-Menominee Indians) claimed "shares" of the year's harvest, "all the applicants," so one Menominee noted, "do not log." Instead, since there were "only certain individuals who are able to carry on logging operations," these entrepreneurs purchased most of the contracts. Given that the cost of conducting business included the price paid for contracts (usually between fifteen and thirty dollars), this amounted to a "tax or tribute to a few members of the tribe." It also undermined the drive to instill values of work and thrift, now evidently prized by some entrepreneurs. "One great evil that results from this," so this same Menominee argued, "is that, many of our young men, by selling their contracts, receive money, which is all spent for whiskey."[35]

For those unable or unwilling to take on the challenges of logging, earning a living on the reservation remained precarious. Farm production continued to lag, so much so that Agent Kelsey asked to purchase 500 bushels of wheat for "poor and helpless Menominees" in 1891. That same year, William Summers, a lumberman from Hayes, Wisconsin, offered a plan to alleviate suffering then evident in and around Oconto. He asked the interior secretary "to permit them to pick up the tops and butts of the pine," on lands lumbered over, for manufacture into "shingle bolts." Summers predicted that the shingle bolt operation would realize between one and three dollars per cord while making productive use of heretofore wasted pine trimmings. He also suggested that local merchants "would be willing to furnish flour and meat (the staples of life) if they were permitted to take shingle bolts of them in payment thereof."[36]

The Indian Office acted on Summers's proposal. In 1892 it authorized the cut and sale of shingle bolts on a trial basis, granting the operation an exemption from logging regulations. This meant that shingle manufacturers could keep all of their profits save 10 percent for the poor fund, and shingles would not count against the annual production limits. It seemed a promising operation. But just the opposite proved true. Plagued by low prices and charges that Indians were violating regulations by manufacturing shingle bolts out of standing green timber, the Indian Office suspended operations on several occasions and seized proceeds it determined came from illegal cuts. The project also failed to turn a profit in any year, and by 1895 even Mitchell Oshkenaniew withdrew his support, transmitting affidavits from six Menominees "concerning the unlawful felling and cutting of standing pine timber" for "use of shingle bolts." Armed with this evidence, as well as a history of poor returns, the Indian Office closed down operations in 1898.[37]

Menominee loggers also faced continued problems with outsiders. By the middle 1890s, harassment took the form of complaints about the quality of logs and a renewal of "combinations" between purchasers. Neither was particularly new, but the aggravation led Agent Savage to offer a bold proposal: construction of a reservation sawmill and lumber plant. He estimated that while such a project would cost at least $20,000, it would "break up the combination among mill men, . . . give employment to the Indians," and provide a means for selling the finished lumber "for many thousand dollars more" than if sold in the conventional manner. The department, however, declined to act on Savage's proposal just as it had brushed aside a similar plan offered by Agent Stephens a decade earlier.[38]

At the same time, the management of reservation forests was undergoing careful scrutiny. In September 1893, Agent Savage submitted a scathing report on prior management, concluding that former logging superintendent Ganz had taken only the best pine, leaving the rest to waste.[39] His conclusions supported those of an Indian Rights Association investigation from 1894. The Indian Rights Association's representative, Charles C. Painter, charged as well that Kelsey and Ganz had sacrificed profits by accepting bids on the entire 20 million feet prior to completion of the work. According to Painter, this permitted "ample opportunity [for] collusion between the purchasers and the Superintendent." Worse still, Painter asserted that Wisconsin's congressional delegation "gave much of their time, and all of their influence," to "make such robbery possible," a swindle that cost the tribe nearly $30,000 in pine "left on the ground,"

Menominee lumberjacks at work, ca. 1900. (Menominee Historic Preservation Archives)

another $30,000 that the Indians lost by selling standing pine as shingle bolts, and a further $29,000, which he estimated as the increased cost of banking the unsold 13 million feet. All told, losses came to $89,000.[40]

Savage's suggestion was to increase annual appropriations from $75,000 to at least $100,000, and to press Menominee loggers toward clearing already cut lands before moving on. But the Indian Office elected to stand pat; consequently, Menominees harvested only 13 million feet of timber in 1893–94, much of which came from the so-called cut-over district. Gross revenues on that year's work likewise sank to barely $100,000. In the following year, and again in 1895, Savage renewed his case for increasing the yearly appropriation. The Interior Department refused again, leaving the agent to curtail operations.[41] From 1894 until the end of the century, the annual cut averaged between 15 and 17 million board feet, never once reaching the 20-million-foot limit provided for by P.L. 153. While profits remained impressive, and even increased if measured by the prices paid per thousand feet, it was also true that, as Savage had predicted, fewer Menominees found employment in the logging industry. By 1897–98 just 63 Menominees entered into logging contracts, down from the 72 for 1892–93 and 1893–94 and far less than the record 133 recorded for 1890–91.[42]

Oshkenaniew found the consolidation of logging contracts troubling, and in 1895 he backed a Menominee council initiative to limit individual chances to 500,000 board feet. He argued that this would circumvent the advantage held by the few who had access to outside capital. Much to Oshkenaniew's frustration, however, Agent Savage foiled this effort, arguing against it in council and coaxing negative votes from prominent officials, including judges and the chief of police. This was too much for Oshkenaniew, who lashed out, writing that Savage had "killed the motion" so that "a few of his best friends" might still "secretly commence buying up contracts, ahead of time, no doubt for the purpose of giving them all the chance they wanted."[43]

Even as Oshkenaniew and Savage clashed over this issue, they found common ground on paying per capita annuities out of accrued interest in the four-fifths logging fund, money heretofore reserved for financing the agency school. Once a vocal supporter of cash annuities, Oshkenaniew's thinking evidently had changed by 1895. In that year, Agent Savage proposed cash payments to the aged, infirm, and widows with minor children. Able-bodied Menominees, on the other hand, would receive only "premiums for clearing and cultivating farms and for crops raised." According to Savage, this method promised to encourage the young "to pay more attention to farming and inculcate industrious habits," while materially aiding those older Indians who "say, with truth too, that they are too old to learn any new ways of taking care of themselves, and that they should be allowed to receive some direct benefits from their funds before they die."[44]

Restricting cash annuities to those physically able to work corresponded with prevailing ideas about the detrimental impact of "handouts" on Indian progress. In this context, Savage's lament that "it seems that the more that is given them the less they appreciate the chances they have" is less surprising than the fact that Oshkenaniew agreed, at least publicly.[45] In a stinging rebuke that reads as though it could have been written by one of his Haskell schoolteachers, Oshkenaniew minimized the significance of the "one fourth of the whole number of Menominees" who called for per capitas. The "non progressed," he continued, "cling and adhere to the old Indian ways," and "as a consequence of their lazyness [sic]" were "always in want." By contrast, the "progressed" majority "work and support themselves from the products of their labor" and "do not shout for money like their brethren." Oshkenaniew's solution, supported, he wrote, by "many of the intelligent members of the tribe," was to place interest money in an "improvement fund," payable only under specific conditions. Foremost among these was a requirement that all except the sick, poor, and "helpless" work for their living. According to Oshkenaniew, this plan "would be a great inducement for the Indians to work," while acting as "a civilizing process." Failure to link pay with labor would, he concluded, "encourage more lazyness [*sic*] and vice," for "as long as a lazy Indian has a little money he will not work."[46]

In spite of Oshkenaniew's forceful proposal, and repeated entreaties by Savage, the Indian Office declined to grant authority for distribution of interest on logging profits, in any form, until 1906.[47] For the remainder of the 1890s, then, Menominee logging continued, with annual production remaining at roughly 17 million board feet. This is not to say that there were no important changes. By 1897, Menominees were acting as foremen of logging and assistant scalers (there were seven), and new logging rules strengthened the prohibition against transferring logging certificates to non-Menominees, Indian or white. In the following year the tribe, the Indian Office, and the State of Wisconsin finally settled the sixteenth-section disputes. This opened new opportunities for Menominee lumberjacks, who cut and delivered some 8 million feet from these lands during the 1898–99 and 1899–1900 seasons. These "special contracts" also paid some $35,000. As part of this settlement, the lumbering companies also agreed to transfer title of the land to the tribe upon completion of the work.[48]

With this, the 1890s ended on a positive note. The 1898–99 season brought record prices for Menominee timber, meaning that accumulated earnings from log sales now surpassed $2 million. These funds supported the agency hospital and the reservation school, and made possible a steady, if not dramatic, rise in home building on the reservation.[49] As skilled lumbermen, Menominees not only proved able to make a living for themselves but also were up to the task of working for outsiders. Shortly after the turn of the century, one agent summed up the Menominee situation:

> During my brief experience here, I have found the Menominee Indians handy workmen. They are expert woodsmen; they excel on the drive; they make good carpenters and blacksmiths, and in fact seem to be able to turn their hand to most anything that a white man can. Their opportunities are ample. With an abundance of labor right at their hand; with their splendid reservation, with its fertile soil and vast timber resources, they have simply to cultivate habits of industry and sobriety to become a prosperous and thriving community.[50]

Mitchell Oshkenaniew could have found himself in substantial agreement with this evaluation. Indeed, the most significant development during this decade arguably was his rise to prominence along with Menominee entrepreneurs. Ambitious, outspoken, and politically astute, Oshkenaniew was the prototypical Indian capitalist and "modernizer," a less flamboyant version of the notorious Elias C. Boudinot, the "Cherokee Jay Gould," according to at least one author. Like his Cherokee contemporary, Oshkenaniew came along at a time of economic and political uncertainty, and took advantage of opportunities that came his way. In a way, he was in the right place at the right time. But while the arrival of logging as the community's most important commercial activity accounts in part for Oshkenaniew's position, drawing the conclusion that political influence flowed from economic power fails to appreciate the full dimensions of this development. Oshkenaniew owed his position at least as much to a change in values among some Menominees, a shift in cultural orientation that embraced, quite simply, individuality and an entrepreneurial "spirit." Even here, however, our mental framework remains crude, insufficiently subtle to appreciate the complexity of cultural change. For while the entrepreneurs gravitated toward combinations of ideas and perspectives that more closely resembled those of their non-Indian neighbors, they did so within a decidedly Menominee context. Clan and lineage relationships still mattered, as did ties to, and a sense of collective ownership of, the reservation land. With few exceptions Menominee loggers chose to work in, and in a sense *for,* the reservation community rather than for outsiders. Logging was a Menominee activity, with shifts in values understood and promoted in terms that still emphasized the importance of community. So it was a rather idiosyncratic individualism that Menominee entrepreneurs, and their spokesman Oshkenaniew, symbolized. And if they ever forgot who they were, or who owned the timber, or their responsibilities as Menominees, others would remind them. This, in fact, is what happened during the next decades, as we will see in the next chapter.[51]

CHAPTER FOUR

Creating Indian Entrepreneurs

As the Menominees prepared to enter the twentieth century, they found themselves enmeshed in a constellation of forces linking their experiences with those of Indians across North America. Both the dramatically expanding American economy and shifting policy objectives undermined local authority while limiting individual and collective prospects for making a living. Although varying degrees of economic dependency had characterized Indian life for generations, Washington's shifting, contradictory, often repressive policies enhanced economic trends forcing Indians into literal and figurative "corners" where a sense of impotence must have been palpable, if not completely overwhelming. This was, after all, the era of allotment in the United States and marginalization in Canada, practices fueled in both countries by racialist thought that denigrated Indians' cultural lives and predicted their not so ultimate demise in one way or another. As the seminal study of the era notes, by the early decades of the twentieth century, the optimism felt by reformers regarding the salutary benefits of severalty, off-reservation schooling, and integration came to be replaced by a pessimistic assessment of Indian prospects, a gradual acceptance of a permanent separate and inferior status for Indians in North American societies. Limited by culture or doomed by genetics, Indians now were seen as destined to fail. Out of sight, out of mind, isolated and on the way to extinction, there was nothing anyone could do about it.[1]

If marginalization represents trends operating at the macroeconomic and "macropolicy" levels, considerable variation nevertheless manifested itself from place to place and from group to group. Communities still needed leaders, individuals still sought direction and meaning for their lives, and whatever impotence Indians may have felt regarding the direction of policies or the operations of the cash economy did not automatically translate into local or personal passivity. Drawing upon long histories, really "traditions," of adaptation and survival, Indians came to terms with the consequences of uneven "power," forging new futures where cultural values informed, and supported, innovations. New leaders emerged as well, individuals who, according to one study of the Crow experience, were not "romantics seeking a return of the buffalo or a rollback of white settlements." Instead, they marked off cultural enclaves, "regions of refuge" to world-systems theorists, and defended them by "utilizing the instruments of 'civilized' American life."[2]

But leaders must have followers, and adaptation quite logically requires some correspondence with shared community values. For while Crow bands could forge a national identity out of the reservation experience, or Indians could find that becoming cowboys was a powerful means to express "Indian-ness" in a changing world, cultural values are not infinitely flexible. This is the tricky part for the ethnohistorian. Even as we have come to appreciate that "real Indians" did not cease to exist long ago and grasp, intuitively anyway, that native peoples have stubbornly fought to adapt "on their own terms," we struggle when attempting to isolate those values that endured, even in an attenuated form. What is the nature of adaptation, and when does change become so substantial that it shades into what older generations of scholars called "acculturation"? Are we speaking of a process where cultural values "manage" change, or where individuals and communities interpret change, "after the fact" as it were, so that it "fits" familiar ideals? Maybe it is both, or neither. Perhaps it is simply a matter of pragmatic choice: what is right is what works.[3]

For the nearly 1,800 Menominees living on the reservation by 1900, logging had become the signal element in this unfolding interplay of change and continuity. It allowed men to make a living in a fashion similar to their white neighbors, but did not require them to leave the community. It generated income for the reservation population, financing some services and fueling a growing investment account. But logging also influenced Menominee sociopolitical arrangements. By distributing income unevenly, it rewarded values differentially. "Entrepreneurs," those whom I have described as gravitating toward, and promoted by, the expansion of logging, also came to exert considerable influence over reservation politics. While this produced societal tensions, it was a creative tension, at least when observed with the benefit of hindsight. The rise of the group headed by Mitchell Oshkenaniew, itself a testimony to the power of logging, still was balanced by a general concern that logging should benefit all Menominees, not just those who labored. What is more, even as changed values permitted Oshkenaniew to confront established authority figures aggressively and openly—showing little regard, it seemed, for cultural strictures against such behavior—his growing influence did not signify disintegrating ideals or loss of shared identity. Oshkenaniew, as it turned out, was not the harbinger of assimilation and dissolution but really a "midpoint" in this ongoing dialogue. As the twentieth century accelerated the pace and substance of change, Menominee values continued to shape responses, collective and individual, even as cultural conventions were themselves shaped *by* logging. The sands were shifting; tidal action was creating a new beach, a different cultural landscape, even as it eroded parts of the old one.

If sands were shifting, they were being pulled, pushed, and sifted by profits, or so it might have seemed. After nearly a quarter century of logging, and a decade under the landmark 1890 act, the tribal log fund stood at just under $3 million, on sales of over 270 million feet of timber. A record $17.27 per thousand feet received in 1902 sales[4] promised continued prosperity and improved standards of living. This was increasingly significant given stagnant farm production and the declining importance of other types of subsistence activities such as wild ricing and maple sugar manufacturing. During the 1890s, increasing numbers of Menominees replaced their log cabins with frame houses and used their earnings to purchase consumer goods, while profits supported a reservation hospital and a boarding school at Keshena. Skills learned in cutting timber, driving logs to market, and managing small enterprises also allowed some to secure jobs with private logging companies.[5] No wonder, then, that successive Indian agents made heady plans for the future. In 1898, D. H. George proposed building roads and bridges to remote segments of the reservation and suggested constructing a pulp mill, to utilize "low-grade" timber and "give employment to a large number in preparing the wood and working in the mill."[6] His successor, Shepard Freeman, envisioned a dramatic plan for "industrial development" and attempted to convince the Green Bay, Oshkosh, Madison and Southwestern Railroad to extend tracks into the reservation's heretofore "underutilized" hardwood district.[7]

While agents sought ways to expand operations, community members reorganized governmental structures, capping this drive with a new constitution. Similar in many respects to the 1892 proposal, the 1904 document aimed, so the preamble stated, to replace the "old form of government . . . in which the ruling power has been under the control of hereditary chiefs." In its place, Menominees intended to institute government "organized according to civilized principles," reflecting the sense that the community was now "far enough advanced in civilization." The charter's most salient feature was the creation of a fifteen-man business committee, to be appointed at first but elected in the future. This committee, a de facto civil government really, held management authority over reservation logging.[8]

Passage of the 1904 constitution represented a clear victory for Menominee entrepreneurs. The inaugural business committee listed Mitchell Oshkenaniew among its members, along with familiar political actors Steve Askinet, Louis Keshena, Moses Corn, and Alex Peters. Included as well were Reginald Oshkosh, the elderly Chief Neo'pit's oldest son, and Wieskesit, perhaps the most influential person from Zoar. His inclusion reveals that entrepreneurs, despite considerable success in shaping the Menominee political dialogue, still sought approval from the community at large. And they needed it. Oshkenaniew could brag, as he did to a panel of United States senators, "that there is not one particular work you might mention in the line of lumbering but what the Indian can do," but the fact was that logging divided Menominees as much as it brought them together. By 1905, for instance, just thirty-three Menominee logging contractors controlled the bulk of logging operations, and three years earlier fifty-three loggers petitioned to be "released" from tribal rolls. Claiming that "no community of persons has ever existed that could all be brought up to a common high and ideal standard," and distinguishing themselves from the bulk of the Menominee population, the petitioners called for an end to "the injustice that would be done to the majority of such persons if they were all held in restraint because of the indisposition or tardiness of a certain portion of their number to acquire civilization." Their solution involved granting allotments, pro rated shares from the tribal funds, and United States citizenship to "competent" individuals.[9]

Nothing, it seems, came of this request, perhaps because, like earlier such proposals, allotment failed to engage the support not only of a majority of Menominees but of commercial timber firms still maneuvering to purchase the forests. In any event, all arrangements, social, political, economic, received a harsh jolt when a severe windstorm hit on 16 July 1905. This "cyclone" swept through the remote northwestern portion of the reservation, downing an estimated 25 to 40 million board feet of timber, most of it hardwood and hemlock but also some 5 million feet of pine. Given that hardwood logs do not float, and are known to deteriorate rapidly, the absence of rail or road links to that area rendered salvage problematic. The complicated legal matter regarding "ownership" of reservation resources and the legislative ceiling on Menominee timber harvests therefore recommended a congressional settlement. Within six months, Indian Commissioner Francis E. Leupp, working with Joseph R. Farr, the Indian Office's general superintendent of logging for Wisconsin, and E. M. Griffith, superintendent of forests for the State of Wisconsin, had drafted a proposal providing for the outright sale of the "blown-down" timber as stumpage. The proposal also authorized the harvest and sale of standing pine intermingled with damaged hardwoods.[10]

From the Menominee loggers' perspective, the proposal's most important feature concerned their role, or lack thereof. In a clear break from past logging practices, Congress now intended to offer reservation timber to outside loggers contracting directly with the Interior Department. Commissioner Leupp and Secretaries Griffith and Farr defended their decision to bypass Indians altogether by suggesting that Menominee loggers already had more than they could handle under the old

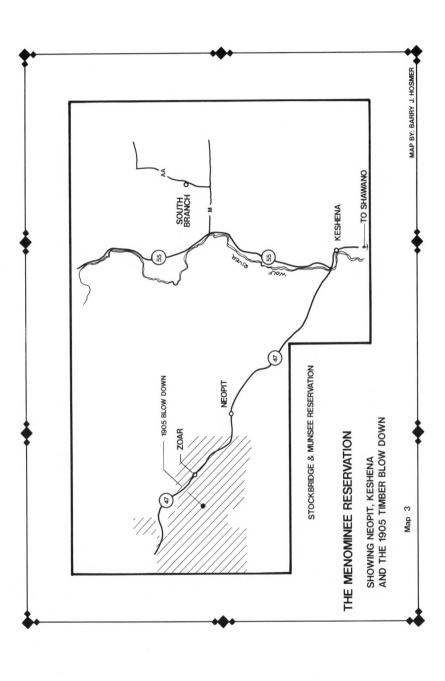

THE MENOMINEE RESERVATION

SHOWING NEOPIT, KESHENA
AND THE 1905 TIMBER BLOW DOWN

Map 3

STOCKBRIDGE & MUNSEE RESERVATION

MAP BY: BARRY J. HOSMER

SOUTH
BRANCH

AA

M

55

55

WOLF RIVER

KESHENA

TO SHAWANO

47

NEOPIT

ZOAR

1905 BLOW DOWN

47

arrangements. Farr also contended that the expense of constructing roads to the "blown-down district," necessary before any timber work could proceed, eliminated the chronically undercapitalized Indian operators from serious consideration.[11]

These arguments notwithstanding, Congress rejected the bill and passed an alternate version that placed responsibility for letting contracts in the hands of the business committee of the Menominee tribe. Oshkenaniew seems to have played an important role in these deliberations, arguing, effectively as it turned out, against implementing a version of the now notorious "La Pointe System." That plan, named after the La Pointe Indian Agency in Minnesota, sold Anishinaabe (Ojibwa) timber to non-Indian companies, "on the stump," and was widely considered responsible for the subsequent denuding of these forests. By contrast, the Oshkenaniew-backed alternative, which passed Congress on 28 June 1906, substantially elevated the profile and authority of the business committee.[12] Control over logging contracts for the blown-down district now rested firmly in the hands of Menominee entrepreneurs, who could enter into contracts with whomever they chose, the only stipulation being that non-Indian loggers had to take on at least one Menominee partner.[13]

Passage of the 1906 law represented the apex of Mitchell Oshkenaniew's influence, the culmination of a decade's activities. It also formalized the business committee's central role in coordinating logging and, by extension, Menominee political activity. While the business committee included Wieskesit,[14] granting voice, it seems, to those least connected with the enterprise, loggers framed the new logging regulations. With Oshkenaniew acting as secretary and chief spokesman, the committee secured authority to appoint a separate logging superintendent for the "blown-down" district and to sublet contracts to outsiders. It also defeated a proposal requiring that all contracts be awarded to the highest bidder on the grounds that better-financed off-reservation lumber companies could underbid Menominees and thereby undermine the central goal of promoting tribal employment. Finally, the committee asked for and received an order suspending green timber logging. "Whereas it is the opinion of the Business Committee of the Menominee Tribe of Indians that the Menominees have all the timber they can handle," they wrote, "be it resolved that the cutting of green timber under the act of June 12, 1890, be suspended until the dead and down timber and the scattered standing green timber . . . has been cut down."[15]

Joseph Farr and E. M. Griffith objected, charging that the business committee was "apparently organized for the purpose of getting as much as possible for themselves out of the tribe," and thus unequal to the monumental task at hand. Griffith predicted as well that members of the group planned to let contracts to themselves at an inflated price, sublet the contracts to outsiders, and thereby realize a profit through "speculation." Both men then recommended suspending logging pending revised legislation. The request was honored in practice if not formally, as it took a full year to begin the salvage work. In the meantime, logging during the 1906–7 season operated under the old rules, with eighty-one Menominee contractors harvesting 17.5 million board feet that sold for $325,000, a new record. After deducting costs, the tribe still cleared nearly $230,000.[16]

By late summer, John W. Goodfellow, late director of logging on the Lac de Flambeau Ojibwa (Anishinaabe) Reservation, had taken his place as superintendent of logging, the business committee began issuing contracts, and millers set up operations at three different sites awaiting an estimated 25 million feet of blown-down timber. Yet barely one month into the logging season, Joseph Farr presented the commissioner with an alarming report. Detailing numerous abuses, from cutting green timber but leaving damaged logs to rot, to attempting to float "unfloatable" hardwoods, Farr suggested that if Goodfellow "could start over again, commencing at the time he made the first logging contract, he would have much less connection with the business committee, and certain of its members." Oshkenaniew's group, so Farr claimed, had blatantly assigned contracts to its own members, whose clear aim was speculation rather than logging. Proof, he wrote, lay in evidence that a clear majority of the thirty-eight contracts went to business committee members or their relations. Mose Tucker, president of the business committee, was both "party of the first part" and "party of the second part" on one agreement, while relatives Louis and Peter secured contracts as well. Other contracts went to business committee men Peter LaMotte, Thomas LaBelle, Louis Keshena, and Joe Corn.[17]

More troubling to Farr were indications that Indian contractors sought white partners rather than taking on logging work themselves. Farr observed that "white men have arranged to do the logging" in most cases and, more troubling, that of the 250 lumbermen, just "one out of every ten, 25, are Indians." Equally damaging was the fact that subcontracting had added an estimated $15,000 to $20,000 to the cost of logging. This additional cost, so he claimed, came as a consequence of the white subcontractor's natural incentive to exaggerate expenses and maximize profits. After all, "if the contractor is forced to take an Indian partner, or partners, who do not assist in any way, and only take part to the extent of taking one-half of the profit, the contractor must have the contract price increased enough above what it should be, to pay his Indian partners." In the case of Wisconsin logger L. F. LaMay, this meant a profit of $1,000 to his Indian partners Louis and Peter Tucker, even though the brothers "do not furnish anything or take part whatever." Moreover, since LaMay had to collect $6.75 per thousand board feet cut and banked when it should have cost "less that $5.00 per thousand," the $1,000 difference had to "come out of the tribe." For Farr, the results were unequivocal, and depressingly so. Concluding that "the business committee . . . does not stand for the interest of the tribe, and is controlled by three or four of the most undesirable Indians on the reservation," he called on the department to dismiss Goodfellow and cancel all current contracts.[18]

Although Goodfellow defended his management, citing expenses involved in beginning such an ambitious project, his reply failed to forestall either a second investigation or the eventual suspension of activities in the blown-down district. In late 1907, J. A. Howarth, United States forest supervisor, confirmed Farr's finding of widespread "speculation" and offered the example of Shawano lumberman August Anderson. A man already linked with unethical lumber dealings on the neighboring Stockbridge and Munsee Reservation, Anderson now was said "to own the outfit and pay all the bills at Joe Gokie's camp," even though Gokie officially held the contract. Howarth went on to document wasteful and sometimes fraudulent cutting practices, all made possible by Goodfellow's lax supervision. It was, he wrote, a relatively simple matter for loggers to "deliberately cut more than their required number of logs and hold them back in the woods until the scaler has been around for the last time or even until just before the drive," at which point "they haul them to the landing and put a special mark on them having previously sold them to another party down the river." Wasteful logging practices only worsened the scandal as a disgusted Howarth concluded that one camp looked "as if an attempt had been made to see how much could be left in the woods."[19]

Turmoil over management of blown-down timber could not have come at a worse time for Agent Shepard Freeman, who also felt the sting of J. R. Farr's pen. As early as April 1907, Farr warned against the evils of speculation and called upon Freeman to cease issuing "clearing patents" permitting Indians to cut and sell timber on the pretext of clearing lands for cultivation. He argued that these "private sales" encouraged the "denuding" of timber while depriving the tribe of needed income. But the men's relationship really deteriorated following Farr's assertion that Freeman had collaborated with August Anderson and the former logger, formerly enrolled Menominee, and full-time "speculator" J. H. Tourtelotte in a scheme to deprive the Menominees of fair prices for their timber. This plan involved "discrediting" the value and quality of marketable logs so as to sell them to Anderson as less valuable pulpwood. Anderson then resold that timber, but at prices more in accord with its original value and, of course, realizing a substantial profit for himself. Farr implied, but stopped just short of charging outright, that Freeman and Tourtelotte received compensation in return for approving the original transactions.

He did, however, accuse Freeman of incompetence, a scalding rebuke that closed with the charge that "a man, who could not sell this timber at better prices than you received and who handled the cutting, scaling and the entire situation as you did, is not fit or competent to manage such transactions." This was enough. A frustrated Freeman denied Farr's accusations but also turned over operations to the reservation logging superintendent William Farr, who reported to his brother Joseph.[20]

Amid charges of waste and fraud, not to mention warring between federal officials, the government acted. In January 1908 the Forest Service assumed control over logging on all Indian reservations. Under this "cooperative agreement," between the Departments of Agriculture and Interior, Forestry assumed responsibility for the supervision and protection of Indian timberlands, and this involved authority over sales as well. While the Indian Office maintained its hold over most other aspects of reservation management, those of its employees connected with logging now either reported to Forestry or lost their jobs. The latter claimed Goodfellow, and Forestry followed his dismissal with a thorough review of existing logging contracts. This survey led to recommendations that final payments to contractors be reduced substantially, as a way of making at least partial restitution to the tribe. The contractors, however, objected to this action and eventually filed breach of contract suits against the federal government. These suits ultimately resulted in settlements favorable to the white contractors.[21]

But some 40 million board feet of blown-down timber never made it to the sawmills and instead remained in the woods, where it continued to deteriorate. An additional 7.5 million board feet of green timber, cut from stands interspersed with the damaged hardwoods, also remained unsold. More significantly, Menominees now began expressing concern over possible fallout from business committee scandals. Howarth noticed a "general impression prevailing that a conspiracy exists to defeat the present operations by the Indians under their own business committee for the purposes of hereafter letting outsiders get a better chance at the timber here." As if on cue, several Menominees not affiliated with the business committee prevailed upon Robert M. La Follette, United States senator from Wisconsin, to use his influence to amend or repeal the 1906 law. La Follette's intervention, which ultimately produced a thorough reorganization of reservation logging operations, marks the beginning of a new era in which Menominees added sawmill laborer and producer of finished lumber to the familiar occupations of lumberjack and timber merchant.[22]

La Follette sold his idea by appealing to Congress's continuing determination to promote Indian economic self-sufficiency and cultural assimilation. On the one hand, he argued, the Menominees' evident "aptitude" for logging and lumbering supported the conclusion that "they might readily be taught to manufacture the logs into lumber." Valuable in and of itself, this plan also promised to free them from "the mercy of the mill men to whom they must sell," reducing expenses while opening "an unlimited market for [their] finished product[s]." At the same time, La Follette called upon the Congress to consider the mill a "school of industry," whose products included wage-earning, industrious Menominees, prepared to abandon tribal life. While there was nothing new about the desire to promote Menominee assimilation through industrial development, this proposal now offered a comprehensive agenda.[23]

The irony, for the Menominees anyway, was that the "price" of economic self-sufficiency included a return to outside management of their affairs. Approved on 28 March 1908, the La Follette Act (P.L. 74) repealed the 1890 and 1906 statutes and authorized the construction, at tribal expense, of between one and three on-reservation sawmills. Lumber produced in these mills was to be advertised and sold to the highest bidder with proceeds earmarked for a new Treasury fund earning 4 percent interest. As for employment, the act promoted Indian jobs in "forest protection, logging, driving, sawing, and manufacturing into lumber for the market," but at the same time forbade natives from subcontracting with or employing non-Indians. On the other hand, the forest supervisor could hire experienced foresters and offer mill and logging jobs to whites, so long as Menominees received prior consideration. Finally, the act encouraged the Forestry Department to implement "modern" forestry methods but did not require sustained-yield harvesting or replanting.[24]

Events moved quickly after the passage of P.L. 74. During a 26 June 1908 council meeting, called by and presided over by Agent Freeman, tribal leaders voted overwhelmingly to disband the Menominee business committee. This effectively suspended the 1904 charter and restored the agent's influence over Menominee governance. Certainly attractive to Freeman and his superiors, this move seems to have been spearheaded by Reginald Oshkosh, Chief Neo'pit's Carlisle Indian Industrial School–educated son. A logger himself at least until 1889, the younger Oshkosh evidently remained a background figure following his return home five years earlier. But with his father ailing and prohibited by Indian Office protocol from exerting formal influence, the thirty-five-year-old man who as a boy had written "when I was on the farm I played with white boys. They play kick wicked and so I know soon, how to play kick wicked," emerged by 1900 as a major political figure in his own right. He authored petitions complaining about the behavior of the logging superintendent and protesting the enrollment of off-reservation individuals or those with questionable Menominee heritage without tribal approval. From his position as interpreter for council meetings, he was able to translate his Carlisle education into political action, perhaps most notably

Photograph of Reginald A. Oshkosh, taken in 1905. (State Historical Society of Wisconsin, negative WHi(X3)26180)

in a 1901 effort to realize per capita distributions from the old four-fifths account.[25]

Reginald Oshkosh's budding career demonstrates a sometimes over-looked consequence of the off-reservation boarding school experience. Although many students certainly found bitter isolation upon their return home, some became leaders, accepted by their peers as possessing a useful understanding of American economic and political arrange-ments. Such was Oshkosh's situation. Able to combine his education with the prestige inherent in his family background, he used his new platform in a variety of ways, not the least to strike at Mitchell Oshkenaniew. Citing evidence of corruption and collusion with outside contractors, Oshkosh declared his intention to "withdraw that contract that Mitchell Oshkannanieu [*sic*] got and banish the committee entirely, so that they will never see daylight any more." Significantly, Oshkosh also castigated the committee for excluding so-called pagans from its deliberations, thereby demonstrating his own commitment to respecting the rights of nonloggers while affirming publicly the suspicion that Oshkenaniew's group was bent only on serving its own interests. These arguments were effective. Those present at the meeting voted not only to do away with the Menominee business committee but, by a vote of 62 to 0, resolved the following: "That Mitchell Oshkenaniew is hereby forever barred from representing the Menominee Tribe of Indians in any way, shape, or manner in any of their tribal affairs, either on or off the Menominee Reservation."[26]

Mitchell Oshkenaniew attempted to convince the Senate to overturn his censure and reinstate the business committee, on the grounds that Agent Freeman had orchestrated the whole affair to undermine what he clearly understood as an effort at Menominee self-government. Senator La Follette refused to be drawn into the tribe's internal business, but the exchange presents an opportunity to consider Menominee "logging politics" as it developed in connection with the business committee. How, for instance, do we evaluate that body's performance? Ample evidence supports charges of questionable dealings and nepotism, if not outright malfeasance. But is that all? Certainly Farr and Griffith, not to mention other officials in and outside Washington, were uncomfortable with Menominee expressions of self-determination, and it takes little imagination to believe that they welcomed evidence of disaster. Suggesting that these officials were gratified when their predictions seemingly came true, however, is not to exonerate the business committee, nor does it offer much sense of how the Menominees understood Oshkenaniew's actions and their consequences. Conclusions here are ambiguous. In disbanding the business committee, not to mention publicly censuring Oshkenaniew, some Menominees added weight to charges of corruption and mismanagement. But since Agent Freeman called the meeting and presided over deliberations, can we assume that these actions constitute an unambiguous repudiation? Maybe Menominees simply sought the avenue of least resistance.[27]

Reginald Oshkosh's emergence adds another element to the equation. We may interpret his vocal repudiation of Oshkenaniew as personal and political rivalry, an emerging contest between one who claimed authority by virtue of heritage versus a "man on the make." It is equally logical to understand Oshkosh as reacting against that individualistic ethos, embodied by loggers and pursued, many may have felt, to the detriment of the collective good. In this context Oshkosh assumed his family's mantle, becoming a guardian of the collective welfare. Here we can discern a link between personal conduct and the continuing dialogue over values, or cultural orientation, a contest brought to the forefront by this latest crisis. Viewed from this perspective, Oshkosh was reviving the practice whereby Menominees avoided direct confrontation with outside authority, preferring instead to negotiate a settlement. Oshkenaniew, then, emerges as an insurgent, one whose ideas may have reflected those of substantial numbers of Menominees but whose methods challenged established manners and mores. They also invited reprisals. Censuring Oshkenaniew, and disbanding his committee, then, may have been directed toward the Indian Office, an effort by Oshkosh to prove that the Menominees were responsible people. It also demonstrates an acute awareness of the constraints under which Indian leaders operated. While he may have appreciated Oshkenaniew's determination to capture for the Menominees a role in directing their own affairs, Oshkosh still could have recoiled against the prospect of direct confrontation. This strategy sacrificed Oshkenaniew in the hopes of preserving a modicum of tribal control over logging.

With the controversy seemingly resolved, the Forest Service appointed E. A. Braniff as forest supervisor and director over all phases of the new operation. A graduate of Yale's school of forestry, Braniff lacked managerial experience and possessed a chilly, some said abrasive, personality. He was decisive, however, and right away committed to a single large sawmill and settled on a site twenty-three miles north and west of Keshena, along the Wolf River and serviced by the Wisconsin and Northern Railroad. Construction began in 1908, and the mill, the center-piece of a new town dubbed Neopit, opened for business in January 1909. Costing just over $200,000, the plant's main building housed two band saws and a host of other lumbering equipment; it boasted an annual pro-duction capacity of 40 million board feet of lumber. Directly adjacent stood a large brick structure housing six large boilers and a Corliss steam engine—the plant's powerhouse. The Forest Service also constructed roads, a log pond, a boardinghouse for 200 men, and an electric plant to serve the mill and the surrounding town. Forestry also proposed build-ing a commissary but backed off when Menominee storekeepers protested that it threatened to put them out of business. All told, the mill and other reservation "improvements" cost just over $1 million, all of it withdrawn from tribal funds.[28]

Planning and construction aside, operations got off to a shaky start. Salvaging the blown-down timber foundered for a lack of adequate roads and a depressed lumber market. Braniff also had to contend with Joseph Farr, who harbored a personal disdain for university-trained foresters and resented the younger man's intrusion on what had been his turf.

Their relationship deteriorated further after the Ballinger-Pinchot controversy set employees of Interior and Agriculture against one another. The result was to throw Braniff, a close associate of the chief forester, into the middle of a controversy he neither wanted nor could control.[29] Fallout could be severe. An investigation commissioned by the Interior Department alleged that manifold instances of mismanagement had cost the tribe over $730,000, and that Forestry never should have appointed him in the first place. Although Braniff steadfastly defended his reputation, attributing a $280,000 deficit to the difficulties in starting the operation from scratch, he clearly lacked the support of the most vocal Menominees. In late August, Reginald Oshkosh and Peter LaMotte headed 100 petitioners who accused Braniff of mismanagement and misappropriation of tribal funds, demanding his removal. Besieged from all sides, Braniff resigned under pressure in October 1909. His replacement, A. M. Riley, touted as a "practical" lumberman, actually improved upon Braniff's fiscal performance. But Riley's relationship with Menominee workers was exceedingly poor—he called them "lazy" to their faces—and he resigned under pressure after just one season.[30]

Angus S. Nicholson, agency superintendent and a career civil servant, took over for Riley in July 1910, and his appointment consolidated mill and agency operations under one man. This probably improved efficiency, but it also isolated Menominee entrepreneurs from logging operations, accelerating a process that had been under way at least since passage of the La Follette Act. Even so, the mill recorded a $60,000 net profit during Nicholson's first year despite a forest fire and salvage operations that compelled construction of a new logging railroad. Mill production then increased steadily, from some 2 million board feet of lumber manufactured in 1909 to 40 million during fiscal year 1913. This translated into profits, financial aid to schools, and new homes and other material improvements; by the end of 1913, Nicholson boasted of over $245,000 deposited in the new 4 percent fund.[31]

The mill had also generated employment as far back, in fact, as Braniff's controversial tenure. From 270 during the first month of operations, Braniff's Indian workforce held steady at nearly 300 throughout that first year, reaching a high of 339 in March. All told, and including the period between April and December 1908, when Menominees constructed the mill and town, the Indian workforce averaged 221 during Braniff's sixteen months on the job. Aggregate monthly wages ranged from $1,400 to $8,000, totaling $70,000, and average individual wages began at just over $20.00, sank to a low of $12.75 in September 1908, and climbed again to a high of $27.00 for July 1909. These figures held relatively steady. From 1909 to 1912, the logging and milling operations sustained an average 205 Indian jobs per quarter, with peak employment coming from late fall to

Neopit Camp No. 1, 1909. (Menominee Historic Preservation Archives)

mid-summer. In 1913, 322 Indians averaged $29.70 per month, not includ-
ing room and board said to be worth an additional $12.00 per month. Of
the 322 employees, 271 were Menominees, fully two-thirds of the 408
"able bodied males over 18," including forest guard Reginald Oshkosh
and Mitchell Oshkenaniew, who inspected dams. Stockbridges and a few
Oneidas rounded out the Indian workforce.[32]

    Beyond providing jobs, the new mill exerted profound pressures on
Menominee society. Neopit now rivaled Keshena as the reservation's principal community, gathering Menominees who gravitated toward logging
and lumbering and therefore represented a particular segment in society,
particularly in terms of occupation and, probably, cultural orientation. The
town's residents enjoyed modern houses, electric lights, and regular
streets; lots were laid out for homes not yet built but destined to be
financed by a new "reimbursable fund." Proposed by Oshkosh during a
1912 council meeting presided over by Nicholson (now the pattern, given
the demise of the business committee), the reimbursable fund financed a
home-building project where Indians could purchase houses through a
series of monthly payments. White workers also took advantage of the
housing boom even though they could rent, but not own, the homes built

with tribal funds. This "mortgage plan" proved a resounding success, with some 167 Indians becoming homeowners by 1914. Menominees may have invested it with greater significance still, as the continuation of a long-standing "tradition" of sharing profits as widely as practicable.[33]

For the 900 residents of Neopit, about half of whom were Menominees, life was enriched by a variety of clubs and activities that reflected the town's racial mixture and its self-conscious commitment to "modernity." There were two schools, a large assembly hall, a public gymnasium, and several stores, two owned by Menominees. Townspeople organized a marching band, a Returned Student's Club, an Indian lodge of the Catholic Knights of Columbus, a Gun and Drill Club, and five fully equipped volunteer fire-fighting companies. Promoting healthy bodies and healthy forests were an agency physician and a brand-new nursery. By almost any measure, Neopit represented a remarkable accomplishment: a community of hardworking, self-supporting Indians who lived in a town many non-Indians would have been proud to call home (and some did). Agent Nicholson viewed Neopit as a personal victory. "Sixty years ago a blanket Indian," he wrote in an article for the Carlisle Indian Industrial School's monthly newsletter, "today his children and grandchildren receiving education, taught manual work, and, in large measure, to be self-supporting. Is this not a record of which to be proud?" The equally proud agent concluded, "Has not the Menominee reason to carry his head high among his fellow tribesmen?"[34]

A marvelous accomplishment indeed. Yet underneath the clean new homes of Neopit, just beneath the shadow of the mill's twenty-five-foot smokestack, signs of discontent began to appear. In truth, many Menominees expressed deep reservations about the management of their timber resources right from the start. By calling for Braniff's removal, Oshkosh and LaMotte raised fiscal concerns, as did August A. Brueninger, an unenrolled Menominee and secretary of the Progressive Indian Association of Shawano, Wisconsin. Challenging Braniff's decision to build the mill "on a swamp which required thousands and thousands of dollars to get a foundation," Brueninger's 1909 complaint pointed as well to the use of tribal money to construct "palatial houses" for the superintendent and his aides and characterized the whole operation as intended "to bankrupt the tribe in the shortest way possible."[35]

But there was more than money to Menominee concerns. Often, though not always, pitting Menominees against non-Indian administrators, disagreements brought to the surface divergent visions for logging and lumbering, not to mention contrasting sets of cultural values. For loggers, the principal bone of contention concerned employment. On at least two occasions, individual Menominee loggers appealed directly to Senator La Follette, complaining that the best-paying positions had been

Log pond at Neopit mill. (State Historical Society of Wisconsin, negative WHi(X3)52063)

reserved for whites. Yet when Thomas LaBelle, an experienced logger from the late 1880s onward, asked whether "it is true" that "an Indian is entitled to any job which he is capable of holding . . . as I have asked and been refused," he found that administrators openly admitted to employing few Menominees as mill workers. Braniff, for instance, conceded that just one-fourth of Neopit's employees were Indians even as he claimed that "out of the wages paid to employees an increasing amount has been paid to Indians." Another experienced logger, John Kaquatosh, raised the same concern but saw his complaint dismissed by an Indian Office which concluded that while the job offered may not have been to his liking, he could work if he so wanted.[36]

Perhaps most troubling to Menominees was the attitude of mill managers toward Indian workers. While Braniff, Riley, and Nicholson agreed that the La Follette Act mandated Indian preference in hiring, and conceded that Neopit's purpose differed from that of a more typical plant, they nevertheless balked at turning operations over to Indians. Some argued that Menominees mysteriously grew "indifferent . . . so far as the interior of the mill is concerned." A. M. Riley was even more direct. Writing in 1910 that "I have been here long enough to know that a man . . . can never make a success of this business as long as he is obliged to hire Indian labor in preference to other," he expressed the somewhat self-serving opinion that Menominees wanted to be "paid for nothing," that they were poor workers whose participation inevitably drained the mill's financial reserves. Another observer argued that since the average Menominee worker did not "steadily, day in and day out, apply himself to any industrial pursuit" or "continue in employment long enough to qualify himself for a position of more responsibility and consequently, one affording increased compensation," he must be satisfied with jobs at the lower ranks.[37]

In relegating Menominees to the status of common laborers, administrators satisfied themselves that nothing else could be done, that since the Neopit mill, as one wrote, brought together "two subjects that we rarely find successfully associated in life—business and education," some compromises were inevitable. Indians offered a decidedly different interpretation of the situation. Reminded of previous, indeed ongoing, efforts on the part of local lumbering interests to despoil them of their resources, some wondered if the mill's price was not just too high. The 1909 council dominated by Reginald Oshkosh and Peter LaMotte suggests as much. According to Mitchell Oshkenaniew, who, by the way, made certain to distance himself from the complaints, most Menominees gathered on that August day strongly "desired to return to the old way of logging." Decrying wasteful spending, which, they argued, had used up "nearly all the interest on the tribal money," Menominees forcefully condemned what they saw as the salient feature of the new productive arrangements: namely, that "the logging business was taken away from the Menominee tribe."[38]

If Menominee mill workers found disappointment amid limited opportunities, and remembered "the old way" as a time when they did as they pleased, others chose to have little to do with Neopit, town or plant. By 1910, nearly 1,000 of the approximately 1,400 Menominees identified with places like Zoar, South Branch (Oconto), or Keshena, where the mill's future was decidedly less important than present, and local, concerns. After all, the Menominee Reservation remained a "community of communities," where kinship mattered and where the passage of time, not to mention economic change, revealed, even enhanced, divergent interests. In these several intersections of geography, subsistence, kinship, and cultural values, many reactions to Neopit were possible. One is revealed in a 1910 council meeting where delegations representing outlying communities demanded additional funding for local schools. The 400 or so residents of Zoar, still disinclined to participate in logging and probably even less interested in Neopit town, voiced their "desire to re-establish [a local] school . . . maintained and furnished from our funds," and with "a Menominee Indian as teacher." South Branch spokesmen Mitchell Oshkenaniew and Alex Peters asked for a new day school, paid for out of logging profits. They bolstered their case by charging abuse of children at the Keshena government school, claiming that their children grew sick and "lonesome" away from home and that "the tribe would save much expense thereby, because it cost in the neighborhood of $150.00 to teach, feed, clothe and take care of one child at the government school." At the same time, however, Keshena residents asked for money to expand their school, something that Sound Branch residents steadfastly opposed.[39]

Debates over schools suggest, albeit obliquely, that Neopit was a long way from Zoar or South Branch, especially if the new mill seemed to be operating principally for non-Indians, or at best for those Indians who valued, it seemed, clapboard homes and civic clubs more than they cherished the collective good. So when Superintendents Braniff, Riley, and Nicholson focused on investing for the future, Menominees in outlying districts saw instead a drain on tribal finances generally, and perhaps even a dangerous consolidation of influence in the new town. This was a real problem for some, like the seventeen surviving members of Menominee Post Number 261, Grand Army of the Republic, who in June 1913 called upon President Woodrow Wilson to settle, in their favor, an ongoing dispute with Agent Nicholson. The issue, so they wrote, was a reduction in their per capita annuities, from thirty dollars as recently as Agent Freeman's tenure, to just "twelve dollars and one half." The problem, according to the veterans, lay squarely in Neopit—significantly, with the erosion of a social compact that had bound all Menominees to logging. Having "always supposed the funds called the Menominee Indian Funds, belonged to the Tribe, to be used for their benefit," they now found "too many cottages at Neopit, where the Mill is," and wondered why the "Supt. with such splendid logging outfit . . . cannot make enough to meet all expenses without taking so much money out of our trust funds." The answer, so they said, was "there must be a leak somewhere."[40]

The leak was in Neopit, and it squandered more than money. Evaporating public support may offer a context for increasingly vocal demands for native control over the entire logging and milling enterprise.

In a February 1912 petition, twenty-four leading Menominees, including old Neo'pit Oshkosh as well as former business committee members Oshkenaniew, George McCall, Weiskesit, John Grignon, Thomas LaBelle, and Mose Tucker, called on Nicholson "to appoint, or use his influence to secure the appointment of Reginald Oshkosh as manager of our logging and lumbering operations."[41] In a letter accompanying the petition, Oshkosh explained the tribe's reasoning in greater detail. "For many years," he wrote, "the Menominee Indians have had among its members men educated at Haskell, Carlisle, and other leading schools of the country," men who "have successfully conducted logging operations, and demonstrated their business ability in many lines." But all of this was to no avail because "the Government has apparently not seen fit to intrust [sic] them in positions connected with the management of their own tribal affairs," even though "the plant here at Neopit was built for the benefit of the Indians and with a view of intrusting [sic] them with positions of responsibility." What the tribe really desired, he explained, was a chance "to become independent and self-supporting and terminate our relations as wards of the Government."[42] As for his own objectives, Oshkosh summarized them this way:

> I believe that having been born and reared as a child of the woods, having witnessed logging operations from the time of my childhood, having been educated in one of the leading Indian schools of the country, and having been more or less intimately associated with the present manufacturing plant at Neopit, that I am competent and qualified to succeed you as manager of the plant at Neopit. I should prefer to occupy such position under your supervision as general superintendent of the reservation until such time as you deem it advisable to intrust [sic] me with the complete management thereof.[43]

After Nicholson declaimed any authority in the matter, three separate delegations lobbied the commissioner's office. There still were no results, despite an impassioned "if we are ever going to be like you we might as well get into the harness now as later" from Reginald Oshkosh.[44]

Advancing Reginald Oshkosh's career constitutes just one instance where some Menominees came to view logging as a valuable political tool, a potential rallying point for dispersed settlements with their competing agendas. Oshkosh and Oshkenaniew understood this, and by 1912–13 the two men emerged as leaders among a core group of decision makers. Able to count on widespread support, particularly since Weiskesit often joined with this contingent of logger-entrepreneurs, Oshkosh and Oshkenaniew found common ground on a number of issues and even served together on delegations headed to Washington. They agreed, for instance, on a plan to increase per capita payments and to finance the annuities through a $125,000 withdrawal from the Menominee Log Fund. "We are in desperate straits," read the council's resolution; "for several years past the seasons have been bad and such crops as we depend on have failed us." The two men also participated in a rigorous vetting process for evaluating enrollment petitions. Flooded with applications and naturally suspicious of those who would seek to share in timber profits, the tribe's "enrollment committee," according to Peter Pamonicutt, demanded "that all those people who have been admitted recently" must understand that "their duties will be to better conditions of the reservation as well as the betterment of the tribe." Oshkosh and Oshkenaniew seconded this recommendation.[45]

By far the most interesting incidence of cooperation came during a May 1913 council meeting when those in attendance voted unanimously to reverse the 1908 censure against Mitchell Oshkenaniew and to request that Congress recognize a revised version of the old business committee. Attributing the original censure to the actions of "a small faction of the tribe," the 1913 gathering now agreed that "it is the desire of our tribe that this infamous resolution be wiped out, canceled and taken from the records, so that it shall not stand in the way against Mitchell Oshkenaniew, upon whom we place a great confidence." Itself a startling move, this same council voted to invest a revised business committee with "full power and authority to manage [the logging and lumbering] business." The proposed committee therefore claimed broad authority, including the right "to finance the entire industry, or of the Menomonee Log Fund," the ability to "control and manage the employing and discharging of employees," and the "duty . . . to cause or encourage all said Indians on said reservation to be employed." It was, in other words, an effort led by logger-entrepreneurs and dedicated to reinstating an effective, moderately independent, civil government. Or, as Peter Pamonicutt related, "if the committee would have power to employ men to perform the work, they could get good employees," meaning, he continued, "having the Indians do their own logging."[46]

The 1913 resolution constitutes an impressive resurrection for Mitchell Oshkenaniew, demonstrating once again his talent for overcoming controversy. He also played no small role in creating tensions. In September 1913, and joined by Thomas Prickett and Louis LaFrambois, Oshkenaniew hired D. F. Tyrrell, a Gillette, Wisconsin, attorney, and his associate Webster Ballinger of Washington, D.C., to conduct a thorough investigation of the Neopit project. LaFrambois, a mixed blood only recently relocated from Marinette, Wisconsin, was, by his own testimony, an experienced logger and lumberman. His return to the reservation indicated logging's potential for consolidating the Menominee diaspora, and not incidentally to unite Indian opinion against outside authority. Prickett's background was at least as interesting. A mixed-blood descendent of a nineteenth-century trader and his Menominee spouse, the sixty-year-old Prickett secured a position on the old business committee only months after successfully petitioning for enrollment; like Oshkenaniew, he found that trouble followed his rise to prominence. Embroiled in the controversy surrounding logging in the blown-down district, he then came under fire for allegedly pocketing insurance premiums collected from Menominee mill workers. This earned him formal censure from a tribal council while Indian Office personnel tried to banish him from the reservation altogether. Like Oshkenaniew, Prickett engineered his own comeback. He convinced tribal councilmen to revoke his earlier censure, and by early 1913 he was in Washington, joining his old associate on an unofficial delegation to secure larger per capitas from the tribal log fund. A controversial, perhaps unsavory, character, Prickett, and to a lesser extent LaFrambois, embodied that entrepreneurial mind-set produced and enhanced by a half century of logging. If some Menominees found the three men untrustworthy, others apparently valued their initiative and willingness to pressure government officials. Such was the nature of Menominee politics in these times.[47]

Unconcerned with, or perhaps unaware of, their clients' backgrounds, Ballinger and Tyrrell went to work. From his base in Washington, Ballinger examined Indian Office records and informed Oshkenaniew that, all told, the mill had lost nearly $1.5 million since its inception, a revelation the lawyer also promised to make public. Meanwhile, Tyrrell toured the reservation. Finding "splendid" timber left to rot in the woods, roads constructed at tribal expense but then abandoned, Tyrrell laid the blame for this litany of wasteful practices at Nicholson's feet. He also discovered evidence that lumbermen had harvested only the very best trees so as to improve short-term profit margins, but at the expense of wise forest management. "The work," so the lawyer concluded, "has been and is being carried on with little or no regard for profit."[48]

Government officials reacted quickly, and in October the Board of Indian Commissioners selected one of their own, Edward E. Ayer, to organize an official inquiry. A wealthy Chicago lumberman and amateur collector of Indian artifacts who had made his fortune selling railroad ties, Ayer seemed especially well suited to the task at hand. He and his party, which included woodsman L. P. Holland and accountant Philip R. Smith, both affiliated with the Ayer and Lord Tie Company of Chicago, arrived in Neopit in late November. J. P. Kinney, supervisor of forests for the Indian Office, joined them later. Over the next few weeks, the group toured the mill and forests and interviewed a number of tribal members, including several who were reportedly behind the decision to hire Tyrrell.[49]

Ayer's work quickly became more complicated when Ballinger and Tyrrell next accused Agent Nicholson of undercutting Neopit's basic mission by employing whites over Menominees. The two lawyers charged further that Menominee workers typically landed the lowest-paying and most dangerous positions, and that Nicholson treated Indians badly himself, or at least condoned the verbal abuse of Indian employees. Other charges included denying aid to the destitute, even when vegetables produced on the agency farm were otherwise going to waste, permitting whites to purchase items from agency warehouses at reduced prices but not extending the same privilege to Indians, and intimidating critics to keep them silent. Armed with incriminating evidence, Tyrrell demanded that the commissioner replace Nicholson at once.[50]

Ayer's investigation and final report constitute an instructive tale of conclusions matching expectations, of seeing what one expects to see. As such they provide a revealing glimpse into dramatically differing conceptions of the mill's purpose, the rationale for logging generally, and evolving relationships within the community. For Ayer, the principal issue was whether the mill operated efficiently and according to its legislative mandate. On this score he cleared Nicholson of any wrongdoing. Ayer's team of "experts," Nicholson's spirited testimony, and affidavits from a number of Indians all supported the conclusion Ayer seemed to have formulated going in, namely, that "the government has done a very wise thing in having this mill built." When Kinney supported Nicholson's claim that he did his best to employ qualified Menominees, Ayer concurred, citing employment statistics and highlighting the forest supervisor's impression that "the Menominee tribe has often suffered because of Nicholson's trying Indians after they had failed." Similarly, Kinney's analysis of Neopit's financial condition corresponded with his own. Both men discounted evidence of "deliberate maladministration" and concluded that, *excluding* costs incurred in mill construction and another $270,000 lost in salvaging blown-down hardwoods, the mill had actually turned a profit of some $440,000. Proof enough, wrote Ayer, that the project "has been of tremendous value to the Indians."[51]

When interviewing Menominee witnesses, Ayer pursued these conclusions with considerable vigor, determined, it seems, to protect both the mill and Nicholson. To retail salesman Charles Chickeney's statement that "I think the reason the tribe are [sic] dissatisfied is that the annuity is decreasing every year," Ayer replied, "There are several hundred thousand dollars added to your credit in Washington in the last three years; so that it isn't true that this mill has decreased your annuity." This was a rather typical exchange. When Peter Lookaround, Haskell graduate and

Neopit merchant, expressed concern that logging "costs more money now," or policeman Joe Gristo said, "I think the idea is that the mill ought to be making money, instead of running behind every year," Ayer lectured his witnesses, expressing a paternalism that must have been hard to take. "Don't you think that if the men knew that the last two years the mill had added to the funds at Washington $444,000 they would have been more satisfied with the management?" he asked Gristo. Addressing Lookaround, he asked, "Do you think that you can preserve the timber for the next fifty years . . . better, by having the mill, than without one?" The Neopit merchant replied simply, "Yes sir."[52]

Not all Menominees were as polite. Thomas Prickett warned Ballinger and Tyrrell that Nicholson ordered the mill and yard cleaned up prior to the investigation (presumably, he wrote, to hide damning evidence), and he held firm in the face of Ayer's questioning. He resisted revealing the source of retainers for the two lawyers, and when asked why hire attorneys at all replied, "We Indians can come up here to Mr. Nicholson but cannot get information; but Mr. Tirrell [sic] . . . knows what we Indians want and can find out from Mr. Nicholson." Some exchanges became testy. "I have been a woodsman for twenty years and yet a man comes here for twenty minutes and tells me I don't know anything about it," exclaimed Louis LaFrambois during his interview. "And I want you [Ayer] to put this down too, that I have been a citizen of the United States and voting for 21 years!"[53]

Ayer seemed unperturbed by such exchanges, satisfied that unscrupulous attorneys had duped some Menominees into following along. He attached significance to evidence that Tyrrell and Ballinger also represented Wallie Cook and August Anderson in their ongoing suits arising out of the abortive timber harvests of 1908. The notorious lumbermen, so Ayer's reasoning went, hoped to secure financial recompense out of any settlement the tribe might reach with the Indian Office. To this apparent conflict of interest Ayer's investigation added indications that the lawyers had collected some $400 to defray expenses, $250 of that from a mortgage on Louis LaFrambois's home. LaFrambois denied the accusation, but linking one of the leading "agitators" with what seemed an underhanded scheme was enough for Ayer. The entire motive for the investigation, he concluded, "is the same one that has been at the bottom of every attack on Indian property—the desire and hope of getting some of it."[54]

So Ayer was understandably pleased when Mitchell Oshkenaniew suddenly distanced himself from Prickett and LaFrambois, Tyrrell and Ballinger. Whether the politically agile Oshkenaniew recognized that the suit was headed nowhere or simply lost faith in his lawyers remains unclear.[55] More certain, however, is Reginald Oshkosh's position. In his final report, Ayer highlighted a letter from "a full blooded Indian and

Tribal Chief" who "has been pulling himself together and doing good work." The now middle-aged Reginald Oshkosh denounced Tyrrell's connection with Wallace Cook ("better known as the Lumber Crook," he wrote); just as important, he linked the scheme with Menominee political and cultural tensions. That he used the language of blood quantum was meaningful, even if questionable in terms of late-twentieth-century scholarship, and reflected popular notions regarding racial heritage and behavior. Perhaps reflecting his own suspicions that mixed "blood" bred avarice, Oshkosh wrote that

> Mr. Tyrrell's solicitation among the Indians is being entertained entirely by the descendants of the mixed bloods who withdrew from the Menominee Tribe under the treaty of 1849, and who, through the sympathy of the generous Menominee Tribe, have just recently been adopted into the tribe. . . . [and they] are employing every means to conceal from the full-blood and original members of the tribe the inside facts of their real purpose.

The design, he concluded, was to "approach the lazy, shiftless and low-bred half-breeds who are as a general rule easy victims [sic] to small bribes, and who are to be the tools (Tom Prickett and others)." From here, it was a comparatively easy matter to "create dissatisfaction, . . . induce them [Menominees] to terminate their relations with the Government as wards, and divide the reservation resources" among themselves.[56]

Oshkenaniew's change of heart notwithstanding, other Menominees still found the investigation distasteful and its conclusions biased. Frank Gauthier, identified as a mixed-blood trader and logger, found Ayer a biased observer and claimed that "there is no limit for [his] praises on the part of Nicholson's good management." According to Gauthier, "every Menominee Indian says that the man Mr. Ayers [sic] is here . . . to whitewash Nicholson's doings." Louis LaFrambois accused the commissioner of spreading "dirty lies" about his ties with the lawyers and claimed that Ayer, "no lover of fair play," had deliberately misquoted him, failing, he wrote, "to take anything that might be damaging" to Nicholson. "The feeling against Mr. Ayer and Nicholson is not very good," warned LaFrambois, and "I would not like to answer for what might happen to Mr. Nicholson if the department sees fit to keep him here." A Keshena missionary also predicted violence and suggested that the Menominees were "very suspicious and revengeful if anyone says a word they do not like," a concern echoed by lawyer Ballinger.[57]

Despite these dire warnings, calm prevailed. Nicholson held his job, the mill continued operating, and the "minirebellion" of 1913–14 seemingly dissipated soon after Ayer submitted his report. A 1934 audit

Menominee Indian Mills (Neopit), ca. 1920. (Menominee Historic Preservation Archives)

supported Ayer's contention that the mill actually generated a small profit during this period. Moreover, while Menominee workers appeared to be concentrated in the lower-paying positions in logging camps, the Neopit project still generated 200 to 300 jobs, along with houses and other amenities, at least in the new town. Combined with evidence that Tyrrell and Ballinger sought a settlement beneficial to their white clients, the investigation certainly appealed to those who equated the mill's worth with its profit statement, or saw numbers of jobs generated and concluded that opportunity followed, at least for Menominees willing to work hard.[58] And, it is true, some Menominees undoubtedly understood the situation in substantially these terms. Even so, we cannot shake the nagging suspicion that this analysis might be missing something. Can it be that focusing on the mill's financial statement is a red herring, a false path leading ethnohistorians toward conclusions that more accurately describe the non-Indian conceptual universe than an Indian one, whatever that may be? If so, can we "turn the picture inside out" and highlight Menominee perspectives? How did Menominees come to understand the Neopit project, what were *their* objectives, and did the mill meet those expectations? Where, to put it differently, can we find that cultural "dialogue" that might provide a handle for deeper analysis?

A council meeting called by veteran Indian Office inspector E. B. Linnen on 2 September 1915 offers one such opportunity, and a convenient coda for the first half of this study. The response to dissatisfaction over Ayer's conclusions and to renewed calls for Nicholson's ouster, this meeting reveals the Menominees' perspectives on the relationship, as they understood it, between economic development and cultural values. Their concerns were severalfold: first, that qualified Menominees continued to be denied responsible positions and were regularly dismissed for trivial offenses; second, that white employees received favorable consideration for these same positions and, as a consequence, enjoyed standards of living financed, so they said, by the Menominees; third, that in diverting scarce resources toward running the mill, the Neopit project hampered the development of other means of subsistence, thereby reducing the financial prospects of non–mill workers (in other words, the mill promoted one kind of labor and thus favored one set of values over others). Finally, Menominees expressed considerable bitterness over their alienation from all levels of decision making. That they were not consulted on even the most minute details fueled the suspicion that Neopit, by either design or default, operated to benefit the interests of whites, whose interest lay in deriving maximum profits from Menominee timberlands, whatever the cost.[59]

Menominee critics were not so much challenging the importance of the mill as equating its utility with tangible improvements in general welfare. And in this respect, what emerges from this council meeting is less a cultural "dialogue" than two separate, though certainly interrelated, "monologues." When Ayer and Nicholson correlated healthy balance sheets, not to mention fulfillment of the project's educational mission, with hiring experienced non-Indians to fill the most responsible positions, Mose Tucker bristled at the implication that Indians were lazy or incompetent. "I think," he said before the council gathering, "the fact that the Indians saved up nearly three million dollars in about eighteen years [prior to the La Follette Act] should be sufficient to prove to the Department that the Indian is competent." While Sam Pywaukee could distinguish profit from loss, he chafed at Nicholson's paternalistic management practices. "Whenever you have a proposition or scheme on hand you start right on without consulting anybody about it," he said, and this bothered him, particularly since "this timber belonged to the Indians." Louis LaFrambois went further. Remembering when Nicholson turned away a Menominee applicant with the comment "'If I give you this job it will be like taking this white man's bread away from him,'" LaFrambois wondered if whites "were educated [by the project] instead of Indians."[60]

If evidence that whites drew disproportionate benefits from the mill fueled suspicions about the use of tribal funds, it also renewed a debate about cultural values. For every Peter Pamonicutt who spoke of Menominees deriving "no benefit" from the operation, even though "our lumber built it," there were at least as many who wondered if the "price" of enjoying the mill's very real benefits might be higher than some supposed. So when Louis LaFrambois found "the Pagan Indians . . . in critical condition," when Sam Pywaukee said "it hurt me and made me feel bad to see the timber these men were destroying," they were expressing a frustration born out of a perceived impotence to shape their collective destiny. Likewise Frank Waubano, who interpreted Nicholson's boast that "he had no [Menominee] friends, did not intend to have friends," less as a promise of evenhanded management than simple arrogance. No wonder, then, that when Mose Tucker observed farmers who "cannot earn enough to support their families," he concluded, "All that I can see is that the proposition is a damage to the tribe. A few gets [*sic*] their daily wages there, but that is all."[61]

The irony here is that at the very moment when individualistic or entrepreneurial values were supposed to reach their apogee, propelled as they were by the Neopit project, Menominee cultural conventions, something we have termed "communitarianism," still influenced the trajectory of that vehicle. Not so much dormant as ignored by those who saw what they expected to see, Menominee values remained the gravitational force shaping the path of social change. This helps explain why, during that 1915 council meeting and indeed all through the latter half of the second decade of the twentieth century, Menominees repeatedly asked for increased annuity payments. To Nicholson, and probably to an Indian Office bureaucracy determined to transform Menominee values, such requests were the work of those "who just hang around, display no ambition and will not work for their own or other's [*sic*] support." But what Nicholson interpreted as a contest between the industrious and the lazy, some Menominees understood as a question of right and wrong. For beyond balance sheets, aside from understandable bitterness over a perceived plundering of tribal resources lay a more fundamental question: For whom is the mill to operate? And toward what end?[62]

In a sense, "Who owns the trees?" had always been the basic concern. From Chief Neo'pit's determination to set aside a portion of timber profits for a poor fund through Mitchell Oshkenaniew's repeated efforts to take charge of lumbering operations, Menominees wrestled with the implications of economic change. Seeking neither to slow the intrusion of entrepreneurial values nor to endorse them wholeheartedly, Menominees performed a delicate balancing act in which they attempted to make economic development conform to certain fundamental values, to distribute timber profits to every "owner" while simultaneously confronting divergent cultural orientations, produced, in no small measure, by logging and lumbering. This was no easy task, for while the mixed-blood logger Tom LaBelle could argue forcefully that "the time has arrived that the Indians should have some voice in the way [lumber] is manufactured," Frank Waubano denounced "the way the white man works to earn money" with equal vigor. The white man, so Waubano argued before a 1915 council meeting, "steals money from other people, and murders and gambles to earn it. There is no Menominee here that will do that."[63]

In his important article documenting Northern Ute tribal politics, David Rich Lewis warns ethnohistorians away from simplistic "dichotomies" based on blood quanta or the equally familiar "progressives" and "traditionalists." More broadly, anthropologists Morris Foster and Loretta Fowler, among numerous others, council caution when we conceive of "Indian-ness" as a continuum, plotting values on a graph, as it were, in ways that equate change with assimilation, or persistence with cultural purity.[64] We would do well to apply these admonitions to Menominees and timber exploitation. In an age when any economic vitality on Indian reservations was rare indeed, the Menominee case offers a glimpse into the dynamic relationship between cultural values and financial stability. While Menominees were engaged in a spirited debate over the consequences of economic change, it would be a mistake to characterize this as a zero-sum game, where one set of values overcame another, where the modern displaced the traditional. The dialogue was more complex than that. For as much as Frank Waubano and Tom LaBelle seemed to be speaking past one another, or Neo'pit Oshkosh and Mitchell Oshkenaniew can be understood as representing divergent ideals born of differing experiences, there remained a level at which Menominees operated in concert. From fur trade days, when this community struggled to weave new technologies and new "peoples" into the social fabric, Menominees demonstrated a talent for innovation, for integrating the new into the old, altering the shape of that which is adopted just as they were changed by those same forces. Menominees demonstrated a tradition *of* change, we might argue, and then extended this formulation to other Indians as well.

But detecting native "agency," valuable as it is, can obscure even as it illuminates. We should remain cautious that innovation is not the same as choosing from a wide range of possibilities. Power matters, and in these times, as before and after, Indians generally possessed precious little. While Menominees faced no Nelson Act or Clapp Rider, which Melissa Meyer demonstrates as providing the legislative mechanism for dispossessing the White Earth Anishinaabeg of their timberlands, they still played a minimal role in shaping laws touching upon the disposition of their resources. Power, or access to it, remains an essential, if sometimes overlooked, factor. So even as we consider the Menominees' success in defending their homeland against allotment or forces pressing for their political disintegration, perceiving an important distinction between their story and that of Oklahoma tribes during these same times, we should be careful to distinguish between what the Menominees accomplished and what, for lack of a better phrase, just happened. Menominees could, and did, seek to make logging work for them, and according to a reasoned, if contentiously expressed, understanding of their interests or fundamental values. They did not, however, prevent allotment so much as benefit from the fact that those who could have forced this issue chose not to, for whatever reasons.[65]

This is not to suggest a return to analyses portraying Indians as acted upon, as passive pawns in the unfolding of history. Rather, it is a call for analytical rigor, a suggestion that we distinguish what Indians could control from what they could not. More important, we must search for subtleties, probing more deeply into ways Indian societies deflect or transform outside pressures. Here, it seems, is where comparison may prove valuable. As we will discover in the second half of this study, Menominees were not alone, either in confronting dramatic change while seeking to preserve their sense of identity (albeit in new forms and expressions) or in perceiving manifold opportunities in rather dramatic economic change. Like the Menominees, the Tsimshians from Metlakatla did not so much resist change as learn to live with it. As they came to terms with pressures for radical change, they too found ways to transform what was not "Indian" into something that was—or at least as they came to define what it meant to be Tsimshian.

CHAPTER FIVE

The Tsimshians of British Columbia

In his study of unfree labor in the American South and imperial Russia, Peter Kolchin succinctly observes that "comparison enables one to weigh the impact of different variables and hence to distinguish the specific or incidental from the general or inherent." Although separated from the present work by distance, cultures, and conditions, Kolchin astutely apprehends a cardinal principle behind comparative history. That is to say, by isolating divergence as well as convergence, and reflecting upon both similarities and differences, comparison advances understanding. This is, in a sense, one primary purpose behind historical analysis. But the trick lies in framing issues in ways that advance inquiry without resorting to such broad generalizations as to inflict violence upon particulars. Thus the need to balance a theoretical framework with empirical data.[1]

My hope here is to strike just that balance, making use of the convenient starting point provided by world-systems theory. By offering a model to understand the process whereby peoples became "incorporated" into global market capitalism, this framework combines flexibility with analytical rigor, all in the service of comprehending what may seem logical: that, confronted with powerful market forces whose instruments operated outside their control, native peoples in the Americas and elsewhere found themselves swept into an economic tide that produced poverty and dependency, even as it offered material goods and, seemingly, opportunity. This is fine so far as it goes, but we aim for more. My analysis strives to suggest that in examining the intersection of economic change and cultural identity as observed in two distinct places, a critical, and sometime overlooked, variable was the degree to which Indian individuals and social groupings made their own choices. Not that all choices were available to them—they certainly were not—but the process of coming to terms with economic change involved manifold adaptations in behavior, changes that, by necessity, individuals and societies had to integrate into their respective identities. In concrete terms, this means that as Menominees and Tsimshians sought material and cultural security amid rapidly shifting circumstances, they redefined what it meant to "be" Menominee or Tsimshian. And it is this process that continues to occupy our attention.[2]

At roughly the same time that the Menominees were wrestling with the transition from fur trading to logging, thousands of miles to the north and west another native group was embarking on a similar, and no less challenging, journey. The name Tsimshian describes culturally and historically related peoples inhabiting the northwest coast of British Columbia, from the Nass River to the Milbanke Sound, and from the Pacific Ocean inland to the headwaters of the Nass and Skeena Rivers. Although specific settlements have appeared and disappeared since the advent of sustained contact with whites, these territories correspond roughly to aboriginal homelands. Their international neighborhood includes Tlingits to the northeast, Tsetsaut Athapaskans to the north and west, Wet'-suet'en (Carrier) Athapascans to the east, Haisla, Haihais (Xaixai), and Heiltsuk (formally Bella Bella) groups to the south, and the Haida of the Queen Charlotte Islands.

Archaeological evidence suggests continuous occupation of the region for at least 10,000 years, with cultural features consistent with historical forms appearing by 2,000 years ago. Tsimshians remember a more distant past, tracing their ethnic origins to a time when the world was far different, and a place they call Temlaxham (Temlaxam, Prairie Town). Located at the confluence of the Bulkley and Skeena Rivers, and near today's Hazelton, British Columbia, Temlaxham was a place of great abundance and happiness, and the origin point for familiar houses and clans. But the ancestors grew arrogant and contemptuous of supernatural spirits; they even abused animals, killing them for fun rather than for food. Terrible cataclysms followed—floods, avalanches, famine, all the work of angry spirits—and in their aftermath the people scattered and, among other things, produced the subdivision of Tsimshian peoples into four "nations" and numerous "tribes."[3]

The nations—Coast, Southern, Gitxsan, and Nisga'a—are geographically separate, linguistically distinct, but similar culturally, and together they constitute the broader Tsimshian world. Each is subdivided further into tribes, sometimes termed "villages." For the nine Coast Tsimshian tribes (Gitwilgyoots, Gitzaxlaal, Gitnadoiks, Giluts'aaw, Gitando, Gispaxlo'ots, Gits'iis, Gitlaan, Ginax'angilk), home territories included fishing and hunting stations along the Skeena River and its estuaries as well as winter villages surrounding Metlakatla (Maxlakxaala) Pass, near today's Prince Rupert harbor. Indeed, "Tsimshian" is derived from the native terms *ts'm* (those inside) and *ksiaan* (the Skeena). South of the Skeena stood the three Southern Tsimshian towns (Gitisu, Gitk'a'ata, Gitkxaala), whose inhabitants spoke a language similar to the coastal dialect but virtually extinct as of a century ago. To the north and east live the Gitxsan (*git*, meaning "people," and *xsan*, meaning "of the Skeena"), peoples who inhabited villages along the upper Skeena in close association with "Tsimshianized" Wet'suet'en and the Nisga'a (also Nisga, Nishga), whose homeland was the upper Nass.[4]

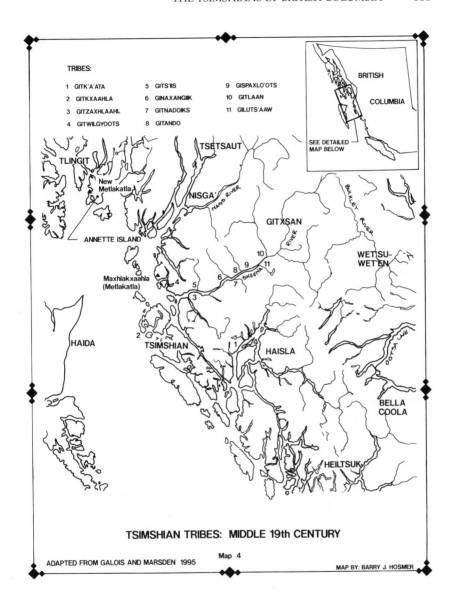

TSIMSHIAN TRIBES: MIDDLE 19th CENTURY

ADAPTED FROM GALOIS AND MARSDEN 1995

Map 4

MAP BY: BARRY J. HOSMER

Anthropologists place Tsimshians within the Northwest Coast complex, where coastal peoples from northern California to southeastern Alaska manifest a distinctive set of social, economic, and cultural expressions. This was a rich environment, with rivers teeming with salmon and *oolichan*, ready access to pelagic and riverine mammals and birds, dense forests of redwoods, hemlock, cedar, spruce, and fir, and abundant supplies of berries and other edible flora. Various Tsimshian households exploited these resources in an annual cycle that took them from *oolichan* stations along the Nass in early spring to seaweed gathering and salmon spawning grounds during the summer and fall, then to hunting territories, and finally to winter villages where, supplied with stocks of preserved salmon and other foods, the tribe settled in for a season of intensive ceremonial activities. So bountiful was their environment that the Tsimshians had the security to support dense populations, build permanent towns featuring large cedar plank dwellings, and produce a rich cultural and artistic life.[5]

As with the Menominees, Tsimshian life was organized around shared principles, beliefs, a sense of identity manifested in a distinctive social structure, patterns of intra- and intergroup relationships, and means of organizing productive activities. All were understood through the telling of sacred histories *(adawx)* and the workings of supernatural wonders *(naxnox)*, as displayed in totemic crests *(p'teex)* and manifested in spiritual potency *(halaayt)*. Basic principles included hierarchy, reciprocity, and an expansive notion of corporate ownership of tangible and intangible properties. In other words, Tsimshians considered ceremonial prerogatives, names, songs, and sacred histories—not just territories—as the exclusive property of corporate groups but held in trust by the highest-ranking individuals. Also of fundamental importance was the social, spiritual, political, and economic institution of feasting, the potlatch *(yaakw)*, which confirmed statuses, relationships, and prerogatives. These principles, of course, were intertwined in the minds and shared cultural identity of all Tsimshians, combining with the fundamental importance of sea, sky, rivers, and animals to produce a tightly integrated whole.[6]

Just as folklore reveals something of the Menominee mental universe, Tsimshian peoples possess rich traditions accounting for the shape of their present world and relationships between human beings and the natural and supernatural realms. These tales are of two principle varieties. *Adawx* (true traditions) are historical, even though they may contain supernatural elements, and they frequently concern encounters between *naxnox* spirits and notable ancestors. Since they provide force and meaning to crests, *adawx* are private property, jealously guarded, and revealed only by those so entitled. *Ma'lesk*, on the other hand, generally take place in those times when animals appeared as human beings, or before the existence of mortal men and women. In this sense they may be considered analogous to "myth." Both are invaluable aids in uncovering the Tsimshian worldview and, since a group continually adds to its storehouse of *adawx*, native perspectives on historical events.[7]

Many *ma'lesk* concern the activities of Txamsem (also Txaamsm), a supernatural trickster and transformer who ranks among the most important *naxnox* beings. Also known as Raven, later as Wiget or "giant," Txamsem was a being of great appetites and complicated moral and ethical sensibilities. But he is responsible for the shape and functioning of the universe, and in this sense his exploits are of fundamental importance to Tsimshian people, outweighing, it seems, a concern with "creation" per se. Of Txamsem's many accomplishments, his most important was stealing the sun, moon, and stars and then releasing light to illuminate the world. A transforming act of fundamental importance, in that light provided meaning and order to the universe, Txamsem's action made possible the world of human beings and all that has come since. So pervasive is this theme that the most recent interpretation places illumination, light, as the paramount integrating force in Tsimshian culture. Thus it follows that Txamsem must occupy a particularly central cosmological role, at least during those times when *ma'lesk* still helped Tsimshian peoples understand their world.[8]

Myths also reveal something about relationships between humans and the natural and supernatural worlds, thus offering cultural outsiders some entrée, however approximate, into Tsimshian modes of understanding. One particularly well-known tale takes place during a time of famine.[9] In the town of Gitsiis on the lower Skeena River the son of a chief was left home when his parents went away in search of food. He was kept company by a slave boy who was to remain with him whenever his parents were away. But the slave boy was hungry, and to stop him from crying, the chief's son gave him a piece of dried salmon, which his mother had placed in a small box. When his parents returned home, the boy's mother opened the box, found a piece missing, and cried out, "Who has stolen my salmon?" She was angry because she had saved that salmon for two years and had meant to use it only in the worst of emergencies. At last the prince confessed, but his mother continued to scold him. He commenced crying and determined to run away from home.

That evening the prince went away and spent the night alone, on the shore below the village. After a time he heard the sound of a canoe making its way up the river. Inside sat four men who invited the prince to come with them. He agreed, got into the canoe, and after a long journey found himself in a large village, its houses painted and carved with the figures of spring salmon. In the center of the village stood the house of the great chief. Then the canoe men said to the prince, "Come up with us to our great chief's house. He invites you in." So they did, but after entering the house, the prince could see that the chief was very ill. He had, in fact, been sick for two years. Soon, an old woman, also known as Mouse Woman, approached and whispered, "The Spring Salmon have brought you here, for their chief has been sick because your mother has kept him in her little box for two years. When you unfolded the salmon the other day, the chief got a little better because you did so." She also gave him some advice. "Some time when you are very hungry," said Mouse Woman, "take a club to one of the children who are playing on the sand-hill behind the house. Make a fire and roast it. Then eat it. Gather all the little bones and cast them into the fire."

Not much time had passed before the prince grew hungry. Remembering Mouse Woman's advice, he went behind the village, finding children playing on a sand hill. When a boy rolled to the bottom of the hill, the prince clubbed him. Instantly the little boy was transformed into a nice spring salmon, which the prince then roasted over a fire. After he had eaten, the prince gathered all the bones and burned them in the fire, just as Mouse Woman had instructed.

That evening, as he was settling down, the prince heard someone cry, "Oh, my eye is sore, my eye is sore." Mouse Woman appeared and said to the prince, "Go and search in the hole at the foot of our roasting-spit." He did so and found the eye of the little spring salmon he had just eaten. Throwing it into the fire, the prince soon discovered that the boy whose eye was sore had now recovered.

One day the chief sent a few slaves to see if the leaves of the cotton-wood had fallen into the Skeena and Nass Rivers. When this party returned, they reported seeing many cottonwood leaves, which to Salmon people are the salmon themselves. With this, the chief of the Spring Salmon gathered his people together and explained that the time had come to make their journey from their village in the deep sea all the way to the rivers. The chief also promised to take the young prince with him, which he did.

As the Spring Salmon people proceeded toward the rivers, they encountered other villages and other peoples. To the chiefs of the Silver, Humpback, and Coho Salmon, the Spring Salmon brought word of the cottonwood leaves, and each responded by preparing to travel toward the rivers. They also encountered the Steelhead Salmon, whose canoes were then returning from the rivers, having made their journey earlier in the spring. The Trout asked that they be allowed to precede the Spring Salmon, to which request the chief assented. When at last the Spring Salmon reached the mouths of the great rivers on the mainland, they divided into four groups, parted company, and began making their way upstream.

While all this was happening, the father of the prince remained deeply distressed, not knowing whether his son was dead or alive, and therefore enlisted the aid of a great shaman. This shaman danced and sang, searching for an answer. After a time he told the father and mother, "Your boy is not dead. He is now in the house of the Spring Salmon peo-ple; for your wife was angry with the boy because he took a little piece of her large dried spring salmon; and if you do not eat the dried spring salmon, your son will not come back this spring." He then instructed the father and mother to eat the dried salmon, promising that this would cure the chief of the Spring Salmon people, who would then reciprocate by returning their son. This they did.

The Spring Salmon chief recovered. As he prepared to lead his people up the river, he also noticed that the shaman had strung such a great net that he was certain to be caught. So he told the prince, "Now, my son, don't let your father dry my flesh. Let him invite the people of all ages, and let them eat my flesh at once, and throw my bones into the fire." Since he had seen all this in a vision, the great shaman told the people to be careful killing the salmon he was about to catch, because it was the chief of the Spring Salmon whose belly contained the small prince. The people listened and treated the salmon carefully, and when two old women opened the fish, they did indeed find a small child, no larger than the span between a man's middle finger and thumb. That boy grew quickly and soon reached his normal size. The prince told his remarkable tale and turned to his mother. "Now mother," he said, "don't keep dried salmon in your box any longer; and if any one cooks fresh salmon of any kind, throw the bones into the fire. Then the salmon will go home, and will revive again safely."

This complex tale reveals a great deal about the way Tsimshians understand their world. Away from human beings, salmon live as people, in villages, with chiefs, organizing their lives around the annual runs, which appeared to them as cottonwood leaves. It is only when the humans and salmon are in contact that salmon "people" take on their familiar form. Their relationship is reciprocal. Salmon runs would continue only so long as humans remain faithful to rituals, in this case the proper disposal of earthly remains. It was a message that emphasized the unity of all creation and humankind's essential role in maintaining the balance of natural and supernatural forces.

The story also provides a glimpse into the workings of the temporal world. Like salmon people, Tsimshians also organized themselves hierarchically, with intersecting relationships that bound together individuals, families, and larger corporate units. Yet explaining the constituent pieces of the Tsimshian world, without doing violence to the whole, has presented a challenge for generations of scholars. Often contradictory, sometimes nearly impenetrable, most interpretations nevertheless begin with the observation that all Tsimshians belonged to one of four matrilineal, exogamous clans: Blackfish (Orca)-Grizzly *(Gispwudwada)*, Wolf *(Laxgibuu)*, Raven *(Ganhada)*, and Eagle *(Laxsgiik)* for the Southern and

Coast groups. These names corresponded with the principal totemic representations, or crests *(p'teex)*, as observed on totem poles and painted house fronts, for instance, which each clan claimed the exclusive right to display. Having originated in myth time, clans and *p'teex* also symbolized a relationship with a particular *naxnox* spirit, as revealed through *adawx*. Clans themselves were subdivided into literally hundreds of subclans, each associated with particular *p'teex*, and ranked in relation to others. This, in turn, produced an interlocking sequence of relationships of both temporal and timeless significance. Since clans and subclans were exogamous, they governed relations between and among lineage groups and village/tribes. Rules of exogamy also applied to unions with neighboring peoples, as, for instance, Haidas, Tlingits, Gitxsan, and Nisga'a.[10]

While the four matriclans were nonlocalized, meaning that clan affiliation cut across residence and therefore promoted kinship linkages throughout the region, the basic social, political, ceremonial, and economic unit remained the household group, or *waalb* (sometimes *walp*), a matrilineal kin group that, in many cases, lived communally in a cedar plank structure. Each of the hundreds of *waalb* was associated with one of the four matriclans and functioned as a repository for material and spiritual properties, from fishing, hunting, and gathering locations to songs and *adawx* whose more visible manifestations included *p'teex*, masks associated with *naxnox*, and assorted regalia having to do with the various *halaayt* cults, dances, and personages. A chief, or a particularly high-ranking person, presided over each household, and the *waalb* usually took his (rarely her) name as its own. Headmen managed economic, political, and ceremonial activities, coordinated relations with other *waalb*, protected and revealed a house's most prized possessions, and in this fashion symbolized the integration of individuals into the larger whole.[11]

Houses generally came together to form villages, or "tribes" to Tsimshians. These are the nine Coast Tsimshian village/tribes as indicated earlier, each associated with winter ceremonial villages and inland hunting and fishing territories. Southern, Gitxsan, and Nisga'a peoples developed a similar organization. Although anthropologists once posited the presence of each of the four matriclans in each village, this conclusion probably reflected social upheaval associated with trading forts and missionary establishments. Current thought supports a dual, or moiety, structure, with only two of the four matriclans present in any particular village, or where Blackfish joins with Wolf, and Raven with Eagle. A case in point is Gitk'a'ta, where most people were, and still are, either Blackfish or Raven. This corresponds as well to Tsimshian traditions, which consider Blackfish and Raven as "original" clans and *p'teex* but suggest an Athabascan origin for Wolf and understand Eagle as arriving through contacts with Haidas.[12]

Recalling the tale of the prince and the salmon, villages organized themselves in established patterns, with the highest-ranking *waalb* chief occupying a preeminent position village-wide. A historical development dating from the late eighteenth century, the institution of village chief distinguished Tsimshians from their neighbors and most probably reflected the ability of a few families, through control over the most productive fishing stations, to mobilize the productive activities of village and kinsmen. This authority corresponded, in turn, with the Tsimshians' heavy reliance on salmon and a chief's responsibility as collector, and distributor, of goods. In addition, the village/tribal chief coordinated matters of mutual concern, such as settling interhouse disputes, conducting diplomacy with other Tsimshian villages or foreign nations, and presiding over ceremonial events and feasts. Consequently, chiefs were in a position to amass, display, and redistribute considerable wealth, and succession to this highest position was a major ceremonial occasion attended by representatives from many tribes and nations. They did not, however, hold rights to crests or properties belonging to other houses or lineage, which were jealously protected and never traded.[13]

If crests were one manifestation of a group's eternal identity, hierarchy may be considered an obvious expression of Tsimshian social organization. Names, too, were property, known to be eternal in such a way that they were not so much given to individuals as the reverse; in other words, a person acted as the temporary repository of a name and all that went with it. But not all names were equally valuable; not all individuals had access to the "storehouse" of names. Houses, names, crests, individuals, perhaps even whole villages—all were ranked according to one another and in accordance with sacred histories, individual feats, and any number of events. Scholars have long recognized four "classes" among Tsimshians, positing the emergence of "royalty" (*sm'oogyit*, "real person") from lesser nobility (*lgu-ya'ks*, "other people") during protohistoric or historic times, then descending toward a "middle class" (*wa-e'in*, "without origin," or "unhealed ones"), whose status, in turn, differed markedly from that of slaves (*lu'nkit*, or *laluungyt*). Even so, Tsimshian hierarchy is probably best described not as rigid "castes" but as a series, perhaps even a continuum, of ranked statuses, where each individual occupied a unique place in the larger social fabric. This fabric extended from house to village to nation, and even internationally, as each status, or confluence of characteristics contributing to a particular status, was measured against others and confirmed publicly and through proper behavior.[14]

Since names, crests, ceremonial prerogatives, and rights to resources resided in clan, lineage, and house, it followed that access to rank and privilege followed birth. Similarly, given that wealth was a natural concomitant of ancestry, and vice versa, relative prosperity was both a necessary precondition for and tangible evidence of high birth. Members of the chiefly class held the highest-ranking names, crests, and prerogatives, passed them down via the maternal line, and tended to marry others of similar rank, be they individuals from their own village, members of other tribes, or scions of leading families from other nations. Status also connoted a special relationship with *naxnox* spirits. Considered *smhalaayt*, or the "real" manifestation of spiritual power, chiefs were *naxnox* dancers and holders of *halaayt* paraphernalia. Chiefs also acted as *wihalait*, or "great dancer," for the *mila* (dancers), *nulim* (dog eaters), *ludzista* (destroyers), and *xgyedmhalait* (cannibals). These were secret societies of Heiltsuk origin whose members "ascended" by invitation and thus were, in themselves, badges of status. All of this made for a comparatively self-perpetuating system, where prospective heirs advanced to positions of authority so long as they could claim an unblemished family heritage, were, as one anthropologist suggested, "skilled in all things, energetic and ambitious," and had changes in status confirmed publicly.[15]

If, as anthropologist Philip Drucker suggests, social distinctions can be described in terms of relative "participation," as, for instance, "one of less than the highest in rank, participated less fully," while "a person above the lowest participated . . . a bit more than one on the bottom rung,"[16] the lesser nobility (*lgu-ya'ks*) shaded into *wa-e'in*. Composed of men and women holding names and crests of lesser rank than chiefly families, *lgu-ya'ks* accounted for the bulk of a village's population and were linked with the chiefly class by broader clan and lineage relationships. These affiliations carried reciprocal responsibilities where, for instance, chiefs "exchanged" protection and material aid for goods, labor, and assistance that not only enhanced a chief's wealth but also elevated the prestige of all members of a house, lineage, clan, and village. *Wa-e'in*, by contrast, lacked important ancestral names but were "free" in the sense that they participated, however marginally, in broader social interactions. While they sometimes moved from house to house, seeking better accommodations, their labor added to a house's prestige and, in return, derived some small benefit from association with higher-ranking persons.[17]

At the bottom of the Tsimshian social structure were slaves, or *lú'nkit*. Estimated at 5 percent of a village's population, slaves were either war captives, individuals purchased from other peoples, or the children of slaves. They also were chattel property, could be killed with impunity (although it is unclear how frequently this happened), had no access to wealth and ceremonial privileges, and as such played no part in Tsimshian societal and religious life. Indeed, some have likened the "status" of slaves to blankets, canoes, sea otter skins, or other manner of "property." While the condition of slavery was perpetual and inherited, it is likely that some slaves were persons of high birth captured for the express purpose of demanding ransom or avenging an insult or injury. To capture a member of an influential lineage was to inflict serious injury on that kinship group, a "stain" that could be erased only through liberal gift giving. These individuals might also be adopted into similarly ranked Tsimshian families. For those captives from lower-ranked matrilineages, or from faraway groups, however, the prospects for escaping slavery were dim indeed. They and their children remained outside the social relationships because it was unthinkable for anyone of higher rank to marry a slave.[18]

What remains unclear, however, is the economic importance of slaves and slavery. One view has it that since all members of a household shared in the labor necessary to keep a village functioning, there developed no "leisure class" dependent on others for material support. This interpretation also suggests that while slaves added to the wealth of their masters through their labor, keeping slaves for what they could produce was not a well-developed concept. A more recent argument favors an economic value for slaves. After all, they contributed to the accumulation of property, made possible a more intensive exploitation of resources, and freed some individuals to produce specialized and highly sought-after crafts. While it is not certain that this amounts to sufficient evidence to support the notion of slaves as "productive property," it does raise the possibility for an economic motive for holding slaves.[19]

Gender intersected this interplay of class status and subsistence. Matrilineal descent sometimes translated into leadership roles for women in that high-ranking females could accumulate the requisite crests, names, and prerogatives. This was unusual, however, because women's roles tended to be distinct, considered complementary to men's. As "crest carriers," women occupied an essential position in the transfer of authority between generations, and this meant that they played an important role in house and tribal politics, although principally as advisers to husbands, brothers, fathers, and sons. Economic activities were likewise separate. Beyond the rather common bifurcation (to hunting and gathering peoples) of gender roles—men hunted, fished, and engaged in war, and women raised children, processed food supplies, and gathered berries, tubers, and seaweed—females derived considerable influence from their control over production and distribution of food supplies. According to one study, berries, seaweed, nuts, bark, and other items gathered by women constituted about 20 percent of the Tsimshian diet, while preserved fish added another 50 percent. Moreover, groups of women managed a house's food supply throughout the year, a particularly important responsibility during lean winter months. The story of the salmon and the prince suggests as much, while rules prohibiting male participation in any phase of production and distribution of *oolichan* reveal links between spirituality and women's subsistence activities.[20]

Women, therefore, occupied a critical location in Tsimshian economic relationships. This translated into political influence as networks of women exchanged not only foodstuffs but also prestige items. The accumulation and distribution of prestige items fueled the feasting cycle, which, in turn, lay at the heart of Tsimshian politics; this meant that women's productive activities directly affected rank and status for house, lineage, and village. The onset of the fur trade seems to have accentuated this pattern. Directly and indirectly, women's productive activities increased the storehouse of novel items. This enhanced their impact on village politics even at time when objects like metal pots and blankets probably undermined the demand for some women's manufactures. Separate exchange networks provided women with the means to participate more fully, and perhaps independently, in feasting, and thus in the operations of the Tsimshian social hierarchy. This amounts to convincing evidence that while Tsimshian women were, in a sense, excluded from certain male pursuits, prohibitions that extended even to membership in two of the four secret societies (cannibals and destroyers), it would be a mistake to draw too close an association between separate "spheres" and comparative "status." Similar conclusions apply to Menominees and other Indian societies even if specific details differ. Gender activities were distinct yet complementary.[21]

Given that rank and status were critical elements in Tsimshian society, it follows that the process of assuming the badges of prestige—such as names, crests, and other ceremonial or material prerogatives—was an important, and highly formalized, affair. For the Tsimshians, as for most Northwest Coast peoples, the "potlatch," or feast complex, was the chief means of announcing and validating all changes in societal relationships. Whether grand affairs involving peoples from several villages or the more limited, and more common, feasts for family members and in-laws, Tsimshian potlatches (*yaakw*) commemorated any number of events, from naming individuals, house building and dedication, and the perforation of ears, nose, and lips for ornaments, to the bestowal of supernatural power, formalizing marriages, settling conflicts between competing groups, erasing shame from a house, village, or individual, and, perhaps most important, validating succession and inheritance upon the death of important individuals. On each occasion, "hosts" accumulated possessions for the purpose of giving them away, sometimes soliciting contributions from clan, lineage, and village relations. The next step was to invite guests, whose purpose was, in a sense, to witness, and thus validate, those changes being commemorated. Once assembled, participants were divided into two groups—hosts and guests—and, in keeping with the stratified nature of Northwest Coast societies, all were seated and introduced according to rank. After witnessing a series of activities, such as speech making, *halaayt* displays, songs, and telling of *adawx*, the celebration climaxed with the ritualized distribution of gifts from hosts to guests, again according to status, who thus were "compensated" for their participation.[22]

In a manner, potlatches functioned as celebrations of renewal, when peoples gathered to affirm their shared values, symbolized at least partly by the bestowal of immortal names upon a new generation. They also constituted a powerful statement of one's social position and, by extension, of his or her right to the prerogatives in question. Conversely, it was unthinkable for an individual to lay claim to an important name, and its associated prerogatives, without demonstrating publicly his or her "fitness" to lay claim to that honor. To circumvent established conventions opened that person to ridicule and brought shame and dishonor to lineage, house, and perhaps village. Potlatching thus played a critical role in integrating Tsimshian society and culture. By demonstrating and reaffirming social distinctions, it contributed to stable and regular leadership, while the combination of hereditary rights and accumulated wealth reserved positions of authority to those with access to names and crests that, in turn, owed their status to myth and legend. At the same time, chiefs affirmed their reciprocal responsibilities even as they redistributed material goods. Finally, since feasting was a regional phenomenon, and was linked with corresponding clan and moiety relationships among other peoples, it also played an important role in diplomacy.[23]

It is possible to understand potlatches in economic terms. After all, the emphasis on concentrating and redistributing accumulated goods set up a complex system of exchange that coordinated a group's labor while rewarding all those who took part. These same objectives encouraged far-reaching trade networks and supported the activities of skilled craftsmen who were compensated for carving totem poles, painting house fronts, constructing canoes, and producing any number of items displayed, and sometimes exchanged, during potlatches. Having argued that case, one should proceed cautiously when transposing economic concepts associated with specific cultural values. While potlatching promoted the accumulation of surpluses, equating wealth with social and political status, it was neither capitalism nor "upside-down capitalism," as is sometimes suggested. Rather, the economic component of potlatching, namely, accumulation and redistribution, stood in a subordinate position to decidedly nonmarket functions, namely, social integration and cultural continuity. Northwest Coast peoples feasted for reasons having to do with fundamental cultural values not necessarily reducible to economic concepts. I am not arguing against an indigenous Tsimshian "economics," but rather suggesting an interpretive space somewhere between the once-warring formalist and substantivist camps in which we accept a perceived "universality" of economic motivations so long as we understand that they are deeply imbedded in broader cultural values.[24]

Change, gradual and dramatic, sometimes highlights these cultural values. Contact between the familiar and the other stresses these same conventions but in heterogeneous ways. A comparative framework offers unique opportunities for understanding the relationship between change and fundamental cultural values, where similar experiences point the way toward broader principles, differences offer intriguing pathways for analysis, and the unexpected, such as links in unforeseen places or discordance where convergence might be anticipated, prompts serious reflection. In the cases under consideration here, one important independent variable is trade, as commerce with Europeans shaped earliest contacts for Menominees and Tsimshians. In both places, trade could be reciprocal, with native tastes, interests, and modes of interaction predominating for a time. It is also possible to describe the initial outcome more as an elaboration of prior cultural forms than as a "rupture" in the historical thread, or a sharp break with that which had been.

Tsimshian contact with outsiders followed Menominee experiences by roughly a century, in the half century following the 1741 arrival of Russian explorers Alexi Chirikov and Vitus Bering. Attracted by the fur trade, seeking to outflank British and Spanish competitors, and driven at least in part by a desire to spread Orthodox Christianity, Russians established trading contacts with Inuits and Aleuts before finding their way among the Tlingits of southeastern Alaska. Erection of a fort at Sitka in 1799 followed upon the heels of landfall at Yakutat Bay eleven years earlier and set the stage for long-standing, if not always peaceful, trading relations between Russians and the autonomous Tlingit villages, or *kwaan*. Tlingit hostility toward the Russian presence, manifested in attacks on Sitka in 1802 and Yakutat in 1805, demonstrated native distaste for the outsiders' apparently permanent land establishments, not to mention their efforts to control Tlingit labor, but did not constitute antipathy toward trade. After all, Tlingit war parties used firearms, obtained in some numbers from Americans, to great effect. While Russians abandoned Yakutat permanently, an 1804 military strike reversed the earlier setback at Sitka and prepared the way for Novo-Arkangel'sk (New Archangel), Russian-American Company headquarters beginning in 1808 and administrative center for Russian America until 1867.[25]

For rather mysterious reasons, Russian imperial interests bypassed the Nass and Skeena Rivers, but attractive goods, like iron and copper, blankets, cloth, and guns, made their way to Tsimshian villages through aboriginal networks or offshore contacts with Spanish, British, and American merchantmen. Following Captain James Cook's 1778 voyage, publication of his journal in 1784, and the discovery that sea otter pelts brought handsome profits in China, a maritime-based trade on the north Pacific coast exploded, with merchants plying their goods to coastal peoples from Nootka Sound on Vancouver Island northward to Tsimshian country. The maritime trade thus enjoyed a brief period of prosperity before destruction of sea otter populations prompted an inland reorientation during the 1820s.[26]

Outside of Russian America, where permanent forts, missionaries, and the employment of native hunters constituted unique modes of interaction for a time, the north Pacific maritime trade proved only moderately disruptive to Indian societies. Merchantmen anchored their ships in accessible harbors, and this rendered Europeans dependent on coastal Indians for supplies, including food, and ultimately for the success or failure of their own ventures. Tsimshian-speaking peoples drew upon a long history of coastal and inland exchange, kinship links with partners and "suppliers," and a facility for integrating novel goods to secure an upper hand over trading relationships. Tlingit-Russian trade operated similarly, as coastal peoples guarded their relationships with interior Athapascans, and in this way forestalled ruinous dependence on the outsiders' forts and products. Able to determine the basic parameters of trade (when, where, and for what), Tsimshians and their neighbors reputedly drove a hard bargain (nineteenth-century observer Albert Niblack considered them "expert traders" who "show rare good sense in their selection of better qualities, mere cheapness being in itself no recommendation"), pitted trader against trader, and forced Europeans to adapt to native social customs. Explorer George Vancouver noted as well a primary role for women in negotiations. Visiting Kaigani Tlingits in 1794, he observed women taking "a very principal part" in commercial transactions, "proving themselves by no means unequal to the task." Adjusting to the cultural environment also required the distribution of gifts in advance of negotiation, carrying a wide variety of items to correspond with changing native "tastes," and trafficking in "contraband" articles like firearms. It also meant dealing through high-ranking persons, which sometimes diminished competition on the Indians' side while driving up prices for animal pelts.[27]

The maritime trade, with its episodic and less intrusive patterns, provides an analogy between Tsimshian-European interactions and the Menominee "protohistoric" period of indirect, periodic contact. In both places, space and time allowed for the development of the economic and political status quo, not necessarily disruptive to native modes of behavior. The mental universe was another matter as Europeans impressed themselves upon the Tsimshian consciousness right away. Contact proved a profoundly important experience, so much so that Tsimshians incorporated these early events into their folklore, with Europeans transformed, in a sense, into *naxnox* personages, and as expressed in new *adawx*. One particularly well-known tale takes place at a Gitkxaala fishing station and concerns the experiences of Saaban, a prince in the high-ranking Tsi'basa household. Absorbed with their task, Saaban and his slave failed to notice the arrival of a huge being with white wings until it was nearly upon them. Paddling furiously toward shore, they attempted to flee on foot from the "monsters," which also had made landfall. Only an accident—in his excitement, Saaban tripped and fell after failing to untie his lifeline to the boat—allowed the "monsters" to catch up. They then asked the prince to make a fire, which he did in the usual way, spinning his drill, using ear wax for friction. But the strangers acted mysteriously, producing fire by way of a long tube that roared. The prince fainted.

When he revived, a hairy, white-skinned stranger made motions to his mouth and Saaban offered halibut, which the stranger cut up quickly by means of a special knife. Those supernatural men also produced cooking pots, which they placed directly on the fire. Understanding the strangers as beneficent, although clearly supernatural, beings, Saaban gathered people from his village.

Some Gitkxaala visited the strangers' ship and found it disconcerting, understanding its creaking to be human skulls crying out in agony. But they proceeded below deck, where they confronted a strange meal: maggots (this was rice), a black substance that appeared to be dried human blood (molasses), and tree fungus (sea biscuits). The strangers consumed this odd meal and offered some to Chief Tsi'basa, who, with considerable trepidation, joined in the unlikely feast. What followed were exchanges and feasts, and in one Tsi'basa presented his guests with a dancing headdress, and with it his name. A high honor indeed, but one befitting the arrival of *naxnox*. In return, that commander presented Tsi'basa with a uniform, accompanying the gift with a hearty "Hail! Hail!" Understanding "Hail" to be a name, Tsi'basa saw this as an exchange of names, and claimed the appellation "Hale" for his family."[28]

This tale demonstrates the Tsimshian facility for interpreting contact according to their own cultural perspectives as well as the dynamic nature of *adawx* traditions. But if Tsimshians initially considered Europeans as supernatural beings, they soon saw the visitors as men, albeit possessors of powerful knowledge and useful technologies. We know, of course, that trade proved just an opening wedge, leading over time to economic dependency, cultural disruption, and social disorganization for

Tsimshians, Menominees, and "colonized" peoples across North America and beyond. At the same time, however, linking trade with dependency may be simply a "truism" that falls well short of illuminating discrete, or interconnected, "processes at work." Put differently, discerning evidence for economic dependency might not explain how one society got there, nor does it offer a sense of local idiosyncrasies, or ways in which a particular culture accommodated economic change. For Tsimshians, three intertwined questions emerge: first, whether the introduction of novel products "enriched" Northwest Coast cultural life generally, enhancing artistic, political, and social patterns already in operation; second, whether a nineteenth-century Gispaxlo'ots trade "monopoly," under the control of a series of chiefs holding the name Ligeex, was of aboriginal origin or a product of European contact; and third, when, how, and whether trade promoted an incipient Tsimshian "confederacy," an expression of political centralization uncommon among Northwest Coast peoples.

These questions touch on many of the fundamental issues surrounding native adaptations to trade generally, and in that sense they defy facile answers. Nevertheless, recent research suggests that trade certainly *contributed* to an elaboration of existing forms and practices well before the unequal exchange degenerated. Contact with seaborne merchantmen placed a premium on diplomacy, and while this theoretically presented opportunities for any number of ambitious individuals, Tsimshian hierarchy meant that benefits probably flowed toward highest-ranking houses, through persons for whom established prerogatives offered an "inside track" to take advantage of new wealth. In the simplest of formulations, contact provided the means to command the productive capacity of lineage, house, and village, and to stage elaborate feasts that in and of themselves confirmed existing, albeit supercharged, social relationships. In all probability, the fact that houses already owned resource-gathering grounds and trading relations promoted continuity—at least early on.[29]

Novel manifestations of wealth still might be transforming. Considerable evidence of more elaborate potlatching, particularly by the 1850s, may constitute a situation where incremental change ultimately produced more fundamental alterations, or where an accumulation of differences in degree becomes differences in kind. This means that feasting might constitute evidence for considerable "reordering" of social relationships, as some houses acquired favorable positions in trade and thus staked claims to preeminence. On occasion, access to trade might even provide unconventional avenues for social advancement, as in the case of Neshaki, a high-ranking Nisga'a woman who married William McNeill, chief factor for Hudson's Bay Company, in 1851 and subsequently used the position as intermediary to elevate her status in both societies. Remembering the dynamic nature of Tsimshian political, economic, and social conventions, we might conclude that trade with Europeans constituted both an elaboration of existing patterns and the beginnings of more discordant change.[30]

A case in point concerns holders of the name Ligeex, of the Eagle clan and Gispaxlo'ots tribe, and probably the most famous of all Tsimshian "chiefly" families during the nineteenth century. Drawing upon a rich storehouse of Ligeex-oriented *adawx*, as well as evidence from Hudson's Bay Company records, scholars posit that, by the 1780s, the Gispaxlo'ots ranked among the most dominant of Coast Tsimshian tribes. They built this position upon a series of trading prerogatives, including a favored relationship with the interior Gitxsan, which also provided indirect access to the Wet'suet'en, the Gitxsan's Athapascan neighbors and trading partners. While this relationship should not be construed as a Gispaxlo'ots "monopoly" over interior trade—that came later—regular access to valued potlatch items like marmot skins combined with control over key Nass River *oolichan* fisheries to provide means for extending tribal, and personal, influence. A regional network of Eagle clan houses, or *Gwinhuut*, a series of strategic marriages, and confirmation through dramatic *halaayt* displays and elaborate feasts furthered these relationships.[31]

The Ligeex name and the steady accumulation of prerogatives to family, clan, and tribe constitute discrete historical phenomena. According to relevant *adawx*, and supported by scholarly treatments, the name was of Heiltsuk origin, the first Ligeex being the product of union between his mother, K'amdmaxl, a captive of Tsimshian heritage, and a high-ranking Heiltsuk man. Taunted as "without origin," this Ligeex ultimately made his way to the home of the Gispaxlo'ots just as a leadership crisis overtook that community. Their own highest-ranking name, Nisbelas, suffered fatal dishonor when its holder was captured and beheaded. Grasping the opportunity, Ligeex ascended through existing family prerogatives (passed down matrilineally), which were confirmed through a series of potlatches, several impressive displays of personal *halaayt*, and the painting of his portrait on a cliff at Ktsiyanexl (Flat-Bold-Cliff) on the Nass River, in full view of canoes traveling to and from *oolichan* fishing stations. One *adawx* suggests that this act followed the uncovering of an assassination plot against Ligeex. After completing the portrait, Ligeex staged a feast, pointed to the display, and said, "To those who wanted to overthrow me and my tribe I wish to reveal to them my great wealth and power. . . . That is why I have painted my picture here. My power shall travel both on the Skeena and the Nass Rivers. Over both waters I am the master." It was a powerful manifestation of Ligeex's power, even as it demonstrated that jealousy accompanied his achievements.[32]

The expansion of sea otter trade effectively shifted "geopolitical" alignments, as holders of the Ligeex name faced competitors on several fronts, most notably Tsi'basaa (Killerwhale clan), leader of the Southern Tsimshian Gitkxaalas, who advertised his position by adding a bar of soap, a butcher knife, and the new family name Hale to their storehouse of crests. Gitkxaala also benefited from control over an important harbor and their well-known skill as sea otter hunters. Other challenges came from the Ginaxangiik tribe, strategically located at the entrance to Metlakatla Pass, and from Tlingit *kwaans* to the north whose leaders pursued a parallel strategy with regard to Russian trade. Ligeex countered these moves with a series of strategic marriages, gaining at least limited access to trading privileges held by other tribes, especially to sea otter grounds, which he had lacked. These he combined with prerogatives among Skeena and Nass groups to produce a series of relationships placing the Gispaxlo'ots astride trade between the coast and the interior. He had, so Tsimshians remember, "married many of his nieces into other tribes, thus controlling these through marriage, and in every way Legaix [*sic*] became very powerful among all the nations."[33]

Reorienting trade from sea to land benefited Ligeex and the Gispaxlo'ots by rendering their Skeena and Nass privileges all the more valuable. Once again, the chief utilized strategic marriages to strengthen the Gispaxlo'ots' position with Gitxsan and Wet'suet'en suppliers while working to prevent an eastward flow of trade toward Hudson's Bay Company forts. In 1823, for instance, some thirty Gitxsan warriors convinced Babine Lake tribes to trade with them, and thus with the Gispaxlo'ots. Ligeex also began making regular trips to the interior, affirming his prerogatives and distributing gifts. This corresponded as well with the creation of a new Wet'suet'en village at Hagwilget, near the fork of the Bulkley and Skeena Rivers, and increasing intermarriage between the Wet'suet'en and Gitxsan, a development that also benefited Ligeex.[34]

These, and undoubtedly many other, strategic moves meant that, by the time the Hudson's Bay Company inaugurated the era of terrestrial trade with Fort Nass in 1831, the Gispaxlo'ots had forged a formidable position in regional politics and trade. Based on aboriginal relationships, forged through culturally appropriate means, but driven by the novel strains and opportunities produced by the fur trade, Ligeex's moves, not to mention similar strategies pursued by his Tsimshian and Tlingit contemporaries, represented conscious adaptations to changing circumstances. It is therefore appropriate, as one recent interpretation notes, to consider these developments as the working out of a Northwest Coast "geopolitics." In this context, the Hudson's Bay Company's residence within the region takes on added significance. Constructed several miles upstream from *oolichan* fisheries, and astride the "grease trails" linking by land the various Tsimshian, Nisga'a, and Gitxsan villages, Fort Nass marks an important turning point for the Gispaxlo'ots particularly, and regional geopolitics generally, and not the least because of Ligeex's most famous response. Seeking to draw the newcomers into his burgeoning set of relationships, Ligeex in 1832 arranged the marriage of his daughter Sudaahl to Dr. John Kennedy, the fort's clerk and surgeon. This extended Ligeex's trading prerogatives to include the newcomers, or, as one *adawx* suggests, "Since [Kennedy] had taken as his mate the Tsimshian chief's daughter," Ligeex became "an ally of the Company's officials." There is little doubt that both sides perceived the strategic advantages of such a union: for the company, it meant an association with the most powerful headman in the region; for Ligeex, an alliance, forged in the "traditional" way, and seemingly without much risk. Since crests, names, and privileges passed through Tsimshian society matrilineally, there was, after all, little apparent danger of a diminution of the chief's hard-won victories.[35]

Fort Nass survived just three years, a victim mainly of poor location, but not before it probably stimulated Northwest Coast fur production. Although totals for Fort Nass alone remain obscure, they probably accounted for a third of all production from Hudson's Bay Company posts in the region, totals that rose from 3,642 in 1831 to 14,314 in 1833. Inclement weather and distance from the coast doomed Fort Nass anyway, and so in 1833 the company accepted Ligeex's offer of a site at the mouth of the Skeena. One scholar suggests an instrumental role for Sudaahl, who communicated her husband's desire for a coastal location and then convinced her father to offer tribal lands on Rose Island (Laxhlgu'alaams, also Lax Kw'alaams). At Laxhlgu'alaams, the company sat within Gispaxlo'ots territory, or at least within the coastal trade networks they dominated. Fort Simpson's importance grew, both Ligeex and the company benefited from a symbiotic relationship, and as the Anglo-Canadians outflanked their American rivals, the Gispaxlo'ots headman outdistanced his rival Tsi'basaa.[36]

Fort Simpson distinguished itself as the company's busiest outpost north of Fort Vancouver by the late 1830s. A nexus for regional prosperity, it brought blankets, cloth, beads, metal implements, and firearms, and stimulated an efflorescence in artistic and ceremonial activities. As such, its success also constitutes a dividing line in Tsimshian history, or an acceleration in the pace and substance of change, most clearly manifested in an alteration in settlement patterns. Drawn by this apparent prosperity, the nine autonomous Coast Tsimshian tribes took up permanent residence around the fort, whose Indian population swelled to 3,000 individuals, living in 240 houses, by 1835. This figure probably represents at least two-thirds of the entire Coast Tsimshian population. At the same time, trading patterns nearly reversed, with Gispaxlo'ots and their coastal neighbors staying put while Gitxsan and Haida suppliers, among others, journeyed to Fort Simpson. Out of this emerged the Ligeex-led

trading monopoly as the Gispaxlo'ots transformed their trading prerogatives with the interior Gitxsan, coastal neighbors, and the Hudson's Bay
Company into a force for political centralization. Gispaxlo'ots "home
guards," for instance, made certain that goods—including potatoes
grown by the offshore Haidas—flowed through established channels and
effectively prevented the Hudson's Bay Company from trading directly
with interior suppliers until the company purchased that right in 1868. In
all this, we detect as well a remarkable parallel with Kwaguls (Kwakiutls)
in and around Fort Rupert, Vancouver Island. So, as Tsimshian middlemen controlled commerce in some thirteen tons of Haida potatoes in 1835,
or attacked company gardens the following year, the message was the
same: protecting the trading monopoly required political centralization.[37]

There was much to protect. The "great emporium of trade," according to one primary source, was responsible for shipments of some 1,300
furs in 1835, 2,300 in 1836, 2,800 in 1837, and 3,400 in 1838. But it should
be noted that only a minority of furs came directly from Coast Tsimshians and so recommends caution when speaking of a fully evolved Gispaxlo'ots trading monopoly. Even so, volumes of trade goods, passing
through a region nominally under his authority, meant that Ligeex *could*
stage more elaborate potlatches, and in a sense *mandated* that he do so
with increasing regularity as the Fort Simpson environment came to
encourage more and more feasting. Thrown into closer, more constant
interaction, the nine coastal tribes, themselves conglomerations of intersecting relations between clan, house, lineage, and individual, found it
necessary to resolve rivalries, establish and reestablish relationships, and
work out a more inclusive social hierarchy. The infusion of wealth accelerated this cycle by financing ever more elaborate feasts, shortening the
time needed to accumulate goods, therefore promoting overtly competitive potlatching. According to anthropologist Viola Garfield, Tsimshians
staged so-called challenge feasts, or rum feasts, for no other reason than
to display wealth and insult guests. Such events naturally invited competition, as houses sought to cleanse their names or promote claims to
preeminence, and then an accelerating cycle of feasts as Tsimshians
sought to reorder their world, but according to established precepts. In
this contest Ligeex, commanding significant resources and prerogatives,
came out on top: not so much "head chief" as first among equals.[38]

Other circumstances contributed to the unsettled social order and the
increase in potlatching. Infectious diseases wreaked havoc on all the
coastal tribes from the beginning of contact, with one estimate suggesting
that, by the end of the particularly severe smallpox epidemic of 1836–38,
the Coast Tsimshian population had fallen to around 2,500, down from
4,200 in 1800. Demographic catastrophe created "gaps" in the social fabric,
threw Tsimshian society into disarray, and led to mortuary and accession

potlatches while creating new opportunities for individuals to improve their social standing. Just as trade presented opportunities for individuals to increase their material wealth, then, depopulation encouraged competitive potlatching.[39]

Out of this grew the Coast Tsimshian "confederacy." The working out of cultural forces over time, this spatial and organizational centralization had at its core economic motivations, and produced some political innovation as well as a moderate adjustment in cultural identity. Robert Grumet, in fact, describes the result as "a highly bounded Coast Tsimshian ethnicity," which encouraged "inter-group endogamy, solidarity," and a nascent "national sense" that ultimately permitted the group "to present a united front to the world." In any case, Tsimshian political and economic reorganization arose out of the fur trade environment around Fort Simpson even as it elaborated upon processes already in operation. Viewed from this perspective, determining whether Ligeex's actions constituted continuity with precontact modes of behavior or creative reactions to novel circumstances may represent a false dichotomy. More than a seamless transition from one era to another, but less than a rupture in time, Ligeex's Tsimshian confederation can be understood as an innovation pursued according to cultural values. In this sense, it resembles Menominee reactions to reservation life, when the various bands, fractured for a time by the fur trade, forged a degree of unity that was both new and rooted in shared cultural values. That the parallel is inexact bears less significance than the process it reveals; in both cases culture was, to a certain extent, "managing" change.[40]

Managing change is, of course, precarious, and was increasingly so for Tsimshians of the middle 1850s. Placer gold strikes along the Fraser River touched off the 1858 frenzy, and scores of miners proved the vanguard of an immigration boom. Gathering in small settlements along the coast and Fraser River valley, and in larger centers like Victoria, whites moved into British Columbia in such numbers that by 1885 they outnumbered the Indians. Gold rush and settlement marked the end of the old regime in British Columbia and as such was greeted with alarm by Indians and white fur traders alike. James Douglas, the Hudson's Bay Company's chief factor in Victoria and later governor of the colonies of Vancouver Island and British Columbia, lamented the passing of the old era and predicted that the rush of settlement would set off interracial conflicts. As governor, Douglas earned a reputation for treating Indians fairly, at least as he understood it, and feared that the influx of miners and settlers would ruin the fur trade by destroying profitable relationships. Only minimally linked with Canadian Indian policy prior to the 1875 Confederation, British

Columbia charted a course that reflected the priorities of settlers and commercial interests rather than Canada's stated intention of recognizing Indian rights and, ultimately, integrating Indians into the mainstream society. Desiring land over trade, British Columbia's new arrivals demonstrated little interest in preserving older relationships and ultimately viewed Indians as impediments to settlement, menial laborers, producers rather than partners.[41] The fact that settlement in British Columbia coincided with a hardening of racist attitudes in Great Britain and North America only helped justify the marginalization of Indians. One tract promoting immigration offered the following chapter headings to the regions' Indians:

Slaves Horribly Abused

The "Medicine Man" and the Dead

Mode of Scalping

Young Indians More Savage Than Old

Horrible Modes of Torture

Barbarous Conduct of an Old Squaw

Shocking Cruelties to an Old Man and Instance of Cannibalism

Horrible Massacre of Emigrants

Cruel Custom of Getting Rid of the Aged[42]

No wonder, then, that many whites felt little remorse for the passing of an era.[43]

For Tsimshians, the influx of whites brought on the beginning of a downward slide into social decay and comparative poverty. Although they were sheltered by geography from the worst aspects of mining and settlement, decades of contact had rendered them increasingly dependent on Fort Simpson, subject to the corrosive influences of alcohol, disease, and inflationary pressures that eroded the value of their trade. Moreover, an increasingly prominent, and sometimes threatening, presence by the British navy clearly suggested that the balance of power was slipping out of their hands. Some Tsimshians attempted to combat the reversal of fortunes by journeying southward to Victoria, where a growing white population offered a market for furs, handicrafts, manual laborers, and prostitutes. On the outskirts of Victoria, Tsimshians gathered with other refugee Indian groups in squalid camps that were marred by violence and disease, while their absence from home hit the Fort Simpson trade hard. Conditions grew worse still when smallpox ravaged the Victoria Indian communities in 1862 and fleeing Tsimshians brought the disease home. The result was a serious outbreak of the dread disease, and in the end an estimated 500 of the slightly more than 1,000 Fort Simpson Tsimshians succumbed.[44]

The 1862 epidemic constituted a serious "shock" to the Tsimshian world. Combined with declining conditions in and around Fort Simpson, and a generally more threatening environment, it constituted a dramatic acceleration of the rate of change, the substance of Tsimshian-white interaction. While it would be an exaggeration to posit cultural "collapse," it is clear that Fort Simpson Tsimshians entered the 1860s in a state of social distress, vulnerable to influences they would have had the strength to resist in happier times. As it turned out, the principal source of such new influences came in the person of a twenty-five-year-old British lay missionary who arrived in the fall of 1857. A representative of the Anglican Church Missionary Society, William Duncan was a remarkable individual: energetic, committed to preaching the gospel of Christ and the ways of English civilization, and tremendously gifted in his ability to learn the language and ways of his native charges. For the next sixty-one years he also would prove to be the single most influential individual in the lives of many Tsimshians. And it is this story, with its dramatic impact on native economics and cultural identity, that constitutes the balance of this study.[45]

CHAPTER SIX

William Duncan and the Genesis of Metlakatla

> I am of Metlakahtla
> I wish all to know
> Sweet is the sound
> Of my village name
> Wherever I go
> A Home so sweet as mine
> I cannot find
>
> Good roads are spread
> For the people's use
> The Guest-house stands well
> For our new brethren to lodge in
> Wherever I go
> A Home so sweet as mine
> I cannot find
>
> —Metlakatla Village Song[1]

By the latter half of the nineteenth century, the various Tsimshian tribes had already embarked on a journey where economic change and cultural identity intersected, dynamically and creatively. Like the Menominees, the Tsimshians found that change is multifaceted, complex, and "dialogical" in the sense that the sum of numerous cultural interactions proved transforming. Yet while these transformations were many, and intersecting, economics still lay at their heart, even as we observe divergent manifestations. This is not to suggest that economics trumps all else, but rather that material wants and needs drew native communities into a broader system of commercial relationships over whose rules and parameters they exerted comparatively little influence. In its most obvious manifestations, this process ultimately produced such substantial social, political, and cultural change as to marginalize peoples and communities. In the sense that they link commerce with culture, "the market" with social disorganization, economically oriented avenues of inquiry have proved useful, even essential.

Particularly enlightening when considering broad trends, materialist approaches sometimes falter when applied to local conditions. Menominees found that economic change might translate into a creative tension between entrepreneurs and "communitarians," but that these conflicts were not necessarily an indication of cultural dissolution. Community members certainly wrestled with the implications of economic change for cultural values and identity, but "markets" sometimes offer room for adjustment, at least at the margins. So, while Menominees lacked the means to influence the composition, and functioning, of the regional and national timber commerce, or the construction of federal Indian policies, they nevertheless made any number of local, though no less significant, decisions. It was here that Menominees, as individuals and in combination with one another, arrived at varying accommodations with economic change.

Tsimshians found themselves at a similar crossroads. Enmeshed in broader webs of international trade, their lives increasingly revolved around Fort Simpson, with the nine formally autonomous tribes living in closer quarters and where the Gispaxlo'ots trade monopoly and Ligeex's rise to prominence exemplified a series of social and political rearrangements. But just as we understand Menominee adaptations as neither acculturation nor cultural persistence, complexity marks Fort Simpson Tsimshian adjustments. Differences, however, do matter. There was no William Duncan among the Menominees, and so comparing the two cases must take into account the obvious absence of such a singular figure. Nevertheless, contrasts can be enlightening and in this connection serve as a timely reminder that as native peoples adjusted to economic change in divergent, if sometimes parallel, ways, their experiences demonstrate the multiplicity of relationships between non-Western peoples and the market.

The outlines of William Duncan's life are well known. Born in 1832 to an unwed servant girl or housekeeper in the hamlet of Stokes Burton, near Beverly, England, Duncan attended the local National School but left at age fourteen to work for George Cussons, a Beverly tanner and dealer in hides and leather. The youth proved an able apprentice, and in time Cussons promoted him to traveling salesman, a position he coveted because it broadened his horizons and helped him escape from "the dunghill" of his origins, as he wrote later. Between working hours he attended the Beverly Mechanics' Institute and immersed himself in contemporary literature, technical manuals, and popular self-help tracts, while finding inspiration in evangelical Protestantism. In 1853 he met the Reverend Anthony T. Carr, a Beverly evangelist, who introduced Duncan to the Church Missionary Society (CMS), an Anglican organization dedicated to spreading the gospel to the native peoples across Britain's far-flung empire. Impressed by what he heard, Duncan abandoned his promising business career, enrolled in London's Highbury College in

William Duncan in 1885. (NA-APR, RG200, Archival Photograph Album 1, Print 4, page 1)

1854, and commenced training for what he thought would be a missionary assignment to Africa.[2]

Duncan cast his lot with the CMS at a most propitious moment in that organization's life. Founded in 1799 as the Society for Missions to Africa and the East, it became the Church Missionary Society in 1812 and gained prominence following the 1841 appointment of the Reverend Henry Venn as honorary secretary. Venn held that position for thirty-one years, presided over a dramatic expansion in CMS activities, and helped devise a systematic approach toward missionary activities. This approach affirmed Victorian-era notions regarding the unity of all of mankind and the idea that culture, not biology, accounted for the apparent "degraded" condition of native peoples. Victorian missionaries thus assumed that meaningful instruction produced cultural transformation, and they approached that task with a sense of urgency, convinced that England's preeminent place in the world brought solemn responsibilities as well.[3]

Among those values missionaries hoped to transmit, few were as important as work. Victorians considered habits of industry an essential underpinning of the Christian ethos, at once imparting self-discipline, thrift, independence, and a desire to acquire and reproduce the trappings of civilized life as they understood it. Inculcation of the work ethic, and growing familiarity with the material benefits of modern society, also promised to draw natives into Britain's widening commercial sphere, and in this way missionary strategy dovetailed with broader imperial objectives. It is for this reason that missionaries held an expansive view of the purpose of their contact with non-Western peoples. Stated simply, the colonial enterprise reflected a conviction that discrete elements of Anglo civilization were unified and interdependent in such a way that the whole was greater than the sum of its parts. It was largely for this reason that while missionaries and colonial officials often debated whether training in civilization should precede conversion to Christianity, or vice versa, most found it inconceivable that one could survive without the other.[4]

Influenced as well by the efforts of Samuel Marsden, the celebrated CMS missionary to the Maoris in New Zealand, Venn concluded that inculcating work habits and training native artisans were at least as important as religious instruction. The society's missionaries thus were encouraged to employ Bible and plow, not to mention saw, hammer, hoe, twine spinner, and fishing net. At the same time, Venn aimed to create "self-governing, self-supporting, self-propagating" mission establishments, where native pastors gradually assumed tasks related to running the church, and where the ultimate goal lay, as he wrote, in the literal *"euthanasia of a Mission."* So, as Venn sought permanent conversions and self-sustaining Christian communities, he also hoped to sidestep potential conflicts between religion and "nationality." His solution lay in adapting the church to "national tastes" (so long as adjustments conformed to fundamental Anglican principles), relaxed "standards" for appointing native preachers and lay officials, and a distinctive plan for social and political reorganization. The latter involved organizing converts into "companies," each headed by an elder (preferably Christian) headman, whose responsibilities ranged from ensuring proper moral and religious behavior to collecting contributions for the material support of the company and mission. Later on, and assuming that the community gained in strength and numbers, Venn envisioned forging companies into a "model Christian village," where the process of social change ultimately produced among converts a distinctive national identity. Isolated from corrupting influences of frontier settlements, and with members united under a common purpose, Christian villages provided missionaries with a controlled environment where they would be free to enforce rules of behavior, and where prosperity and stability might draw ever more individuals into the fold.[5]

As a practical matter, Venn's plan relied upon demonstrating the village's material prosperity and institutional stability. This required missionaries to learn native languages, enlist the support of established leaders, and stimulate cultural change by promoting material prosperity. A cornerstone of efforts to replace the African slave trade with "legitimate" enterprises, encouraging native commerce supported the conclusion that inculcating industrious values constituted an essential component in cultural "uplift." These notions were fundamental to United States Indian policies and American philanthropy as well, and can be detected in manifold ways, from the desire to remake Indians into farmers and laborers to off-reservation boarding school experiments. Also like American policy makers, Venn hoped to conserve scarce resources by employing native labor and resources; for the CMS this meant that missionaries were to explore commercial applications for native manufactures and traditional trade goods while also stimulating manufacturing with money, training, and "experts" such as weavers, carpenters, blacksmiths, and the like.[6]

These were the ideas that formed the substance of Duncan's preparation at Highbury, and in 1857 the unordained twenty-four-year-old missionary received the unexpected assignment among the Tsimshians at Fort Simpson. Location of the new mission followed advice from Captain (later Admiral) James Prevost, who described the West Coast of British Columbia as "most promising" (despite an embarrassing incident in which the visiting captain was deliberately tripped, and publicly humiliated "much to the amusement of the Gispaxloats [sic]") and offered the prospective missionary free transport to Victoria. Arriving on 13 June 1857, Duncan introduced himself to James Douglas, governor of Vancouver Island, and the Reverend Edward Cridge, a local chaplain. Three more months passed before Duncan secured transport northward, and in that time Douglas tried to dissuade the young missionary from journeying to the notoriously violent Fort Simpson. Duncan, however, remained steadfast in his determination to take on his assignment, and on 1 October he arrived in Tsimshian country.[7]

Duncan assumed his post at a particularly difficult moment. At least one-half of the nearly 2,500 Tsimshians spent parts of each summer in Victoria, seeking better prices for their furs and wages but just as often, it seems, falling prey to alcohol abuse, violence, prostitution, and exploitative working conditions. While one recent scholar has argued, rather forcefully, that travel to Victoria afforded natives the opportunity to recast their middleman role more widely, it seems equally plausible that the prolonged absence of so many individuals undermined both the Fort Simpson economy and native subsistence patterns, particularly *oolichan* fishing. At the same time, the Gispaxlo'ots' commercial monopoly, only recently solidified, now began to unravel. Gitxsan and Wet'suet'en trappers began to trade directly with Hudson's Bay Company officials, as did Nisga'as through Neshaki (also Nisakx, or Martha McNeill), William McNeill's Nisga'a wife. Competition also came from independent operators, including some former company men, who also labored to supplant the Gispaxlo'ots middlemen. Add in the baneful impact of greater quantities of rotgut liquor, and an acceleration of competitive potlatching, and it is little wonder that William Duncan described Fort Simpson as "a perfect hell." This characterization probably applied to white residents as well, for they too drank heavily and, much to Duncan's dismay, sometimes participated in *halaayt* ceremonies.[8]

Duncan's tenure in Fort Simpson lasted five years, but for the first few months he remained within the fort, setting up residence in a cabin supplied by the Hudson's Bay Company while observing his prospective charges. Journal entries from those first years reveal keen powers of observation and an accountant's interest in figures—for instance, he compiled an 1858 "census," which placed the Fort Simpson Tsimshian population at 2,156. They also reveal fairly predictable cultural biases. Regarding the potlatch as "folly," he concluded that "they never think of appropriating what they gather to enhance their comforts but are satisfied if they can make a display like this now and then." The result, "a vast amount of dead stock . . . doomed never to be used," offended both his Victorian sensibilities and his merchantman's background. More lurid stories found their way back home, where readers of missionary magazines could recoil at the murder of slave women "sacrificed to satiate the vanity of their owners," a "dog eating party," tearing at animal flesh "in a most doglike manner," and incidents of cannibalism where "inhuman wretches" engaged in the "horrid work" of "tearing [a corpse] to pieces with their teeth." Leaving the scene "with a depressed heart," Duncan noted—simply, forcefully, and tellingly—"What a dreadful place is this!"[9]

But Duncan also perceived a willingness among Tsimshians to hear his message. These "half naked and painted savages," he wrote, "long[ed] for instruction" and offered him a "truly wonderful and encouraging" reception. Among those was his erstwhile tutor, friend, and conduit to the Tsimshian world, Arthur Wellington Clah, sometimes known as T'amks. Born in 1831 at Laghco, ten miles south of Laxhlgu'alaams (later Fort Simpson), Clah was of the Gispwudwada (Blackfish) clan, the house of T'amks, and the Gispaxlo'ots tribe. Although the T'amks *waalb* was of Gidestsu (Southern Tsimshian) origin, it had become linked with the Gispaxlo'ots, and Clah grew up in that Tsimshian world marked by the conglomeration of the nine coastal tribes and, not incidentally, direct or indirect interactions with white traders. His remained, nevertheless, a world defined by clan and house, where intersecting relationships linked him with a broader Tsimshian world, from the southern coast at Gidestsu to the upper Nass and Skeena. As one of the four principal totemic clans, the Gispwudwada linked Coast and Southern Tsimshians, Nisga'a, and Gitxsan, as well as Haida, Tlingit, and Wet'suet'en. Through the Gispaxlo'ots Clah benefited from membership in the most influential Fort Simpson tribe, and through his adoptive father's membership in the Laxsgiik (Eagle) clan, a close association with Ligeex. Connections with Ligeex meant that Clah had access to Gispaxlo'ots upriver trading prerogatives, and to these he added links with the Nass by virtue of his marriage to Dorcas (or Catherine Datacks), a Nisga'a from Gitlaxdamks. A niece of Neshaki, William McNeill's native wife, Dorcas strengthened his connections with the Nisga'as while offering the most solid of associations with the English newcomers. On at least one occasion, McNeill accompanied Clah on an excursion into Nisga'a country where the two men brought home ninety-eight salmon on 25 September 1861 and another sixty-three just five days later.[10]

Clah took advantage of these contacts to become a successful trader, a boatman ferrying customers up and down the Skeena and Nass, and a day laborer at outposts from Fort Simpson to Victoria. He also began to learn English and emerged as a cultural intermediary almost by definition or "profession." This, of course, rendered him invaluable to Duncan, who sought him as a language tutor and even requested that Clah interpret his first public sermon, delivered in 1858. But according to Duncan, Clah became "so unnerved at my proposal that I quickly saw I must do the best I could by myself." Clah, too, benefited from the relationship.

Valuing English as a powerful tool with which to maneuver in the new multiracial world, he exchanged lessons in Tsimshian for instruction in Duncan's language. By the latter 1850s he could read and write and began keeping a journal. Duncan also compensated him. Financial records from 1857–58 indicate that Clah earned a "salary" paid in soap, a gun, a cloth cap, tobacco, and clothing, goods that ranged in value from three shillings for one bar of soap, two pounds, four shillings for the gun. Duncan wrote later that he paid Clah a blanket and one-half per month, worth about 24 cents. For Clah, a man with an eye toward capitalizing upon novel opportunities, Duncan was more than a curiosity; he was benefactor, a source of material goods, and, possibly, a friend.[11]

This helps explain Clah's cautious but steady movement toward the newcomer. Tsimshian *adawx* offer the sense that Clah benefited from Duncan's strange knowledge, or, as one passage suggests, that "a new thing was about to be shown, and only Duncan and Tamks really knew what this power was going to be." But oral records also portray Clah as an isolated, singular, perhaps arrogant man. Remembered for "enhanc[ing] his position because of his strong character and open disregard for any that opposed his views," Clah was instrumental in the provocative act of constructing Duncan's first schoolhouse upon Gispaxlo'ots property generally used for secret society meetings. Clah knew this, advised Duncan to build anyway, and suffered "many taunts . . . which he disregarded."[12]

But the incident also indicated that at least some found his message attractive, perhaps interpreting his facility with reading and writing as evidence of a strange, powerful *halaayt*.[13] Students flocked to the schoolhouse, Duncan's roll lists 140 children and 120 adults for 1859, and although it is likely that most students attended lessons intermittently, at least one demonstrated consistent interest. Sugunaats (Shooquanahts), a Gitnadoix adolescent, evidently found some comfort or satisfaction in the school's strict diet of the three R's, daily scrubbing with rough soap, and teaching that urged him to believe, as he wrote, that "bad people no care about Son of God." The mission's star pupil, he accepted baptism in 1861 and, significantly, took the name Samuel Marsden. But not everyone found the message so appealing, and the year 1859 brought a dramatic confrontation with Ligeex and a significant intervention by Clah. This incident arose out of the Gispaxlo'ots chief's request that the school be closed during the *halaayt* season, and particularly, as Duncan recalled, "while his daughter was away in the Moon—whither she had been taken to be initiated to the craft of a secret superstition." The situation was sufficiently threatening that chief factor William McNeill counseled assent. But Duncan refused, and when Ligeex came to the door brandishing a knife, only Clah's timely intervention, and the missionary's steady resolve, prevented violence.[14]

Tsimshian *adawx* offer a more nuanced account, even if they agree on fundamental details. Following Duncan's determination to open his school on schedule, but, more important (according to Tsimshians), his refusal to cease ringing the school bell for one week, Ligeex reportedly threatened violence, vowing to "teach that man of unknown origin, that I am the chief here and I own this land, not he." When the next day arrived, and while "the naxnox whistles began to blow about the Gispaxloats village, announcing Legaix's daughter's return from her initiation," Duncan went ahead and rang the bell. As the chief made his way toward the school, Clah received the warning that "'Legaix has now gone to kill Mr. Duncan, your friend. There is no one to help him.'" Grabbing his pistol, Clah raced toward the schoolhouse and entered through the back just as Ligeex appeared at the front door, knife drawn. "Pistol in his hand," Clah stood behind his friend, and the chief backed down. "Seeing Tamks, he turned and went out, thoroughly defeated and embarrassed. He had lost face with the people, and had been shamed by one of his own tribesmen." Perhaps significantly, this *adawx* implies a direct link between Ligeex's embarrassment and his later conversion.[15]

The incident, particularly as Tsimshians remember it, reveals something of the budding relationship between Duncan and Clah, and, by extension, the state of Fort Simpson Tsimshian society. For Clah's part, confronting Ligeex amounted to an extraordinary public statement that challenged the existing social order in a way that, more than likely, would have cost him his life in former times. That he did so with seeming impunity suggests that Clah already identified with the newcomers, perhaps by necessity. He was thought to have sought refuge among company men, reportedly the consequence of committing a murder, but it is equally plausible that economic opportunity "pulled" Clah in a new direction as much as public shame "pushed" him. Clah had, after all, discovered new avenues toward accumulating wealth, and possibly prestige, pathways that, significantly, operated both within and outside the Gispaxlo'ots hierarchy.[16]

By the later 1850s, in fact, and as commercial ties rendered him a familiar figure from Victoria to the upper Skeena and Nass, Clah still worked closely with Ligeex. Diary entries identify Ligeex as "chief" of the various hunting and fishing stations even as it was Clah who compensated Tsimshian helpers. "I made them satisfied and they will please with Clah," he wrote in March 1861 in reference to paying Tsimshian fishermen five salmon "from my canoe." This suggests that while Clah relied on his Gispaxlo'ots connections, and at least a cordial relationship with Ligeex, he was an independent operator, perhaps even an "entrepreneur" whose social values may have shifted along with his economic interests. This necessarily affected his relationship with Ligeex, but the two men should be considered neither deadly rivals nor archetypes of a new order. Clah still operated within a Tsimshian world and still understood his position according to Tsimshian values, so if he understood his new position as threatening to Ligeex, he also may have reasoned that close association with Duncan both confirmed and supported the economic, political, social, and cultural choice Clah had already made.[17]

Emphasizing the importance of economics should not be understood as denying the significance of other motivations, but it does offer context and suggestions of broader motivations, and, as such, contributes to our understanding of what happened next. It is well understood that by 1861–62 William Duncan had attracted a number of Tsimshians—in 1862 visiting preacher L. S. Tugwell baptized twenty-two of them—and was well on the way toward resettling his followers at Metlakatla, his celebrated "model Christian village." By 1863, Metlakatla boasted a population in excess of 600 and was proof positive, it seems, of the wisdom of Duncan's decision to demonstrate that material advantages followed religious conversions. Writing in 1858 that "our schools will be of little real utility" if students remain "little better off than the Indians who have had no such education," Duncan struggled simultaneously with the rocky, wet Fort Simpson landscape and with dependence upon Hudson's Bay Company stores. As the area's sole importer and market for Indian products, the company typically set low prices for furs and fish while demanding exorbitant fees for "necessities" like guns, powder, clothing, and even soap, where one mink skin, valued at roughly a dollar, reportedly purchased a single bar about the size of a man's finger. Difficult for Tsimshians certainly, commercial conditions directly affected Duncan's work. His financial records indicate that most of his annual salary of 100 pounds (about $500) went toward purchasing basic supplies, leaving precious little for building a mission establishment or compensating helpers.[18]

Tsimshians, of course, could seek alternative markets by traveling to Victoria, that is, if natives could withstand the violence (in 1862 Clah wrote, "All my friends fighting in the night for whiskey"), which had grown worse following the 1858 Fraser River gold strikes. Political winds shifted as well. By 1860, Governor James Douglas was in retreat, his program of exchanging aboriginal title to lands on Vancouver Island for lump-sum payments and rights to small reserves—the famous "Douglas Treaties"—now under attack from British Columbia's growing settler population. This affected Duncan and the Tsimshians, both directly and indirectly. His novel proposal to limit Indian immigration to Victoria while gathering those who remained into economically viable communities organized along cultural and linguistic lines, and supervised by administrators dedicated toward promoting cultural change, faltered even though the governor had appealed to Duncan for help and had financed his excursion to the south. In the longer term, the abrupt reversal in British Columbia's Indian policy, signified by Governor James Truch's 1864 decision to halt treaty making altogether, left open the question of Indian land tenure throughout the colony.[19]

Duncan's solution lay in isolating his followers, and in 1860 he broached this proposition with Tsimshian leaders. Chiefs reacted "favorably" and offered a site seventeen miles south of Fort Simpson, a place they knew as "Metlakatla," meaning *metla* (between) and *kah-tla* (salt), or a peninsula bounded by sea water, which it is. Abandoned for a generation, Metlakatla once was a trading nexus and location for the autumn *halaayt* season. Duncan found it an ideal location, so he recorded in his diary, to isolate his followers "from the deadening and enthralling influence of heathen customs." He also sold Metlakatla to CMS officials as a Venn-inspired plan for "a model community," where he might "break up all tribal distinctions and animosities," cement "all who came to us, from whatever tribe, into one common brotherhood," and finally "establish the supremacy of the law, teach loyalty to the Queen, conserve the peace of the country around, and ultimately develop our settlement into a municipality with its native corporation." With this plan in mind, the missionary and fifty Tsimshians set out for Metlakatla on 27 May 1862. Within a few weeks, another 300 followed, most notably scores of Gitlaans led by Chief Nislanganos and the nobleman Leequeneesh. By June and July a severe outbreak of smallpox led to further migrations, first a Gitnadoiks contingent fleeing the pestilence that had claimed their chief (and an early supporter of Duncan's efforts), Nieswexs, and then Giluts'aaws and Gitwilgyoots, Ginax'angilks and Gitandos. More tellingly, July 1862 saw the arrival of Ligeex, his principal wife Wahtlh, and a number of Gispaxlo'ots. Recently baptized as Paul Legaic, this "head chief of all the Tsimshians" now cast his lot with the Metlakatlans.[20]

Scholars have devoted considerable attention to considering Tsimshian motivations for migrating to Metlakatla and have reached a general consensus that follows a "social anomie" hypothesis first advanced by anthropologist Homer Barnett and the Tsimshian scholar William Beynon in the 1940s. Drawing upon interviews conducted with the elderly Metlakatlan Matthew Johnson, Barnett and Beynon concluded that "outcasts" constituted a natural vanguard of converts. Disconnected from the main currents of social interaction for one reason or another, these individuals eagerly grasped the opportunity to escape rigid social convention, or crushing shame, and lay claim to an otherwise unattainable level of prestige. Following this formulation, Clah emerges as the archetypal convert whose personal "status revolution" derived both from disorganized social conditions in and around Fort Simpson and from his own determination to reshape existing trading prerogatives into a source for personal enrichment. His success, and that of those who followed Duncan, encouraged others to move, thereby accelerating the social trauma already in evidence and creating, in effect, still more potential followers. Driven as well by degraded conditions in Fort Simpson, converts saw Metlakatla as a "sanctuary," a place where they might escape drunkenness, violence, disease, and despair, and where conversion amounted to a determination to reform, repent, and rebuild.[21]

Available data support all of these conclusions, at least to a degree. Duncan's baptismal records reveal a high incidence of the young, and unmarried, among his first converts. Of his first group of twenty-two, baptized in 1861, men outnumbered women eighteen to six, and together they represented seven of the nine coastal tribes. Significantly, eighteen were aged 30 or younger, only one was over 50, and just three were married. Expanding the sample to include the eighty-four receiving sacraments by 1863, fully fifty-seven were under the age of 30, with twenty-four falling in the 19 and under age cohort and another thirty-three aged 20 to 29. Approximately half of this first group were unmarried (although the data are less complete here). The 30 to 39 age cohort consisted of nineteen individuals, most of them married; five, including Ligeex and Wahtlh, were between 40 and 50; and just three individuals were listed as over 50, one of whom was the 70-year-old Nisleganos. Although limited to those actually announcing religious conversion, and therefore not reflecting the entire set of immigrants, baptismal records probably highlight those with deepest attachments to Metlakatla. They also exclude "periodic" residents of Metlakatla, and in this sense may more directly correlate with those of Duncan's most committed followers.[22]

If the high incidence of the young and unmarried among the core group of Metlakatlans supports the anomie hypothesis, considering the immigration and conversion of at least three high-status individuals, Ligeex, Nisleganos, and Leequneesh (four if one considers Wahtlh as a separate case) complicates matters. So, too, does the fact that Clah, the archetypal "outsider," remained in Fort Simpson. Given the apparent success of his commercial endeavors, Clah simply may have perceived little advantage in immigrating, But the fact that the thirty-two Gitlaans and seventeen Gispaxlo'ots constitute the heaviest representation among Metlakatlans suggests less anomie than the persisting importance of chiefly authority. Nisleganos and Ligeex certainly had their own, probably personal and complex, reasons for accepting baptism and moving to Metlakatla, but it is reasonable to conclude that one motivation was to gain access to the missionary's peculiar spiritual power and thus retain some modicum of accustomed influence. Ligeex's recent public shame at the hands of Clah and Duncan no doubt influenced the head chief's behavior, as did a prior incident that followed the death of this particular Ligeex's illustrious predecessor and a contentious struggle for succession. In order to secure confirmation of his claim to this name, the Ligeex who became Paul Legaic promised, but failed, to exact revenge upon Haidas, who had killed a number of Gispaxlo'ots. His rival, also an uncle, apparently convened a secret meeting of Gispaxlo'ots chiefs and as a consequence of that meeting convinced the newly installed chief to migrate to Metlakatla. This shame may explain that particular Ligeex's attempts upon Duncan's life. As for Nisleganos, his motivations may have been similar (Barnett suggests mismanaged revenge against another Tsimshian tribe), but at least one study highlights a gift of Gitlaan property for the site of the first Metlakatla settlements. Nislaganos and the Gitlaans may, then, have assumed that Duncan owed them something in return.[23]

Contemporary Metlakatlans stress, at least in retrospect, that conversions were genuine, and linked as well to the perception of Metlakatla as a sanctuary from debilitating conditions in Fort Simpson.[24] Even Clah admitted to "Quarling [sic] because I trinking [sic] bad spirit and whiskey" and reported an incident where, after threatening a campmate with a pistol, Ligeex received a gunshot wound to the hand. "Legaic," he suggested on another occasion, "he is crazy. Him drinking too much." Added to this, of course, was the catastrophic smallpox epidemic of 1862, which was traced to the Indian camps on the outskirts of Victoria. Tsimshian traders brought it home, and before the end of 1863 fully 500 Indians had perished. Clah's diary for 20 May 1862 includes the chilling entry: "Some Tsimshians come from Victoria, bring lot Small Pox. Killing all Indians at Fort Simpson." Available data confirm that Fort Simpson suffered the worst effects of the outbreak, but disease also spread north, south, inland, and to offshore islands, with high mortality reported among Nisga'a, and Gitxsan, Tlingit, Haida, and Haisla.[25] Although spared, Clah observed the course of the disease, providing Duncan with mortality figures from each Tsimshian community and recounting the considerable psychological "shock" in yet another diary entry. "Saturday, the 21 of month," he wrote in June:

> and all the Indians. . . . Burned . . . lots of things with fire about in half Day and thee wants Sacrifices to God and want the will God tak away Sickness from them, this the way burned all bad things an all the Chiefs in Tsimshen burn all [his] music with Fire. Called Nokhnakh [naxnox] and other kinds we called Ahamelk [halaayt] burnt them all, poor all Tsimshen. Thee make God angry an in every year thee always telling lies an stealing. Murder killing another. Drunkeness an fighting an we never do Right In God Sight.

After the spectacular destruction of ceremonial items, Clah remembered returning home, where he prayed, "O God look upon poor Tsimshens.

Tak away Sickness from them an save them an make clean our hearts. Make us good and give us Thy Holy Spirit for Christ's Sake."[26]

Metlakatla remained remarkably, perhaps notably, healthy—even though the Gitlaan Waksh and Gitsiis Nahks and Teloon (baptized Stephen, Martha, and Jacob Ryan, respectively) perished—and became a sanctuary for Tsimshians fleeing the disease. Whether because of isolation, Duncan's determination to isolate the new community (even from Clah, it seems; professing a concern for his safety, and probably wondering if he too might be infected, Duncan sent Clah away), or the missionary's good fortune to have inoculations at the ready, the incident probably rebounded to his advantage. Writing some years later, Moses Hewson (Gitlaan), son of one of Duncan's earliest followers, Leequeneesh (baptized as Robert Hewson), considered smallpox the principal reason for emigration and credits Duncan with making "up his mind to move south east of Fort Simpson," establishing an effective "quarrantine" against the disease. There, Hewson wrote, his Gitlaan forebears "start[ed] to build little huts of barks."[27]

Whatever the combination of factors, Metlakatla soon embarked on a course of development inextricably linked with the dominating presence of William Duncan while he was alive, and laboring under his considerable legacy thereafter. As a consequence, Metlakatla can seem to be an extension of the missionary's personal will, where local culture and scholarly analysis effectively replicate Duncan's own concept of himself as leader, Tsimshians as followers. Partly the result of available resources—in other words, Duncan's voluminous papers and a comparative paucity of native voices—equating person with place hinges as well upon the missionary's energetic brand of "social reform." This program, so any number of studies have concluded, produced committed converts by encouraging a sense of civic-mindedness at least in part by substituting celebrations at Christmas, New Year's, and Queen Victoria's birthday for Tsimshian ceremonials, including the potlatch, while it replicated, but replaced, house, crest, and lineage with an integrated system of municipal government and patrilineally based nuclear families. Left unexplored, however, are Tsimshian perspectives. For instance, why remain in Metlakatla once the "price" of membership became clear? Phrased differently, why did Tsimshians come to identify with Metlakatla and this program of cultural transformation? How did Metlakatlans forge a distinctive identity?

Addressing this question draws us back to the fundamental issue of why Tsimshians, and natives generally, accepted conversion, and just how sincere these conversions were. Competing analytical frameworks channel this discussion in two directions, each with strengths and drawbacks. On the one hand, characterizing Indians as essentially passive receptors of Christianity, whose freedom of action was constrained by unequal "power," disintegrating social structures, or a combination of like factors, denies natives the facility for molding outside cultural influences to fit their needs or interpreting novel ideas according to fundamental cultural values. It also ignores the clear possibility that natives converted for seemingly "nonreligious" reasons, such as the desire to enhance one's political or economic position. Ligeex may have perceived conversion and migration as a means for furthering, or preserving, his own position, and the same can probably be said for Clah, even as he chose to remain in Fort Simpson.[28]

But emphasizing agency, or its variant "creative resistance," also leads to problems, namely, by diminishing the importance of unequal power, overt or covert coercion, not to mention social disorganization. In response, several scholars have endeavored to produce a theoretical model that considers cultural contact as flexible and dynamic or, as anthropologist William Simmons explains, "externally induced yet indigenously orchestrated." In a slightly different context, Michael Harkin offers a similar evaluation. Highlighting Heiltsuk women's apparent facility for producing "new ideas about sacredness, power, morality, and gender," he cautions us to apply the term "syncretism" with care. Adaptations, in other words, are not simply manifestations of transcultural identity but must be seen, more properly, as "unique and original attempts to construct an idea of society that reflected a rapidly changing and threatening world."[29]

The point is that while Duncan's followers certainly found meaning in conversion and exodus, these meanings were plural, individualistic, shifting, contradictory, and related to gender, social position, and personal circumstance as much as to culture generally. They involved any number of adjustments, accommodations, and means for creative resistance. The Tsimshian "strategy" constituted neither passive acceptance nor unadulterated agency, and not simply a combination of these poles, splitting the difference, as it were. Here it may be productive to place Metlakatla in comparative counterpoint. I have suggested already that the intersection of economic change, material opportunity for some perhaps, and cultural values produced a dialogue of remarkable force among Menominees. This same process of examining cultural identity and political behavior through the prism of economic relationships may yield similar results for Metlakatla. If, for instance, the development of logging and lumbering produced a conversation on cultural values among Menominees, can it be that migration and immersion in Duncan's Metlakatla "system" generated something similar? If not, why not? Optimally, comparison offers an opportunity to move the scholarly discussion

Canoe building on the beach at Metlakatla, British Columbia (NA-APR, RG200, Archives Box 69, Print 698)

away from what Duncan did to, or for, Metlakatlans and toward a consideration of native perspectives.

Returning to historical events, migration seems not to have attenuated prior social and economic relationships, at least at the outset. Metlakatlans maintained ties with Fort Simpson relations and even participated in potlatches. Clah reports an 1865 feast held at Ligeex's old house where one chief "give away all is [sic] property, 100 blankets, to all Tsimshen [sic] chiefs," and one scholar suggests that Fort Simpson Tsimshians may have attempted to convince their chief to return home and thus preserved his house. Clah staged his own potlatch in 1868 and invited Ligeex to a feast confirming his claim to the celebrated name T'amks. The feast earned him Duncan's condemnation, but it suggests as well that Clah perceived opportunity in the fragmented Tsimshian social structure. Ligeex's presence indicates as well that, in spite of their migration, Metlakatlans had not severed their ties to home and extended family.[30]

Economic ties operated similarly. Duncan's financial records indicate continued reliance on the Hudson's Bay Company in Fort Simpson, from which the new community purchased $795 worth of supplies in 1864, as well as Victoria trading houses. We might presume with some confidence that Metlakatla's southern contacts had a history of dealing with Indian traders from the north coast. Clah also frequented Metlakatla, sometimes purchasing a few items (one cloth cap, a tin of biscuits, seven pounds of soap, a "sowester" hat, and five days' anchorage cost $10.34 in 1863); on at least on one occasion he stopped there on the way home from Victoria (bringing with him seven passengers and $500 in cash). Metlakatla, therefore, found an economic "niche" for itself as its inhabitants, operating according to accustomed prerogatives, naturally drew the new community into regional trading networks. This provided, in theory at least, the possibility of economic security. But it might also lead to conflict. Clah and Ligeex, for instance, frequented Gispaxlo'ots resource-gathering territories just as they had in prior times. Sometimes they worked together, but not always. In April 1864 Clah wrote, "Paul Legaic angry against me. Speaking with Duncan about me and about Indians interior, and thee never telling the truth." They aired the disagreement before Duncan, and in Metlakatla, and while its resolution is lost to history, it suggests conflict over trading contacts with interior tribes. Metlakatlans, and in this case Ligeex (Paul Legaic), persisted in exploiting claimed fishing and hunting territories and possibly argued that the "entrepreneur" Clah may have been attempting to circumvent *pt'eex, waalb,* and tribal prerogatives. Metlakatlans understandably were not so ready to surrender these rights and so did not equate migration with an end to tribal relations in the broadest sense. Clah, on the other hand, may well have assumed just that, namely, that following Duncan constituted an act of renouncing prerogatives.[31]

If migration failed to interrupt established resource-gathering patterns, it did shift the flow of goods somewhat as the community gradually laid claim to products and profits, and William Duncan came to direct commerce. For example, in 1864 Ligeex (Paul Legaic) exchanged $242.50 worth of furs for manufactured products—not remarkable in and of itself, of course, but this transaction took place within Metlakatla, and under Duncan's auspices. Other Metlakatlans apparently donated $68 worth of deer, salmon, fish grease, ducks, and potatoes. Although still "owned" by native producers, goods fell under the control of the community, meaning that Metlakatla, through Duncan, conducted the commerce in the name of the community. Operating collectively, Metlakatla also sold $85 worth of cypress planks to the Irving and Meyer Company of Victoria; fifty-four gallons of fish oil, at fifty cents per gallon, to the Hudson's Bay Company; and four fur seals ($2 each), along with two barrels of fish oil ($68 in total), to the Victoria firm of Lawrence, Clark and Joyce in that same year. Even more impressively, two shipments of furs to Sifkin and Brothers, Victoria, brought $1,500 in 1864 and $1,810 the next year, funds that financed, in part anyway, purchases of $6,687 from that same trading firm.[32]

But if Duncan gradually assumed control over Metlakatla's commercial relations, native converts realized certain benefits from those arrangements. The simple act of migrating, after all, secured for Metlakatlans access to useful, sometimes valuable, articles. Community accounts for 1864 show wages of $89.13 to selected Indians for performing servants' duties, while records for 1865 include $51.00 paid to "gardeners" and another $53.25 to a servant named "Andrea." Contacts with the Church Missionary Society and the government of British Columbia only enhanced Duncan's ability to reward followers, demonstrating again the material advantages of becoming "Metlakatlan." Duncan's annual salary of $500 constituted an infusion of independently derived capital that partially underwrote the Metlakatla economy. Other CMS contributions included $254 to board Indian students in 1865 and a grant of $887 in 1866, much of which went toward constructing a mission house and other "capital improvements." Duncan's contacts with Governor Douglas paid off as well. A housing allowance of $262.50 in 1862 financed the construction of thirty-seven new homes. In 1863 Metlakatla received another $970 in government grants, mostly dedicated toward another round of housing and "promoting industries" like hunting, gardening, shoe making, and smith work. Still more support came from Duncan's 1863 appointment as local magistrate, and with this one-half of all fines collected and fees for trading licenses made their way into Metlakatla's coffers. The British Columbia government also provided uniforms and covered a portion of constables' salaries, refunded expenses incurred in watching prisoners, and contributed substantial funds toward building and maintaining a prison.[33]

What this means is that there was every incentive for Tsimshians not only to migrate but also to *stay*. From the outset, Metlakatla's economy promoted both community and individuality in a way that roughly recapitulated Tsimshian patterns of social integration. A parallel operates as well in the person and activities of William Duncan. Just as Tsimshian societies were organized hierarchically, but with legitimate leadership rested on the ability to provide a stable, productive social environment, Metlakatla's appeal hinged upon William Duncan's ability to do the same. For their part, Tsimshians brought to Metlakatla not only a commitment to build a new community but also the "tools" to do so. These tools included claims to fishing and hunting territories, the skills to exploit locally available resources, and trading contacts from Fort Simpson to Victoria and including networks of exchange that long preceded contact with Europeans. As an embodiment of Duncan's considerable efforts and perhaps a unique *halaayt*, Metlakatla may have confirmed the missionary's accession to a position resembling "head chief," or *sm'oogyit*. Ironically, it is here that the association of person with community may make sense from a Tsimshian perspective. After all, it was common for an aboriginal village to take the name of its most prominent chiefly family.[34]

So their commitment was genuine, their determination clear. Working with scant resources but ample manpower, Metlakatlans constructed homes, a church, and a meetinghouse, as well as roads, canoe rests, and a school, and they did this within just a few years. An annual tax, first assessed on New Year's Day 1863 and set at one blanket or $2 for adult males, generated $5.50 in cash, 100 blankets, one dressed elk skin, and sixteen shirts, resources now consolidated to fund projects of mutual importance. Material improvement also proved a magnet for new settlers, as 52 newcomers enrolled as citizens by 1867, with another 372 by 1879. Motivated, so Duncan wrote, "by a desire to rise with their advancing brethren," Metlakatla welcomed Gitxsans "from Kitsahlam and Kitsamakalum on the Skeena" and "the whole of the Kitkaht [Gitk'a'ata] tribe." Migrating from their homes far to the south, the Gitk'a'atas pledged, "in the presence of W. Duncan and the council of Metlakatla," to "put away for ever the abomination called ahlied [*halaayt*] or cannibalism and dog eating orgies."[35]

Whether abandoning these "abominations" constituted a substantial sacrifice for migrants, or was perceived as such, is difficult to discern. But like the Menominees who came to understand that commercial opportunities were not necessarily inconsistent with fundamental cultural values, Metlakatlans may have found prospects for economic and social security sufficiently attractive to outweigh understandable concerns. This is not to suggest that change came without cost, or that individuals embraced change without trepidation. But it does suggest that change was not so mysterious, not so utterly destructive to Indian values, as to be resisted at every step. In part, Menominee gravitation toward logging and the economic appeal of Metlakatla derived at least partly from a prior experience with the fur trade, a mode of commerce both groups shared. Enmeshed in a widening world economic system, and with all that meant for economic independence and cultural integrity, many Menominees and presumably most Metlakatlans chose to continue along this path, hoping, perhaps, to transform economic change into material and cultural security.

But Metlakatla was not the Menominee Reservation. There was no one like William Duncan in northern Wisconsin, and this was a critical difference. So, too, was the fact that those Tsimshians who followed Duncan did so because they embraced, to the extent that they could understand it, what he offered. By contrast, all Menominees did not have to accept, or pursue, logging personally. They had options, and thus there was a greater variability to the early Menominee experience than in Metlakatla. This element of choice, of individual variability, came to distinguish the Menominee experience from that in Metlakatla, and where William Duncan's energetic effort to transform Tsimshian culture sets the two groups apart. It is this component of the Metlakatla "system" that will next occupy our attention.

CHAPTER SEVEN

Metlakatla and the Market

If material security motivated some Tsimshians to pull up stakes for Metlakatla, what took place there was more than economic development. William Duncan, of course, had in mind a more comprehensive set of social and cultural reforms, and it is quite likely that he viewed economic security as a means toward reaching more ambitious ends. Acting in concert with the strategy set out by Henry Venn, and finding correlations with missionary activities across place and time, from South American "reductions" to the work of Oblate Father Paul Durieu in southern British Columbia, and including missions supported by the Church Missionary Society in Africa and China, and from New Zealand to Palestine, Duncan aimed at a self-propagating native community where Anglo-Christian modes of religious belief and social interaction gradually supplanted indigenous forms. And he was influential. The Methodist Thomas Crosby applied a similar concept among natives in Nanaimo, Vancouver Island, before taking it to Fort Simpson, where he ministered to those Tsimshians who declined to move to Metlakatla. Later, U.S. Indian agent and amateur ethnologist James G. Swan praised Duncan's "system" as "eminently superior to any system we now have regarding Indian management," pointing in particular to village "industries," which, he noted, "rendered [Metlakatlans] independent of any outside support."[1]

In a sense, Metlakatla operated "holistically," with reforms of mind, body, and spirit reinforcing each other. Phrased differently, Metlakatla's political economy constituted a complicated mix of social reform and economic change, where resettlement ultimately produced a distinctive ethnic identity, and therefore stands in apparent contrast to the Menominee situation. The Menominee cultural dialogue certainly involved a reciprocal interplay of social forces and fundamental values that altered Menominee life but it did so according to clear boundaries or where ideals channeled the direction of change. With no corresponding migration of a discrete segment of the Menominee community, cultural adaptation operated "unevenly," if by this we take it to mean that there developed a multiplicity of personal accommodations. By contrast, cultural change in Metlakatla may appear "uniform," particularly if we conclude, quite reasonably, that migration constituted an *active* decision to sample a new way of life. It would be as if Menominee entrepreneurs decided to pick

152

up stakes, sever ties with the larger community, and then pursue an independent path and all that might entail.

But surface distinctions sometimes mask broader similarities. Market forces, over which Indian communities exerted little direct control, demanded adaptation in both locations, sometimes establishing the parameters for this interaction between social forces and cultural values. By conglomerating around Keshena and Neopit, Menominee entrepreneurs effectively set themselves apart from those less inclined to embrace economic change. Residence patterns, therefore, amount to a rough indicator of cultural orientation even as they remain crude instruments, to be employed judiciously. After all, Menominee entrepreneurs still took into consideration the needs of the broader community, cultural values shaped accommodations with the market and interactions with others, and the overall objective of economic change (so far as one can be discerned) remained not assimilation but, ultimately, a bolstering of Menominee ethnic identity. Economic modernization did not equal assimilation, nor should scholars confuse the two.

If this recipe applies to Metlakatla, it must do so differentially so as to consider Duncan's effort to produce comprehensive social and cultural transformation. More a series of ad hoc solutions that reflected a constancy of purpose than a comprehensive program devised in advance, social reform in Metlakatla nevertheless operated according to two main principles: a determination to forge civic-mindedness by encouraging collective responsibility, and an effort to reshape public and private behavior according to Anglo-Victorian sensibilities. "Rules of Metlakatla," set forth in 1862 and operating as a combination town charter and preconditions for migration, illustrate just how these two objectives intertwined. Under the heading "Forbidden," Duncan decreed an end not only to "The Demonweal Rites Called Ahlied [halaayt]," "Gambling," "Painting Faces," and "Giving away property for display" but also to "The use of intoxicating liquor." At the same time, the code set forth ten requirements having as much to do with community affairs as with personal conduct. Observing the Sabbath, attending church, and sending children to school figured prominently, as did the requirement to pay a yearly tax ("one blanket or $2\frac{1}{2}$ dollars," or "one shirt or one dollar" for "males approaching manhood"), to submit disagreements to "Arbitration or by recourse to the Civil Force by Law," to "build neat homes and cultivate gardens," and to be "cleanly in their habits," "industrious," "peaceful and orderly," and "honest in their dealings with each other and with Indians of other tribes."[2]

A demanding code to be certain, but one tempered by a system for local government and social organization that paralleled the Tsimshian notions regarding the interplay of collective action and social hierarchy.

Beginning in 1865, Duncan apportioned his male followers, by lot, into a series of "companies," each of which elected one member to a collective governing body. Steady in-migration led to periodic reorganizations, and by 1881 members in each of ten companies elected three village councilmen, two church elders, two constables, two native teachers, two musicians, and ten volunteer firemen. Rules charged company leaders with promoting "improvement and industry," caring for their sick and aged, devising solutions to company problems, and raising subscriptions for village projects. Commanded to "strive to be great in everything good," company leaders were to "shun all evil doers," "learn to be a servant and help to the village," and, if need be, "excommunicate" backsliders. A parallel system of ten "classes" organized women similarly even as they indicate Duncan's intention to alter gender relations by distinguishing clearly female from male roles. Even so, all "civic organizations," male and female, provided "advice—help and sympathy" to new immigrants who, upon declaring loyalty to Metlakahtla and fealty to its strictures, were assigned, again by lot, to one of the ten companies.[3]

William Duncan undoubtedly considered village organization a powerful means for directing cultural change. An 1881 letter boasted that "these measures tend to destroy all tribal chiefs; secure the sick a visitor, and the erring a monitor; uphold the law; bring suitable bye-laws [sic] into operation; [and] provide pleasure for, and promote the safety of the village." The result, he predicted, would be "a general feeling of brotherhood . . . prompting each man to assist his fellow in time of need," and native Metlakatlans agreed, or at least seemed to. The system of constables, councils, elders, and firemen—rules and all—recapitulated previous bonds to clan, house, and tribe, albeit in altered form; more broadly, collective responsibility became the hallmark of Metlakatlan social organization, a critical component in their developing identity. So when respected citizens Henry Ridley and James P. O'Reilly posted bond guaranteeing the good behavior of a wayward youth named Alfred Auclaire, or when ten adult men promised "to do our utmost to watch them [a group of five boys] and guide their conduct aright—that they offend not again nor do anything contrary to the Christian morals and regulations of Metlakahtla," residents affirmed both Duncan's determination to reshape native mores and their own desire to make Metlakatla succeed. And success meant expressing a communal ethos, or the belief that it was just as "natural" for the village council to monitor personal conduct—as in the case of the immigrant Shimpowst, who in 1871 was "forbidden to be with Cushnanlak until it can be ascertained that his heathen wife in Fort Simpson has got another husband"—as it was to settle civil matters like property disputes.[4]

But the case of Shimpowst, Cushnahlak, and that "heathen wife" points to the complexity of social reform in Metlakatla, and nowhere was

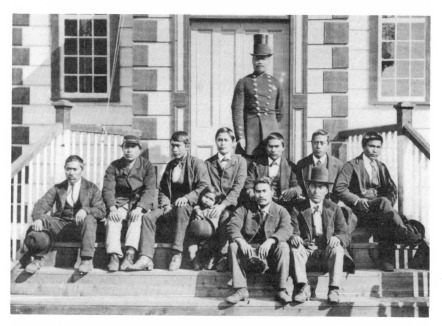

Group of Tsimshians in front of the town hall, with Paul Legaic standing at the back wearing a constable's uniform. (NA-APR, RG200, Archives Box 69, Print 660)

this more evident than in gender relations. On the one hand, Metlakatla restricted citizenship to males, and the assessment of a village tax to men only suggests a relative decline in women's status. This corresponds as well with Duncan's intention to substitute nuclear households, headed by men, for a Tsimshian system that recognized women's political and property rights through extensive kinship networks organized matrilineally. This practice, so one scholar concludes, also undermined women's economic role by separating them from resource rights while offering ancillary occupations that offered little prospect for independent action. What is more, Duncan also sought to prevent divorce, and one scholar of the subject detects evidence suggesting that Metlakatla courts, dominated by the missionary, punished women who sought to leave their husbands. Clah recorded one such incident from 1870: "News came up today from Metlekatlah. They was trouble about taking up 2 women but those 2 women used married before. But both running away from 2 younger men." Resolution came the following day as the two male Metlakatlans "taken back 2 wives belong to them. . . . One woman and little child was in Jail." Even though Clah thought this punishment too severe, Metlakatla's action supports the notion that missionization adversely impacted women's status.[5]

Accurate in its details, this conclusion equating missionization with persecution of women misses several points, some peculiar to Metlakatla, others more generally associated with the larger question of women and Christian missions. Women as well as men followed William Duncan to Metlakatla, and there is little evidence to suggest that they left the mission in greater numbers than their male counterparts. What is more, some women may have perceived Metlakatla as a sanctuary, offering safe haven from the violence in Fort Simpson and Victoria, where, it must be remembered, they could be, and were, forced into prostitution. Metlakatla also offered security to women fleeing prostitution or abusive husbands. Here again, suggestive evidence comes from Clah's diaries. In 1871 he recorded an incident in which a wife of Chief Weeshaks, whom Clah identified as Sarah Legaic's sister, fled her husband for Metlakatla and "a nice house." The chief, he continued, "cried every day for Lost his wife," but the absence of contrary evidence suggests that the woman and her child remained in Metlakatla. While this should not be taken to mean that most Tsimshian women perceived safety and security in Metlakatla, or found life there satisfying in all respects, it does recommend a more complex picture of the mission, William Duncan, and what converts, men and women, found there. Equally important is the possibility that women, as much as men, did not interpret conversion as separating them from older kinship ties. Both women and men attended feasts still taking place in Fort Simpson, and trading networks, organized around matrilineal relationships, continued to operate. Thus, female Metlakatlans, like their husbands, brothers, and fathers, lived parallel lives, and their "status" associated with Tsimshian relationships did not just disappear following migration and conversion. This story also reminds us that women could be sincere converts, that the relative impact of missionization upon women versus men was complex and varied, and that women, in anthropologist Michael Harkin's words, might "cooperate with the missionaries to forge new ideas about sacredness, power, morality, and gender."[6]

Similarly complicated is the question of Metlakatla and Tsimshian social status. While converts seemingly came from all levels of society, it is clear that those of noble heritage not only influenced the migration of lower-status village mates but also retained some ability to act independently of Duncan. Here again, kinship networks offered the prospect for accumulating wealth, and with that came some autonomy. Ligeex's family, for instance, maintained a home in Fort Simpson, a place for feasting and affirmation of kinship ties even as Duncan attempted to forge novel arrangements.[7] By contrast, lower-status persons, particularly those who fled slavery or migrated individually, may have found a level of security and acceptance in a community where ascribed status held little meaning, at least formally. With or without the active support of Metlakatlans who previously enjoyed high status, William Duncan actively recruited former slaves, sometimes agreeing to purchase their freedom. In 1867 he paid a Haida chief fifty dollars for a slave named Yah-kom, and in the following year eight dollars went toward food and clothing for unfree persons "rescued from the Kithratla" tribe. Another Haida slave, Kahlp, became a devout Christian for whom Metlakatla represented salvation. "I was a slave, . . . poor in spirit, and drawn to cry to God take my heart," he wrote in later years, happy to have left behind a life where "those who die in their sin go to darkness and to fire." Even considering the possibility that Duncan "coached" Kahlp's testimony, Metlakatla still meant different things to different people. If lower-status individuals were more dependent on Duncan and the community than their higher-status counterparts, they also benefited from social and economic arrangements that distributed goods widely and without regard to prior associations.[8]

It remains unclear whether Metlakatla's governing bodies were dominated by higher-status persons, but their functioning suggests a complex melding of old and new, where the village council embodied Tsimshian notions regarding reciprocal obligations even as ascribed position faded away. Dominated of course by William Duncan, the village council oversaw tax assessments, then allocated funds and manpower toward construction projects large and small, maintained public spaces, and saw to the needs of the aged, sick, and poor. Like tribal governing bodies, it promoted community harmony and forged interethnic relations, on one occasion allocating seven dollars toward the "purchase of land to divide between 4 houses to keep peace,"while commissioning an 1870 mission to "the chief of the Keetquahclah on the other side of the Nass river," because "he wish to try to fighting the Metlakahtla people." The community also devoted scarce funds toward staging annual celebrations and invited guests who were treated to food and lodging at the community guest house. These festivals, marking Christmas, New Year's, and Queen Victoria's birthday, not only attracted potential converts but also bound Metlakatlans together by replicating the Tsimshian *halaayt* season and *naxnox* displays, what with their gift giving, speeches, singing, and performances by the village brass band. Athletic contests, like soccer matches pitting one wing of the village against another, recapitulated competition between village moieties, and New Year's Day amounted to a secular alternative to midwinter rites. That village-wide feast set the tone for Metlakatla's annual business meeting, where company leaders detailed progress made during the previous year and introduced new members. Afterward came the collection of taxes, speeches by Duncan and native notables, the singing of the village song and "God Save the Queen," and finally a magic lantern show.[9]

Means for enforcing community standards also set Metlakatla apart from neighboring villages, raising its profile substantially, but here, too, concrete practices rested on this ongoing conversation between missionary and residents. Internally, constables patrolled the streets, rounding up violators of town strictures and sending them before magistrate Duncan, who administered reprimands, fines, whippings, and jail sentences. In particularly troubling cases, he employed ridicule, hoisting a black flag, "with fingers pointing to the black-hearted villain," with great effect, because "such is the Indian sense of shame that this device always rendered the employment of force unnecessary." Metlakatla's reputation for totalitarianism derives from this determination to publicly censure transgressors and to use the native constabulary to monitor personal behavior.[10]

External relations operated similarly. Armed with his appointment as a provincial officer, his authority backed up by Metlakatla's corps of constables, Duncan moved vigorously to enforce provincial laws, even if his aggressive stance sometimes earned Metlakatla the enmity of local non-Indians. Of particular note were prosecutions under the provincial statute prohibiting the sale of intoxicants to Indians and the apparent use of Metlakatla citizens to entrap suspected violators. On several occasions during the latter 1860s, Metlakatla constables testified to having purchased spirits (sometimes even verifying the drink's potency personally), and their testimony was taken seriously and used to secure convictions. Clah performed a similar task in 1870 in a case involving a Skeena River merchant, and Metlakatla's reach extended as well to at least one Indian woman convicted of working in tandem with Hudson's Bay Company storekeeper Robert Cunningham to provide Indians with liquor. Cunningham was, by this point, a repeat offender, having been convicted of a similar offense in 1868. Although he paid that earlier fine of $400, "in protest," and appealed his conviction to provincial officials in Victoria, Duncan's ruling held, and so too, apparently, did his authority. Metlakatla's coffers also benefited, from their one-half share of fines collected, fees paid native witnesses, and allowances from the provincial government to house inmates.[11]

One measure of Metlakatla's authority undoubtedly derived from the backing of the Royal Navy. Gunboats watched over a murder trial in 1864 and in 1876 intervened to "impose law and order among the Hydahs." But Duncan's standing rested at least as much on a reputation for treating natives fairly. He noted with pride that "Indians from every quarter who feel themselves aggrieved come here for redress or advice," and he sometimes injected himself into disputes between natives. He heard a case in which a Gitlaan "chief" named Yakahdates sued to recover property extorted from him following the kidnapping of his wife Gom. On another occasion he assessed forty dollars in fines and awarded twenty-four dollars to Neashyakahnaht of Fort Simpson following the destruction of a ceremonial pole. The fact that the four defendants admitted to destroying property because "they are vexed with their chief . . . because he joins the Metlakahtla Christians" may have influenced the magistrate's decision, but the larger point, in both these cases, was that Tsimshians other than those who migrated to Metlakatla respected Duncan's deliberations.[12]

And they respected him, it seems, because he periodically upheld native rights, or at least considered Tsimshian values. In 1877 Duncan rejected the proposition, advanced in this instance by a native, that colonization abrogated native claims to resource territories. Ruling against the plaintiff Melumkaupa, he "decided to sustain the ancient Indian law, in that remote part of the Province, until such times as the Dominion and Provincial Governments have settled the Indians on their respective Reserves; and therefore I forbade Melumkaupa from again trespassing on the Kinahtocks [Gitnadoiks] hunting grounds." On another occasion Duncan upheld Tsimshian inheritance practices. In 1875, Metlakatlan Oliver Scott filed suit, arguing that Methodist missionary (and sometimes Duncan's rival) Thomas Crosby had acted unlawfully by permitting a native, William Kighnow of Fort Simpson, to reside in a home previously owned by Scott's now deceased brother Cushahwalah (?). The case turned upon whether Scott, as the sole adult relative of the deceased, retained ownership of the property, even though Crosby claimed that Scott was estranged from his brother, had since moved to Metlakatla, and had removed six boards from the Fort Simpson home, using them to construct his new home. Duncan found for Scott on all counts. Relying on the testimony of Metlakatlans Charles Ryan (Gitlaan) and John Tait (Gispaxlo'ots), he determined that neither distance, nor supposed estrangement, nor a deathbed request that Crosby manage the contested property outweighed Tsimshian inheritance practices. As Ryan explained, "Nothing could prevent a brother having [his] say about his deceased brother's effects"; similarly, according to Tait, "There is the law of the Indian that a male in the family can speak about the [brother's] property and his voice must be heard about the disposing!" Duncan fined Crosby for his inappropriate actions, and Tsimshian law affirmed the proposition that the act of migrating did not abrogate any Metlakatlan's right to family property or prerogatives.[13]

None of this should be taken to mean that the vigorous extension of Metlakatla's influence went unchallenged. Tsimshians from Fort Simpson evidently reacted angrily to migrations, sometimes destroying property as exemplified by the ceremonial pole case, other times acting to prevent the removal of prestigious properties. In 1874, Clah reported a dispute over the disposition of Ligeex's house in Fort Simpson. The new owner, Paul Legaic, evidently expressed his intention to move the structure to

Metlakatla, a move Tsimshians in Fort Simpson opposed. According to Clah, "Council says don't take the house down because it not belong to him [Paul Legaic]. Belong old Legaic." Nonnatives also recoiled against Metlakatla's authority. One trader told of "a large force of Mr. Duncan's Constables arriv[ing] at my place of business" and the subsequent arrest of two employees, "without making any previous statements, or producing any warrant." These same constables, identified as Samuel Marsden, Samuel Pelham, and Matthew Aucland, then threatened "to blow the head off" any "white man who dare open his mouth," and announced further that "'the blood of the white men should sleep [on] the banks of the river.'" Duncan not only stood by his constables, maintaining that threats really "meant nothing," but also convicted traders of violating liquor laws and demanded that they apologize for slandering Metlakatla constables. One infuriated convict predicted trouble should "Mr. Duncan persist in instructing Constables of his own creation to do that which white men would decidedly refrain from doing," to which Duncan replied, "It will be a sad state of things when we are forced to let law breakers choose the kind of constables that they will allow to arrest them." Suggesting as well that "the white men at Port Essington have the Indian constables at Metlakahtla to thank for [their] peace and safety," Duncan argued that employing Metlakatla lawmen "tends to enlist their [Indians] sympathies on the side of the law."[14]

This spirited defense of the constables, though no doubt calculated to enhance his stature among Metlakatlans, reveals as well ways in which community structures recapitulated Tsimshian social organization. Whether the consequence of an overt agenda or a matter of complex interactions between missionary and followers, it remains that constables and companies approximated house and crest organizations. Moreover, since material and symbolic benefits followed positions of authority, public service occupied an important place in Metlakatla, and contributions to community welfare were valued and expected, a pattern revealed by the tendency for constables to advance to positions on the village council as a reward for meritorious service. The Metlakatla economy mirrored this same pattern, as hierarchy and reciprocity combined to encourage the flow of material goods toward William Duncan, who then redistributed benefits widely, acting at once as head chief and chief factor of a trading outpost. Neither new nor old, directed by neither Tsimshians nor missionaries, this system essentially appropriated a native understanding of economic relationships but in ways that promoted a sense of collective identity while encouraging cultural change.[15]

Especially instructive examples present themselves in the operations of the community store and, relatedly, Metlakatla's trading vessel. Initially, Duncan managed Metlakatla's finances through his own personal account, a practice that reflected his determination to remain in complete control and the fact that he personally remained the conduit for outside contributions. But the Metlakatla community store appeared within just a few months. While the native role in this decision remains unclear, it is probable that Tsimshians approved of the idea, since, like its predecessor in Fort Simpson, Metlakatla's outlet promised economic independence (meaning lower prices for imports and higher returns for furs) by dealing directly with merchants in Victoria and elsewhere. Hudson's Bay Company, however, vigorously opposed this development and, acting upon the advice of one manager who warned that "if he [Duncan] continues the trade much longer I see no alternative for us but to close up our shop," attempted to strangle the infant enterprise by stifling access to supplies and markets. Duncan responded by purchasing a thirty-five-ton schooner. The vessel cost $1,500, toward which the British Columbia government donated $500 and Duncan added another $600, probably from CMS contributions. More interestingly, Metlakatlans raised the balance, some $400, by purchasing "shares," at $5 apiece, in the schooner, now christened *Carolena*. Shares were redeemable at a later date, with holders promised dividends fixed at a percentage of trade profits. Sixty-seven Metlakatlans purchased shares, and some, most notably Charles Ryan and Paul Legaic, held several. From his home in Fort Simpson Clah bought two.[16]

The gambit paid off. Community members operated the schooner for six years, or until the company agreed to begin regular transportation, and Metlakatlans dubbed the vessel "Kahah," or "slave," signifying, so Duncan wrote, that "it did all the work and they reaped all the profit." When Duncan sold the schooner in 1869, he realized a small profit and distributed dividends averaging one dollar to shareholders. Beyond earning a healthy return on their investment, the schooner encouraged community development in other ways. William Rudland, a white man married to a native Metlakatlan, captained the vessel, but community members John Tait and Samuel Pelham contributed their seafaring skills and earned small salaries, and Pelham served as first mate. The schooner also promoted commercial contacts far and wide. Paul Legaic forged contacts with Victoria merchants, representing Metlakatla in the process but also, perhaps, expressing his personal prerogative as holder of that most important of Gispaxlo'ots names to negotiate on behalf of his fellow Tsimshians. In a broader sense, the *Carolena* experiment offered Metlakatlans a "stake" in the trade, an active interest in the economic success of their community, and the sense that, united, they could compete with the larger trading combinations.[17]

The community store exerted an even more profound influence on the development of a new civic identity among Metlakatlans. By consolidating export revenues and contributions from outside sources, the store generated capital to purchase diverse items. *Carolena's* ship manifest for September 1863 included building supplies: "twenty windows, two hundred pounds of nails, and one hundred pounds of shingles"; provisions for hunters: "ten guns, two thousand percussion caps and one hundred ten pounds of shot"; a quantity of foodstuffs; and various items from washtubs, tin kettles, and crockery, to ink, twelve pairs of black cloth trousers, 800 pounds of soap, twelve silk handkerchiefs, a bottle of "Jaynes Expectorant," wedding rings, and a trumpet, drum, and whistles for the constable corps.[18] These were purchased, at least partly, by what could be rather handsome revenues from exports. In 1863, fifteen native hunters contributed some 400 animal skins, worth $500, and a single shipment from the next February included the skins of 89 martens, 362 minks, 103 deer, 73 seal, 118 marmots, 7 ermine, 2 beaver, 25 bear, 4 otters, 1 fisher, 1 wolf, and 19 sheep. Deposited to the store, and under Duncan's care, these purchased $1,000 worth of goods in Victoria. Subsequent revenues surpassed $3,700 in 1865, individual shipments from 1870 to 1875 regularly earned in excess of $1,000, and one brought $6,139.50 from dealers in Victoria and San Francisco. Such earnings were sufficient to purchase quantities of soap, coffee, tools, and clothing—staples that, along with food and medicines, rank as the most popular items.[19]

With sales of $4,500 in 1870, and inventory worth some $4,000 by the next March, the market house stood alone as Metlakatla's most important economic institution. Moreover, as the community's sole financial institution, the store coordinated fiscal affairs, distributing credit vouchers that allowed cash-poor Metlakatlans to purchase necessities while also "banking" an individual's take of fish, furs, and the like. These "deposits" could be drawn upon in lean times but earned 5 percent interest in the meantime. While this system helped soften shortages of capital typical for extractive economies like Metlakatla's, it also encouraged natives to consolidate their resources, and these kept the store solvent while accumulating funds for more ambitious projects down the line. What is more, William Duncan likely perceived the store, and particularly the extension of credit, as a powerful means for encouraging "consumerism," and thus a critical component for effecting cultural change. This, of course, correlates with varied examples of intercultural interactions, from the fur trade to the deliberate use of debt to force land cessions, and even to the effects of disposable income among Menominee loggers, where non-Indians perceived, and acted upon, the transforming power of market forces.[20]

The greater surprise, of course, would be if Duncan either missed the connection between consumerism and cultural change or refused to act upon it. Either directly, or through store manager William Rudland and his mixed-blood son James, Duncan dictated inventory, and invoices reveal a preference for goods that would influence values. After all, soap, western-style hats, capes, gloves, and silk stockings, foodstuffs like biscuits, tea, and fruits, and manufactured fish traps, guns, and nets not only supplanted native dress, diet, and crafts but also inclined Indians toward certain cultural perspectives. Similarly, soccer balls, photographic equipment, "magic lanterns," and slides directed leisure activities, while dictionaries, lesson books, and Bibles informed the mind and Metlakatla's prohibition against alcohol and smoking (although Duncan did permit chewing tobacco) promoted the development of upright, sober, and industrious "Victorian" Metlakatlans. Headman and head chief, Duncan directed operations, writing at one point, "I am acting simply as their Agent—exporting their productions—importing goods for their Store and spending the profits upon village improvements." It was, perhaps, an example of "applied anthropology" before such a term existed.[21]

Duncan's two roles intersected in any number of instances. He frequently complained about the quality of imports, requesting on one occasion that a supplier ought to absorb "at least one half" the cost of one shipment given "the window glass we found smashed nearly as bad as usual—72 panes gone."[22] Even more common were disputes over returns on Metlakatla's furs. Once he threatened to cut ties with London merchants after learning of "simply ridiculous" prices for mink and marten skins.[23] Realistically, though, Metlakatla could ill afford to sacrifice any potential market, so Duncan sometimes resorted to other means. Following a bitterly disappointing relationship with the Portland, Oregon, firm of Glass and Company and its fur broker, J. H. Meyer,[24] Duncan sent the following notice to other brokers, along with a threat to take his case to the newspapers. It began with "To All interested in the Fur Trade," and continued:

> From a village in the Northern part of British Columbia—in the autumn of 1876—a quantity of furs were sent to Mr. J. H. Meyer in San Francisco and by him sold to Messrs. Glass & Co. of this city. The Autumn of 1875 a quantity of furs from the same village were sent to be sold in England. . . . [When compared, the figures] will be enough to show those who have furs to dispose of the necessity of warning their agents (unless they are honest and very smart) to be careful lest they fall into the hands of Messrs. Glass & Co.[25]

Difficulties with suppliers highlighted the fragility of the Metlakatla economy. Although community savings might cover periodic downturns, bad times still meant that native hunters missed expected income, and the store lost vital capital. This, of course, was no academic issue. Export records from September 1863 indicate that individuals realized meager returns for their labors. For one box of fish grease and ten salmon, Quilbahtsap earned just $2.25. He failed to sell a handmade mat. Frank Allen did somewhat better, earning $11.00 for twelve "cakes" of berries, as did Philip Keith, who realized $8.50 for twenty cakes and two beaver skins, and Thomas Eaton, whose parcel of berries, fish grease, and one wolf skin brought $16.12. But others fared much worse. Shillokahtal earned just sixty-two cents for five salmon, and Paul Legaic's three boxes of berries, one parcel of seaweed, two bags of salmon, and a box of grease went unsold.[26]

These figures indicate that Metlakatlans found it difficult to sustain an internal economy purely upon returns from the local bounty. As a consequence, some apparently began exporting Tsimshian cultural "curiosities." As early as 1863, Duncan revealed his intention to "show the Native Paints to Merchants" in Victoria, but returns here were small as well. In one case, just $23 bought a stone bowl, three spoons, one bracelet, and a carved stick, even though "the carved bowl," so Duncan explained to one collector, "belonged to the head chief of the Kithratla tribe." But the trade continued, perhaps because it represented one of the few areas where Metlakatlans could earn a living. In 1879, natives Paul Sebassoh, Tseets, Wailohits, Peter Simpson, Oliver Scott, Neashtohydah, Abraham Lincoln, and Margaret Macdonald sold twenty-one different "curiosities" to Dr. Israel W. Powell, the federal commissioner of Indian affairs for British Columbia, but earned just $146.50. Whether these "curiosities" were of recent manufacture or family heirlooms is not clear, but in either case the market in Tsimshian cultural artifacts was limited indeed.[27]

Fortunately for the Metlakatlans, they did not have to rely completely on the export trade. The Church Missionary Society continued to underwrite at least a portion of mission expenses, and in 1867 Duncan convinced it to do still more. Fifteen hundred dollars raised by the CMS supplemented another $1,000 in accumulated trade profits and financed the construction of a small sawmill. Duncan and Paul Legaic then journeyed to Victoria in March 1867 to purchase the requisite equipment, and assembly began shortly thereafter. By the end of that year a waterwheel, leather belt, and chain powered three saws, and Metlakatla workmen made good use of augers, files, and other new tools. They opened a sash shop a few months later, and while two millwrights from Victoria oversaw construction, native Metlakatlans provided most of the labor to build the mill, earning a total of $166 for their efforts.[28]

Although not as singularly formative a development as construction of the much larger mill on the Menominee Reservation, Metlakatla's plant marked an important departure from prior activities. It also constituted a capital investment in Metlakatla's economy and a commitment to generating jobs as well as earnings—a critical distinction. But while it would be tempting to argue that millwork built on existing native skills in woodworking, and thus was more an elaboration on existing modes of behavior and not a substantial change, closer analysis suggests something a bit more complex. In terms of its pace, organization, and purpose, industrial work was different, and even if Metlakatlans weathered the transition with apparent facility, it is important to remember that this mill, like the Menominee experiment, was designed to do more than simply produce boards out of trees. Both, after all, were expressions of that set of beliefs that regarded industrial education as critical to promoting cultural change. Robert La Follette believed it, as did William Duncan as well as the missionary's longtime friend Bishop Edward Cridge, who observed with evident satisfaction that Metlakatla sawyers, lumberjacks, planers, and shingle makers "devot[ed] themselves to their daily task, rather with the constancy of the English laborer, than, with the fitful disposition of the savage."[29]

But if the sawmill seemed to be promoting changes in native work habits, it was less successful in generating operating profits. Mill records for 1869–70 show revenues of just $255 on 20,000 feet of lumber produced. Although customers included settlers in Tongass, the HMS *Sparrowhawk*, and Clah, who bought 1,150 feet for $17, the nearly $1,000 earned by Metlakatla loggers came primarily as a consequence of village consumption, where, for instance, constructing a new work shed took 14,000 of that 20,000-foot total. The sawmill, in other words, functioned first to satisfy Metlakatla's demand for building materials and enjoyed a steady "subsidy" to do so. Contributions took the form of home-building allowances from the British Columbia government and CMS backing for a number of projects, including a ninety-by-thirty-foot market house, a guest house, and a mission school for which native mill workers produced some 30,000 shingles. Total value of wood and wages for these projects reached $1,160, and while trade profits, tax revenues, and native donations of time and resources were important, it remains unlikely that the community could have financed the construction on it own.[30]

This pattern, of outside contributions supplementing Metlakatla's own economic activity, reached a particularly important milestone in 1871 with a massive church-building project. Beginning in 1870, Duncan began soliciting donations for the construction of a new church, and over the next five years he received nearly $6,000 from the CMS and the affiliated Missionary Leaves Association, while native Metlakatlans contributed another $800, principally by donating blankets and furs to the community store. This allowed work to begin in the summer of 1871, and for the next three years the project consumed large quantities of timber, offered employment to hundreds of Metlakatlans, and thus stimulated the internal economy. Equally significant was the fact that nonnatives played a comparatively minor role. While Duncan paid a Victoria architect $125 for plans and occasionally sought the help of outside contractors, natives did most of the work. Peter Simpson, Robert Allen, Thomas Eaton, and John Tait led groups gathering logs, rafting them to the site, and "squaring" timbers for the foundation, floor joists, and beams. A native known simply as "Jeremy" earned money by lending his skill in sash and window making, and countless other Metlakatlans took on the hard work of leveling the ground and doing everything from hammering nails, cutting clapboards, and shingling the roof to erecting fences, painting the structure, and installing gas lanterns. For all of this, laborers earned $700 in 1871; $1,690 in 1872; $2,108 in 1873; and $2,285 in 1874.[31]

Construction also pushed sawmill capacity to the limit. Along with window frames, the mill churned out nearly 70,000 shingles and, all told, more than 150,000 feet of lumber. To meet the demand for more waterpower, Duncan authorized the blasting of a channel from a nearby lake to the sawmill stream. But the finished product, which opened officially on Christmas Day, 1874, was something to behold. Built at a total cost of $12,000, seating over 1,000 worshipers, and said to be the largest church on the West Coast north of San Francisco, Saint Paul's, with its gabled roof, high windows, arched door frames, and flying buttresses, was an impressive example of Victorian architecture. One visitor described it as "architecturally pretentious," marveling as much over the fact that "it is wholly of native handicraft" as over its "Brussels carpet in the aisles," stained glass, and "pulpit carved by hand." As an example of Metlakatlans' advancing cultural development, Saint Paul's stood as an impressive monument.[32]

Rising above the pulpit, though, were two poles with carved representations of Wolf and Blackfish, Raven and Beaver. The symbolism was obvious and was made more significant by the substitution of Beaver for the more commonly seen Eagle clan crest. Reputedly done at Duncan's request and recognizing the beaver's importance to Metlakatla's economy, this complex combination of symbols, appearing within an Anglican church, illustrated the community's ongoing dialogue between past and future, the ethnogenesis, as it were, of a new Metlakatla "tribe." And so, too, did Metlakatla's new round of home building. Commencing in 1875 and financed by a $1,000 grant from Canada's superintendent of Indian affairs, this construction project transformed Metlakatla's outward appearance through a single house design, uniformly sized lots, and regular streets, sidewalks, and avenues. Accordingly, all new homes were to be two-story structures, 36 by 18 feet, with two rooms on the ground floor and three bedrooms upstairs. Lots measured 120 by 60 feet and were organized ten lots to a block; a road 50 feet in width divided one block from another. But the plan's most striking feature was its accommodation of Tsimshian residence patterns. On each parcel of land stood not one but two homes, arranged, Duncan wrote, so that "a middle room can be built to connect them and be used in common by both families (the two families being of course related)." This "middle room," Duncan continued, "is to have an Indian open fire in it; to answer all the purposes for which the Indians require such a fire; to save their private rooms for themselves; and to afford accommodations to strangers or temporary workers."[33]

Metlakatla also distributed housing grants in characteristic fashion. Upon applying for a plot of land, each prospective builder received credit for $30 in building materials. Of this, $18 went toward purchasing 100 pounds of nails and eight window sashes. What was left over could be used for lumber, doors, locks, and hinges. The program proved a resounding success. From 1875 to 1878, twenty-five Metlakatlans took advantage of the grant, and by 1881, fueled by a second $1,000 contribution, another eighty-eight homes graced the Metlakatla landscape, with twelve more under construction. One observer described Metlakatla as a "well ordered community," with inhabitants occupying "two story shingled and clapboarded dwelling houses of uniform size . . . with three windows and gable ends, and door in front, . . . enclosed flower gardens, and macadamized sidewalks ten feet wide along the entire line of the street."[34]

Just as local construction stimulated the Menominee lumbering industry, this massive home-building project boosted demand for the mill's products, ultimately to where Metlakatlans completed work on an expanded complex in early 1877. True to form, trade profits provided roughly one-half of the $2,000 needed to build and equip the modernized plant, with the remainder coming from the CMS and individual subscriptions. Native contractors earned nearly $1,000 for their work. The new mill increased annual capacity to over 300,000 board feet, and two years later Duncan spent an additional $820 on a planing machine for producing finished lumber. Metlakatlans wasted no time in taking full advantage of the improvements. From just 8,414 board feet sold to native home builders in 1876, consumption jumped to 147,000 feet the next year, and over the next five years cumulative totals surpassed 1.6 million feet. The value of lumber consumed domestically also shot upward, rising from $113 in 1876, to $415 in 1877, to nearly $18,000 for the years 1878–82. The new plant also proved invaluable as a source of wages. During the plant's first six years in operation, native mill workers earned $7,200, and lumberjacks collected another $7,000 for logs cut and transported to Metlakatla.[35]

A small export business also developed as the mill began supplying commercial canneries with lumber for shipping boxes. Exports for 1878 included 9,427 feet of cedar, 2,073 feet of cypress, and 200 feet of pine to a Victoria firm, and 1,220 feet of pine lumber, 1,300 "ends" for boxes, 250 "boxes for salmon," and 800 box "bottoms" to Windsor's Northwestern Commercial Company in nearby Inverness. But revenues remained meager, reaching just $1,320 for 4,897 salmon cases in 1882.[36] Partly a consequence of Duncan's refusal to ship lumber on credit and his refusal to standardize product lines, shortfalls in the export business did not translate into poverty as community projects consumed most of what the mill could produce. In 1876 the government of British Columbia contributed $631.75 toward a new prison. Of this, $240 purchased 16,000 feet of lumber and another $250 went toward wages. By 1878, Metlakatlans had constructed their new mission house, school, and workshop. The school alone took 17,000 feet of lumber, valued at $255, as well as 15,000 shingles, and native workmen earned $500 for their labor. The workshop cost $13,000, of which well over two-thirds went toward wages and materials produced at home; for the mission, native workers earned $630, while the mill supplied nearly 20,000 feet, or $300 worth, of lumber.[37]

None of this should suggest that Metlakatlans were content with an economy where cash was scarce, where debt was common, and where individuals exchanged labor on public projects for necessities. Duncan, too, had more ambitious plans and in March 1870 commenced exploring the possibility of transplanting small-scale manufacturing to Metlakatla. Taking advantage of a visit to England, where he delivered a progress report to the CMS, Duncan spent most of the next eight months interviewing weavers, clog makers, rope makers, and furniture makers and then purchasing a washing machine and dyes, a model loom, and tools and materials to supply prospective craftsmen. On his way home he stopped in San Francisco, where he learned more about weaving and purchased a full-sized loom. Duncan also bought a boiler, pipes, twenty-four feet of India rubber hose, and a press, all supplies for extracting *oolichan* oil in a mechanical process of his own invention. He also brought back to Metlakahtla $320 in "gifts," from a magic lantern and slides to a camera and "fittings," a "homeopathic Chest and Books," a copying letter press, band instruments, and a bottle of eye lotion. Altogether, Duncan spent $680 on supplies and instruction and another $800 on travel and living expenses, but the CMS agreed to absorb the entire amount. It was, apparently, an expression of considerable support.[38]

Returning home to an enthusiastic reception,[39] armed with loom, tools, and implements, and finding willing weavers, clog makers, and rope makers, Duncan now devoted his attention to an expansion of Metlakatla's domestic manufactures. Native craftspeople drew upon existing social and political structures and organized themselves into several "companies" with small budgets and inventories. There were weaving companies for women, and associations of clog makers, rope makers, coopers, and sawyers. These craft companies can be understood as an elaboration of Duncan's plan to use manufacturing as a means toward promoting cultural change, Tsimshian familiarity with cooperative labor, and a clear commitment toward building the community. But domestic industries also proved expensive to initiate and maintain. Between 1871 and 1879, investments neared $6,000 but produced little in the way of cash returns. As "domestic industries," they may have alleviated the strain upon meager finances by substituting locally produced products for imports, but financial records suggest that they broke even, at best.[40]

Metlakatla, in other words, remained a "colonial" economy, dependent both on exporting the natural bounty and on contributions from well-wishers. Although Duncan's records render a complete accounting difficult, donations forwarded through the CMS during the 1870s certainly exceeded $10,000 and may have totaled twice that amount; government grants added at least another $4,000.[41] This was important because Metlakatla consistently registered trade deficits. In 1872, for example, Metlakatla purchased nearly $8,000 worth of supplies through James Englehardt, one of its Victoria contacts. Profits from exports totaled just over $2,000 leaving the CMS to pick up the remainder, which it did. By 1877 this ratio had changed little. In that year imports surpassed $10,000, exports brought in just under $3,000, and the CMS, private individuals, and the Canadian Indian Commission met the difference, with the CMS contributing the most by far. All through the 1870s and into the 1880s, then, Metlakatla operated under a substantial trade deficit, and it was the CMS that made it possible for Duncan to continue importing what he and his followers needed and desired.[42]

To the extent that Metlakatlans freed themselves from diverting scarce resources toward satisfying basic needs, they may have realized a level of material security comparable with that of the Menominees. But Menominees also drew upon annuities, and their lumbering enterprises ultimately generated substantially greater cash returns, and with that a more "dynamic" economy. This dynamism also may account for the development of an entrepreneurial class, which promoted individualistic cultural values that also influenced political behavior. By contrast, there were few true "entrepreneurs" among Metlakatlans of the 1870s and, perhaps more tellingly, little in the way of an overt dialogue over cultural values. To some extent, William Duncan's position as unquestioned head of a community of believers probably softened any comparable discourse, but the structure of the Metlakatla economy may have played a role as well. Stabilized by infusions of capital and operated in a way that minimized distinctions based on wealth, the Metlakatla economy proved less dynamic than its Menominee counterpart but more conducive to social unity. These two factors may have been inseparable.

Even considering the importance of structures unique to Metlakatla, the broader economy also exerted its influence. And here the question remained: What exactly did Metlakatlans have to sell? An attempt to export local marble foundered upon high expenses and lack of markets,[43] while the *oolichan* oil business proved only marginally more successful. A clear example of Metlakatlans' efforts to transform a "traditional" manufacture into something they could market or at least use as a substitute for imports, a potential market for *oolichan* motivated Duncan to purchase equipment for extracting oil during his 1870–71 trip abroad. He also brought a sample of the oil to England, spent $12.50 to have it analyzed, and in 1875 requested that future shipments of oil lamps be of a kind capable of burning native oils. The potential trade in *oolichan* oil, as well as preserved fish, led to the 1876 purchase of "a set of cooper tools," as, he wrote "one of our Indians here is anxious to commence coopering on his own account." Eighty-three dollars bought an adze, a leveler and cross, a rivet set, spokeshaves, a coopers' ax, and several kinds of knives in 1877; another $275 in 1878 outfitted the shop, paid John Sayyea, a nonnative cannery worker and master of odd jobs, it seems, to oversee instruction, and extended loans and store credit to John Tait, James O'Reilly, Sydney Campbell, and Luke Summer, the coopering company. The native barrel makers seem to have had some success, for between 1877 and 1879 they earned over $100 for their labor, and the community realized $400 in sales of oil, grease, and salted fish, some of which found buyers in Honolulu and Sydney.[44]

Markets, however, continued to bedevil Metlakatla. In 1875 Duncan wrote his agent that "we have about 1000 gallons of Oil," on hand but chose to delay shipment "as we are putting it through a [purifying] process I learnt in San Francisco and which I hope will much increase its value." On other occasions he shipped "samples" of native productions, from casks of oil to one "small case of fresh and pure oolichan grease," and watched carefully the ever-fluctuating demand for these goods. When prices were low he complained but seemed never to threaten to withdraw oil from the market as had been his practice with furs. But his characteristic reluctance to ship goods "on speculation" seems to have been well founded, for with at least one shipment he complained that Victoria customers "*Dr. Ash* and *Mr. Langley* have not yet paid for the Oil and Grease sent them." This was a problem, Duncan continued, for "the grease belonged to an Indian and he no doubt wants the money," and he instructed his agent to tell "him I will write to him and remind him."[45]

Through it all, Metlakatlans expressed their civic pride, and perhaps sincere fealty to William Duncan, through their efforts at community development. Between 1876 and 1882, trading profits partially financed an enlarged trade shop and weaving annex, a new well, seawall, and roads, a stove and utensils for making bread, sash shop improvements, and a brick-making company. Native Metlakatlans not only performed virtually all the labor but in 1883 also contributed nearly $400 in cash and goods toward "village improvements." Subscriptions came from all levels of society, from councillors, elders, firemen, and constables to the band and women's organizations, and ranged from goods valued at as little as fifty cents to $6 each from John Tait and David Leask, Metlakatla's longtime secretary and Duncan's most trusted assistant. The fact that these were voluntary contributions, rather than revenues generated through taxation, offers evidence for the proposition that Metlakatlans valued community over individual gain. It also attests to their satisfaction with Duncan's notion of a hierarchically organized society and economy, where few got rich but most had roofs over their heads and enough to eat.[46]

Still, loyalty to community failed to satisfy everyone, or at least not completely. Reacting against receiving store credit instead of cash, one Metlakatlan, so Duncan admitted in 1878, "requested payment [for goods] in cash and seemed both astonished and vexed that we could not comply with their demands."[47] Others apparently seized the opportunity presented by the Hudson's Bay Company outpost at Fort Simpson and began to "shop around" their goods, particularly furs, hoping that competition would bring higher prices. "Our hunters," Duncan wrote in 1879, "are anxious to sell their hunt to me" if the price was right, but he conceded that "there is a strong feeling among the Indians that furs sent through me don't realize as much as if they went through regular traders."[48] This alarmed Duncan, who complained that "Mr. Hale [chief factor] at Fort Simpson seems determined to get all the fur seal," and would succeed unless Metlakatla's buyers "will be able to give us such prices as will enable us to compete with the Company." His only option, at least on this occasion, was to trade upon native Metlakatlans' continuing need for building materials, revealing in 1880 that "many of our people being busy building have been willing to lose something in price in order to get lumber (which I sell very low)."[49]

Some wanted more and attempted to carve out important niches for themselves. Not strictly "entrepreneurs" in the sense that they operated independently of the broader Metlakatla "system," a few sought to escape the cycle of debt and repayment by producing salable goods, establishing contacts beyond the settlement, and sometimes both. Robert Dundas, for example, began working as a fur trapper and trader, but when the sawmill opened he drew upon his credit with the cooperative store to set himself up as a shingle maker and logger. Fred Ridley likewise parlayed profits from hunting to a career in the lumber business, led a company of sash makers, and used his skills to emerge as Metlakatla's principal supplier of building materials. In 1878 he produced 60 window sashes, which he then sold for $45, and in the following year earned $84 on sales of 108 sashes. Ridley also employed two assistants, kept the mill busy filling his orders, and even had contacts as far away as Victoria. Others took advantage of different aspects of Metlakatla's expanding economy. Roger Pearson and Henry Ridley led companies of fur hunters and fishermen and made considerable profits in what remained Metlakatla's principal export. By 1882 Ridley's eight-man fishing company sold $215 worth of salmon; two years later he added three more employees and recorded $644 in sales. He also doubled as a semi-independent trader and in 1877 purchased $944 worth of goods from the store, products he then resold to surrounding communities. Echoing the pattern exhibited by Mitchell Chickeney, the Menominee storekeeper who parlayed family connections into a vibrant business, James Rudland, the mixed-blood son of Metlakatla's first storekeeper William Rudland, followed in his father's footsteps and carved out an important position for himself as a trader and manager of the cooperative store. By 1883 he was earning $10 per week and was responsible for nearly $1,000 worth of supplies.[50]

Native Metlakatlans also proved active and aggressive traders. Working in units often composed of related individuals, native traders forged contacts with surrounding villages and succeeded in large part because they combined access to valuable manufactured goods with relationships that often predated Duncan's arrival. So active were Metlakatla's traders that they often ran afoul of military and customs authorities in Alaska. In 1876 the acting deputy collector and inspector of the United States Customs Service in Sitka complained that "Mr. Duncan makes a business of sending goods to Alaska" and had been "smuggling goods in Chilcat and other places in Alaska for a great number of years." In response, Washington sent a delegation to investigate the charges, and while admitting that Duncan "may not have been directly interested pecuniarily in the success of the venture," the report of the delegation added that it could not "be disputed that these Indians would not have departed upon this expedition with canoes heavily laden without Mr. Duncan being cognizant of the whole transaction."[51] The commissioners also expressed concern that traders stood to benefit from illegally supplying local potlatches. "In October 1879," they contended,

> there is to be given in the Chilcat territory a grand potlatch. Preparations for it will have consumed two years by the time it is had. Large quantities of rich and valuable furs and peltries of all kinds will be traded and given away. The usual amount of Hoochenoo [an alcoholic drink] will be consumed. This will be a rich field for the Metlacatlah [sic] Indians to work in, and unless we have a revenue-cutter there at this time, the coast will be swarming with Hudson's Bay blankets and other foreign goods.[52]

In order to protect "the Chilcat trade [which is] too valuable to permit it to be the source of clandestine importations [*sic*] from a foreign province," the commissioners recommended forcing Duncan either "to enter his goods at our custom-houses, and prevent his Indians from a repetition of these offences," or "else there will be some seizures, and perhaps bloodshed, in Alaskan waters."[53]

While it is not clear how, or if, Duncan responded to these charges, the concern expressed by American authorities indicates that Metlakatla was rapidly becoming a principal nexus of economic activity in the region. Fueled by subsidies and well-established trading contacts, Metlakatla likely boasted the most stable economy in the region and this produced a unique opportunity to dominate local commerce. Native traders held an edge over whites when it came to contacts with local tribes, and access to large quantities of manufactured goods simply added to this disparity. Moreover, full inventories and their apparent wealth enhanced the stature of Metlakatla merchants among other natives. Indeed, by the late 1870s and into the next decade, Metlakatlans were selling not just goods but an entire lifestyle. The fact that natives benefited from Duncan's program was all the proof some needed that Metlakatla represented an attractive choice for the future, one that combined material benefits with independence from whites.

Nowhere was this combination of relative wealth and apparent prosperity more obvious than in the community's relationship with the several associated missions that sprang up along the rivers and coastline of western British Columbia. From the earliest days of Metlakatla, Duncan had hoped to spread his message among the various Tsimshian groups farther upstream, and from 1867 he worked to establish missionary outposts at Kincolith on the Nass River, on the forks of the Skeena River at Ankitlast and Aiyansh, and even among the Haidas at Massett and the Kwakiutls at Fort Rupert. Like Metlakatla, these "satellite missions" had strict rules of behavior, organized natives into companies, were funded and staffed by the CMS, and combined religious instruction with training in material pursuits. Significantly, Duncan dominated operations in each mission, including the appointment of missionaries and the management of financial affairs. Indeed, for most of this period missionaries stationed at these remote outposts received compensation through Metlakatla and traded native-produced furs and fish through Duncan's store, for which they received manufactured goods or a line of credit.[54]

Association with outlying districts proved beneficial to the new missions, but particularly to Metlakatla, which profited from access to natural resources outside its borders as well as markets for its goods. Even more significant, though, was the fact that establishing and maintaining these satellites provided certain Metlakatlans with opportunities for wealth and status. Samuel Pelham, leader of the scarlet company, chief of the constable corps, and onetime first mate on the schooner *Carolena*, landed an appointment as native teacher in Kincolith. In addition to earning a salary of ten dollars per week for the time spent away from home, Pelham supplemented his income by transporting men and supplies between the two missions. His also parleyed his contacts into an appointment as district constable for the provincial government, a position that required him to escort prisoners to trial, and for this he earned an additional four dollars per week. Edward Mather, also a constable, likewise earned four dollars per week at Kincolith while extending his trading activities northward to Skidgate. Pelham and Mather, along with others, found that contacts abroad brought them not only additional money but also status back home, as both rose from constables to councillors while serving missions abroad.[55]

Of those who found avenues for advancement through outside contacts, John Tait and David Leask stand out. A Gispaxlo'ots, Tait rose from constable to councillor while earning a living as a cooper, fur seal hunter, and trader. Perhaps seeking to capitalize on the Metlakatlan's far-flung associations, as well as his evident interest in embracing community values in 1876, Duncan dispatched Tait to Fort Rupert, where he was to forge relationships with Kwakiutl chiefs. Paid $20 for his service, Tait returned with two leaders, and the journey led to the creation of the Fort Rupert "satellite" the next year. Not formally stationed among the Kwakiutls, Tait nevertheless made frequent visits as an assistant and teacher and earned $10 per month while away from home. More important, Tait combined his missionary duties with business and by 1878 was earning over $400 per year, most of this as a trader.[56]

David Leask enjoyed an even more diverse career. One of Duncan's first students in Fort Simpson, the mixed-blood Gitlaan emigrated to Metlakatla in 1862; his many ventures there included marble prospecting, coopering, fishing, trading, teaching, and, of course, village administration. By the early 1870s Leask was purchasing furs from natives, exchanging them for goods from the Metlakatla store, and then transporting these products abroad for resale. These shipments could be substantial indeed: one manifest from 1877 records a hefty return of $562 from "Furs Assorted" and an accumulation of capital to purchase a small boat, hire Tait and two other assistants, and commence trading with the Hudson's Bay Company directly. Leask also rose from constable to councillor and finally to village elder, becoming, in effect, Duncan's principal "lieutenant" for the administration of Metlakatla's internal affairs. As secretary-treasurer for the village council, he earned $6 per week and was responsible for collecting taxes and assigning tasks to those citizens who pledged labor in lieu of cash or in-kind payments. He also managed Metlakatla's community business during Duncan's periodic absences.[57]

David Leask and family. (NA-APR, RG200, Archives Box 74, Print 195)

In 1878, perhaps drawing upon the success of Tait's mission and most certainly as a demonstration of his distinguished position, Duncan called upon Leask to assist the Reverend W. H. Collison in establishing a mission among the Haidas at Massett, on the Queen Charlotte Islands. Leask seems to have relished the opportunity and over the next few years earned $480 per year as a native teacher. This was a considerable sum, second only to Duncan's annual salary among Metlakatlans, and, together with profits from his trading ventures, probably made him the wealthiest native in the village. And the mission proved successful. Writing in 1879 that "many of the people here have manifested a desire to know and learn the truth," Leask related the support of Haida chiefs Edenshew and Weeah, who accompanied him, via a convoy of canoes, to several villages. The chiefs "were very kind to me," Leask wrote to Duncan, "and tried to help us in any way they could in explaining to others the meaning of the scriptures." Leask also reported that, just as Tsimshians once abandoned their homes for the security of Metlakatla, some Haidas now viewed Massett similarly. "Leaving their villages," he wrote with evident satisfaction, several Haidas now "came to live with us for the 'Gospel's sake.'"[58]

If Leask's mission shows Duncan simultaneously rewarding a trusted assistant and acting upon Henry Venn's ideas regarding native preachers, it also suggests a purposeful extension of Metlakatla's influence, where commercial motivations were never far from the surface. As with other satellite missions, the Metlakatla store financed efforts at Massett, and Leask himself counseled against relying on Hudson's Bay Company merchants. His 1879 evaluation, "I find every thing dear in prices," probably amounted to an accurate representation of the situation, but it was a powerful reminder of Metlakatla's own experiences with company merchants, and perhaps even more. It is, after all, possible to conclude that Metlakatlans, themselves beneficiaries of financial largesse from abroad, sought to share these benefits with outsiders while establishing their community as the center of regional commerce. In a pattern roughly approximating that of Gispaxlo'ots efforts of an earlier generation, Metlakatlans may have perceived opportunity in changed circumstances. After all, the store not only financed spreading the gospel but also generated new customers, at least potentially. Admittedly speculative, this conclusion corresponds with other evidence where native Metlakatlans actively, and aggressively, pursued trading opportunities, transforming their own subsidized economy into a machine for extending influence. Duncan suggested as much, for while he recommended Leask as "the most qualified native we have" to direct Massett operations, he also feared that since his missionary also was "engaged in industrial enterprises," he might better serve as Collison's assistant rather than directing the mission himself, a position Leask seems to have desired.[59]

Beyond communications from Massett, Leask's letters from 1879–81 also reveal something of the Metlakatla economy. Directing the community during one of Duncan's periodic absences, Leask forwarded several large requisitions, reporting "very brisk" sales as "many outsiders came to trade." Writing on another occasion that "you [Duncan] will be astonished to see what a heavy requisition we sent," Leask detailed a variety of decisions, from supplying hunters and fishermen "on credit," to returning a shipment of boots of inferior quality, to allocating $27.75 for a "marriage feast." Metlakatlans, he reported in 1879, "are busy at their houses," and all was well. Or at least partly so. Despite a shipment of 20,000 logs to the Hudson's Bay Company in Fort Simpson, lumbermen experienced considerable difficulties, as bad weather cost "Roderic & Co." its raft and 120 logs, with similar misfortune afflicting "Alfred Aucland & Co." and "R. Dundas & Co." Sash shop production suffered as well, and Leask was forced to purchase windows from abroad, while "Frederic," a Metlakatla millworker, "is not commenc[ing] making them." More troubling was Metlakatla's seeming inability to generate jobs or to pay market price for furs and fish. "We are still giving $62\frac{1}{2}$ for a full size [deer] hide," he reported in 1880, while competitors offered "75 [cents] to $1.00 which we cannot afford."[60]

Low prices for furs were not the only problem. Following the 1876 opening of the Inverness cannery, the first Skeena River operation, Metlakatla found itself in competition with better-funded operations that threatened to draw away both fish and workers. This concerned William Duncan on at least two counts. For one, he feared that contact with whites, and ever-increasing numbers of Asian workers, would undo the moral and spiritual training he had worked so hard to instill. He especially objected to demands that Metlakatlans break the Sabbath by working on Sundays. When native workers refused, cannery managers turned to Chinese laborers. Duncan condemned the dismissals as "unreasonable" and begged managers "to seriously take to heart the awful responsibility which rests upon you as manager of the cannery when you are either promoting or permitting others in your employ to ignore the plain command of God himself." He also worried that opportunities for outside employment might undermine Metlakatla's economic base. "The canneries at Skeena Mouth are prospering," he wrote early in 1881, but their very success "threaten[s] to draw our natives away from permanent settlements" like Metlakahtla.[61]

Leask offered a similar evaluation. Calling upon Duncan to purchase "salmon twine," he observed that Metlakatla fishermen were "very anxious to have the twine," which "the canneries would not let them have unless they make arrangements to be supplied with salmon caught by the twine." But if Metlakatlans felt squeezed by the presence of canneries, they also searched for remedies that, significantly, held out the prospect for strengthening the local economy and keeping people home. "The people are still talking of starting a small cannery for themselves," began one letter to Duncan, "so please if you have time enquire what the prices of materials required for the business, also if silver salmon will sell as the big salmon." Duncan had proposed just such a measure as early as 1877. Since "exploitation of salmon" was "bidding to become an important industry in this Province, and as salmon abounds in the neighborhood of Metlakatla, and the preparing it for the market is . . . within the range of Indian skills to manage," he thought of operating a cannery. "I propose (God willing) to start the business for the benefit of our settlement." Five years later, and with a loan of $3,000 from his old friend John Macdonald, Duncan realized this dream. It proved at least a partial antidote to Metlakatla's financial worries, and natives gravitated toward this opportunity in greater numbers than they had to any others.[62]

The activities of Leask and Tait, as well as those of Samuel Pelham, Edward Mather, and Henry and Fred Ridley, illustrate the degree to which natives at Metlakatla had embraced the forms and substance of changes demanded by Duncan. All were at least nominal, if not devout, Christians, and they, like many of their brothers and sisters, had come to understand and take advantage of many of the opportunities presented by Duncan's emphasis on the material accoutrements of Anglo-Canadian

General view of Metlakatla, British Columbia, showing (left to right) cannery, wharf, rows of houses, market house. (NA-APR, RG200, Archival Photograph Album 1, Print 63, page 3)

civilization. Yet while Duncan intended to use prosperity to reinforce religious conversion, some native Metlakatlans may have reversed the equation and gravitated more to commerce than to Christianity. Less than independent entrepreneurs, but more than passive receptors of Duncan's message, Metlakatlans influenced the development of their community and indeed the course of regional intercultural interactions. In doing so, they relied upon Tsimshian values even as many apparently became hardworking, God-fearing laborers as Duncan had wished. If it is possible to discern motivations from scattered pieces of evidence, we can conclude that Leask, Tait, and their brothers and sisters in Metlakatla did not aim toward assimilation with the growing nonnative communities in northern British Columbia but instead sought to create a viable, self-sustaining village of their own. Indeed, one of the more remarkable features of Metlakatla by 1880 was the development of a distinctive sense of "identity" among community members. Neither Anglo-Canadian nor Tsimshian, Metlakatlans came to see themselves as something else, and this evolution of consciousness may have operated in two directions, altering Duncan's self-perceptions as well as those of natives. It is here that the relationship between social reform and economic development reveals itself as complex, reciprocal, and dynamic. Less a surrender to the inexorable forces of the white man's ways than a practical means for channeling those changes toward new ends, Metlakatla was, it seems, an example of "ethnogenesis."

But storm clouds remained. Metlakatla's ability to generate the kinds of employment that fueled community development remained in question, particularly as we understand the continuing, and critical, role played by outside contributions. This would prove particularly problematic during the 1880s. Early in that decade, the CMS turned against Duncan in a bitter contest that ultimately ended in a painful severing of the thirty-year-old relationship. Local whites and the governments of British Columbia and Canada likewise found him a troublesome neighbor, and Duncan and his followers battled them as well. After nearly a decade of great difficulties, the missionary finally turned away from his countrymen altogether and, with most of the native Metlakatlans joining him, abandoned the community they had worked so hard to build, re-created their "exodus" of a generation before, and took on the difficult task of renewing their community, and their dream, in Alaska.

CHAPTER EIGHT

Outlines of a Metlakatla Identity

In 1887, looking out upon "small houses, mostly log huts" in New Metlakatla, Alaska, David Leask wrote a heartfelt letter to "Christian Friends" in Philadelphia. Expressing his appreciation for "the sympathy and kindness of the American people to us in our trouble about our land," Leask was passing along the sentiments of the 800 or so Metlakatlans who, just weeks earlier, had packed up their belongings, loaded them into several canoes, and braved the seventy-mile ocean journey northwest, to begin anew in a place known as Annette Island, the southernmost outpost of the United States territory of Alaska. Christening their town as "new" Metlakatla revealed as well the natives' intention to re-create their earlier accomplishments. But it was no easy matter, as Leask readily revealed. "Only [a] few of us have brought over the material of the dwelling houses," he wrote, "and a great number of buildings are still left, including the Church, Saw-mill, Village Hall, Cannery, Guest House, etc. etc." These structures, he made certain to point out, "were built without cost to the British Government or the Church Missionary Society," but even as the structures were "seized and taken from us," Metlakatlans chose "to suffer loss and persecution to avoid further trouble." He now asked for mercy from God and continued assistance from "true christian [*sic*] hearts who feel for our loss."[1]

Leask's letter, written while William Duncan visited churchmen and politicians in the United States, represented another chapter in the Metlakatlans' convoluted tale, a strikingly unfortunate replication of their 1862 migration from Fort Simpson. Dedication to William Duncan the person and to the dream that had become Metlakatla had combined in such a way that natives chose emigration over home and hearth (not to mention church, sawmill, and workshops) when British Columbia no longer afforded them the safety and security they so cherished. Migration also revealed that to be "Metlakatlans" now distinguished them from their neighbors, native and nonnative, if not by ethnicity then certainly by attachment to their missionary and the community all had played a role in constructing. And a critical component of this identity was economic change, perhaps what later generations of scholars and politicians would call economic development. It is here as well that the parallel with Menominees appears, even as we acknowledge the absence of a singular figure like William Duncan in northeastern Wisconsin. That is, as Indian

Excursion steamers docking at Metlakatla, Alaska, with cannery at center. (NA-APR, RG200, Archival Photograph Album 1, Print 130, page 9)

peoples adapted to economic change, producing in these two cases enterprises that generated income and home-based employment prospects, they also came, in one way or another, to equate cultural survival with material security. An expression perhaps of the twentieth-century phenomenon where, in Frederick Hoxie's apt phrasing, Indians transformed reservations from prisons to homelands, Menominees, Metlakatlans, and other peoples across North America not only recognized but also produced a connection between cultural survival and material security that was both innovative and respectful of fundamental values. In these cases, certainly, we can detect evidence for the conclusion that *adaptation* constitutes a "traditional" Indian value.

Measuring the mechanics and complexity of cultural adaptation is, of course, more interesting to contemporary ethnohistorians than it was to Metlakatlans of a century ago. In the years leading up to the second Metlakatla exodus, William Duncan directed his energies toward developing a local economy sufficiently vibrant and diverse to keep natives close to home. Jobs were one thing, but wages alone scarcely guaranteed community survival. Skilled native workers might just as readily gravitate toward commercial operations, and in this sense Metlakatla stood to fuel its own demise by training laborers only to send them away. Despite his interest in promoting cultural transformation, William Duncan apparently had little interest in seeing Metlakatla become a temporary way station toward full assimilation. Judging from their considerable sacrifice and subsequent determination to pull up stakes for Alaska, native Metlakatlans shared this more expansive view of the community and its future. This offers another important link to the Menominee situation, where the objective lay not so much in creating skilled lumbermen capable of surviving in a broader commercial world as in promoting reservation economic development that preserved the community by providing jobs close to home.

Keeping Metlakatla natives close to home proved no simple matter. With new canneries opening along the Skeena and Nass Rivers came new possibilities for employment, and natives from throughout the region left their villages for part-time or seasonal work either in the canneries themselves or as suppliers of fish. As one recent study shows, natives, and women in particular, worked in British Columbia's canneries in numbers second only to Chinese immigrants, and this pattern continued up through the beginning of the twentieth century. Metlakatla's financial records indicate as much. In 1880–81, twenty-four Metlakatlans, led by Fred Verney, Theodore Dundas, Frank Allen, and Thomas Booth, worked for the Northwestern Commercial Company in Inverness, British Columbia. Although Metlakatla's sawmill generated employment in part by selling finished planks to that cannery, jobs were comparatively few, averaging about twenty-five per year.[2]

In response, Duncan moved in 1881 to request a $5,000 loan from the Canadian government to finance a salmon cannery of their own. But despite arguing that "the Indians . . . must have industries or they will retrograde" and promising to employ "hundreds of Indians," he was rebuffed and then turned to more tried-and-true methods for securing capital.[3] To a $3,500 loan from his old friend Senator W. J. Macdonald, he added another $1,000 from a Royal Navy captain and transferred a portion of profits from the community store. He also convinced forty-eight native Metlakatlans to purchase "shares" at $100 each (although they borrowed one-half the money from Duncan and agreed to repay the loan at 10 percent interest) and reorganized the store as a joint-stock company selling shares to natives, once again on credit.[4] By 1884, seventy-seven Metlakatlans had purchased shares in the new store. Most of these shares were valued at $100, although David Leask and Robert Hewson each pledged $1,000. All told, natives raised, or promised to contribute, another $9,200, and, combined with donations from outsiders, funding approached $18,000 to complete the 14,000-square-foot cannery and purchase its machinery and some supplies.[5]

Canning commenced in early spring of 1884, and in that first year seventy-five women and seventy-six men, all organized into six "corps," produced nearly 5,000 cases of salmon. Each case contained four dozen one-pound tins, virtually all of which went to markets in England. Typically, men undertook the heavy work of loading and unloading the fish, running the soldering machine, and readying the cases for export. They also sold fish to the cannery. On the other hand, while some women utilized their skills in cleaning and preparing the fish, most affixed labels to finished cans or loaded tins into wooden trays for export. For this work, women earned rather meager wages: Henrietta Allen earned just $19.18 for filling 959 trays and $5.88 for labeling cans in 1882, and Marcia Booth earned the paltry sum of $10.68. This division of labor drew upon Tsimshians' customary division of labor along gender lines, replicated women's roles in commercial canneries, and corresponded with Duncan's expectations for labor performed by "civilized," if distinctly lower-class, women.[6]

Buoyed by the results of that first year, Duncan again approached Indian superintendent Powell about a loan. Reminding him that it is "painful to see a community of Indians like the Metlakahtlans unable to take up industries at their very doors, for which they are adapted & competent to manage, all because they have not the means to purchase the needful appliances," he asked for $20,000.[7] Rebuffed for a second time, Metlakatlans forged ahead anyway, exploring prospects for hiring an experienced manager and purchasing a soldering machine from a defunct Frazer River cannery. Meanwhile, Duncan corresponded with the manager of the nearby Inverness cannery regarding customary wages. Understanding that the prevailing rates were $30 per month for Indian fishermen on the Skeena and $1 per day for cannery workers, Duncan suggested advancing wages for fishermen to $35. "It is to be remembered," he wrote, "that fishermen have but a *short season* compared to other workmen, nor have they any chance of *making overtime* during their short season as others have." Finally, he began investigating the market for canned clams after learning that "the Alert Bay Cannery found a ready sale for some they put up."[8]

By the end of the 1884 season, operations seemed to be progressing, though not without a few setbacks. Obtaining suitable tin plate for cans was a problem, and defective materials caused spoilage of some 100 cases shipped in late 1884. Sparks from a furnace ignited part of the cannery floor in May 1884, but the damage was minimal and was covered by insurance. Even so, Duncan reported "unusually good" salmon runs, and Metlakatla's cannery workers turned out 8,300 cases, which, while falling short of the hoped-for 10,000 cases, still amounted to 18 percent of the total regional pack. In addition, an operation run by David Leask shipped a few barrels of salted salmon and 35 cases of canned clams. Most went to brokers in England, although Duncan authorized "cautious inquiry" into the Canadian and Australian markets, the latter provided that customs rates in Sydney were lower than those charged for salt salmon in previous years.[9]

Metlakatla fishermen delivering salmon to the cannery. (NA-APR, RG200, Archival Photograph Album 3, print 704, page 21)

Although William Duncan managed the operation, native Metlakat-lans performed virtually all the labor, and the cannery represented the community's most promising avenue toward economic development to date. Fishermen found stable, if seasonal, employment, and in 1884 twelve boats, working a total of seventy days, earned nearly $2,400 in wages on fish valued at $4,975.[10] As in previous commercial activities at Metlakatla, individual companies were organized around family ties. Both Henry and Archie Ridley operated fishing "companies." In 1884 Henry's company sold $174 worth of salmon and employed eleven fish-ermen as well as several women, including his wife, Noas Louise, who mended nets. Fishermen William Alford, Alfred Aucland, Jacob Bolton, and Matthias Simpson earned anywhere from $75 to over $200 for a sea-son's work "fetching fish," and Paul Legaic, perhaps relying on family prerogatives to fishing stations, earned the comparatively handsome sum of $158.50 in July 1883.[11] Cannery wages stood at $1 per week, plus over-time, and Ed Mather cleared $200 during the busy season, from early June to early September 1885.[12]

Even as fishing and cannery work added substantially to opportuni-ties for gainful employment, the new industry did little to alter the essen-tial pattern of Metlakatla financial life. Cannery workers rarely earned cash, and most simply paid with their labor for supplies already purchased on credit. Duncan conceded as much, writing that of the impressive sum of $21,061.26 in wages for 1884 (in all activities), Metlakatlans actually earned "goods" rather than cash.[13] This was especially the case with regard to fishermen. The cooperative store advanced them nets, twine, and virtually all other supplies, while anglers repaid their obligations with salmon, labor, or both. What is more, women appear to have been particularly disadvantaged. While some managed their own accounts, others, like Lucy and Rebecca Auriol, found their cannery wages subject to a man's discretion. Although they worked, their wages were deposited in Solomon Auriol's account, and thus were under the discretion of a "responsible" male.[14]

At the same time, others focused their energies on fur hunting, trading, and work in the store or on community products, and cannery labor supplemented rather than replaced these occupations. Timothy Buxton exemplified what was a common pattern when in 1882 he earned $3.75 in unspecified "wages," $57.25 selling charcoal and cordwood, $22.50 at the cannery, and $7.50 for soldering. Will Morgan earned substantially more from trading furs than working as a fisherman; Edward Achtseay cleared only $4.00 as a cannery worker in 1885 but made substantially more money selling furs and prospecting for gold; and Robert Hewson fished, canned salmon, sold furs, and freighted lumber.[15] Once again, David Leask stood alone among Metlakatla businessmen. He ran a salmon salting business, bought and sold furs, operated a trading business that grossed over $1,000 annually, and even established a personal account with Duncan's Victoria agents.[16] Paul Legaic operated in a similar fashion although on a smaller scale.[17] Finally, while the cannery expanded the range of employment opportunities, it did little to alter that hierarchical, tightly controlled combination of commerce and social control so characteristic of Metlakatla.

Metlakatla, of course, remained a complicated place, its mission characterized as much by social reform as by economic development, with William Duncan technically serving at the pleasure of the Church Missionary Society. Whether Duncan ever considered himself subject to CMS oversight remains an open question, but by the 1870s he clearly had developed a deep antipathy toward what he considered outside "interference." This was not much more than a theoretical problem for more than fifteen years, but in 1879 Anglican authorities dispatched the Reverend William Ridley to Metlakatla—headquarters, so they said, for the new Bishopric of Caledonia (a region encompassing north coastal British Columbia). Shortly thereafter, Ridley submitted a scathing denunciation of Duncan's work. Exclaiming "What hath God wrought!" Ridley described a strange place where "*one strong will is supreme,*" where all Metlakatlans "are expected to attend the public services," and where policemen, "in uniform," reminded all "that loitering during service hours is against proper civil order." While the new bishop conceded great progress in secular matters, he nevertheless expressed alarm at Duncan's refusal to hold Bible classes or to translate Scriptures into Tsimshian, even though few Metlakatlans possessed more than a rudimentary command of English. It appeared that Duncan had given the mission over to business concerns and established himself as supreme leader. "To resist," Ridley concluded, "every Indian feels, would be as impossible as to stop the tides."[18]

Ridley's charges were not particularly novel, as earlier visitors had also noticed Duncan's autocratic tendencies and idiosyncratic methods, but this report raised the stakes to where it became a matter of honor, a contest between missionary and church—at least in Duncan's mind. Mistrustful of High Church Tractarians whom he believed had seized control of the Anglican hierarchy and, following Henry Venn's 1872 retirement, his own missionary society, Duncan reacted by closing Metlakatla's doors, or at least trying to. In 1877 he abruptly canceled religious services meant to commemorate the visiting Bishop George Hills. What followed was an official Anglican inquiry headed by the Reverend William Bompass, bishop of Athabasca. With language that anticipated Ridley's, Bompass discovered a shocking absence of religious instruction, which he proposed to remedy by ordaining William Collison, head of the Massett mission and one of Duncan's assistants. Collison was asked to leave the Haida station and move to Metlakatla.[19]

This just inflamed Duncan's suspicions, reminding him of a prior move to ordain another protégé, Robert Tomlinson. Although Tomlinson, under heavy lobbying from Duncan, refused, the fact remained that Metlakatla was operating outside conventional church standards. Nowhere was this more evident than in Duncan's refusal to administer the holy sacraments. Rooted in his determination to avoid pressing Tsimshians too far, or too fast, persisting with this truncated form of Christianity now appeared—to church officials—as unnecessary and perhaps damaging. When Duncan explained his position, he suggested that Indians still were not ready, that they might confuse the sacraments with cannibalism. For evidence, he contrasted Metlakatla with Methodist Thomas Crosby's mission at Fort Simpson. Crosby, so Duncan claimed, "did not know (perhaps he did not care to know) that the poor Indians were seeking baptisms from his hand to act as a charm for their bodily preservation."[20] He also recalled an 1877 outbreak of religious "fanaticism" in Metlakatla. Trouble began while Duncan was away in Victoria on business, leaving the mission in the hands of the Reverend A. J. Hall, a minister recently assigned to him as an assistant. While there, Duncan received word of "a great religious excitement [then] in progress." Hall, it seems, had delivered "very passionate addresses" to the native parishioners, and, as Duncan reported, "the Indians quickly caught the excitement & soon a fire raged which defied all control." Natives began hearing strange "murmurings," a group of girls claimed that they had seen the "cross of Jesus," and soon many were relating dreams and waking experiences in which they claimed "that the Spirit of God had visited the Church and that the voice they had heard was His voice." A group then took off for Fort Simpson, where they retold their experiences to local natives who "readily accepted the delusion and soon imparted it with fresh vigor." Even Hall claimed that the experience was, in fact, "'the work of the Lord.'"[21]

Duncan rushed home to find that "terrible delusions had seized the people and a fanaticism had resulted which threatened to disorganize the whole mission." To his dismay, he also discovered that of the ten native councillors, "four of them had gone far astray," and two were "somewhat to blame." Determined to halt the movement, Duncan summoned 300 men and condemned their actions in the strongest terms. Although he found "some resistance" to his efforts, including "six of the most painful hours of my life with four of the five leaders of the 'delusion,'" the missionary ultimately succeeded in shaming the Metlakatlans and convincing them to renounce what they had seen and heard.[22]

For Duncan, the incident had far-reaching consequences. It left him convinced that, while Hall's "heart" was right, lack of experience with natives had rendered his judgment "far from sober." Indeed, Duncan claimed "that it is to his premature ordination [that] Mr. Hall's bold conduct is attributable," recommending that the young missionary be sent away. The incident also damaged his confidence in native followers, confirming "that I was not mistaken in representing to you the necessity of still regarding this people" as "children in the Gospel." Duncan also argued, perhaps with some sadness, that "I had overrated the strength of the Native Elders and teachers." In the end, this "terrible" incident convinced Duncan of the rightness of his approach, the danger in trusting his mission to conventionally trained preachers, and the necessity of ruling over his followers with a stern hand. It was an experience that greatly influenced his reaction to Ridley's arrival.[23]

But what of native Metlakatlans? Did embracing enthusiastic religion indicate a susceptibility to "emotional" Christianity or frustration with Metlakatla's straight-laced lifestyle? Were some Metlakatlans casting about for a different kind of leadership? This is difficult to determine, but there are scant indications that the incident damaged relations between missionary and most Metlakatlans. In fact, following the official severing of ties between Duncan and the CMS, a painful "rupture" that reached its final stage in 1882, the vast majority of native Metlakatlans rallied to their missionary's side.[24] Informed of the ecclesiastical breach, a gathering of seven Metlakatla church elders called a general council of adult males to whom Duncan asked "what they wished me to do." Paul Legaic remembered the proceedings this way:

> In the evening we had a meeting in the guest house, on the beach. . . . [Duncan] told us that he had been dismissed, and remarked to us that he did not want to press anything on us, he wanted to leave the matter entirely to us, and that . . . he was going to leave Metlakatlah entirely, unless we wanted him to stay. Immediately after Mr. Duncan left, the people talked, and we considered it amongst ourselves, and came to this conclusion: We bid him to stay, as he had done such good work ever since he was a young man, up to the present time. We all agreed the people of Metlakatlah said he should not go, but he will stay.[25]

To Duncan the message was a clear triumph: "In the face of such proceedings and declarations what could I answer them . . . how could I dare to oppose the earnest and unanimous voice of the people begging me to remain?"[26]

Following that meeting, Duncan's allies demonstrated their support in other ways. With Ridley summoned back to England to report on the situation, Metlakatlans moved Duncan from the rectory to a new house and boarded up the entrance to the church. Duncan also secured legal opinion supporting his contention that Metlakatlans held title to structures located on "Mission Point," a two-acre tract also claimed by the CMS. These buildings included the store, guest house, and marketplace. A welcome development, certainly, the opinion still failed to address the status of Metlakatla's remaining five acres, a "reserve" established in 1864, and the location of most homes and the community church. Although the parcels were distinct in a legal sense, Metlakatlans nevertheless assumed them to be under community control and therefore outside the authority of church, province, and Dominion. Duncan was responsible for this misperception, for, as he admitted later, he had never revealed the historical basis for conflicting claims.[27]

In any event, when Ridley returned in the spring of 1882, he found nine-tenths of the community behind Duncan. Prominent defenders included David Leask, John Tait, Robert Hewson, and Paul Legaic, individuals united by the vigor with which they seized the opportunities presented by Metlakatla's peculiar political and economic arrangements. Entrepreneurs, perhaps, members of "Duncan's Party" also seem to have benefited from the missionary's efforts to reduce the influence of traditional leaders. Legaic, of course, does not fit this characterization, but even he had severed ties with house and community, and his story, along with those of Leask, Tait, and Hewson, suggests that influence flowed toward those who did as Duncan expected and were loyal to him personally. On the other hand, it appears that Ridley's more ardent supporters were a group of well-born (in the Tsimshian sense), generally elderly, men, individuals who may have resented the growing influence of men like Leask and Tait. Duncan certainly interpreted it this way as he wrote, "The first intimation of any dissension that I heard of was three or four chief men who had been offended because they were not made as much of as the elders of the church."[28] In an interesting parallel to a situation that developed among the Menominees, then, age and cultural perspective constituted social and political "fault lines," to which we might add adaptation (or resistance) to economic and social change.

But just as it would be a mistake to produce a static "dichotomy" for Menominees, where progressives embraced economic change and so-called traditionalists opposed it, the Metlakatla situation was similarly complex. There is little evidence that Ridley's followers rejected the substance of Metlakatla's reforms. Rather, men like Moses Venn, Matthiew Aucland, and Samuel Pelham supported the ongoing transformations but objected, it seems, to Duncan's autocratic tendencies. For Samuel Pelham, the onetime trusted captain of the constable corps, a clue to Duncan's true designs lay in the circumstances surrounding the dissolution of ties with the CMS. Alarmed when "Mr. Duncan informed us that the Church of England was hand in hand with the devil" and that " 'the Bishop will take this church,' " Pelham left the meeting convinced "that Mr. Duncan was speaking falsely, and that it was all his own make up." In other words, the issue was whether Metlakatlans should be loyal to person or process, an important distinction by 1882.[29]

But a majority of Metlakatlans still objected to Ridley's presence, and in late November 1882 the native council moved to prevent him from carrying out his intention to turn the schoolhouse into a rival church. To this end, the council posted notices on all public buildings. Addressed to "the Agents of the Church Missionary Society now residing on a piece of land at Metlakahtla," the petition promised not to "allow two churches on our reserve" and declared the council's "intention to remove at once all the buildings belonging to and for the use of our village, from the ground belonging to the Church Missionary Society." These proved no idle threats as Duncan's supporters then threatened, so the bishop claimed, "to cleave his [Collison's] head—to cut it in two" and converged upon the store, market, and guest houses, where they proceeded to empty the buildings' contents, dismantle the structures, and rebuild the store a few yards away, that is, on reserve property. According to Ridley, buildings valued at some $7,000 were "destroyed in the most wanton manner with crowbars and axes, and the front pulled out." Fearing an escalation of the violence, Ridley read the riot act, arrested two natives, and called upon governmental authorities for help.[30]

If Duncan's supporters were indignant over the imprisonment of their compatriots, a second incident added fuel to the growing fire. This time the disagreement surrounded disputed ownership of a ceremonial drum and culminated in a scuffle and the arrest of two more natives. Following this, a group then made their way toward the jail with the intention of releasing the prisoners. Along the way they encountered Ridley, and a struggle broke out. Ridley claimed that "a swarm of Indians," led by Legaic, "came down from Mr. Duncan's house" and "surrounded us— a party of five, three ladies and two gentlemen." In the ensuing confusion, Legaic, so Ridley claimed, "seized me by the shoulder and stopped me." While others "put their hands upon me and I fell backward," Robert Hewson delivered "a blow which paralyzed me," and Sitka Jim "spat in my face, and afterwards stuck me heavily on the back." As Ridley fought to maintain his balance, he hit one of his assailants "heavily," while one of the women in his group exclaimed, "'They are murdering the Bishop!'" By then, however, Legaic had entered the jail and, with the words "'See what we can do,'" released the prisoners.[31]

Legaic and Duncan disputed Ridley's account of the melee. Legaic denied ever touching the bishop and stated that he only wanted to speak to him. Duncan agreed and maintained that "the Bishop had struck Legaic," not the other way around, and, as a testament to his respect for law and order, the Indian still "relied upon the law to defend him." Local magistrates then intervened and fined Legaic and Hewson ten dollars each, and Sitka Jim twenty dollars. Duncan reportedly paid their fines personally and accused the bishop of inciting violence by brandishing firearms. In a letter expressing his hope that reports of him "leaving the schoolhouse with a gun covered up in your hand" were untrue, Duncan also implored his adversary that, "in the interests of peace, . . . you will not repeat the conduct of carrying firearms during the present excited state of the village-mind here." Otherwise, he warned that "I am afraid that in spite of all I can do to prevent it, the Indians, too, will arm themselves, and angry passions will thus be encouraged."[32]

Reports of violence quickly made their way south to Victoria, and on 18 January, Superintendent Powell, accompanied by Alfred C. Anderson, the inspector of fisheries, and Charles Todd, superintendent of the provincial police, arrived in Metlakatla. What they found could not have pleased the bishop. While the commissioners concluded that "serious troubles and the most unhappy religious rancor still exists at Metlakahtla," they also dismissed charges pending against the jailed natives. Moreover, Powell, long a Duncan supporter, continued to praise the work of his old friend. He made clear his assessment that "the secret of Mr. Duncan's great popularity with the Indians at Metlakahtla is his desire and fondness for inaugurating industries, which, after all, is the strongest bond which can be made to unite these people," concluding that "the retirement of either or both would seem the only true solution to the difficulties," and, "as fully nine-tenths of the people are unanimous and determined in their support of Mr. Duncan," the withdrawal of Ridley was to be preferred.[33]

But "retirement" proved unacceptable to both parties. The native council, controlled by Duncan's followers, voted to fine anyone patronizing the bishop's rival store, rewarded Sitka Jim with a seat on the governing body, and tore down homes built by Moses Venn and others who supported the bishop. At the same time, Samuel Pelham particularly resented what he viewed as persecution and blamed Duncan for the violence. "It is quite true," he later charged, "that Mr. Duncan's party are always threatening us, and putting us in fear." Arguing that it "is thoroughly understood by myself, and by all, that Mr. Duncan was teaching them [his supporters] to disrespect the law," Pelham went on to wonder why it was that "a white man [Duncan] is allowed to build a cannery on Indian ground." So great was the fear of reprisals that the CMS asked Ottawa for permission to establish a separate reserve for Metlakatla's minority. The Indian Department denied the request.[34]

Ottawa's response was clumsy at best. In 1883 and 1884 the Indian Department decided to place Metlakatla under the operations of Canada's Indian Act, appointing, for the first time, an agent to oversee community affairs and stripping Duncan of his judicial commission. This only awakened concerns of an alliance between governmental and ecclesiastical authorities. John Tait summarized the views of many when he testified that "there are too many ministers and too many magistrates, and that is the real cause of the confusion." Other Metlakatlans openly rejected Dominion authority, a move Powell denounced as an attempt by natives to "take the law into their own hands," and on "the dangerous advice of those who are, in my opinion, solely responsible for their present unfortunate position." Undeterred, Metlakatlans then expelled government surveyor E. E. Sherburne. Hired to demarcate the reserve from Mission Point, Sherburne was greeted by a letter, "signed by David Leask," questioning his authority to perform his duties. But following a tense meeting with council members, Sherburne abandoned his task.[35] At the same time, the council delivered a notice to Ridley. Signed again by David Leask, it read: "We, the Council and people of Metlakatlah, having had under consideration your continued presence amongst us and its effect in retarding the progress and peace of our village, have decided to inform you that we are not willing you should remain any longer here, and we do hereby notify you to leave Metlakatlah."[36]

Ridley ignored the petition, but, by this time, merely removing him would have had scant effect. By now, the bishop symbolized a more fundamental dispute in which his presence conflated with the Dominion's move to extend its authority over Metlakatla and in a way that clearly threatened the Metlakatlans' accustomed, and cherished, independence. Moreover, the growing presence of miners, settlers, and nonnative fishermen added economic pressure to political instability. Duncan had attempted to forestall the potential erosion of Metlakatla's land base in two important ways. As a consequence of negotiations with Governor James Douglas, Metlakatla was recognized as one of the few Indian reserves on the British Columbia mainland, with land claims extending to fifty square miles surrounding the village.[37] But while settlers received "certificates" to lands on which they could construct homes and plant gardens, they could not "sell, lease, give away or transmit the said lot or any part thereof to any person but an Indian of the settlement of Metlakahtla not already in possession of a similar lot." Since these homesteads belonged to the village collectively, they were similar to, but still substantially different from, the individual allotments that became commonplace on many United States Indian reservations.[38]

None of this would matter, of course, without secure access to fishing and hunting stations, and in this respect the growing presence of outsiders and Dominion hostility toward aboriginal land rights directly threatened Metlakatla's security. To his credit, Duncan journeyed to Ottawa in 1875 and proposed policy reforms designed to protect native subsistence rights. He did so at the request of David Laird, Prime Minister John A. Macdonald's interior secretary, who openly denounced British Columbia's record on aboriginal rights as "unsatisfactory," given "the generous treatment which the Indians have received at Red River and other parts of the Dominion." Duncan's plan aimed at reversing Canada's trend toward locating Indians on small "reserves," which reflected negotiations with band leaders but ignored both subsistence considerations and broader linguistic and cultural relationships.[39] Yet even as he suggested recognizing "the natural division of languages" and proposed "a large district for the use and benefit of all the Indians of one language," political fortunes in British Columbia pulled policy in the opposite direction. Most settlers apparently agreed with former governor Joseph Truch, who advanced the debatable proposition that "the title of the Indians in the fee of public lands, or any portion thereof, has never been acknowledged by Government, but, on the contrary, is distinctly denied." Truch also supported disfranchising Indians on the basis of race.[40]

This proved a problem in Metlakatla, where competition for resources laid bare their vulnerability. In 1878 Duncan accused the manager of the Windsor Canning Company of "completely stopping the salmon from reaching the Indian fisheries up the river" and warned of "a combination of the tribes to redress their grievances," should that cannery's fishermen not "keep their nets within the bounds prescribed by law."[41] In a separate incident, Duncan explained to a frustrated W. N. Neil, manager of the North Western Commercial Company, that, in the absence of equitable fishing practices, "it cannot be expected that the Indians, numerous as they are here, will as a matter of course quietly relinquish their ancient rights and privileges and be jostled into other and new regulations, because somebody tells them they must and especially as when their fears are aroused and under the new arrangements the salmon (their staff of life) will very soon disappear from the streams."[42] Given these conditions, Duncan warned Neil against abrogating an existing agreement. "If the payment of fifty dollars for the use of the stream," he explained, "seems now a bad egg and extravagant waste of money I would remind you that the egg was laid and hatched at Inverness at your cannery last year."[43]

Native Metlakatlans, too, were becoming increasingly fearful of losing hold of their lands. During an 1878 visit by Admiral James Prevost, one of Metlakatla's most loyal patrons, Samuel Pelham observed that just as "white people carry two pockets in their trousers in which they keep their money, . . . the two rivers Skeena and Nass are our two pockets where we obtain our food." Yet today, "white men are now putting their hands into our two pockets and robbing us and we hope you will plead for us among the white chiefs."[44] John Tait was much more direct, stating,

> Our forefathers thought that all the land from the Nass river to the Skeena river was theirs, . . . but now it appears it belongs to our elder brother England. England is strong. . . . We see white men hemming us around and we consider our Reserve too small. We need more land for we are increasing in numbers. We are like a younger son asking the older brother for what we want. Poor people and orphans need help.[45]

"We shall be very poor if not helped," he concluded. "We ask you Sir to help us and plead our cause."[46]

And Metlakatlans had some hope of receiving help. Following an 1876 state visit to Metlakatla, Governor-General Lord Dufferin spoke out in favor of aboriginal land rights. In fact, in an address before leading citizens and government officials in Victoria, Dufferin challenged provincial officials to "raise your 30,000 Indians to the level Mr. Duncan has taught they can be brought," reminding his audience that in the rest of the Dominion, "no government, whether provincial or central, has failed to acknowledge that the original title to the land existed in the Indian tribes and communities that wandered over them." By interfering "with the prescriptive rights of the Queen's Indian subjects," British Columbia stood alone in contributing to "an unsatisfactory feeling amongst the Indian population," who, in his mind, were "entitled to exactly the same civil rights under the law as are possessed by the white population."[47]

While it remains unclear whether Dufferin's remarks reflected his own opinions or were the views of federal officials, it is certain that Ottawa, preoccupied with contentious issues surrounding Confederation, had no intention of forcing the land rights issue. But natives took Dufferin's words to heart, and by the end of the 1870s many became more aggressive in asserting their rights. In the winter of 1877–78, for instance, Tsimshians from the Reverend Thomas Crosby's mission at Fort Simpson went to Duncan after learning that the Hudson's Bay Company regarded them as mere "squatters." Duncan, however, recommended only that Crosby's followers resettle in Metlakatla, advice that, according to the company's representative, "aroused a great deal of excitement."[48]

The upshot of this was that what began as a dispute between bishop and missionary now became a contest over aboriginal land rights, and here Metlakatlans not only rallied behind Duncan but also exerted considerable influence regionally. This marks an important evolution of Metlakatla from mission settlement to regional leader and supports the contention that the community never was truly "isolated." In fact, their extensive regional contacts combined with the village's comparative prosperity to render Metlakatla uniquely well placed to promote their vision of cultural independence through economic security. As operators of a salmon canning industry, Metlakatlans also felt, acutely, the implications of a denial of rights to land and resources. They reacted with the righteous outrage of a people who had done what was expected of them only to find that it still was not enough.

Several incidents from 1881 onward demonstrate Metlakatla's evolving leadership in these regional struggles. Following Duncan's warning that "the Indian fisheries were being taken possession of by whites for cannery purposes," British Columbia dispatched Reserve Commissioner Peter O'Reilly to work out some kind of agreement. Working from a map provided by Duncan and accompanied by David Leask, who served as interpreter, O'Reilly designated a series of reserves along the Nass and Skeena Rivers. Although his results evidently met with Duncan's approval, many Tsimshians seemed less pleased. Metlakatlans complained about the exclusion of Mission Point from their reserve, and Tsimshians from Fort Simpson, so O'Reilly wrote; claimed "the entire peninsula—including Mr. Turner's fishery on the Skeena (the Inverness)." O'Reilly rejected both contentions, explaining that he lacked "the power to deal with lands sold to whites."[49]

But this failed to quell tensions. As O'Reilly himself noted, missionaries had come to support the principle "that all the lands belonged to the Indians." Although he advised Reverend Crosby "to disabuse the Indians' mind from this suggestion," agitation evidently spread across the region. From miners threatened into abandoning their claims to the destruction of a church at Kitkatlah, natives' pronouncements against inadequate reserves spread to the banks of the Skeena and Nass Rivers as well as to Haida settlements on the Queen Charlotte Islands and even as far south as Fort Rupert. And Metlakatla, itself in some turmoil, seemed to lay at the center of this storm. In fact, British Columbia's agent of fisheries warned that local economies "will be affected and perhaps imperiled, should the defiant stand of late taken by a party at Metlakahtla be suffered to continue." Superintendent Powell agreed, adding that Metlakatla's "symptoms of insubordination" now "extended pretty generally to surrounding localities."[50]

These concerns led Victoria to dispatch an official commission, which convened in Metlakatla during mid-November 1884. Native Metlakatlans welcomed the move, believing, as their council petitioned, that the government had an obligation to examine "all the matters which are now disturbing our settlement."[51] But if they expected a full consideration of all issues, Alexander E. B. Davie, attorney general of British Columbia and head of the three-man body, disabused them of this notion right away. "We are told the Metlakatlahs [sic] say all the lands belong to the Indians," he began, but then quickly added, "this is not true." Rather, the Crown had empowered the province to create reserves and added that any "white men who tell the Indians otherwise, are false both to the Indians and whites and make trouble."[52]

Several witnesses added force to complaints against Duncan and native Metlakatlans, adding their support to the notion that the village stood accountable for the recent controversy. Robert H. Hall, the Hudson's Bay Company agent in Fort Simpson, testified that "it was while Mr. Duncan's cannery was in operation" that the Haidas "first showed signs of dissatisfaction." When asked if the Metlakatla cannery employed many Haidas, he replied, "Yes; quite a number." A miner working along the Nass River claimed: "All the Indians that I have spoken to told me that they had been taught by the missionaries that the white men were coming into the country to rob them of the land," that "all the land belonged to the Indians," and that officials in British Columbia "were thieves and robbers." Asked to name those missionaries, he responded, "Crosby at Fort Simpson, Duncan at Metlakatlah, and Tomlinson at Metlakatlah."[53]

Not all evidence came from miners and traders. Ridley's ally Collison suggested that "the influence which Metlakatlah formerly exercised for good has since that time been exercised for evil." Even more compelling was testimony from several natives. Metlakatlans Matthiew Aucland and Samuel Pelham agreed that Duncan had instructed the natives at Kitkatlah to destroy their church, and Neasoise, a resident of that village and witness to the event, confirmed their charges. But perhaps most damning were Duncan's own words, as quoted by Joseph E. White, manager of the Inverness cannery. In the course of one conversation, Duncan asserted that "there were only three ways of acquiring property—by purchase, by finding it, or by stealing it." According to White, the missionary then supposed that since "the Government certainly had not purchased this land from the Indians" and did not "find it uninhabited" or "acquire it by right of conquest," it followed that "they must have stolen it." Indians, then, would "allow one inch of their land to be taken from them," but "would all be hanged at first."[54]

Duncan did not deny the statement but suggested that natives simply were asking for justice, which meant a recognition of land rights in some fashion. "The people here are not Fenians or boycotters," he contended, but rightfully questioned the proposition that "the Queen owns all the land on which the Indians live." To accept this proposition "would be to suppose they are merely slaves or paupers." John Tait and Robert Hewson concurred, and in rushing to Duncan's defense they revealed as well the link some Metlakatlans had made between the ecclesiastical and land struggles, one they expressed in the language of unity, self-rule, and self-reliance. "We have never at all thought, or said," argued Tait, "that there should be a split in Metlakatlah between the churches," but "that law was broken" when Ridley arrived. So he pleaded with the commissioners to halt the proposed survey. Should it be allowed to proceed, so Tait concluded, "half the village site will not then belong to us." Hewson proved even more forceful. "We are not satisfied," he explained, "that the ground is the Queen's ground," and then "a paper stating that this is really a reserve." Davie responded by suggesting binding arbitration to resolve the Mission Point dispute. When Hewson and Tait refused the offer, Davie shot back angrily, "You are men of good sense; do not act like children—always being led."[55]

As an additional rebuke, the commissioners' report not only rejected Metlakatla's land claim but also blamed the native council for encouraging the breakdown of law and order. "The Indian Council at Metlakatlah is productive of trouble," the report read; "it has no legal organization, or status, and assumes to authorize the commission of acts of violence." Accusing Metlakatlans of "mak[ing] laws to themselves and in disregard of the laws of the land," the commissioners concluded further that in refusing to submit to the Indian Act, Metlakatla's councilmen had elected "to rebel against authority generally," and thus had "set an evil example to neighboring tribes." Therefore, and because "the Nass and the Skeena Indians have been moved to take the stand they have regarding the lands, by reason of the example set at Metlakatlah," the commissioners called upon government officials "to assert—and if necessary, by force of arms—the right of the Province."[56]

Completion of the inquiry, and publication of its findings, marked an important turning point in Metlakatla's relations with provincial officials. By 1885, Duncan, David Leask, and Ed Mather were in Ottawa receiving Prime Minister Macdonald's promise to recognize Metlakatla's right to self-government, and to seek Ridley's expulsion. From Ottawa, Duncan proceeded alone to London, where he received praise and support from the Aborigines Protective Society but then returned home to learn that, ill and preoccupied with other matters, Macdonald had chosen not to intervene.[57] In British Columbia, conditions had deteriorated as provincial authorities had already dispatched another surveyor. Metlakatlans pulled up stakes as soon as the surveyor sunk them, surrounded his boat, and then seized his instruments. The surveyor, C. P. Tuck, then called upon provincial authorities, who sent a magistrate, Victoria's chief of police, and a "posse of constables," all aboard the HMS *Cormorant*. Armed with an injunction from the Superior Court of British Columbia, the party arrived in Metlakatla on 2 November, arrested eight of the so-called ringleaders, and transported them to Victoria to await trial. Among those seized were John Tait, Edward Mather, and Fred Ridley. As the ship lay in port, Tuck's survey proceeded without further interruption.[58]

While the eight Metlakatlans awaited trial, others attempted once more to explain their plight and, hopefully, elicit some support. In a letter to the commander of the *Cormorant*, Paul Legaic and four others complained of "an attempt . . . made on behalf of the Dominion and Provincial Governments to take from us by force part of our patrimony and the inheritance which we received from our fathers." Stating their "firm belief" that "no surrender of these lands has been made by us to either government," they asked for the commander's aid in convincing a court to hear their case. "We have no wish to oppose the law or authorities," Legaic concluded; "we are only anxious to prevent our possessions from being taken from us."[59] David Leask offered similar sentiments. In a letter to the Victoria *Daily Colonist*, he asked, "Are we now out of our senses and warring against England's law because we hold fast our title to our inheritance? Is not the love of a bird for its nest a natural feeling given to it by the Creator?" It "is now too late," he warned, for "cheating and underhand dealing with the Tsimshians. That game would have answered thirty years ago when European fur-dealers paid for a prime black bear-skin with a lacquered tin cup." Instead, "what is wanted nowadays in dealing with our fellow-men is a civilized way of doing business, 'a just balance, just weights, a just ephah, and a just hin.' "[60]

But time was running out. After years of being lauded for his work, Duncan now was persona non grata in much of British Columbia, abandoned by all but a few outside the mission community. Dr. J. S. Helmcken, Speaker of the British Columbia Assembly, expressed the views of Victoria's well-to-do establishment when he wrote in an editorial to a local newspaper, "The Metlakahtla question is *not one of pseudo-christianity or pseudo-philanthropy, but* whether Indians shall be allowed at the instigation of their misleaders to set the rule of the province at their defiance." The answer, he said, was no, for "British Columbia has not, during the past thirty-five years, acknowledged any Indian title to land, save that given them by, may I say, their conquerors—not by the sword, but by civilization and commerce." Teach Indians "to work," he concluded, "but to teach them to rebel is against the law." To add insult to injury, in a case involving an application by Ridley to prevent the removal of yet another building from Mission Point, Sir Matthiew Begbie, chief justice of the provincial supreme court, sided with Bishop Ridley and ruled that "the Indians had no rights in the land except such as might be accorded to them by the bounty and charity of the Queen of England." He stated further that Lord Dufferin's views on native land tenure were "simply blarney for the mob."[61]

For the Metlakatlans, this proved the final act in a decade-long struggle for independence and self-determination. By undercutting their position on land tenure, Begbie's ruling not only cleared the way for Ridley's continued presence but also threatened their very economic survival. Absent legal protection for claims beyond village boundaries, miners, fishermen, cannery operators, or settlers could claim, with impunity, their streams and hunting grounds. Alienated from the halls of government as well as from the CMS, Metlakatla now faced an uncertain future, where isolation also meant the loss of critical financial support. In the face of competition from outside firms, the future seemed grim.[62]

What followed was a dramatic step. Led by David Leask, the native council adopted a resolution authorizing Duncan to proceed to Washington, D.C., with the intention of securing a new home in Alaska. Although Indian commissioner J. D. C. Adkins was cool to the idea, Duncan persisted and by February 1887 had enlisted the support of a number of luminaries, including territorial governor A. P. Swineford and Sheldon Jackson, general agent of education for Alaska. Jackson offered a particularly powerful appeal when he reminded the Treasury secretary that Congress already was inclined "to vote a large sum of money to encourage a colony of Icelanders to remove to Alaska." Surely, he continued, "the

Government can afford to encourage these people who ask for no money help."[63]

Perhaps even more important was a massive public relations effort engineered by Henry Solomon Wellcome, an American chemist with strong ties to England's colonial and philanthropic communities.[64] The two met soon after Duncan's arrival in Washington, D.C., and Wellcome was taken with Duncan's story, and perhaps with the prospect of profiting from the publicity. A skilled manipulator of public opinion, Wellcome wrote a polemic entitled *The Story of Metlakahtla* and arranged a whirlwind speaking tour that took Duncan from prestigious churches in Boston, New York, and Philadelphia to a joint meeting in Washington of the Board of Indian Commissioners, the Conference of Missionary Boards, and the Indian Rights Association. The campaign proved an unqualified success. Leading with an urgent appeal to "all who read . . . to see to it, that they [Metlakatlans] be allowed to secure homes in a land where their rights will be defended, where they shall enjoy the blessings of freedom and of peace; where they may work out their own destiny as an independent, and united Christian Community," *The Story of Metlakahtla* went through four editions, raising money all the way.[65]

Duncan proved a star in his own right. Interrupted frequently by applause and chants of "Amen!" and "That is so!" Duncan told a Washington, D.C., gathering of "Friends of the Indian" that "whenever a man speaks to me about the difficulties of civilizing the Indian, I always tell him that the difficulties are on the side of the white man; that the white man is pig-headed, stupid, and doesn't know anything about the Indians at all." Duncan claimed to have learned that "he [the Indian] wants to be treated as a brother" and "wants to be treated as a man." Indians, he continued, "are capable of all the brain power, of all the conscientiousness, and of all the ability to make splendid men of themselves." By contrast, those who would "leave the Indian down in the dirt . . . do not believe in helping the Indians. They believe in paying the Indians to keep quiet. If he has his war paint on, they will pay him money to keep him quiet, but they have given evidence that they do not care for the Indian if he is an improved, civilized, Indian." This condition, he concluded, "is a disgrace to our nation [and] a disgrace to our civilization."[66]

Duncan's tour received considerable coverage in the press, including a declaration from the editorial pages of the New York *World* that "the work of Mr. Duncan has never been equaled in the history of missionary effort; that the thousand Indians under his charge are victims of an oppression more cruel and shameful than that which drove the Pilgrim Fathers to New England." Their cause, the editors concluded, "should appeal to every true American heart." Despite his reluctance to antagonize the British, President Grover Cleveland also lent his support and in the summer of 1887 granted Duncan and his followers "squatters' rights" to Annette Island, formerly the site of a Tlingit fishing village. Duncan had hoped to purchase the island and had raised $1,300 for that purpose, but because fee simple tenure did not yet exist in Alaska, he agreed to the compromise settlement. This arrangement remained until 1891, when an act of Congress designated Annette Island a "reservation" for the exclusive use of the Metlakatlans.[67]

All that remained was the formal exodus. In May, John Tait, Edward Benson, and David Leask led an advance party to the island. Tait and Benson used profits from their trading and fishing ventures to set up a store, and Leask poured his own money into a salting house.[68] Three months later, Duncan set out for Port Chester, later named "New Metlakahtla" (today's Metlakatla, Alaska), and within a few days of his arrival, canoes bearing 800 of his followers left British Columbia ready for a new start. Back in "old" Metlakatla, Ridley attempted to convince the natives to remain with him, but fewer than 100 chose to do so. Among those who stayed were Moses Venn, Alfred Aucland, Samuel Pelham, and the mixed-blood trader James Rudland. Yet they did so with mixed feelings. Pelham expressed the sentiments of many left behind when he wrote Duncan, "Ever since we were separated I did not sleep well nor feel happy because I left you. I missed the true Christians who used to help in God's work. I often said to myself where is the old path, the path of Christian union."[69]

In Alaska, the immigrants rushed to build homes and establish order before the onset of winter. They re-created the native council, with John Tait as chairman, and appointed Edward Mather head of the constable corps, while at the same time planning to return home to remove houses, the church, and other structures they had built and presumably owned. What they found, however, were Ridley and his supporters ready, and willing, to resist any such action, including a stern warning to native Metlakatlan Ed Mather to go away. In response, immigrant Metlakatlans reportedly dismantled a few buildings and made off with some cannery equipment. But that was all. Despite complaints to Governor Swineford and threats of legal action, Duncan and the Alaska Metlakatlans failed to recover any additional property—or steal it, as the case may be.[70]

Despite this setback, New Metlakatla grew and prospered. With a population recorded at 823 in 1891, the town's general patterns of social and economic interaction persisted, reflecting those established over the previous generation in British Columbia. Drawing again upon aid from outside contributors and nearly $22,000 held by William Duncan himself, Metlakatlans built a church, homes, and the commercial plant, including a store, a lumber mill, and a salmon cannery.[71] The lumber mill began operations in 1888 and quickly found customers for its packing crate

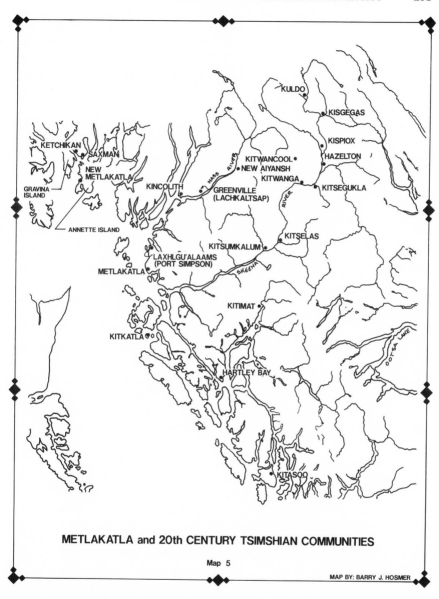

METLAKATLA and 20th CENTURY TSIMSHIAN COMMUNITIES

Map 5

MAP BY: BARRY J. HOSMER

materials among Alaska's fishing establishments, while also providing building materials for community members.[72] Aided by $5,000 worth of boats, tools, and miscellaneous equipment brought from British Columbia but still costing an additional $7,000 to construct, New Metlakatla's cannery opened for business in 1891; by 1912 its total production had reached 298,076 cases, amounting to an average of 13,549 cases per year.

Cannery work also was responsible for most of the nearly $300,000 in wages earned by Metlakatlans from 1891 to the turn of the century; an impressive figure given the impact of mill fires in 1889 and 1892 and a disastrous village fire in 1893. In most years the cannery employed about 100 workers, who earned between $1 and $2 per day for a season running from September to May, and re-created the division of labor established by its predecessor, where women labeled cans and loaded crates while men cleaned fish, packed the cans, and soldered lids. The fifty or so fishermen (on average) organized themselves in companies where individuals earned either $2.50 per day or a set price per fish, and the community store outfitted anglers, generally on credit, distributing profits in goods more often than in cash. The store also helped finance village projects (like church construction), absorbed losses incurred by the sawmill, and funded ancillary ventures in canning clams and operating a hatchery. As in British Columbia, this practice tied laborers to the village while orienting economic activity away from the promotion of independent operators and toward community development.[73]

The communal nature of Metlakatla's industrial activities was enhanced further by Duncan's 1891 decision to organize the Metlakahtla Industrial Company, a joint-stock combination that recalled the old store in that it consolidated community resources (assessed at over $30,000 in 1900) and distributed dividends to shareholders. Unlike the earlier arrangement, however, the company also sold shares to outside investors and turned over some financial decisions to a Portland, Oregon–based board of directors, and its chairman, attorney Thomas Strong. While this facilitated access to investment capital, indeed opened a line of credit, it also created a new distance between native workers and their finances. In fact, just five natives held a total of 180 shares in the new company in 1904, while William Duncan, acting as "trustee" for outside investors, held 1,184.[74]

The centralized structure of finances notwithstanding, some Metlakatlans still operated their own businesses, albeit under community direction and financing. As in British Columbia, John Tait and David Leask emerged as leading "entrepreneurs," at least as that term had meaning for Metlakatla. Tait ran a fishing company, engaged in prospecting, sold lumber, operated a store, and even traveled as far afield as Seattle to purchase merchandise. In that city, Duncan's mercantile contacts praised Tait as "a very bright and intelligent man" who employed "good business, tact" and "surprised" all those who hardly considered "it possible for a man of his nationality to be so intelligent." David Leask supplemented his salary as secretary of the town council and principal assistant to William Duncan with several ventures, including an ambitious, but ultimately ill-fated, effort to export salt salmon and dogfish oil.

Native Metlakatlans working at the New Metlakatla sawmill. (NA-APR, RG200, Archival Photograph Album 3, Print 708, page 22)

At various times between 1890 and 1915, native Metlakatlans operated a variety of semi-independent ventures, from fishing companies run by Ed Benson, Peter Johnson, Daniel Auriol, and Robert Hewson, to combinations organized to hunt and sell furs. Ernest Milton, Mark Fawcett, Louis Sumner, Charles Gibson, Silas Booth, Eli Gordon, Fred Gibson, and Charles Bates were among those who found work as lumberjacks; at least seven Metlakatlans ran stores by 1900; and others found work as steamer repairmen, and, of course, doing odd jobs around the community.[75]

Metlakatlans also continued to ply the waters of the Skeena and the Nass, returning to stations long claimed by *waalb* and *pt'eex* and providing convincing evidence that they did not equate immigration with a relinquishing of their aboriginal resource rights.[76] The report of an 1887 provincial commission investigating ongoing conflicts over land issues indicates no diminution of chiefly claims to fishing and hunting territories, and this despite the relocation of numerous individuals to the various mission communities. In fact, as natives voiced complaints regarding encroachment upon established prerogatives, they generally blamed confusion associated with the creation of mission communities and the subsequent reshuffling of family relations. Moreover, while some Nisga'a apparently resented the return of Alaska Tsimshians to Nass River *oolichan* fisheries, they also praised the Metlakatlans' decision to leave rather than submit. "What we don't like about the Government is their saying this: 'We will give you this much land,'" explained Nisga'a spokesman David Mackay.

After all, "How can they give it when it is our own? We cannot understand it. They have never bought it from us or our forefathers. They have never fought and conquered our people and taken the land in that way, and yet they say now that they will give us so much land—our own land." Natives from Kincolith and Hazelton to Kitsukalum and Fort Simpson agreed, often requesting "strong paper" affirming land rights. Several also threatened to join the Metlakatlans in exile. Charles Russ, listed as a "sub-chief" of those Nisga'a settled in Greenville on the Nass, testified that "what the Metlakatlah people have done, in leaving their lands because the Government said the land did not belong to them, we will do just the same; we will leave the country too." And Alfred Dudoward, a Tsimshian from Fort Simpson, rejected the position "that we cannot have authority [over their lands] until an agent comes among us. But the Tsimpseans do not wish an agent among them; that is why we know we are not free, . . . and this is why the Metlakatlah people have left."[77]

A substantially lower rhetorical temperature, at least toward governmental representatives, prevailed in "old" Metlakatla. Donald Bruce, listed as a "chief" by the commissioners, requested help "to be free from our oppressors—those Indians who have gone across," and Alfred Aucland condemned Duncan and Tomlinson, "bad white men among us who say we are slaves on the reserve." Turning their anger toward the emigrants who, they charged, "stole" and "destroyed" their property, they now looked toward the government for deliverance. As Bruce testified, "It is only the work of the Government that has protected us all along from being destroyed by those people." But if they now considered government emissaries friends rather than adversaries, the remaining residents of old Metlakatla still sought recognition of aboriginal land rights. Paul Legaic promised to "go on talking" about "our land" until the matter was settled. According to Alfred Aucland, "In the old time no one but the owner had the right to go to these places," but lately, he continued, "white people have been telling us that anyone can go to them, and so Indians from Tongas [Tlingits] and all around have been going to these streams, where they were not allowed before." Although tempered by experience, these Metlakatlans still sought "strong paper," even as they now requested, rather than demanded, such agreements.[78]

One conclusion supports Duncan's contention that those most conversant with, and supportive of, the Metlakatla "system" had successfully picked up and relocated, hardly missing a beat. By contrast, old Metlakatla foundered, its commercial life damaged by the destruction of property, the decline in population, and, perhaps, the dilution of its entrepreneurial "spirit." Although Duncan remained in communication with William, James, and Mary Rudland, he also harbored considerable bitterness toward those who had chosen not to join the exodus. "Our

David Leask returned from a visit to old Metlakahtla," he wrote in 1894, "and gave us a woeful account" of conditions. "In secular growth there is only stagnation and decay, and in spiritual matters only division and confusion." In response to a 1901 report of a fire in the old settlement, he wrote caustically, "We hear that the Church and other buildings were destroyed—and if that report is true—the fire only consumed stolen property." Similarly, anthropologists Homer Barnett and William Beynon, comparing the two Metlakatlas during the first decades of the twentieth century, contrasted "progressive" Alaskans with British Columbia's "traditionalists." Viola Garfield discovered much the same thing, and even contemporary Metlakatlans agree, attributing the communities' divergent paths to the emigration of those "with business sense." Old Metlakatla "just fell apart," suggests one informant, and this was due in no small measure to the loss of those who "worked hard," as well as Duncan's firm guiding hand.[79]

It follows, then, that most of the concerns expressed by Alaskan Metlakatlans, even as voiced through William Duncan, centered around making a living. Although Nass and Skeena stations helped supply the cannery with salmon, Metlakatlans also exploited the several small streams on Annette Island, Prince of Wales Island, and other locations along the southern Alaska panhandle.[80] This, however, soured relations with neighboring Tlingit communities, which apparently resented both the incursion of new fishermen and, sometimes, the presence of "foreigners" on Annette Island. Duncan's approach recapitulated strategies in old Metlakatla. On behalf of Metlakatlans, he asserted claims to streams by virtue of the Alaska Organic Act of 1884 (23 U.S. Stat. 24), which protected native fishing rights as well as equal access to all comers, while at the same time encouraging Tlingits to join the community, just as an earlier generation had welcomed Nisga'as, Haidas, and Gitxsan.[81] According to an 1895 census, 95 of the 823 Metlakatlans were "Tlinkits," whose possessions upon arrival presumably included claims to fishing stations. But relations with neighbors remained complicated, and Duncan even conceded that some lived "in fear of coming to us thinking that if they do so they will forfeit their rights in other places where they have been used to fish and hunt." This seems to have been a legitimate concern as the Metlakatlans, Duncan and native alike, came to consider Alaska fisheries as common property. Acting on this presumption, a native Metlakatlan delegation visited Saxman and Ketchikan in 1902, warning Tlingits "against taking any step for settling on this island" in ways other than the "legitimate door of entrance," which was, of course, "joining our community, and obeying our rules of living."[82]

More troubling were relations with commercial canneries, and here the link with the Menominee situation emerges more directly. Just as

Menominees struggled to operate in an economic environment dominated by better-capitalized lumber companies, where they exerted little influence over broader economic forces, Metlakatla found it difficult to compete with the Alaska Packers Association, a politically influential combination of canneries controlled by San Francisco investors, whose fishermen plied the very same waters.[83] Duncan's approach was to appeal for assistance from his own financial backers and to protest the APA's practices on the grounds that they violated the spirit, if not the letter, of the Organic Act by interfering with native claims to fishing streams ("Each stream had its quota of families to support and is jealously guarded by those to whom it has been assigned by the general consent of the Band from time immemorial," he wrote in 1896). The APA's efforts to set commodity prices "are no doubt arranged before hand to trap, and if possible to kill, every cannery outside their Combination," and thus threatened Metlakatla's hard-earned economic progress. What is more, their fishing practices endangered the future health of salmon runs. An 1896 letter captures the spirit of Duncan's protests. After reporting plans by the Loring cannery, located northeast of Ketchikan on Revillagigedo Island and some forty miles north of Annette Island, to double its pack to 60,000 cases (compared with Metlakatla's 16,000), Duncan charged that "this Syndicate" refused to "obey the fishing laws." But worse still, federal and territorial authorities refused to act. "Backed by their great wealth" and "emboldened" by the lenient application of fishing laws, the APA, so Duncan concluded, now was determined "to fish without limits or regard for the rights of others," a situation that would lead to "calamity" as southeastern Alaska's "salmon streams are denuded of Salmon life."[84]

Duncan pursued a contradictory relationship with commercial canneries, however. Even as he protested the Loring cannery's determination to exploit streams claimed by Metlakatlans, he also proposed "an understanding," fixing prices paid native fishermen and wages for cannery operators. This compact, so he revealed in a letter to territorial legislator J. R. Hechman, was in response to activities of "a few of the natives" who "would reap temporary advantage through rivalry of the Canneries, and who, to serve their selfish ends, would do their best to bring about such a rivalry." While it is likely that Metlakatla fishermen also benefited from increased demand, Duncan, nevertheless and repeatedly, sought to roll back prices. "Indians are very apt to carry around false reports as to wages," he wrote, "are never satisfied" despite earning "very great wages," and so "without some arrangement between us the natives will be tempted to misquote us." He even dispatched Ed Benson to Loring in 1902 to negotiate a division of salmon streams, but, apparently fearing adverse reaction among other native Metlakatlans, revealed that "I have not mentioned this matter to any one but Benson." With his dual roles as manager of a cannery and spokesman for native laborers apparently in conflict, Duncan seems to have been more comfortable complaining about unfair competition than advancing the economic interests of individual natives, or even justifying Metlakatla's higher prices for canned salmon by advertising the superiority of his "hand pack" over machine-filled cans. "I think we are fairly entitled to better prices for our salmon which is hand filled and carefully packed," he wrote in 1893, "whereas— the other canneries use machine-filling and chinese [sic] contracted labor which would not pass muster at our cannery at all."[85]

Native Metlakatlans responded in a variety of ways. In addition to "agitating for a rise in the price of Salmon," there is ample evidence that they took advantage of competition to drive up prices. In 1901, for instance, Metlakatla fisherman Peter Johnson informed Duncan of a price-setting agreement with Loring. Responding, Duncan complained that while "these figures ['Red: $5^1/_2$ cents each; Coohoos: $7^1/_2$ cents each; Hump: $3/_4$ cents each—with canneries supplying net and gear'] are much higher than we have given them for salmon, if they are what you have agreed to give I must accept them." Yet competition occasionally led to conflicts between Metlakatla fishermen and those employed by commercial canneries. In an 1899 protest to the APA board of directors, Duncan complained of Metlakatla fishermen being "set upon by your Employees as if they had been a part of thieves or pirates," at the very same time that Loring's manager planned to "send his own fishermen and nets" to Metlakatla's customary fisheries "unless they would agree to sell him half of their catch."[86]

It would be a mistake, however, to characterize commercial relationships as pitting Metlakatla against everyone else. In fact, Metlakatlans apparently joined other natives from the region and hired themselves out to canneries on both sides of the international border. Alfred Atkinson, an experienced pilot and fisherman, Ed Benson, a seasoned cannery worker and sometimes intermediary between Duncan and Loring officials, and fishing company leader Peter Johnson rank among those who found away-from-community employment. Women from Metlakatla also continued to work for commercial canneries, often, it seems, for the Northwest Commercial Company at Inverness, British Columbia, as some had prior to 1887.[87] Less an innovative response to changed circumstances than the continuation of long-established patterns, extracommunity wage labor nevertheless undermined Duncan's determination to use the cannery as a magnet for both current residents and new immigrants. It indicates as well that as the Metlakatla economic "system" fell short of meeting the demand for well-paying jobs, an expanding regional economy drew workers away. "A few days ago we had a steamer here," Duncan wrote in 1903, "seeking for employees and urging our people to go over [to the Skeena River] for fishing. I believe a great number will go—as they talking of raising the price of salmon this season." Although Duncan acknowledged that native Metlakatlans needed to seek employment wherever their skills were in demand, better wages elsewhere also produced periodic labor shortages at the cannery and, sometimes, salmon shortfalls as fishermen sold their catch to the highest bidders. Once again, this forced Metlakatla to enter the regional market for fish and at least entertain the idea of hiring Asian laborers.[88]

As some Metlakatlans looked beyond the community, those who had come to embrace entrepreneurial and individualistic values found the regional economy at least as attractive as Metlakatla's hierarchically controlled "system." While Peter Johnson, Thomas Hanbury, and Joseph Auriol led a group of commercial fishermen with contracts serving canneries in Alaska and British Columbia, Peter Simpson set himself up in Sitka, where he ran a small business in fur sales and used stationery engraved with "Peter Simpson, Boat Builder and Contractor." A letter filed with the report of the commissioner of education for 1898–99 lists Metlakatlans engaged in a variety of trades, from boot and shoe making, cannery work, carpentry, and coopering to clerking, engineering, teaching, storekeeping, and sawmill labor, and a number of individuals so working did so away from Metlakatla. Thomas Hanbury was recorded as building boats in Cape Nome. Gravina Island, across from Ketchikan, was home to carpenters Joseph Campbell, George Eaton, Arthur Milton, and Robert Ridley, and Selina Leask Gamble worked as a teacher in Sitka. Even David Leask, erstwhile companion to William Duncan, apparently transferred his clerical skills into seasonal work for a Ketchikan lumber mill and was not alone among Metlakatlans seeking, and sometimes finding, employment in that industry.[89]

More telling still were the activities of Edmund and Fred Verney, who in 1901 or 1902 opened a lumber mill of their own on Gravina Island and thus joined Peter Simpson among the ranks of Metlakatla's small collection of "entrepreneurs." Duncan attempted to foil the Verneys' venture by warning commercial contacts not to advance them supplies, as "Indians are very reckless in their use of borrowed money." Although Duncan considered the brothers "honest men," he nevertheless expressed his fear that "they are too ambitious and visionary in business affairs." This concern closely repeated an earlier warning, directed toward Peter Simpson and that native's determination to establish a salmon cannery of his own. "I may tell you," wrote Duncan in 1891, "that a cannery requires a lot of money and very careful management. You ought not to begin till you have at least $15,000 to spend," a difficult task, since "no agent will advance you money to work with unless you can give him good security for his loan." While Duncan seems to have successfully dissuaded Simpson from pursuing that risky enterprise, the Verney brothers forged ahead and operated their sawmill for several years before a disastrous and, according to some contemporary Metlakatlans, mysterious fire drove them into bankruptcy sometime after 1912. Significantly, while the Verneys seem to have maintained a productive business arrangement with Metlakatla for a time, even contracting with Duncan for the use of that community's steamer, the relationship eventually imploded, with both sides accusing the other of dishonoring debts, indeed, stealing money.[90]

The Verney brothers' business, combined with the increasing tendency for Metlakatlans to hire themselves out to commercial firms and, indeed, to locate away from the community at least seasonally, suggests that Duncan's system had begun to fray around the edges by the early decades of the twentieth century. In some sense, these problems had everything to do with the fact that the community's manufacturing and commercial infrastructure failed to provide home-based employment for all who sought it, or at least the kinds, and quality, of jobs that some apparently desired. Whether pulled by opportunities elsewhere or pushed out of frustration with Duncan's determination never to relinquish control—or more likely a complex combination of these and other circumstances—the result seems to have been a growing distance between Duncan and the most "worldly" of his native associates. Perhaps impatience with Duncan's peculiarities preconditioned certain individuals toward seeking contacts away from Annette Island, or time spent away from home affected views of the missionary. In any event, the fact is that numbers of Metlakatlans not only sought jobs away from home but also, and increasingly, called Sitka, Saxman, Gravina, and Ketchikan home for at least part of the year.

Just as tellingly, by the first decade of the twentieth century, William Duncan had become more pessimistic about the "capacity" of any of his charges to take on the management of Metlakatla's enterprises. His 1901 confession to Thomas Strong that "my experiences during the last season's operations have fully convinced me that the hope I entertained of finding an ample number of reliable natives to shoulder the responsibility of management must be abandoned" echoed an earlier warning to a Seattle merchant against loaning money to Indians—"as they have no honesty." The fact that even David Leask left a substantial debt when he died in December 1899 only confirmed Duncan's worst suspicions.[91] His response was to explore the possibility of leasing the cannery first to an outside firm and then to the United States government. But in 1912, just when negotiations with the government seemed about to bear fruit, he suddenly changed his mind, grasping and holding his creation more tightly than ever, evidently convinced that the plan was nothing more than a ruse to force him to step aside. This brought a sharp rebuke from old friend and associate Robert Tomlinson, who left the community, condemning Duncan for taking that action without first consulting shareholders and, more tellingly, accusing the old man of "repressing" the will of native Metlakatlans by defying the wishes of the native council.[92]

Increasingly isolated, Duncan responded in characteristic fashion. Citing poor salmon runs and competition from commercial firms, he unilaterally closed both mill and cannery following the 1912 season. An act apparently contrary to the wishes of "the workingmen and residents of Metlakatla," who in 1915 petitioned their old friend "asking to operate cannery and sawmill as usually," it also brought a sharp rebuke from Tomlinson. Accusing his old mentor of withholding vital financial information from native Metlakatlans and of suppressing the will of the native council, Tomlinson wrote, "You have never, they say, gave [sic] them any accounting of the profits for each year nor even showed [sic] them the books."[93] In former times, he continued and with regard to the native council, "though they were still only babes in knowledge, your efforts were to encourage them to assume responsibility, and to think and care for the progress of their place. Now it is a policy of repression. It is like trying to keep overgrown children in an infant class and expect them to be interested and contented. They have no chance; their efforts are carped at, and their least mistakes magnified." As Tomlinson asked, "Why the change?"[94]

Unable to entrust operations to any of those he himself educated, unwilling as well to support either the extension of United States citizenship to Metlakatlans, on the one hand, or an offer to administer Annette Island as just another Indian "reservation," on the other, Duncan sought, as he had in the past, to define the community as his own creation. Native Metlakatlans, however, had come to define the place differently, and so while they still participated in a vibrant community life, continued to expend profits for village improvements, and, working collectively, created a town that impressed visitors, certain individuals forged associations that drew them away from Duncan, if not physically, then perhaps psychologically.

And so it was. Metlakatla remained Duncan's home until he died in 1918. The community exists today, although the cannery closed its doors a few years back. For many Duncan is a revered figure, his memory honored on 8 August every year in celebrations commemorating "Founders' Day." I was fortunate to attend the 1995 gathering and to enjoy the company of Russell Hayward and Arnold Booth, descendants of those "founders" and former cannery workers themselves. Still standing, Duncan's home is a museum, or, more accurately, a shrine. Old Metlakatla also continues, and although the town always suffered in comparison with its more famous namesake, Tsimshians there are engaged in a renewed interest in commercial activities, running a water taxi service in and out of the fishing city of Prince Rupert. I was honored to be the guest of the tribal council, enjoyed a plate of smoked salmon and rice topped with *oolichan* oil, and was pleased to spend a wonderful afternoon with Joyce and Elvin Leask.

Yet the last decade of Duncan's life was not a happy one. Besieged, or so he believed, by government forces attempting to dominate his community, he also faced increasingly restive native Metlakatlans who believed the time had come for natives to take charge of their lives, industries, and community. They had, it seems, internalized Duncan's message of self-reliance, and while they had abandoned potlatch and *adawx* for savings accounts and church services, the restless spirit of Txamsem still resided in their hearts—as it does today.

Conclusion

On 20 October 1913, Governor J. F. A. Strong of Alaska submitted a report on Metlakatla to the United States secretary of the interior. In it, he outlined complaints raised by a number of natives regarding the conduct of their leader, William Duncan. Their remarks, he contended, "all ran the common note that Mr. Duncan was no longer fitted to carry to the fullest fruition this work he had initiated a half century before and which he still directs." More specifically, the Metlakatlans charged that "while they as pupils . . . have gone forward, their teacher has stood still or gone backward," and that his training methods were "totally inadequate for the purpose of making them self-supporting and in broadening their views and quickening their intelligence." Strong bolstered his case against Duncan by citing statements from several native community members. " 'Many have left,' " said one correspondent, " 'because of the arbitrary, old-fashioned methods of Father Duncan, and they have gone elsewhere to find employment which has been denied them at home.' " Another reportedly alleged, " 'We thought we knew something about business following the instructions we had received from Father Duncan,' " but " 'when we tried to conduct business for ourselves we found we knew nothing of practical affairs.' " This witness concluded, "We want this kind of knowledge, we want it for our children so that we and they may be fitted for American citizenship."[1]

The natives' complaints followed several years of increasingly tough times for Metlakatla. Declining revenues and a paucity of outside contributions had led to the closure of the cannery and sawmill, and the subsequent loss of jobs caused the community's population to drop to just over 600 persons as many moved elsewhere. Complaints also surfaced of misuse of village funds and Duncan's increasingly intransigent attitude toward allowing natives to take on a greater share of managerial and governmental responsibilities. At the same time, Duncan's relationship with United States federal authorities deteriorated as he waged a long, and often bitter, battle against the Bureau of Education. Beginning in the second decade of the new century, the bureau had taken steps to start its own school and install an agent to oversee operations in the village.[2] On the surface, this new dispute bore an eerie similarity to Duncan's fight with church officials and the British Columbia government a quarter century before. And as before, Duncan's plight attracted the attention of some outsiders. Henry Wellcome, author of *The Story of Metlakahtla* and architect of Duncan's 1887 public relations tour, rushed to his old friend's side, where he led a campaign to protect the old missionary's reputation.[3] Others took up Duncan's cause and sought, again as before, to enlist the support of well-meaning whites. "A gloomy winter of discontent broods over Metlakahtla," wrote one journalist in 1913, for in this "'Indian Arcadia of Alaska,' . . . Duncan, after devoting fifty-five years of his life to the moral uplift and material welfare of his wards, is now, at four score, forsaken by a generation who know not their Joseph." Damaged by competition from better-funded canneries and ignored by a government that had once acted as its protector and benefactor, Duncan's experiment faced a dismal future. As one observer remarked, "Nearly all his younger colonists have emigrated to new districts of industrial activity, where higher wages and freedom from restraint have proven stronger attractions than the conditions of living under the strict and uncompromising rule of their religious and temporal overlord."[4]

But despite the similarities with earlier trials, this new wave of discontent was different in important ways. Duncan's attitudes regarding native capabilities had, of course, hardened, and he even mocked the natives' aspirations. To Thomas Strong he wrote, "They think they would like to become doctors, or lawyers, or missionaries," but sarcastically concluded that "they would make great doctors and lawyers, or preachers, now would they." Characterizing them as mere "children," Duncan seemed to confirm charges of his increasingly autocratic manner when he closed the interview with the words "I know them and I know what is best for them. I am myself teaching them the things they ought to know, and only those things."[5] He also lashed out at his critics. "Go away," he wrote to shareholders in the Metlakahtla Industrial Company (MIC), the community's joint-stock operation, when he dissolved that body in 1912 but refused to reimburse its native creditors. This led Alfred Baines, Ellen Hanbury, Edward Benson, Jacob Scott, Aldophus Calvert, and Catherine Marsden to bring suit against Duncan and the MIC in 1916 for recovery of investments.[6] Unlike the earlier dispute in British Columbia, then, this time Duncan seemed to be at war not with outsiders but with his followers.

To complicate matters, Duncan's chief antagonists included many of his most successful followers. John Tait, Ed Verney, Mark Hamilton, Benjamin Haldane, Edward Benson, and Adolphus Calvert, all of them active in business enterprises, now joined the chorus against him. Led by Alfred Atkinson, mayor of Metlakatla, eight prominent Metlakatlans made it clear that "our trials do not come from our enemies but from one whom we have always considered as our best friend. We refer to Father Wm. Duncan and the type of religious and industrial tyranny he represents."[7] At the head of this faction was Edward Marsden, the newly appointed secretary of the Metlakatla native council. In a 1916 memorandum, Marsden charged Duncan with "the deliberate misuse of public funds," a "policy of repression," the "use of God's Holy word to suit his own purposes," a "constant distrust of his own converts," and a pattern of "false dealings in regard to the incorporation and disincorporation of the Metlakahtla Industrial Company." He also made it clear that as "Father Duncan's present authority as a gospel minister rests on the will and consent of his Indian congregation," neither he nor those who shared his sentiments would accept another "white minister" as a replacement.[8]

Marsden's accession to the leadership of the "anti-Duncan" faction was a significant step in the evolution of Metlakatla society and politics. The son of Samuel Marsden, Duncan's first convert and trusted associate, Edward was born in 1869 and established an especially close relationship with Duncan, particularly after the elder Marsden's death in 1878. From that time on, the missionary acted as a surrogate father to the young man, directing his education and grooming him to take an important place in community affairs. Edward and his widowed mother, Catherine (Gitlaan), also were among the earliest immigrants to Alaska, and in that first year Marsden so impressed N. H. R. Dawson, United States commissioner of education, that he offered to send the teenager to the Sitka Indian Industrial School. Although troubled by the prospect of losing his star pupil, Duncan assented to Dawson's request, and Marsden enrolled in the Indian school the next fall. Once there, his talents shone so brightly that in 1891 he earned admission to the Lane Theological Seminary, a Presbyterian college in Marietta, Ohio.[9] Although Duncan was proud of Marsden's accomplishments, he admitted to having reservations about the value of higher education, particularly for Indians. In an 1895 letter, Duncan warned Marsden against "indulging the idea that learning, and the spread of knowledge, are the cure-all for the world's degradation, and especially important for the uplifting of the Indian race." While conceding that "learning is not an evil," Duncan went on to write: "Depend upon it, Edward, it is not an extensive acquaintance with book-lore, but a consecrated spirit we need, first of all, to do effectual work for the uplifting of mankind." Duncan also called upon Marsden to abandon his plans to study theology and pursue orders as a minister in the Presbyterian church, the former because examining "abstruse theological questions [would] unhinge your mind and impede your usefulness," the latter because "our people want nothing to do with exclusive allegiance to any sect or denomination."[10]

Despite these rather stern admonitions, Marsden ignored his mentor's advice and became an ordained clergyman. Following the completion of his education in 1898, Marsden finally returned to Alaska—but not to Metlakatla. Instead, the Presbyterian Board of Home Missions sent him to Saxman, a Tlingit village located just fifteen miles east of Met-lakatla.[11] If the desire had been to cause problems, the choice could not have been more opportune. Beginning in 1899 and continuing for over fifteen years, the two men engaged in a most bitter struggle for control over Metlakatla and, in no small measure, Duncan's legacy. Duncan complained that Marsden spent more time stirring up trouble in Metlakatla than working for the betterment of Saxman, and, indeed, a sizable anti-Duncan faction, which included the Verney brothers and Mark Hamilton, grew up around the young preacher. By 1914 tensions had resulted in the destruction of property belonging either to Duncan or to the community at large. The following year, officials representing Secretary of the Interior Franklin K. Lane (who relied on Marsden for information) arrested, but then released, Duncan, seized control of most of the public property in Metlakatla, and abolished the old native council. In its place they established a town council form of local government and a new company, the Metlakatla Commercial Company. With the backing of federal officials, and his own followers, Marsden became secretary of the town council in 1916 and held this nonelective position until his death in 1932.[12]

For years following the takeover of Metlakatla, scholars and Duncan's supporters suggested that Marsden's rise to power was a consequence of a "conspiracy" on the part of federal officials to take control of what was the "showcase" native community in all of Alaska. Although further research is necessary to firmly establish this contention, correspondence between Marsden and government officials lends at least some credence to coordinated activity, and Duncan's most recent biographer substantially accepts this conclusion.[13] Marsden's motivations in this saga are less clear. While his detractors vilified him as a crafty manipulator of his followers and a willing dupe to more nefarious designs of federal officials, available evidence indicates that Marsden was expressing doubts about Duncan's leadership as early as 1895. "It is eight years since I left my home," he wrote to Duncan in that year, "and my fellow boys, then in ignorance like myself, are now young men still in ignorance, while I have received an education."[14] Twenty years later he had not changed his views and in an article printed in the Ketchikan *Progressive*, said, "Our school was a farce, and was always a farce. If we were a little too religious we were found fault with. Our youths blindly took to the vices of civilization. Our girls especially, in many cases, from lack of any home training, became victims of these vices."[15] In 1916 Marsden acted on his fears that Duncan's methods encouraged vice and ignorance by suspending his mentor's license to preach in Metlakatla.[16]

Marsden's animus did not end there. On several occasions prior to the events of 1915 and continuing up to Duncan's death in 1918, Marsden's letters to federal officials were filled with invective toward the old man. "I am doing all I can to help and I fear Duncan not a single bit," he wrote to W. T. Lopp of the Bureau of Education in 1913. "I have clashed with him many times now [and] conclude that of all human beings he is foxy, dishonest, tyrannical, and a hopelessly bigoted preacher. He looks after William Duncan's affairs very carefully but is unmercifully sacrificing the welfare of my own people."[17] Just months before Duncan died, Marsden fired off still one more shot. In a letter to Richard Henry Pratt, he wrote:

> Poor old Duncan. He is still existing, and he thinks that the world will go to pieces without him. Little does he know that he is only hampering the progress of affairs at Metlakahtla. His complete retirement by the Interior Department will bring many good and rich blessings, to the over 700 persons in this Indian town—a town that once had a population about twice what it has today.[18]

Yet when Duncan finally died, Marsden was an honored member of the funeral party. In 1927, after the heat of battle had cooled, Marsden offered his own eulogy to his mentor. "The memory of Father Duncan as a friend, brother, and Christian missionary, lives in our hearts," he wrote. "He will ever be associated with things upright, godly, and progressive. The fact that he ended his long life in our midst calls for our sincere gratitude and occupies within our hearts a tender place."[19]

The last decade of William Duncan's life, which climaxed in the bitter struggle with his protégé and star pupil, presents us with an instructive place to end this narrative and offer conclusions and comparisons with events on the Menominee Reservation. In an important respect, Marsden's rise to power mirrored the situation in Wisconsin, where two native leaders, Mitchell Oshkenaniew and Reginald Oshkosh, initiated efforts to seize control over their community, and its considerable economic potential, from inept and sometimes corrupt white administrators. Like Marsden, both Oshkenaniew and Oshkosh were products of off-reservation education, and all three returned home convinced that familiarity with the white man's "world" suited them to assume the mantle of leadership. The three natives also were linked by their conviction that their brethren, by virtue of a long period of tutelage and evident successes, had earned the opportunity to manage their own affairs. For Oshkosh and Oshkenaniew, the issue was federal management, or rather mismanagement, of the tribe's sawmill and rich stand of timber. In a similar fashion, Marsden sought to free himself and his people from what he viewed as William Duncan's outdated and restrictive methods. Viewed together, both situations illustrate a dramatic maturation of political awareness and the realization on the part of Indians, schooled in the white man's ways, that through self-determination, not paternalism, their people could survive, and indeed prosper.

In the drive to awaken a new "consciousness" among their brethren, Marsden, Oshkenaniew, and Oshkosh adopted similar methods, if with varying results. All three took advantage of dissatisfaction and a vacuum in leadership to forge political "constituencies" dedicated to advancing a decidedly modern, but still native-centered, program. They also sought to influence white policy makers by presenting themselves as democrats, capitalists, and exemplars of what whites hoped for when they, to paraphrase Richard Henry Pratt, sought to "save the man by killing the Indian." As so-called educated Indians, all three understood that real power resided elsewhere; they knew that success, both personally and in terms of furthering their programs, lay in presenting themselves to policy makers as reasonable, thoroughly modern, men. It was for this reason that Marsden maintained close contacts with officials from the Bureau of Education, and both Menominees authored petitions and cultivated relationships with agents on the spot and administrators elsewhere. That all three, and particularly Oshkenaniew, occasionally provoked and irritated whites has less to do with a supposed inability to deal effectively with outsiders than with their increasingly spirited demands for self-determination.

At home, leaders like Oshkenaniew, Oshkosh, and Marsden promoted their programs with at least equal vigor. As Richard White notes in the conclusion to *The Roots of Dependency*, one of the few choices open to natives when confronted by severe pressures from the outside was to attempt to maintain a degree of cultural independence through "purposeful modernization." This avenue, he argues, was particularly difficult because it mandated that natives undertake what amounted to a "revolution in values."[20] For the Menominees this revolution involved not only accepting wage labor but also finding ways to satisfy those who did most of the work, while at the same time understanding that preserving tribal unity necessitated an explicit, material recognition that reservation resources belonged to the collective whole, and all tribesmen deserved to share equally in profits and decision making. In the two Metlakatlas, the situation was a bit different, since Duncan effectively created a new "tribe" out of the disparate clans, families, and ethnic groups that chose to follow him and adopt his vision. But unity and a sense of collective responsibility were no less important among Metlakatlans than with the Menominees. As with the Menominees, Duncan's followers labored to balance the needs of the individual with the realization that sacrifices and benefits had to be distributed as widely as possible.

But in neither place was this "revolution in values" an easy or seamless process. In Metlakatla, individuals like John Tait and David Leask proved more willing and able to adopt the capitalist "ethos," as Duncan at first rewarded them with council offices and investment capital, only to grow suspicious of their intentions, and indeed independence. Suspicion proceeded from several directions. For while "entrepreneurs" like the Verneys, Haldane, Atkinson, and Benson led the opposition to Duncan, others were equally vociferous in his defense. Moses Hewson, a native Metlakatlan storekeeper, was particularly critical of the activities of the anti-Duncan faction. Referring to Marsden as "an old Lucifer," Hewson even blamed "Kitlan Trouble Makers" for the turmoil, a thinly veiled attack on Marsden, who was, of course, a Gitlaan by virtue of his mother's ethnicity. Even Salina Leask Gamble—David's daughter, a schoolteacher, and a graduate of Sitka Indian Industrial School—condemned Marsden. "Mr. Marsden," she wrote, "you can judge my surprise as well as being shocked, for you, Mr. Duncan's own convert, who had given you your start in life which you are enjoying now . . . should be the first to throw him out." Conceding that she, too, "have had many disagreeable times with him," she still called upon Marsden to demonstrate Christian charity, closing with the particularly cutting remark: "It has been said many times that as soon as an Indian learn his A B C then he turns around and considers himself above his teacher." And to Duncan, Salina Leask Gamble wrote, "I have blamed Edward Marsden for the whole thing and have told him so, that's what an over-educated Indian amounts to, when his education is given him without any effort on his part to earn it."[21]

The point here is that the conflict did not simply reflect a dichotomy between "entrepreneurs" and "communalists," or between those who were educated in boarding schools and those who were not. After all, Moses Hewson ran a store, Salina Leask Gamble and Edward Marsden attended the same boarding school, and Arthur Wellington Clah, ending a long estrangement from his old compatriot, sent along a letter of support.[22] In a very real sense, positing such distinctions, especially between entrepreneurs and those not so inclined, was somewhat artificial in Metlakatla's cultural climate. All Metlakatlans were "entrepreneurs" in a way, and by virtue of following Duncan in the first place. Rather, the issue seems to have turned on the question of legitimate leadership, where the anti-Duncan side seemed to support *native* control over *native* affairs. Edward Marsden addressed this point directly when he wrote:

> One thing I am certain. I will not abandon my poor people. My skin is just like theirs. I will work for their best interests as well as those of the other Indians here in Southeastern Alaska. The system that has been fattened on the expense of our Indian rights and one that considers us as its legal chattels only to be subjugated, governed, and

disposed of at will, will hereafter be given wide publicity and be fearlessly exposed. We will then leave to the judgment of the christian [*sic*] public wherein the whole fault lies.[23]

Similar fissures plagued the Menominees as they wrestled with modernization, and, as among the Metlakatlans, the issue cannot be understood simply as a clash between those old adversaries: "progressives" and "traditionalists." Although cultural orientation was indeed a critical issue, comparatively few Menominees opposed lumbering outright and absolutely. Rather, disputes centered around the distribution of profits from industry, and indeed legitimate leadership. As with Marsden, a goodly number of Menominees mistrusted Oshkenaniew and regarded his brand of modernization as self-serving individuality, a threat to deeply held values. Unity returned to the Menominee Reservation only when Reginald Oshkosh, Neo'pit's son but a true modernizer himself, asserted his right to lead and recast many of Oshkenaniew's ideas in a more communal, and hence palatable, form. A similar process was not possible in Metlakatla, although a continuing commitment to maintaining Duncan's legacy may have tempered Marsden's individualistic tendencies.

The point is that political divisions in both places did not indicate significant opposition to economic development, or even hostility to market arrangements. In fact, while political reorganization was important, its primary significance is as an indicator of more fundamental changes. It was economic transformation, in other words, adjustment to the market, that stands out as the principal agent for social, cultural, and political modifications. Economic change mandated cultural adaptations, and Metlakatlans and Menominees altered political institutions to fit new circumstances. That it often was a tumultuous, uneven process testifies to the overwhelming power of economic forces and the difficulty with which cultures incorporate novel concepts or sets of relationships.

Even so, the Menominees and Metlakatlans did incorporate new ideas, and by the first decades of the twentieth century both groups emerged as significantly different, but still "native" in terms of evolving identities. To an important degree, both societies found in economic development a way to preserve unity, independence, and indeed survival. For the Tsimshians who elected to follow Duncan to Metlakatla, his "system" provided a way out of a downward cycle of economic dependency, cultural disorganization, and political impotence. In fact, for all his emphasis on conversion to Christianity, the most compelling aspect of Metlakatla remained its promise of material prosperity and freedom from white domination. As the Metlakatlans learned that labor in service of the community also produced goods for sale in the regional market, they reveled in their independence and resisted efforts to equate their community with Canadian Indian reserves, which, in their estimation, suffered from too great a dependence on the goodwill of whites. The Menominees also came to understand that exploiting timber resources promised a measure of independence that was rare among other tribes in the United States. They, too, used profits to fund needed services such as schools, hospitals, and housing, and in doing so they mitigated the demoralizing consequences of relying on the federal bureaucracy for the necessities of life.

Adaptation to the market also proved a spur to political action. As Menominees and Metlakatlans realized that the key to independence lay in the utilization of natural and human resources, and as individuals in both places grew accustomed to the benefits provided by economic change, they mobilized to protect their livelihood. For the Menominees, political action took the form of pressing for responsible management of timber stands, a greater role for native workers in directing logging and lumbering, influence in developing policies affecting the exploitation of resources, and an accurate accounting of costs and profits associated with reservation enterprises. When these efforts failed, or when Menominees grew dissatisfied with the nature of their relationship with white officials, the tribe hired lawyers and filed suit against the federal government. Metlakatlans, too, employed political action to protect their rights. As far back as the 1870s, William Duncan appealed to British Columbian and Canadian bureaucrats for aid to promote economic development. Metlakatlans pressed provincial and dominion lawmakers to recognize their rights to land and resources. When it became clear that they could not count on whites to help them preserve their rights to fisheries, and even to the lands on which Metlakatla stood, Duncan and his native followers appealed to governments for help, suffered a stinging rebuke, and chose to move to Alaska rather than subject themselves to restrictions, particularly those pertaining to Indian landholding, inherent in Canada's Indian policies.

Economic change also created circumstances favorable to the ambitions of native leaders. Oshkenaniew and Oshkosh benefited from the opportunities made possible by reservation enterprises, and their drives to assume political leadership were fueled by this same prosperity, uneven though it often was. In this respect, they challenge prevailing assumptions about natives who returned home after being educated in off-reservation settings. Both in their times and later, many have argued that these "returned students" generally failed because they were victims of substandard and irrelevant education, were isolated from friends, relatives, and culture, and came home to an environment devoid of possibilities or even hope. Neither Oshkenaniew nor Oshkosh faced this situation. While it is true that they clashed with those espousing more communal values, most Menominees apparently held aspirations for the future, desires that depended, to some degree, on participating in broader, "mainstream," commercial arrangements. Oshkenaniew and Oshkosh provided leadership, and in turn they found a productive avenue for their talents and training.

The situation in Metlakatla was somewhat different in that the first generation of "new leaders," such as David Leask and John Tait, did not leave the community to pursue an education. But under new economic arrangements they, too, found satisfying outlets for talents learned under Duncan's tutelage and in turn worked diligently in the service of their compatriots. And evidence of numerous, semi-independent, business enterprises suggests an ongoing "education" via commercial contacts. Duncan's program for economic change also made possible Marsden's aspirations for higher education. When he returned home, his first project involved establishing a "mini-Metlakatla" in Saxman, where he hoped to duplicate Duncan's successes but this time under Indian direction. Moreover, Marsden's subsequent conflicts with his mentor may indicate a frustration with Duncan's reluctance to allow him to utilize his talents. It is difficult to imagine even the existence of this bitter conflict had Metlakatla's future not been worth fighting for.

In the larger context, the Menominee and Metlakatla cases challenge the widely held notion that natives were "temperamentally" unsuited to capitalism or to wage labor. Here, this work stands with those pertaining to the United States and Canada, authored, respectively, by Leonard Carlson and Sarah Carter, both of whom argue that natives demonstrated considerable interest and talent for commercial agriculture. Carter even suggests a parallel between the rise and fall of native agriculture in North America and similar developments in East Africa. In all these cases, native agriculture "failed" not because Indians, or Africans, were "culturally" hostile to the notion of a settled life, or so-called tedious work, or planning for the future. Rather, they argue that ill-conceived, and often punitive, governmental policies conspired to strip them of their land base, to make it virtually impossible for individuals to raise sufficient capital (by preventing natives from mortgaging property or using it as collateral for loans) or to gain fair access to markets. Even so, Carlson and Carter demonstrate that, in what often was a self-fulfilling prophecy, whites assumed Indians could not or would not become farmers and, acting upon these assumptions, did little to aid native farmers while directing their energies toward securing massive transfers of Indian lands to the supposedly more "productive" whites.[24]

Similar problems plagued native enterprises among the Metlakatlans and Menominees. In an age when governments north and south of the border were allocating millions of dollars to finance the construction of railroads and promote the development of western lands, projects on native reservations and reserves received scant support. While Duncan was generally reluctant to tie Metlakatla's fortunes too closely to the shifting will of policy makers, his entreaties for financial support for native enterprises, and in particular the salmon cannery, often came to naught. So, too, did his efforts to convince whites to reorient Canadian native policies in ways that would promote self-reliance and economic self-sufficiency. As for the Menominees, aid from federal agencies most often went toward supporting agents and to more traditional projects, such as efforts to promote farming. To a large degree, the Menominees used timber sales to fund construction and operating costs for their sawmill, and profits eventually subsidized a whole range of community services. Ironically, then, while whites consistently castigated natives for failing to achieve a measure of financial independence, they also turned their backs on natives who tried to do for themselves.

In tracing the web of events that shaped the lives of Metlakatlans and Menominees during the decades surrounding the turn of the twentieth century, it often may seem that we are suggesting that economic interests ultimately outweigh all other considerations in the "evolution" of societies. Yet such was not the case in either place. While it appears clear that adaptation to the market set the stage for broader changes, it is equally important to caution against economic determinism in any overarching manner. Menominees and Metlakatlans may have acted as "economic men and women," but, like other peoples in other places, "culture" remains central to understanding their choices. In aboriginal times, both Menominees and Tsimshians pursued economic interests, trading goods and even people (in the Tsimshians' case), but they conducted these activities within a context influenced by cultural priorities. The Northwest Coast potlatch, for example, was an economic institution that also served important societal needs. Elites accumulated goods and in so doing cemented claims to prestigious titles, rituals, and resource-gathering sites. But they also redistributed these goods to more needy clan and lineage members. Moreover, the act of giving away vast stocks of goods demonstrated the givers' fitness to hold exalted positions in society and thus completed an equation that linked economic activities with social needs.[25] Similarly, Menominee headmen were expected to provide for fellow tribesmen and in doing so validated their own claims to leadership. For both groups, then, culture set the parameters within which they conducted economic activities.

What emerges, then, is a complex interplay between cultural and economic change, where each informed the other and where identity, or identities, proved evolving concepts and yet still rooted in certain fundamental values. As both Morris Foster and Loretta Fowler point out, cultural identity is both persistent and changing, and indeed community members "decide" what constitutes legitimate membership, or agreed upon sets of values. Ties holding people together are not necessarily what outsiders, including ethnohistorians, expect. For Menominees, this meant distributing profits as broadly as possible and financing community services. It also moved them to insist that reservation resources, including houses, belonged to the collective, not to individuals. Moreover, Reginald Oshkosh may have emerged as principal leader because, as the eldest son of Chief Neo'pit, he best exemplified the Menominees' efforts to integrate the new with the old. Metlakatlans, too, labored to chart a course for the future without abandoning the past. Even though part of Duncan's "system" envisioned the dismantling of traditional leadership structures, Metlakatlans often valued unity above pure profit and, like the Menominees, believed that all held an equal interest in community property, regardless of one's economic standing. For both groups, then, culture remained a central factor in organizing society, and while the market changed many things, it did not dismantle this old and cherished ideal.

Just as we are to be cautioned against interpreting the actions of these Indians as motivated solely by the drive for profit, so too must we avoid romanticizing their struggles lest we conclude that Indians held power over their affairs in ways they clearly did not. Influence over "big issues," be they policy or the operations of regional and national markets, is something exceedingly few Indians possessed. At the same time, Indians do render a whole series of what we might consider local "choices" as they adapt to changes, and it is here where Indians exercise some influence over the course of their lives. In a sense, this study argues that economic development does not equal assimilation, even as it is transforming. Although it is possible to conceive of a point when cultural changes are so comprehensive that they eradicate most of what makes a particular group distinctive, identity is such a complex, flexible concept, that documenting "when an Indian is no longer an Indian" is a truly monumental task. That early-twentieth-century Menominees and Metlakatlans lived very differently from their ancestors is self-evident but that does not mean that individuals from both groups ceased thinking of themselves as "Indian" peoples, not simply white men with red skin. The fact that both groups wrestled with changes and attempted to incorporate the market into existing, albeit evolving, structures indicates both the importance of heritage and their very real concern that they not abandon their pasts.

Similarly, concepts regarding culture that emphasize a rigid dichotomy between the traditional and the modern also rob natives of important parts of their histories, and indeed their very humanity. It is under these outdated constructions that Indians emerge as passive pawns, fighting against all odds to preserve a way of life that is out of step with new realities. Natives were, and are, more creative than that. They were, and are, actors in their own affairs, and they make the kinds of choices that help determine later events. It is for this reason that this work presents the view that Menominees and Metlakatlans, native peoples separated by great distance, understood the forces affecting their lives and chose economic modernization as the best possible way to preserve, not abandon, distinctive identities. That theirs was a circumscribed, even precarious, independence tells us more about the tremendous task before them than about the supposed inability of native cultures to adapt to changed circumstances. Their success in conserving traditions while working within the white man's market system also bears witness to the flexibility of culture, and to two peoples' creativity in reinterpreting culture to fit new ways.

Notes

1. Angus S. Nicholson, "The Menominee Indians Working Their Way," *The Red Man* 5, no. 1 (September 1912): 19, 23.
2. Ibid., 19.
3. Ibid., 19, 21.
4. Ibid., 19, 22.
5. Ibid., 22.
6. Ibid., 23.
7. Ibid.
8. A note on the spelling of "Metlakatla." During the nineteenth and early twentieth centuries, the predominant spelling was "Metlakahtla," with an "h" inserted before the second "t." This was William Duncan's spelling and as such was "official." By the mid–twentieth century, however, that "h" had disappeared, and "Metlakatla" became the modern spelling for both the British Columbia and the Alaska communities. More recently and in combination with land claims cases, British Columbia Tsimshians have begun to substitute "Maxhlahxaahla," a spelling more reflective of native phonemes. As of this date, however, both communities continue to use "Metlakatla" as an official spelling. For purposes of consistency, I have chosen to use "Metlakatla," except, of course, in direct quotations. The most recent full-length study of Duncan and Metlakatla is Peter Murray's *The Devil and Mr. Duncan: A History of the Two Metlakatlas* (Victoria: Sono Nis Press, 1985).
9. George T. B. Davis, *Metlakahtla, A True Narrative of the Red Man* (Chicago: Ram's Horn, 1904), 118.
10. Ibid., 119.
11. Ibid., 119–20.
12. Ibid., 120.
13. Ibid., 123.
14. Ibid., 123; S. E. Bridgeman, *Rev. William Duncan, the Alaskan Pearl Seeker*, 55th Cong., 2d sess., S. Doc. 275, 15.
15. On this subject, see especially Ronald L. Meek, *Social Science and the Ignoble Savage* (Cambridge: Cambridge University Press, 1976); Roy Harvey Pearce, *Savagism and Civilization: A Study of the Indian and the American Mind*, rev. ed. (Baltimore: Johns Hopkins University Press, 1971); Robert F. Berkhofer Jr., *The White Man's Indian: Images of the American Indian from Columbus to the Present* (New York: Vintage Books, 1978); Lewis Henry Morgan, *Ancient Society; or, Researches in the Lines of Human Progress from Savagery Through Barbarism to Civilization* (New York: Henry Holt, 1877), v–vii, 9–12, 18–27, 30–37, 40–41; Frederick E. Hoxie, *A Final Promise: The Campaign to Assimilate the Indians, 1880–1920* (New York: Cambridge University Press, 1984), 1–39; George W. Stocking Jr., *Race, Culture and Evolution: Essays in the History of Anthropology*, rev. ed. (Chicago: University of Chicago Press, 1982), 69–132; Nancy Oestreich Lurie, "Relations Between Indians and

Anthropologists," in *History of Indian-White Relations*, ed. Wilcomb E. Washburn, vol. 4 of *Handbook of North American Indians*, ed. William C. Sturtevant (Washington, D.C.: Smithsonian Institution Press, 1988), 549–61.

16. Lurie, "Relations Between Indians and Anthropologists," 549; Berkhofer, *White Man's Indian*, 52–54.

17. Stocking, *Race, Culture, and Evolution*, 72–88, 116–25; Berkhofer, *White Man's Indian*, 51–54; Lurie, "Relations Between Indians and Anthropologists," 549–51. For a full-length account of Morgan's thinking, see Thomas R. Trautmann, *Lewis Henry Morgan and the Invention of Kinship* (Berkeley: University of California Press, 1987).

18. Berkhofer, *White Man's Indian*, 63; Lurie ("Relations Between Indians and Anthropologists," 551) credits Margaret Mead's influential work *The Changing Culture of an Indian Tribe* (New York: Columbia University Press, 1932) with drawing attention of anthropologists to the question of cultural change.

19. See Ralph Linton, ed., *Acculturation in Seven American Indian Tribes* (New York: Appleton-Century, 1940), 463–520; Robert Redfield, Ralph Linton, and Melvin J. Herskovits, "A Memorandum on the Study of Acculturation," *American Anthropologist*, n.s., 38 (1936): 149–52; Edward H. Spicer, *Perspectives in American Indian Culture Change* (Chicago: University of Chicago Press, 1961), 517–44; C. Matthew Snipp, "Changing Political and Economic Status of the American Indians: From Captive Nations to Internal Colonies," *American Journal of Economics and Sociology* 45 (April 1986): 148.

20. Snipp, "Changing Political and Economic Status," 148; Loretta Fowler, *Shared Symbols, Contested Meanings: Gros Ventre Culture and History, 1778–1984* (Ithaca, N.Y.: Cornell University Press, 1987), 6.

21. Fowler, *Shared Symbols*, 6.

22. Ibid.

23. Walt W. Rostow, *The Stages of Economic Growth* (Cambridge: Cambridge University Press, 1960).

24. Snipp, "Changing Political and Economic Status," 148.

25. For more on this see Hoxie, *Final Promise*; R. Douglas Hurt, *Indian Agriculture in America: Prehistory to the Present* (Lawrence: University Press of Kansas, 1987), 96–151; William T. Hagan, "Private Property, the Indian's Door to Civilization," *Ethnohistory* 3 (Spring 1956): 126–37; Loring Benson Priest, *Uncle Sam's Stepchildren: The Reformation of United States Indian Policy, 1865–1887* (New York: Octagon Books, 1969); Joseph Jorgensen, "Century of Political Economic Effects on American Indian Society, 1880–1980," *Journal of Ethnic Studies* 6 (1978): 1–82; Larry W. Burt, *Tribalism in Crisis: Federal Indian Policy, 1953–61* (Albuquerque: University of New Mexico Press, 1982); Marjane Ambler, *Breaking the Iron Bonds: Indian Control of Energy Development* (Lawrence: University Press of Kansas, 1990); and Vicki Page, "Reservation Development in the United States: Periphery to the Core," *American Indian Culture and Research Journal* 9 (1985): 22.

26. Fowler, *Shared Symbols*, 6

27. See Reinhard Bendix, "Tradition and Modernity Reconsidered," *Comparative Studies in Society and History* 9 (1967): 292–346; Thomas D. Hall, "Peripheries, Regions of Refuge, and Nonstate Societies: Toward a Theory of Reactive Social Change," *Social Science Quarterly* 64 (1983): 586–87; Snipp, "Changing Political and Economic Status," 148; Page, "Reservation Development," 22; For an application of this in an unusual setting, see Michael Hechter, *Internal Colonialism: The Celtic Fringe in British National Development, 1536–1966* (Berkeley: University of California Press, 1975).

28. Snipp, "Changing Political and Economic Status," 148. The quote is from Evan Z. Vogt, "The Acculturation of American Indians," *Annals of the American Academy of Political and Social Science* 311 (1957): 139.

29. While there are important differences between dependency and world-systems theories, their general outlines are quite similar. For that reason I have chosen to group them together. Snipp, "Changing Political and Economic Status," 149; Hall, "Peripheries, Regions of Refuge," 586–87; Page, "Reservation Development," 22–23.

30. André Gunder Frank, *Capitalism and Underdevelopment in Latin America: Historical Studies of Chile and Brazil* (New York: Monthly Review Press, 1967); Immanuel Wallerstein, *The Modern World-System: Capitalist Agriculture and the Origins of European World Economy in the Sixteenth Century* (New York: Academic Press, 1974); See also Paul Baran, *The Political Economy of Growth* (New York: Monthly Review Press, 1957).

31. The literature on dependency and world-systems theories is extensive, indeed unwieldy. For this reason, I have decided to rely on several short articles to construct this section. They are Hall, "Peripheries, Regions of Refuge," 582–95; Page, "Reservation Development," 21–35; Snipp, "Changing Political and Economic Status," 457–74; Thomas D. Hall, "Native Americans and Incorporation: Patterns and Problems," *American Indian Culture and Research Journal* 11 (1987): 1–30; and Stephen Gudeman, "A View of the North from the South," in *Overcoming Economic Dependency*, The Newberry Library, D'Arcy McNickle Center for the History of the American Indian, Occasional Papers in Curriculum Series, Occasional Paper No. 9 (Chicago: Newberry Library, 1988), 8–24. Also useful is James A. Carporaso, "Dependence, Dependency, and Power in the Global System: A Structural and Behavioral Analysis," *International Organization* 32 (Winter 1978): 13–43.

32. Hall, "Peripheries, Regions of Refuge," 586.

33. Ibid., 586–87; Gudeman, "View of the North," 11–12; Page, "Reservation Development," 22–23. See also Cardell Jacobson, "Internal Colonialism and Native Americans: Indian Labor in the United States from 1871 to World War II," *Social Science Quarterly* 65 (1984): 159.

34. Snipp, "Changing Political and Economic Status," 150; Hall, "Peripheries, Regions of Refuge," 586; Frank, *Capitalism and Underdevelopment.*

35. Snipp, "Changing Political and Economic Status," 150.

36. Hall, "Peripheries, Regions of Refuge," 586.

37. Ibid.; Snipp, "Changing Political and Economic Status," 150. See also Joan W. Moore, "American Minorities and 'New Nations' Perspectives," *Pacific Sociological Review* 19 (October 1976): 449–55; and Jacobson, "Internal Colonialism," 159.

38. Hechter, in *Internal Colonialism,* has also employed the internal colony model to explain the continued existence of underdeveloped regions within Great Britain. He lays particular emphasis on the role of ethnocentrism in deepening underdevelopment in peripheral regions.

39. See Joseph G. Jorgensen, "Indians and the Metropolis," in *The American Indian in Urban Society,* ed. Jack O. Waddell and O. Michael Watson (Boston: Little, Brown, 1971), 66–112; Joseph G. Jorgensen, *The Sun Dance Religion: Power for the Powerless* (Chicago: University of Chicago Press, 1972); Jorgensen, "Century of Political Economic Effects." See also Page, "Reservation Development," 22–23.

40. Jorgensen, "Century of Political Economic Effects," 5–7; Page, "Reservation Development," 22–23; Snipp, "Changing Political and Economic Status," 150–51.

41. Jacobson, "Internal Colonialism," 167–68; Moore, "American Minorities," 451–53; H. Craig Miner, *The Corporation and the Indian: Tribal Sovereignty and Industrial Civilization in Indian Territory, 1865–1907*, 2d ed. (Norman: University of Oklahoma Press, 1989), passim.

42. Hall, "Peripheries, Regions of Refuge," 587; Gudeman, "View of the North," 14; Hall, "Native Americans and Incorporation," 2–3; Eric R. Wolf, *Europe and the People Without History* (Berkeley: University of California Press, 1982), 23–24; Richard White, *The Roots of Dependency: Subsistence, Environment, and Social Change Among the Choctaws, Pawnees, and Navajos* (Lincoln: University of Nebraska Press, 1983), xvi–xvii; Fowler, *Shared Symbols*, 6.

43. A recent work that offers a compelling account of pre- as well as post-white contact culture change is John H. Moore's *The Cheyenne Nation: A Social and Demographic History* (Lincoln: University of Nebraska Press, 1987). See also Wolf, *Europe and the People Without History*, 18.

44. Among other works, see Ronald L. Trosper, "The Other Discipline: Economics and American Indian History," in *New Directions in American Indian History*, ed. Colin G. Calloway (Norman: University of Oklahoma Press, 1988), 199–222; Rolf Knight, *Indians at Work: An Informal History of Native Indian Labour in British Columbia, 1858–1930* (Vancouver: New Star Books, 1987); Daniel L. Boxberger, *To Fish in Common: The Ethnohistory of Lummi Indian Salmon Fishing* (Lincoln: University of Nebraska Press, 1989); Arthur McEvoy, *The Fisherman's Problem: Ecology and Law in the California Fisheries, 1850–1980* (Cambridge: Cambridge University Press, 1987); Thomas Vennum Jr., *Wild Rice and the Ojibway People* (St. Paul: Minnesota Historical Society Press, 1988); Roxanne Dunbar Ortiz, ed., *Economic Development in American Indian Reservations* (Albuquerque: University of New Mexico Press, 1979); David Rich Lewis, *Neither Wolf nor Dog: American Indians, Environment, and Agrarian Change* (New York: Oxford University Press, 1994); Ambler, *Breaking the Iron Bonds*. See also Hall, "Native Americans and Incorporation," 5–6; White, *Roots of Dependency*, xv–xvi.

45. White, *Roots of Dependency*, xv–xvi, 318–19.

46. Boxberger, *To Fish in Common*; McEvoy, *The Fisherman's Problem*; Lewis, *Neither Wolf nor Dog*; William Cronon, *Changes in the Land: Indians, Colonists, and the Ecology of New England* (New York: Hill and Wang, 1983); Wolf, *Europe and the People Without History*.

47. Hall, "Peripheries, Regions of Refuge"; Hall, "Native Americans and Incorporation"; Duane Champagne, *Strategies and Conditions of Political and Cultural Survival in American Indian Societies*, Cultural Survival, Occasional Papers, No. 21 (Boston: Cultural Survival, 1985); Snipp, "Changing Political and Economic Status."

48. Christopher Chase-Dunn and Thomas D. Hall, *Rise and Demise: Comparing World Systems* (Boulder, Colo.: Westview Press, 1997); Christopher Chase-Dunn and Thomas D. Hall, "World Systems in North America: Networks, Rise and Fall and Pulsations of Trade in Stateless Systems," *American Indian Culture and Research Journal* 22 (1988): 23–72.

49. Alice Littlefield and Martha C. Knack, eds., *Native Americans and Wage Labor: Ethnohistorical Perspectives* (Norman: University of Oklahoma Press, 1996).

50. Fowler, *Shared Symbols*, 2. See also Loretta Fowler, *Arapahoe Politics, 1851–1978: Symbols in Crises of Authority* (Lincoln: University of Nebraska Press, 1982); Marshall D. Sahlins, *Islands of History* (Chicago: University of Chicago Press, 1985); Clifford Geertz, *The Interpretation of Cultures* (New York: Basic Books, 1973).

51. Fowler, Shared Symbols, 10.

52. Richard White, *The Middle Ground: Indians, Empires, and Republics in the Great Lakes Region, 1650–1815* (New York: Cambridge University Press, 1991), 95.

53. Morris W. Foster, *Being Comanche: A Social History of an American Indian Community* (Tucson: University of Arizona Press, 1991); Melissa L. Meyer, *The White Earth Tragedy: Ethnicity and Dispossession at a Minnesota Anishinaabe Reservation, 1889–1920* (Lincoln: University of Nebraska Press, 1994); Daniel K. Richter, *The Ordeal of the Longhouse: The Peoples of the Iroquois League in the Era of European Colonization* (Chapel Hill: University of North Carolina Press, 1992).

54. Fowler, *Shared Symbols,* 8.

55. Robert H. White, *Tribal Assets: The Rebirth of Native America* (New York: Henry Holt, 1990), 277.

56. Knight, *Indians at Work,* 16.

57. Ibid., 23, 26.

1. THE MENOMINEES

1. Nicholson, "Menominee Indians Working Their Way," 19, 23.

2. This version of the Menominee genesis was recorded by the anthropologist Alanson Skinner through his informant-interpreter John V. Saterlee and was told by Näkuni, aged eighty-four in 1912. See Alanson B. Skinner, "Social Life and Ceremonial Bundles of the Menomini Indians," in *Anthropological Papers of the American Museum of Natural History,* vol. 13, pt. 1 (New York: American Museum of Natural History, 1913), 8–10. I have also used Skinner's syllabary.

3. Ibid., 10.

4. While scholars remain unsure as to the meaning or etymology of Omä'nománéo, they agree that it does not derive from the Menominee word for wild rice, which is *mano'm h.* The tribe seems to have accepted "Menominee" since very early in the contact period, and use it to identify themselves. For Mamaceqtaw, see Verna Fowler, "Menominee," in *Encyclopedia of North American Indians,* ed. Frederick E. Hoxie (Boston: Houghton Mifflin, 1996), 371. For early uses of "nation de la folle avoine," or "Folles Avoines," see Reuben G. Thwaites, ed., *The Jesuit Relations and Allied Documents: Travel and Explorations of the Jesuit Missionaries in New France, 1610–1791,* 73 vols. (Cleveland: Burrows Brothers, 1896–1901), 55: 102 [henceforth, *JR*]. For a survey of Menominee synonymy, see Louise Spindler, "Menominee," in *Northeast,* ed. Bruce G. Trigger, vol. 15 of *Handbook of North American Indians,* ed. William C. Sturtevant (Washington, D.C.: Smithsonian Institution Press, 1988), 724.

5. In constructing this section on Menominee culture, I have relied on several classic ethnographies as well as more recent studies. The best recent study is David Robert Martin Beck, "Seige and Survival: Menominee Responses to an Encroaching World" (Ph.D. diss., University of Illinois, 1994). Classic works include Walter James Hoffman, "The Menomini Indians," in *Fourteenth Annual Report of the Bureau of Ethnology, for the Years 1892–93* (Washington, D.C.: GPO, 1896); Skinner, "Social Life and Ceremonial Bundles"; Alanson B. Skinner, "Associations and Ceremonies of the Menomini Indians," in *Anthropological Papers of the American Museum of Natural History,* vol. 13, pt. 2 (New York: American Museum of Natural History, 1915); and Alanson Skinner and John V. Satterlee, "Folklore of the Menomini Indians," in *Anthropological Papers of the American Museum of Natural History,* vol. 13, pt. 3 (New York: American Museum of Natural History,

1915). See also Spindler, "Menominee," 708–24; Albert E. Jenks, "The Wild Rice Gatherers of the Upper Lakes: A Study in American Primitive Economics," in *Nineteenth Annual Report of the Bureau of American Ethnology, for the Years 1897–98* (Washington, D.C.: GPO, 1900); Patricia K. Ourada, *The Menominee Indians: A History* (Norman: University of Oklahoma Press, 1979); Felix M. Keesing, *The Menomini Indians of Wisconsin: A Study of Three Centuries of Cultural Contact and Change,* Memoirs of the American Philosophical Society, No. 10 (Philadelphia: American Philosophical Society, 1939); and M. Inez Hilger, "Some Early Customs of the Menomini Indians," *Journal de la Société des Americanistes de Paris,* n.s., 49 (1960): 45–68. Charles Callender's *Social Organization of the Central Algonkian Indians,* Milwaukee Public Museum, Publications in Anthropology, No. 7 (Milwaukee: Milwaukee Public Museum, 1962), discusses Menominee culture in a comparative framework. The population figure is from Nicholas C. Peroff, "Menominee," in *Native America in the Twentieth Century, An Encyclopedia,* ed. Mary B. Davis (New York: Garland, 1994), 329–30.

6. For this section I have relied on Jeanne Kay's invaluable "Wisconsin Indian Hunting Patterns, 1634–1836," *Annals of the Association of American Geographers* 69 (1979): 403–5, 414–15. See also Callender, *Social Organization,* 12, 33; Spindler, "Menominee," 708–9, 713. For early accounts of the Wisconsin environment and Menominee subsistence patterns, see *JR* 44:245–51; 56:121; 57:265–67; 58:273–75; 59:93. The quote is from Claude Charles Le Roy, Sieur de Bracquevile de la Potherie, "History of the Savage People Who Are Allies of New France," in *The Indian Tribes of the Upper Mississippi Valley and Region of the Great Lakes,* ed. Emma Helen Blair (Cleveland: Arthur H. Clark, 1911), 2:305.

7. The best source on wild rice remains Jenks, "Wild Rice Gatherers," 1013–137. See also Hoffman, "Menomini Indians," 290–91; Vennum, *Wild Rice and the Ojibway People;* United States House of Representatives, 20th Cong., 2d sess., 1829, H. Doc. 117; *Annual Reports of the Commissioner of Indian Affairs* [henceforth, *ARCIA*], 1838, 16; 1845, 494. See also Jenks, "Wild Rice Gatherers," 1048–49.

8. Jenks, "Wild Rice Gatherers," 1058–71; Hoffman, "Menomini Indians," 290–91; Skinner, "Social Life and Ceremonial Bundles," 25–26; Callender, *Social Organization,* 33.

9. Hoffman, "Menomini Indians," 286–92; Spindler, "Menominee Women"; Spindler, "Menominee," 708–9, 718. For more on women's roles and economic activities, see Nancy Shoemaker, ed., *Negotiators of Change: Historical Perspectives on Native American Women* (New York: Routledge, 1995); Carol Devens, *Countering Colonization: Native American Women and Great Lakes Missions, 1630–1900* (Berkeley: University of California Press, 1992); Priscilla K. Buffalohead, "Farmers, Warriors, Traders: A French Look at Ojibway Women," *Minnesota History* 48 (1983): 236–44.

10. Hoffman, "Menomini Indians," 39–43; Skinner, "Social Life and Ceremonial Bundles," 17–22; Callender, *Social Organization,* 35; Spindler, "Menominee," 713; Keesing, *Menomini Indians,* 40.

11. Hoffman, "Menomini Indians," 43; Skinner, "Social Life and Ceremonial Bundles," 22–25; Callender, *Social Organization,* 35–36; Spindler, "Menominee," 40.

12. Skinner, "Social Life and Ceremonial Bundles," 6–8, 73–85; Hoffman, "Menomini Indians," 87; Spindler, "Menominee," 714–17.

13. Skinner, "Social Life and Ceremonial Bundles," 42–47; Skinner, "Associations and Ceremonies," 191–92; Hoffman, "Menomini Indians," 151–52; Spindler, "Menominee," 714–17.

14. Skinner, "Associations and Ceremonies," 192–97; Hoffman, "Menomini Indians," 138–40; Spindler, "Menominee, 714–17.

15. George D. Spindler and Louise S. Spindler, *Dreamers with Power: The Menominee*, 2d ed. (Prospect Heights, Ill.: Waveland Press, 1984), 54–62; Hoffman, 11, 66–84, 151–52; Spindler, "Menominee," 715–16, 718.

16. Spindler, "Menominee," 718–19; Kay, "Wisconsin Indian Hunting Patterns," 403–5, 414–15. The best treatment of the Great Lakes demographic "revolution" and Indian-white diplomacy during the fur trade period is Richard White's book *The Middle Ground*. For a detailed account of the Iroquian expansion westward, see Richter, *The Ordeal of the Longhouse*.

17. Kay, "Wisconsin Indian Hunting Patterns," 415–17; Spindler, "Menominees," 713, 719; See also Ourada, *Menominee Indians*, 13–41; and Stephen J. Hertzberg, "The Menominee Indians: From Treaty to Trusteeship," *Wisconsin Magazine of History* 60 (Summer 1977): 268–69.

18. One Catholic missionary reported that Menominee women resisted Christianity, and particularly its impact on gender roles. See Anthony Marie Gachet, "Five Years in America (Cinq Ans en Amérique): Journal of a Missionary Among the Redskins, 1859," trans. Joseph Schafer, *Wisconsin Magazine of History* 18 (1834–35): 66–76, 191–204, 345–59. For insights into the changing roles of women and the question of women's "autonomy" in the fur trade era I have relied on Sylvia Van Kirk, *Many Tender Ties: Women in Fur Trade Society, 1676–1870* (Norman: University of Oklahoma Press, 1980); Jennifer S. H. Brown, *Strangers in Blood: Fur Trade Company Families in Indian Country* (Vancouver: University of British Columbia Press, 1980); Devens, *Countering Colonization*; Kathryn Holland Braund, "Guardians of Traditions and Handmaidens to Change: Women's Roles in Creek Economic and Social Life in the Eighteenth Century," *American Indian Quarterly* 14 (1990): 239–58; and Meyer, *The White Earth Tragedy*. More recently, Nancy Shoemaker and Lucy Eldersveld Murphy have demonstrated that women were able to maintain a measure of autonomy by adapting to changed economic circumstances. See Nancy Shoemaker, "The Rise or Fall of Iroquois Women," *Journal of Women's History* 2 (1991): 39–57; Nancy Eldersveld Murphy, "Autonomy and the Economic Roles of Indian Women of the Fox-Winnebago River Region, 1763–1832," in Shoemaker, *Negotiators of Change*, 72–89.

19. Hoffman, "Menomini Indians," 33; Keesing, *Menomini Indians*, 225; Spindler, "Menominee," 708–10, 718–19; Callender, *Social Organization*, 8–9; Hertzberg, "Menominee Indians," 270–72; Ourada, *Menominee Indians*, 32, 40, 47, 51–58. For more on the genealogy of the Thomas Carron "clan," see Hoffman, "Menomini Indians," 50–60.

20. Kay, "Wisconsin Indian Hunting Patterns," 416–17; Spindler, "Menominee," 719; Hertzberg, "Menominee Indians," 267–74. For a more detailed discussion of Menominee land cession treaties, see Ourada, *Menominee Indians*, 75–77, 88–89, 94–97, 107–10.

21. Hertzberg, "Menominee Indians," 274–75; Ourada, *Menominee Indians*, 110–22, with Oshkosh's quotation on page 99.

22. Kay, "Wisconsin Indian Hunting Patterns," 416–17; Hoffman, "Menomini Indians," 31–36; Ourada, *Menominee Indians*, 122–23; Spindler, "Menominee," 708–9, 719–20.

23. *ARCIA*, 1870, 776; 1871, 928–29; Spindler, "Menominees," 708–9, 719–20; Hoffman, "Menomini Indians," 47–48; Ourada, *Menominee Indians*, 123–26, 135–36, 147–48; Hertzberg, "Menominee Indians," 275–76.

24. *ARCIA*, 1870, 776; Ourada, *Menominee Indians*, 147–48; Hoffman, "Menomini Indians," 47–48.

25. *ARCIA*, 1870, 777; 1871, 927–28, 1050, 1059, 1079; 1872, 58–59; 1873, 545–46; J. P. Kinney, *Indian Forest and Range: A History of the Administration and Conservation of the Redman's Heritage* (Washington, D.C.: Forestry Enterprises, 1950), 1–6; Ourada, *Menominee Indians*, 142.

26. *ARCIA*, 1873, 545–46; 1874, 494–95; 1875, 873; 1876, 550–51. See also J. P. Kinney, *A Continent Lost—A Civilization Won: Indian Land Tenure in America* (Baltimore: Johns Hopkins University Press, 1937). Bridgeman's quotation is from *ARCIA*, 1876, 550–51.

27. *ARCIA*, 1874, 187, 495; 1875, 370; 1876, 551; Kinney, *Indian Forest and Range*, 8–9. For studies on the Wisconsin "pine ring," see Robert F. Fries, *Empire in Pine: The Story of Logging in Wisconsin, 1830–1900* (Madison: State Historical Society of Wisconsin, 1951); and Charles E. Twining, "Plunder and Progress: The Lumbering Industry in Historical Perspective," *Wisconsin Magazine of History* 47 (Winter 1963–64): 116–24.

28. *ARCIA*, 1874, 495. Bridgeman's quotation is from *ARCIA*, 1875, 872.

29. *United States v. Cook* (1873), 19 Wallace 591; *ARCIA*, 1876, 551; Kinney, *Indian Forest and Range*, 7–9; Kinney, *A Continent Lost*, 256.

30. *ARCIA*, 1880, 292; "Statistical Supplement, " *ARCIA*, 1880, 350–51.

31. "Statistical Supplement," *ARCIA*, 1871–80; Jenks, "Wild Rice Gatherers," 1075–77; Hoffman, "Menomini Indians," 269.

32. E. Stephens to Commissioner of Indian Affairs, 12 January 1881, National Archives, Record Group 75, Letters Received, Office of Indian Affairs, 1881–1907, Accession 754 [henceforth, NA, RG 75, LR, OIA, Accession number].

33. The standard treatment of the Menominee Dream Dance is S. A. Barrett's "The Dream Dance of the Chippewa and Menominee Indians of Northern Wisconsin," in *Bulletin of the Public Museum of the City of Milwaukee*, vol. 1, article 4 (Milwaukee: Milwaukee Public Museum, 1911), 253–406. See also Spindler and Spindler, *Dreamers with Power*, 61–68; Hoffman, "Menomini Indians," 157–61; and Skinner, "Associations and Ceremonies," 173–81.

Because the Dream and Ghost Dances shared many features and were contemporaneous, scholars have considered the possibility of a link between the two movements. Barrett, "Dream Dance," 279–301, discusses this in some detail, and while he concedes that a connection was "possible," he also notes that the dances were quite different, ritually as well as philosophically. At this point, it is possible to argue only that certain vague ideas regarding the importance of rituals in regenerating a religion, or society, in crisis found expression in many places, among many peoples, throughout the nineteenth century, and even earlier. Given the preponderance of such movements the world over, however, it can be (and has been) argued that revitalization movements may be a very common psychological response to pressures of cultural change. For a sampling of the vast literature on North American "messianic" movements, see Anthony F. C. Wallace, *Culture and Personality*, 2d ed. (New York: Random House, 1970), 191–96; and William A. Haviland, *Cultural Anthropology*, 3d ed. (New York: Holt, Rinehart and Winston, 1981), 365–66. Studies of specific movements include James Mooney, "The Ghost Dance Religion and the Sioux Outbreak of 1890," *Bureau of American Ethnology, Annual Report for 1892–93* (Washington, D.C.: GPO, 1896), vol. 14, no. 2; R. David Edmunds, *The Shawnee Prophet* (Lincoln: University of Nebraska Press, 1983); Jorgensen, *The Sun Dance Religion;* Anthony F. C. Wallace, *The Death and Rebirth of the Seneca* (New York: Vintage Books, 1972); and Gregory Dowd's fascinating book *A Spirited Resistance: The North American Indian Struggle for Unity, 1745–1815* (Baltimore: Johns Hopkins University Press, 1992).

34. Barrett, "Dream Dance," 295–98; Hoffman, "Menomini Indians," 157–58; Spindler, "Menominee," 716; Spindler and Spindler, *Dreamers with Power*, 62–68.

35, Spindler and Spindler, *Dreamers with Power*, 62–68. The quote is from Hoffman, "Menomini Indians," 160–61.

36. Hoffman, "Menomini Indians," 161.

37. Stephens to CIA, 25 August 1881, NA, RG 75, LR, OIA, Accession #15033; Stephens to CIA, 27 August 1881. NA, RG 75, LR, OIA, Accession #15219; Keesing, *The Menominee Indians*, 170–73.

38. *ARCIA*, 1881, 235–36.

39. Ibid., 235; *Shawano County Advocate*, 16 April 1882. Melissa Meyer's *White Earth Tragedy* is the best treatment of logging and its impact on Ojibwa communities. A dated but still useful study is Edmund Jefferson Danziger Jr., *The Chippewas of Lake Superior* (Norman: University of Oklahoma Press, 1979).

2. COMMERCIAL LOGGING DURING THE 1880s

1. I am indebted to Frederick Hoxie's masterful book, *A Final Promise*, for this analysis of policy objectives during the latter third of the nineteenth century.

2. David Rich Lewis, in *Neither Wolf nor Dog*, explores at length the place of agrarianism in nineteenth-century discussions of Indian cultural change. See also Hoxie, *A Final Promise*.

3. Martha Knack has influenced my thinking on the impact of wage labor in Indian societies. See Littlefield and Knack, *Native Americans and Wage Labor*. An earlier work, Rolf Knight's *Indians at Work*, suggests as well that Indians were far more involved in the mainstream wage economy than previously thought. For more on logging and wage labor in the Great Lakes, see Meyer, *White Earth Tragedy*, and Lewis, *Neither Wolf nor Dog*.

4. David Rich Lewis, in "Reservation Leadership and the Progressive-Traditional Dichotomy: William Wash and the Northern Utes, 1865–1928," *Ethnohistory* 38 (1991): 124–42, warns us away from relying on the "traditionalist vs. progressive" dichotomy. I am indebted to Thomas Hall for articulating the notion of "purposeful modernization." Among a plethora of articles on this topic, see particularly Hall, "Peripheries, Regions of Refuge," 582–95; Hall, "Native Americans and Incorporation," 1–30; and Vicki Page, "Reservation Development," 21–35.

5. In *United States v. Cook* (1874), the Supreme Court ruled that Indians possessed only a "right of occupancy" to reservation lands and resources. This meant that reservation resources such as timber, minerals, and the like remained the trust property of the United States government. The opinion was consistent with a series of precedents establishing Indian "right of occupancy" and the federal government's role as guardian over Indian lands. In 1882, Secretary of the Interior Henry M. Teller approved an exemption for "dead and down" (i.e., damaged) timber, and it was under this exemption that Menominee, and Anishinaabe (Chippewa), logging could resume. See *United States v. Cook* (19 Wallace 591) 1874; *ARCIA*, 1888; Kinney, *A Continent Lost*, 253–56. See also the series of precedents upon which it rested: *Johnson v. McIntosh* (8 Wheaton 543) 1823; *Cherokee Nation v. Georgia* (5 Peters 1) 1831; *Worcester v. Georgia* (6 Peters 515) 1832; and *United States v. Rogers* (4 Howard 567) 1846.

AMERICAN INDIANS IN THE MARKETPLACE

6. Stephens to CIA, 29 December 1881, NA, RG 75, LR, OIA, Accession #290.

7. *ARCIA*, 1882, 232; Stephens to E. Stevens, 1882, NA, RG 75, LR, OIA, Accession #295; Stephens to CIA, 1882, NA, RG 75, LR, OIA, Accession #1986; Stephens to CIA, 3 March 1882, NA, RG 75, LR, OIA, Accession #4577; Stephens to CIA, 23 March 1882, NA, RG 75, LR, OIA, Accession #4754; Stephens to CIA, 7 April 1882, NA, RG 75, LR, OIA, Accession #64742; M. Wescott (agency trader) to Stephens, 29 December 1881, NA, RG 75, LR, OIA, Accession #290; Stephens to CIA, 14 February 1882, NA, RG 75, LR, OIA, Accession #2630.

8. "Statistical Supplements," in *ARCIA*, 1881–85. The tribe also realized an additional $5,000 from logs cut during the abortive 1876–77 season. A separate act provided for the sale of logs cut in 1876–77 under Agent J. C. Bridgeman's authority, for which the tribe realized an additional $5,000. *ARCIA*, 1882, 232.

9. *ARCIA*, 1885, 433.

10. Stephens to CIA, 30 May 1882, NA, RG 75, LR, OIA, Accession #9790; Stephens to E. Scheffels and Son, 26 February 1883, NA, RG 75, LR, OIA, Accession #9987; A. G. Wescott (attorney) to CIA, 30 October 1883, NA, RG 75, LR, OIA, Accession #19988. For band leaders and Menominee genealogy, see Hoffman, "Menomini Indians," 44–60. Also useful is an appendix prepared by David Robert Martin Beck in his dissertation, "Siege and Survival," 556–94.

11. Stephens to CIA, 23 January 1882, NA, RG 75, LR, OIA, Accession #1851; Stephens to CIA, 31 January 1882, NA, RG 75, LR, OIA, Accession #2425; Agent D. P. Andrews to CIA, 11 December 1883, NA, RG 75, LR, OIA, Accession #22694.

12. "Statistical Supplements," in *ARCIA*, 1881–85.

13. A. G. Wescott (attorney) to CIA, 30 October 1883, NA, RG 75, LR, OIA, Accession #19988; Agent Thomas Jennings to CIA, "Statistics relating to logs banked on the Wolf and Oconto Rivers," 13 June 1889, NA, RG 75, LR, OIA, Accession #16024; Hoffman, "Menomini Indians," 11, 34. Hoffman records Mah Chickeney as headman of the Aqka'mot band, one of eleven bands in existence at the time of his fieldwork in 1890.

14. Lewis, "Reservation Leadership," 140–42; Meyer, *White Earth Tragedy.* See also Fowler, *Arapahoe Politics*; Foster, *Being Comanche.*

15. Hoffman, "Menomini Indians," 48.

16. Stephens to CIA, 23 May 1882, NA, RG 75, LR, OIA, Accession #9422; *ARCIA*, 1885, 433; Spindler and Spindler, *Dreamers with Power*, 18–35, 179–92; Beck, "Siege and Survival," 185–86.

17. Ohopahsa, Louis Oshkenaniew, Joseph F. Gauthier, and Ahkonemi Oshkosh to CIA, 2 June 1882, NA, RG 75, LR, OIA, Accession #10089.

18. Petition signed by ninety-seven Menominees to CIA, 29 June 1882, NA, RG 75, LR, OIA, Accession #10710.

19. Neopit, Mah Chickeney, Ne-ah-tah-wah-puny, Ohopahsa, John Shawanopash, Wytahsha to CIA, 19 January 1883, NA, RG 75, LR, OIA, Accession #2308.

20. *ARCIA*, 1885, 433.

21. This analysis is based on close reading of the following documents: Ohopahsa, Louis Oshkenaniew, Joseph F. Gauthier, and Ahkonemi Oshkosh to CIA, 2 June 1882, NA, RG 75, LR, Accession #10089; Petition signed by 97 Menominees to CIA, 29 June 1882, NA, RG 75, LR, Accession #10710; Neopit, Mah Chickeney, Ne-ah-tah-wah-puny, Ohopahsa, John Shawanopass, Wytahsha to CIA, 19 January 1883, NA, RG 75, LR, Accession #2308; Agent Thomas Jennings to CIA, "Statistics relating to logs banked on the Wolf and Oconto Rivers," 13 June 1889,

NA, RG 75, LR, OIA, Accession #16024. Also helpful is Beck's dissertation ("Siege and Survival") and its appendix.

22. E. Stephens to CIA, 27 February 1883, NA, RG 75, LR, OIA, Accession #4326. Others, like Louis Gokey, were not so fortunate. Ruling he "was never enrolled as a member of the Menominee tribe, [and] neither has he ever been considered a member of said Menominee tribe," Chiefs Neo'pit and Mah Chickeney denied Gokey's application. Neo'pit and Mah Chickeney to CIA, 9 July 1887, NA, RG 75, LR, OIA, Accession #17534.

23. D. P. Andrews to CIA, 19 November 1884, NA, RG 75, LR, OIA, Accession #21836.

24. The ethnologist William Hoffman concluded that there were very few genetically "full blooded" Menominees by the latter 1880s. See Hoffman, "Menomini Indians," 34–35; D. P. Andrews to CIA, 11 December 1883, NA, RG 75, LR, OIA, Accession #22694.

25. D. P. Andrews to CIA, 11 December 1883, NA, RG 75, LR, OIA, Accession #22694.

26. Robert S. Gardiner, to the Secretary of the Interior, 8 May 1884, NA, RG 75, LR, OIA, Accession #9154.

27. Robert S. Gardiner to the Secretary of the Interior, 8 May 1884, NA, RG 75, LR, OIA; W. Wescott, agency trader, to D. P. Andrews, 8 May 1884, NA, RG 75, LR, OIA; both from Accession #9154; Oho-pa-sha to CIA, 7 December 1883, NA, RG 75, LR, OIA, Accession #22621.

28. *ARICA*, 1884, 222.

29. For more on Menominee credit problems, and the Menominees' rocky relationship with local merchants, see Stephens to CIA, 29 December 1881, NA, RG 75, LR, OIA, Accession #4434; Stephens to CIA, 24 May 1882, NA, RG 75, LR, OIA, Accession #9690; Stephens to CIA, 30 May 1882, NA, RG 75, LR, OIA, Accession #9790; Stephens to CIA, 9 June 1882, NA, RG 75, LR, OIA, Accession #10592; A. G. Weisert, attorney, to CIA, 30 October 1883, NA, RG 75, LR, OIA, Accession #19988; D. P. Andrews to CIA, 30 November 1883, NA, RG 75, LR, OIA, Accession #21933. L. A. Shankman and Co., Lanamer and Co., Cohen Brothers and Co., Henry Scheftels and Co., Bradley and Metcalf to Hon. P. V. Deuster, 21 May 1884, NA, RG 75, LR, OIA, Accession #19634.

30. D. P. Andrews to CIA, 11 February 1884, NA, RG 75, LR, OIA, Accession #3184; Andrews to CIA, 26 February 1884, NA, RG 75, LR, OIA, Accession #4059.

31. D. P. Andrews to CIA, 30 November 1883, NA, RG 75, LR, OIA, Accession #21933; *ARCIA*, 1885, 222, 433; D. P. Andrews to CIA, 11 May 1885, NA, RG 75, LR, OIA, Accession #11032. Beck, in "Siege and Survival," 484, reports that the Keshena sawmill was capable of cutting 25,000 board feet of timber daily.

32. *ARCIA*, 1885, 433, 1886, xlii, 1887, 45–46; D. P. Andrews to CIA, 22 April 1884, NA, RG 75, LR, OIA, Accession #8051; Kinney, *A Continent Lost*, 256–57. The Menominees were not the only Indians accused of violating the prohibition against taking green timber. The Chippewas (Anishinaabeg) of Minnesota and Wisconsin were likewise implicated in this matter and were accused further of deliberately starting fires to increase the "supply" of dead and down timber. For more on Anishinaabeg logging, see Meyer, *White Earth Tragedy*.

33. *ARCIA*, 1887, 46.

34. Ibid., 46–47, 307–8.

35. *ARCIA*, 1888, 237–38.

36. *Op. Atty. Gen.* 194, 195 (1888); Hertzberg, "Menominee Indians," 283; *ARCIA*, 1890, 88.

37. C. C. Painter to John H. Oberly, 16 October 1888, NA, RG 75, LR, OIA, Accession #26143; *ARCIA*, 1889, 89–90; Kinney, *A Continent Lost*, 256–57. President Cleveland authorized Menominee logging in 1889, and Benjamin Harrison followed suit in 1890. For more on the Indian Rights Association's involvement in this issue, see William T. Hagan, *The Indian Rights Association: The Herbert Welsh Years, 1882–1904* (Tucson: University of Arizona Press, 1985), 72–73.

38. *ARCIA*, 1889, 298–99. In 1888–89, log sales also added $15,000 to the tribal stumpage fund designated to support the agency hospital and poor relief.

39. Suspicion of wrongdoing was well founded, however, as throughout the 1880s the average annual cut for purposes of clearing land was approximately 300,000 feet. Kinney, in *A Continent Lost*, repeats this suspicion but notes also that nothing ever came of it. See, *ARCIA*, 1889, 90–91; "Statistical Supplements," in *ARCIA*, 1880–89; Kinney, *A Continent Lost*, 257; Thomas Jennings to CIA, "Statistics relating to logs banked on the Wolf and Oconto Rivers," 13 June 1889. NA, RG 75, LR, OIA, Accession #16024.

40. Gross sales for the 1889–90 season totaled nearly $220,000. Of this, some $22,000 went to the tribal "stumpage" fund. *ARCIA*, 1890, 235.

41. *ARCIA*, 1888, 238.

42. Hagan, *Indian Rights Association*, 71–72. Hertzberg, "Menominee Indians," 282–84. Dawes supported this measure because he hoped it would promote both allotment of Menominee lands and the transformation of Menominees into farmers.

43. Jennings to Sen. H. L. Dawes, 7 February 1888, NA, RG 75, LR, OIA, Accession #4112.

44. Petition signed by 187 Menominees, to H. L. Dawes, 6 February 1888, NA, RG 75, LR, OIA, Accession #4112.

45. Copy of Myron McCord's open letter to the Milwaukee *Sentinel*, in McCord to Interior Secretary John W. Noble, 16 November 1889, NA, RG 75, LR, OIA, Accession #33991; Rep. Myron H. McCord to President Benjamin Harrison, 18 November 1889, NA, RG 75, LR, OIA, Accession #33991.

46. McCord to CIA Thomas Jefferson Morgan, 10 March 1890. NA, RG 75, LR, OIA, Accession #7621. See also Affidavit of John Wapoose, 23 November 1889; Henry Hankwitz to Myron McCord, January [n.d.]; Affidavit of Marion Wescott, 18 November 1889; Affidavit of F. F. Green, 28 October 1889; Affidavit of John Dick, 25 October 1889; Affidavit of Myron Hill, 29 October 1889; Affidavit of Bernhard Melkhorn, 29 October 1889; Affidavit of Charles E. Perry, 22 October 1889; Affidavit of Otto Schoenfeld, 28 October 1889; Henry Hankwitz to Myron McCord, 24 January 1890; Col. W. S. Wood to McCord, 20 November 1889. All in NA, RG 75, LR, OIA, Accession #7621.

47. McCord to President Benjamin Harrison, 18 November 1889, NA, RG 75, LR, OIA, Accession #33991. Religious bigotry was a prominent feature of Gilded Age politics in general and became particularly virulent in the Indian Service during Thomas Jefferson Morgan's tenure as commissioner (1889–93). For more on Morgan, religious bigotry in the Indian Service, and the Bureau of Catholic Indian Missions, see Francis Paul Prucha, *The Great White Father*, abridged edition (Lincoln: University of Nebraska Press, 1984), 238–41. The Wisconsin and Menominee links to this general phenomenon can be seen as well in Col. W. S. Wood to M. McCord, 20 November 1889, NA, RG 75, LR, OIA, Accession #7621; and in Jennings to CIA, 21 February 1890, NA, RG 75, LR, OIA, Accession #5844. Here the agent denounced McCord as "a pronounced Christian hater of the most malignant type," who hated "God or any one who worships God in any manner, and particularly the Catholics."

48. Jennings recorded expenditures of $51,495 for "permanent improvement and home comforts" and $7,500 for "constructing dwellings and stables." *ARCIA*, 1889, 298; Jennings to CIA, 21 February 1890, NA, RG 75, LR, OIA, Accession #5844.

49. Jennings to CIA, 13 March 1888, NA, RG 75, LR, OIA, Accession #7257.

50. Petition signed by 139 Menominees to CIA, 15 October 1888, NA, RG 75, LR, OIA, Accession #13559; *ARCIA*, 1889, 300; Petition signed by 162 Menominees to CIA, 29 January 1890, NA, RG 75, LR, OIA, Accession #3785.

51. This analysis is based on examination of the following documents: Petition signed by 139 Menominees to CIA, 15 October 1888, NA, RG 75, LR, OIA, Accession #13559; *ARCIA*, 1889, 300; Petition signed by 162 Menominees to CIA, 29 January 1890, NA, RG 75, LR, OIA, Accession #3785; Agent Thomas Jennings to CIA, "Statistics relating to logs banked on the Wolf and Oconto Rivers," 13 June 1889, NA, RG 75, LR, OIA, Accession #16024; Agent Charles S. Kelsey to CIA, "Schedule of logs cut and banked by the Menominee Indians, during the last winter, on the Wolf and Oconto Rivers and tributaries," 14 July 1890, NA, RG 75, LR, OIA, Accession #21740. I have also relied on Beck's appendix, "Siege and Survival," 556–94; and Hoffman's genealogy, "Menomini Indians," 44–60.

52. Ibid.

53. Mitchell Oshkenaniew to Commissioner J. D. C. Atkins, 23 November 1887, NA, RG 75, LR, OIA, Accession #31592; John Corn to CIA, 24 February 1890, NA, RG 75, LR, OIA, Accession #6028. Joseph Oshkenaniew and Neo'pit were cousins. Hoffman records Oshkenaniew's father as Oshkiq'hinaniu ("young man"), younger brother of Chief Oshkosh (Neo'pit's father). Thus, both families, Oshkosh and Oshkenaniew, were of the bear clan. Hoffman, *The Menomini Indians*, 46–48.

54. Jennings to CIA, 21 February 1890, NA, RG 75, LR, OIA, Accession #5844; *ARCIA*, 1889, 299. See also Beck, "Siege and Survival," 188–89.

55. Fred T. Ledergerber to Interior Secretary John W. Noble, 21 September 1889, NA, RG 75, LR, OIA, Accession #5709; Acting Commissioner [?] to Noble, 21 September 1889, NA, RG 75, LR, OIA, Accession #5671; Noble to CIA, 15 October 1889, NA, RG 75, LR, OIA, Accession # 6512; Noble to Commissioner T. J. Morgan, 23 January 1890, NA, RG 75, LR, OIA, Accession #2304.; Fred T. Ledergerber to secretary of interior, 26 May 1890, NA, RG 75, LR, OIA, Accession #17174. See also Meyer, *White Earth Tragedy*.

56. J. W. Noble to T. J. Morgan, 1 February 1890, NA, RG 75, LR, OIA, Accession #3166; M. McCord to T. J. Morgan, 13 February 1890, NA, RG 75, LR, OIA, Accession #4542.

57. Joseph Oshkenaniew and Joseph Gauthier to T. J. Morgan, 14 March 1890, NA, RG 75, LR, Accession #8164; Neopit, Chickeney, and Nah ya taw aponey [*sic*] to J. W. Noble, 22 May 1890, NA, RG 75, LR, OIA, Accession #17174.

58. F. T. Ledergerber to T. J. Morgan, 26 May 1890, NA, RG 75, LR, OIA, Accession #17174; Neopit, Chickeney, and Nah ya taw aponey [*sic*] to J. W. Noble, 22 May 1890, NA, RG 75, LR, OIA, Accession #17174.

59. Milwaukee *Sentinel*, 5 May 1890, in NA, RG 75, LR, OIA, Accession #14739.

60. Ibid.

61. "Agreement between Phil. B. Thompson and the Menominee Tribe (Neopit, Neahtahwapany, Jos. Oshkenaniew, Jos. Gauthier, reps.), 29 January 1890. NA, RG 75, LR, OIA, Accession #9978.

62. Jennings to CIA, 14 February 1888, NA, RG 75, LR, OIA, Accession #4560.

63. Petition signed by Ahkonemi (Oshkosh), Kah we, Kit, Wy boy tuck to CIA, 15 March 1888, NA, RG 75, LR, OIA, Accession #7453.

64. Frank D. Lewis to T. J. Morgan, 5 June 1890, NA, RG 75, LR, OIA, Accession #17886.

65. In his annual reports, Jennings consistently argued that Indian loggers were turning a profit. See *ARCIA*, 1888, 237–38; 1889, 288–89.

66. "With Words of Fire: How the Indians at Keshena Defended Their Property," Milwaukee *Daily Journal*, 2 July 2 1890, NA, RG 75, LR, OIA, Accession #20531.

67. Ibid. Shawano, a city ten miles south of the reservation, was considered the "headquarters" for those lumbering interests seeking to deprive the Indians of their pine lands.

68. Ibid.

69. Act of 12 June 1890 (26 Stats. 146); *ARCIA*, 1890, CXI; Menominee Commission to CIA, 9 July 1890; E. Whittlesey to J. W. Noble, 27 August 1890; Charles S. Kelsey to CIA, 11 August 1890; George Chandler to CIA, 27 October 1890; all NA, RG 75, LR, Accession #29535. See also Hagan, *Indian Rights Association*, 72–75; and Hertzberg, "Menominee Indians," 283–84.

3. MITCHELL OSHKENANIEW AND LOGGING DURING THE 1890s

1. "An Act to authorize the sale of timber on certain lands reserved for the use of the Menominee tribe of Indians, in the State of Wisconsin," P.L. 153 (26 Stats., p. 146). See also *ARCIA*, 1890, 387; "Statistical Supplements," in *ARCIA*, 1890–1901. For the contrasting situation on the Anishinaabe Reservation, see Meyer, *White Earth Tragedy*.

2. P.L. 153 (26 Stats., p. 146). See also *ARCIA*, 1890, 387.

3. Ibid. Under regulations devised following passage of P.L. 153, prices paid to Menominee contractors were not to exceed five dollars per thousand feet. See *ARCIA*, 1890, 90.

4. Ibid.

5. Menominee Commissioners (E. Whittlesey, J. T. Jacobs, and Charles Kelsey) to CIA, 9 July 1890; E. Whittlesey to CIA, 27 August 1890; Interior Secretary John W. Noble to CIA, 24 September 1890; Acting Interior Secretary George Chandler to CIA, 27 October 1890; all in NA, RG 75, LR, OIA, Accession #29535.

6. Menominee Commissioners (E. Whittlesey, J. T. Jacobs, and Charles Kelsey) to CIA, 9 July 1890; E. Whittlesey to CIA, 27 August 1890, NA, RG 75, LR, OIA, Accession #29535; Louis B. Kahquatosh to CIA, 16 July 1890. NA, RG 75, LR, OIA, Accession #21994.

7. Beck, "Siege and Survival," 189–95. See Meyer, *White Earth Tragedy*, and Edmund Danziger, *The Chippewas of Lake Superior*, for elaboration on the allotment of Ojibwa (Anishinaabe) reservations.

8. Miner, *The Corporation and the Indian*, 100–101, 118–42.

9. "Orders of Agreement accompanying the Act of June 12, 1890" in *ARCIA*, 1891, 90–91. Neither the agent nor the Indian Office could, under these rules, be held responsible for debts, but they were empowered to assist individual contractors in meeting obligations when circumstances demanded. See also Charles Kelsey, George Gans, and Charles Montclair to CIA, 15 November 1890, NA, RG 75, LR, OIA, Accession #35874.

10. Charles Kelsey, George Ganz, and Charles Montclair to CIA, 15 November 1890, NA, RG 75, LR, OIA, Accession #35874.

11. In February 1891 the interior secretary requested that the tribe be granted authority to cut and sell timber in excess of the 20-million-foot limit. His reasoning was that, given that this was the first year under the new act, the federal government ought to exercise some leniency in this matter. On 13 February Assistant Attorney General George H. Shields ruled that the wording of P.L. 153 rendered it inflexible in this matter and rejected Noble's appeal. See George H. Shields to Assistant Secretary of the Interior George Chandler, 13 February 1891; J. W. Noble to CIA, 13 February 1891; both in NA, RG 75, LR, OIA, Accession #6119; *ARCIA*, 1891, 91, 463–64. See also James I. Cisney, Indian Office inspector, to CIA, 27 April 1891, NA, RG 75, LR, OIA, Accession #17395.

12. Mitchell Oshkenaniew to John W. Noble, 4 May 1891, NA, RG 75, LR, OIA, Accession #16867.

13. Resolution dated 6 April 1891, in NA, RG 75, LR, OIA, Accession #17395.

14. Ibid. The issue involved disputed ownership of the ten sixteenth, or "school," sections on the Menominee Reservation. Wisconsin claimed that all such sections, including those within reservation lands, belonged to the state, as "school lands." Therefore, the state was free to sell them as it saw fit. Henry Sherry purchased one such section and the state court upheld his claim in 1890. Controversy over sixteenth sections within the Menominee Reservation dated from at least the mid-1880s and continued through the 1890s. See *ARCIA*, 1890, 235–36; Thomas Jennings to CIA, 19 February 1890, NA, RG 75, LR, OIA, Accession #5777.

15. Resolution dated 6 April NA, RG 75, LR, OIA, Accession #17395. The Menominee council also requested the reinstatement of several Catholic "sisters" who had acted as teachers in the agency school. Kelsey had them removed when he took charge of the reservation.

16. James I. Cisney to Secretary John W. Noble, 27 April 1891, NA, RG 75, LR, OIA, Accession #17395. Cisney served as an assistant to Indian Office inspector Frank T. Lewis during the installation of Kelsey in 1890. On the Henry Sherry matter, Cisney found that the assistant superintendent had been involved in "a scheme to have roads cut," probably because he had "worked for years for Sherry." But Cisney still declined to recommend any disciplinary action.

17. Ibid.

18. Herbert Welsh to T. J. Morgan, 10 June 1891, NA, RG 75, LR, OIA, Accession #21136.

19. *ARCIA*, 1891, 463–64. It is important to remember that, under the terms set by P.L. 153, the tribe was responsible for this $77,174.05, which was deducted from the tribal log fund. *ARCIA*, 1891, 93.

20. *ARCIA*, 1891, 92–93. See also Charles Kelsey to CIA, 12 April 12, 1891, NA, RG 75, LR, OIA, Accession #30048. The Oconto Company also threatened to "take" the full amount promised it and, according to Kelsey, began cutting the "booms" holding the Menominee logs on the bank of the Oconto River. See Kelsey to CIA, 25 April 1891, NA, RG 75, LR, OIA, Accession #15123.

21. Charles S. Kelsey to CIA, 12 August 1891. NA, RG 75, LR, OIA, Accession #30048.

22. Ibid.; *ARCIA*, 1892, 85–86.

23. George Chandler, Acting Secretary of the Interior, to CIA, 26 June 26 1891, NA, RG 75, LR, OIA, Accession #22790; Charles S. Kelsey to CIA, 7 September 1891. NA, RG 75, LR, OIA, Accession #33238. Eighty-five Menominees, including the most influential men on the reservation (Neo'pit and Mitchell

Oshkenaniew in particular), endorsed this proposal. See Charles S. Kelsey to CIA, 19 October 1891, NA, RG 75, LR, OIA, Accession #38034. The Interior Department approved this change later that month. See George Chandler, Acting Secretary of the Interior, to CIA, 27 October 1891, NA, RG 75, LR, OIA, Accession #38810.

24. Charles S. Kelsey to CIA, 21 February 1891, NA, RG 75, LR, OIA, Accession #7581; George Chandler, Acting Secretary of the Interior to CIA, 26 June 1891, NA, RG 75, LR, OIA, Accession #22790; *ARCIA*, 1891, 93–94.

25. *ARCIA*, 1884, 222, 1891, 465; Hertzberg, "Menominee Indians," 299–300; Keesing, *Menomini Indians*, 176, 191–93; Rachel Reese Sady, "The Menominee: Transition from Trusteeship," *Applied Anthropology* 6, no. 2 (Spring 1947): 3.

26. Mitchell Oshkenaniew to Herbert Welsh, 31 July 1891, NA, RG 75, LR, OIA, Accession #27966.

27. Charles S. Kelsey to CIA, 2 November 1891, NA, RG 75, LR, OIA, Accession #39569. Kelsey reported that some of those half-breeds were descendants of these Menominees who, after the treaty of 1848, had renounced tribal membership in exchange for cash.

28. Mitchell Oshkenaniew to E. Whittlesey, 16 October 1891, NA, RG 75, LR, OIA, Accession #39570; Mitchell Oshkenaniew to CIA, 30 November 1892, NA, RG 75, LR, OIA, Accession #44684.

29. Charles S. Kelsey to CIA, 13 December 1891, NA, RG 75, LR, OIA, Accession #44684.; Mitchell Oshkenaniew to E. Whittlesey, 16 October 1891, NA, RG 75, LR, OIA, Accession #39570; Alexander Peters (Menominee) to CIA, 1 December 1894; Peters to Secretary of the Interior, 7 December 1894; both in NA, RG 75, LR, OIA, Accession #48580.

30. Peters to Secretary of the Interior, 7 December 1894, NA, RG 75, LR, OIA, Accession #48580.

31. Petition signed by 84 Menominees granting power of attorney to Mitchell Oshkenaniew, Peter LaMotte, Neopit, Chickeney, Shunion, and Wyuskesit, approved, 24 October 1891, NA, RG 75, LR, OIA, Accession #9278; Charles S. Kelsey to CIA, 31 December 1891, NA, RG 75, LR, OIA, Accession #173; Petition signed by 150 Menominees to Secretary of Interior, 20 July 1891, NA, RG 75, LR, OIA, Accession #27848; Resolution signed by Joseph Oshkenaniew, Joseph LaMotte, John Dick, John Tomah, Philip Nicato, and John King, 5 March 1892, NA, RG 75, LR, OIA, Accession #9278.

The proposed amendment to P.L. 153, Senate Bill 2929, and its companion in the House, H.R. 4847, never made it out of committee. See *Congressional Record*, vol. 23, 52d Cong., 1st sess., pp. 3405, 4805; and S. Rep. 573, 52d. Cong., 1st sess., 1892, Serial 2913. Communication signed by Mitchell Mahkimetas, Shunion, Louis Oshkenaniew, and Wyuskesit, 21 March 1892, NA, RG 75, LR, OIA, Accession #10808; also William G. Raines, attorney, to Acting Commissioner R. V. Belt, May 28, 1892, NA, RG 75, LR, OIA, Accession #19750.

32. Charles S. Kelsey to CIA, 31 December 1891, NA, RG 75, LR, OIA, Accession #173; Mitchell Oshkenaniew to CIA, 12 September 1892, NA, RG 75, LR, OIA, Accession #33625; Petition signed by 68 Menominees, 19 May 1892, NA, RG 75, LR, OIA, Accession #19502.

33. Resolution creating a "business committee" for the Menominee Tribe of Indians, signed 29 September 1894. See also Dudley and Michener (attorneys) to CIA, 15 October 1894; both in NA, RG 75, LR, OIA, Accession #40393; Contract between the Business Committee of the Menominee Tribe of Indians and Mitchell Oshkenaniew, Signed by Wyuskesit, Joseph LaMotte, and Steve Askinett, members of the Business Committee, and Mitchell Oshkenaniew, 2 October 1894, NA,

RG 75, LR, OIA, Accession #40393. In fairness to Agent Kelsey, he too had been calling for a resolution of the claims against the State of Wisconsin and the Stockbridge-Munsee tribe. See *ARCIA,* 1890, 235; 1891, 463; 1893, 342.

34. *ARCIA,* 1892, 82–84; 1893, 39–42.

35. Alexander Peters to Secretary of the Interior, 1 December 1892, NA, RG 75, LR, OIA, Accession #48580.

36. By 1895, farm production had increased only incrementally, and this despite the clearing of new lands for cultivation. See "Statistical Supplement," in *ARCIA,* 1885–95. Charles S. Kelsey to CIA, 28 August 1891, NA, RG 75, LR, OIA, Accession #31700; William Summers to Secretary of the Interior, 10 September 1891, NA, RG 75, LR, OIA, Accession #33307.

37. *ARCIA,* 1898, 366. Citing poor results of the shingle bolt experiment, the Indian Office denied Agent Savage's request for authority to permit Menominees to cut and market "hoop poles" from pine cuttings. See Thomas Savage to CIA, 24 January 1895, NA, RG 75, LR, OIA, Accession #3631; Hoke Smith, Secretary of the Interior, to CIA, 12 April 1895, NA, RG 75, LR, OIA, Accession #16065. Oshkenaniew originally supported the shingle bolt operation but then reversed himself. See Oshkenaniew to CIA, 11 August 1893, NA, RG 75, LR, OIA, Accession #30634; Oshkenaneiw to CIA, 9 November 1895, NA, RG 75, LR, OIA, Accession #6422. For more on the shingle bolt experiment, see *ARCIA,* 1892, 84–85; 1893, 36, 38–40; 1894, 53–56; 1895, 55, 325; 1896, 54, 323; Thomas Lynch to T. J. Morgan, 19 September 1892, NA, RG 75, LR, OIA, Accession #34429; Edward A. Bowen, Acting Commissioner, General Land Office to CIA, 6 June 1893, NA, RG 75, LR, OIA, Accession #20538; Thomas Savage to CIA, 20 March 1895, NA, RG 75, LR, OIA, Accession #12478; Thomas Savage to CIA, 19 April 1895, NA, RG 75, LR, OIA, Accession #17974.

38. *ARCIA,* 1896, 321–23, 1897, 325; Thomas H. Savage to CIA, 8 April 1895, NA, RG 75, LR, OIA, Accession #15911. See also U.S. Representative Thomas Lynch to CIA, 22 September 1893, NA, RG 75, LR, OIA, Accession #35771; Paine Lumber Company to Secretary of the Interior, 18 August 1894; Acting Commissioner Edward Bowers to CIA, 28 August 1894; both in, NA, RG 75, LR, OIA, Accession #32911. Notice as well: W. A. Holt to Secretary of the Interior John W. Noble, 24 November 1891, NA, RG 75, LR, OIA, Accession #42010; W. A. Holt to Commissioner Thomas J. Morgan, 1 January 1892, NA, RG 75, LR, OIA, Accession #176; George N. Ganz to Charles S. Kelsey, 14 January 1892; Charles S. Kelsey to CIA, 15 January 1892; both in NA, RG 75, LR, OIA, Accession #2008.

39. Thomas H. Savage to Commissioner D. M. Browning, 18 September 1893, NA, RG 75, LR, OIA, Accession #35396. Also *ARCIA,* 1894, 47–48.

40. "Menominee Logging," *Eleventh Annual Report of the Indian Rights Association,* 1894, 50. See also Charles C. Painter to Commissioner D. M. Browning, 29 October 1891, NA, RG 75, LR, OIA, Accession #35396.

41. Thomas H. Savage to Commissioner D. M Browning, 30 November 1894, NA, RG 75, LR, OIA, Accession #48421; Savage to Browning, 7 October 1895, NA, RG 75, LR, OIA, Accession #41324; *ARCIA,* 1894, 48; 1895, 51–52.

42. Under rules approved for the 1894–95 season, Indian contractors were paid up to $6.50 per thousand feet for logs cut and banked. This was an increase from the maximum of $5.00 paid in earlier years. *ARCIA,* 1892, 513; 1894, 47–56; 1895, 51, 325; 1898, 309.

43. Mitchell Oshkenaniew to Secretary of the Interior, 4 November 1895, NA, RG 75, LR, OIA, Accession #47667.

44. *ARCIA,* 1895, 324–25. See also Thomas H. Savage to CIA, 24 March 1894, NA, RG 75, LR, OIA, Accession #12437.

45. *ARCIA,* 1896, 322–23. For more on late-nineteenth-century attitudes toward "handouts" and their supposed effect on Indian initiative, see Hoxie, *A Final Promise.*

46. Mitchell Oshkenaniew to CIA, 23 March 1894, NA, RG 75, LR, OIA, Accession #11809. Interestingly, one of the leaders of the faction proposing straight cash annuities was none other than Ahkonemi Oshkosh. See petition signed 22 June 1895, NA, RG 75, LR, OIA, Accession #26989.

47. Thomas H. Savage to CIA, 28 June 1895, NA, RG 75, LR, OIA, Accession #26989. Also *ARCIA,* 1896, 323; 1897, 303; 1906, 389.

48. Records do not reveal the role, if any, played by Mitchell Oshkenaniew in resolving this dispute. *ARCIA,* 1898, 54–55; 1899, 53–54; 1900, 72–73. Also E. G. Mullin, Wisconsin Chief Inspector of Lands, to Commissioner W. A. Jones, 13 August 1898, NA, RG 75, LR, OIA, Accession #37642.

49. *ARCIA,* 1900, 403–4; The higher prices realized for Menominee timber were largely a function of an industry-wide rise in lumber values. For more on this see William G. Robbins, *Lumberjacks and Legislators: Political Economy of the U.S. Lumber Industry, 1890–1941* (College Station: Texas A&M University Press, 1984), 16–34. For more on the various "improvements," see *ARCIA,* 1896, 322; 1897, 303.

50. *ARCIA,* 1904, 345.

51. For details on Elias C. Boudinot, see Miner, *The Corporation and the Indian,* 44–46, 81–83, 120–21.

4. CREATING INDIAN ENTREPRENEURS

Portions of this chapter appeared as "Creating Indian Entrepreneurs: Menominees, Neopit Mills, and Timber Exploitation, 1890–1915," *American Indian Culture and Research Journal* 15 (1991): 1–28; and as "Reflections on Indian Cultural 'Brokers': Reginald Oshkosh, Mitchell Oshkenaniew and the Politics of Menominee Lumbering," *Ethnohistory* 44 (Summer 1997): 493–509.

1. This evaluation of American Indian policy, and the thought that underlay it, draws upon Frederick Hoxie's essential study, *A Final Promise.* For a corresponding study of Canadian Indian policy, see James R. Miller, *Skyscrapers Hide the Heavens: A History of Indian-White Relations in Canada* (Toronto: University of Toronto Press, 1989).

2. For a sophisticated analysis of this process, see Frederick E. Hoxie, *Parading Through History: The Making of the Crow Nation in America, 1805–1935* (New York: Cambridge University Press, 1995). Quotations are from Hoxie, *Parading Through History,* 355.

3. Ibid. The references to Indians becoming cowboys is from Peter Iverson, *When Indians Became Cowboys: Native Peoples and Cattle Ranching in the American West* (Norman: University of Oklahoma Press, 1994). For a provocative discussion of this, see Foster, *Being Comanche,* 19. Foster also relies on the work of Loretta Fowler, whose *Arapahoe Politics* and *Shared Symbols* explore these issues in a compelling fashion.

4. *ARCIA,* 1902, 71.

5. "Statistical Supplement," in *ARCIA,* 1890–1905; *ARCIA,* 1902, 371; 1903, 344–45; 1904, 369; 1905, 371.

6. *ARCIA,* 1898, 308.

7. *ARCIA,* 1903, 345; 1905, 371. Citing limitations imposed by the law, the

department denied Freeman's request to expand the harvest. A. G. Turner, Acting Commissioner, to Shepard Freeman, February 17, 1903; Turner to Freeman, October 6, 1903; Turner to Freeman, February 15, 1904; all in Copies of Letters Received by the Superintendent, Green Bay Agency; National Archives—Great Lakes Branch, Records of the Bureau of Indian Affairs, Record Group 75 [henceforth, NA-GLB, RG 75].

8. "Constitution of the Menominee Tribe of Indians of the State of Wisconsin, 1904," cited in Beck, "Siege and Survival," 202–3, 208–9.

9. Ibid.; "Statement of Mitchell Oshkenaniew," in *Conditions of Indian Affairs in Wisconsin: Hearings before the Committee on Indian Affairs, United States Senate,* 60 Cong., 2d sess., Sen. Res. 263 (Washington, D.C.: GPO, 1910), 809 [henceforth, Hearings, Sen. Res. 263, 1910]; Petition signed by 53 Menominees, 24 January 1902, NA, RG 75, LR, OIA, Accession #17261.

10. Kinney, *Indian Forest and Range,* 117, 127–28, 133–37; Hertzberg, "Menominee Indians," 284. Logging experts called for authority to cut the 100 million feet of standing timber on the grounds that it would be more economical to harvest all the timber in the "blown-down district" at once. U.S. Congress, 59th Cong., 1st sess., 1906, H. Doc. 287, p. 1; F. E. Leupp to Gifford Pinchot, 24 August 1906, Letters Sent and Reports of J. R. Farr, General Superintendent of Logging, Menominee Mills, NA-GLR, RG 75.

11. Kinney, *Indian Forest and Range,* 117–18; United States Congress, 59th Congress, 1st sess, 1906. House Doc. 287, p. 9.

12. P.L. 327, June 28, 1906 (34 Stat. 547); F. E. Leupp to Gifford Pinchot, 24 August 1906, Letters Sent and Reports of J. R. Farr, General Superintendent of Logging, Menominee Mills, NA-GLB, RG 75; U.S. Congress, 59th Cong., 2d sess., 1907, H. Rep. 7280, pp. 2–3. See also Kinney, *Indian Forest and Range,* 118. Wisconsin State Forester E. M. Griffith, no supporter of P.L. 327, nevertheless was determined that the "slaughter" of Ojibwa timber not be repeated on the Menominee Reservation. See E. M. Griffith to Gifford Pinchot, 19 September 1905, Records of the Forest Supervisor, Menominee Mills; Copies of Reports and Letters of E. M. Griffith, State Forester, NA-GLB, RG 75.

13. P.L. 327; J. R. Farr to CIA, 2 April 1907, RG 75, CCF, Keshena, Accession #43289-07 [henceforth, RG 75, CCF, Keshena, Accession number]. It is important to note that P.L. 327 did not repeal the 1890 act. P.L. 153 remained in force as the guiding legislation regarding the green pine harvest. P.L. 327 governed only logging in the "blown-down district." For a time, both enterprises operated side by side. See Kinney, *Indian Forest and Range,* 118–19.

14. Subsequent testimony indicates that Wieskesit exerted very little influence over business committee deliberations and may have been included primarily for symbolic reasons. See *Hearings Before the Joint Commission of the United States to Investigate Indian Affairs,* pt. 8, Menominee Indian Reservation, 63d Cong., 2d sess. (Washington, D.C.: GPO, 1914), p. 775 [henceforth, *Hearings,* 1914); Ourada, *Menominee Indians,* 122–23.

15. "Rules and Regulations for the Logging, Sawing, Hauling and Sale of Dead and Down Timber on the Menominee Reservation in the State of Wisconsin, as Provided for by Act of Congress, Public Law No. 327; E. M. Griffith to F. E. Leupp, Commissioner of Indian Affairs, 2 October 1906, Records of the Forest Supervisor, Menominee Mills, Copies of Reports and Letters of E. M. Griffith, State Forester; NA-GLB, RG 75; "Resolution of the Business Committee of the Menominee Indians," Mose Tucker, Chairman, to CIA, 23 May 1907, RG 75, CCF, Keshena, Accession #49800-07. See also Shepard Freeman to CIA, 25 May 1907,

RG 75, CCF, Keshena, Accession #49800-07; and E. M Griffith to CIA, 1 July 1907, RG 75, CCF, Keshena, Accession #59562-07.

16. E. M. Griffith to F. E. Leupp, Commissioner of Indian Affairs, 2 October 1906; E. M. Griffith to Overton W. Price, Forest Service, 3 October 1906; both in Records of the Forest Supervisor, Menominee Mills; Copies of Reports and Letters of E. M. Griffith, State Forester, NA-GLB, RG 75; James A. Carroll to Commissioner R. G. Valentine, 9 November 1909, RG 75, CCF, Keshena, Accession #91339-09-339. See also Beck, "Siege and Survival," 494.

17. Acting Commissioner C. F. Larribe to Secretary of the Interior, 6 April 1907, RG 75, CCF, Keshena, Accession #31920-07; John W. Goodfellow to CIA, 18 June 1907, RG 75, CCF, Keshena, Accession #59562-07; Joseph R. Farr to CIA, 5 November 1907, RG 75, CCF, Keshena, Accession #88433-07-339.

18. J. R. Farr to CIA, 5 November 1907, RG 75, CCF, Keshena, Accession #88433-07. See also Farr's "final report" on 1907–8 logging: J. R. Farr to Chief Forester of the United States, 10 March 1908, RG 75, CCF, Green Bay, Accession #15912-08-339.

19. John W. Goodfellow to CIA, 23 November 1907, RG 75, CCF, Keshena, Accession #93064-07; J. A. Howarth, Jr., "Report on Logging in Recent Years on the Menominee Indian Reservation, Wisconsin (1907)," Records of the Forest Supervisor; Reports, Memoranda, and Letters of J. A. Howarth, Jr.; NA-GLB, RG 75. See also Kinney, *Indian Forest and Range*, 119; and Hertzberg, "The Menominee Indians," 285.

20. See, J. R. Farr to CIA, 2 April 1907, RG 75, CCF, Keshena, Accession #43289-07; J. R. Farr to CIA, 20 May 1907, RG 75, CCF, Keshena, Accession #48323-07; J. R. Farr to CIA, 8 June 1907, RG 75, CCF, Keshena, Accession #54678-07; J. R. Farr to Shepard Freeman, 10 June 1907. Letters Sent and Reports of J. R. Farr, General Superintendent of Logging, Menominee Mills; NA-GLB, RG 75; Shepard Freeman to CIA, 4 June 1907, RG 75, CCF, Keshena, Accession #52848.

21. Hertzberg, "Menominee Indians," 286–87; Beck, "Siege and Survival," 214. Goodfellow was suspended on 19 April 1908 and dismissed from the Indian Service on 16 November 1908. Kinney, *Indian Forest and Range*, 119.

For more on the "cooperative agreement" of 22 January 1908, see H. H. Chapman, *The Menominee Indian Timber Case History: Proposals for Settlement* (New Haven, Conn.: Yale University School of Law, 1957), 16.

In 1919 the United States Court of Claims awarded $50,362.55 to the twenty-nine claimants in this dispute. The court ruled that the contracts entered into by Superintendent Goodfellow, the Menominee Business Committee, and the various contractors were valid and that the tribe had no authority to withhold the balance of payments due. See *Wallace P. Cook and Charles W. Chickeney, et al. v. the Menominee Tribe of Indians and the United States of America*, Court of Claims of the United States, decided 17 February 1919, RG 75, CCF, Keshena, Accession #76255.

22. J. A. Howarth to E. M. Griffith, 2 December 1907; Records of the Forest Supervisor; Reports, Memoranda, and Letters of J. A. Howarth, Jr.; NA-GLB, RG 75; John H. Hannon to F. H. Abbott, 18 November 1913. Papers concerning the United States Board of Indian Commissioners, collected by Mr. Edward Everett Ayer, 1913–19, Newberry Library, Chicago, Ill. [henceforth, Ayer Papers]; U.S. Congress, House, "Cutting Timber on the Menominee Indian Reservation," 16 March 1907, *Congressional Record*, XLVIII, 3410–14; Public Law 74, Chap. iii, 60th Cong., 1 sess., *Statutes at Large*, vol. 35, no. 51 (1908); Hertzberg, "Menominee Indians," 287; Ourada, *Menominee Indians*, 170.

23. Robert M. LaFollette, "Cutting and Sale of Timber on Menominee Indian Reservation, Wis.," Report to 59th Cong., 2d Sess., S. Rep. 6669, 14 February 1907.

24. P.L. 74, 28 March 1908 (35 Stat. 51); John H. Hannon to F. H. Abbott, 18 November 1913, Ayer Papers; Hertzberg, "Menominee Indians," 287; Kinney, *Indian Forest and Range*, 120, 124.

25. See Menominee Delegation, represented by Reginald Oshkosh, to CIA, 2 April 1901, RG 75, LR, OIA, Accession #17520; Menominee Delegation, represented by Reginald Oshkosh, to CIA, 8 April 1901, RG 75. LR, OIA, Accession #18737; Menominee Delegation, represented by Reginald Oshkosh to CIA, 27 April 1901, RG 75, LR, OIA, Accession #22927; *ARCIA*, 1906, 389. For Reginald Oshkosh's boarding school experience, see "Carlisle Indian Industrial School, Descriptive and Historical Record of Students"; "Record of Graduates and Returned Students, United States Indian School, Carlisle, Pennsylvania," Carlisle Indian Industrial School, Student Record, file no. 791, "Ahqwinimy Neopet (Reginald Oshkosh)," NA, RG 75. The quotation is from an essay Reginald Oshkosh penned for the Carlisle Indian Industrial School newsletter. See *School News* (Carlisle Indian Industrial School), July 1882, p. 4. I have discussed Reginald Oshkosh's career in Hosmer, "Reflections on Indian Cultural 'Brokers.'"

26. Hearings, Sen. Res. 263, 1910, 857, 865; *Hearings*, 1914, 775. The "contract" referred to here seems to be the one designating Oshkenaniew as the tribe's sole representative in Washington. See chapter 3. Copy of the resolution of 26 June 1908, transmitted to M. Oshkenaniew by F. H. Abbott, Acting Commissioner of Indian Affairs, April 25, 1913, Hearings, 1914, 772. Also Hosmer, "Reflections on Indian Cultural 'Brokers.'"

27. Hearings, Sen. Res. 263, 1910, 872.

28. Kinney, *Indian Forest and Range*, 122; Hertzberg, "Menominee Indians," 287. See E. A. Braniff to Chief Forester, 2 April 1909, RG 75, CCF, Keshena, Accession #26304-09; R. G. Valentine, Acting CIA to P. S. Everett, Special Disbursing Agent, 28 April 1909, RG75, CCF, Keshena, Accession #26304-09; Peter Lookaround, George McCall, Thomas LeBell, Sr., Mrs. Louisa Richmond, Al Boyd, and Thomas LaBell, Jr. (Menominee storekeepers) to Commissioner Francis E. Leupp, 6 May 1909, RG75, CCF, Keshena, Accession #35698-09; T. B. Wilson, Superintendent, Keshena Indian School, to CIA, 8 May 1909, RG 75, CCF, Keshena, Accession #35698-09; E. A. Braniff to CIA, 28 August 1909, RG 75, CCF, Keshena, Accession #93992-09.

29. Kinney, *Indian Forest and Range*, 91, 120–21. Samuel P. Hays describes the impact of the decline in lumber prices on the industry as a whole; see Hays, *Conservation and the Gospel of Efficiency: The Progressive Conservation Movement, 1890–1920* (Cambridge, Mass.: Harvard University Press, 1959), 263–64.

For a more complete discussion of the Ballinger-Pinchot affair, see George E. Mowry, *The Era of Theodore Roosevelt and the Birth of Modern America, 1900–1912* (New York: Harper and Brothers, 1958), 250–59; and Hays, *Conservation and the Gospel of Efficiency*, 152–65. According to J. P. Kinney, even the Indian Service was divided between pro-Ballinger and pro-Pinchot partisans. Commissioner Valentine sympathized with Ballinger and was at odds with his assistant, Frederick H. Abbott, who was a Pinchot supporter. Abbott also was Joseph Farr's chief sponsor in the Indian Service, and this relationship eventually cost Farr his job in 1911. Farr returned the favor by testifying against Valentine in the 1912 congressional hearings investigating Valentine's conduct. Valentine resigned at the end of 1912. See Kinney, *Indian Forest and Range*, 84–96.

30. E. A. Braniff to CIA, August 28, 1909, RG 75, CCF, Keshena, Accession #93992-09; Mitchell Oshkenaniew to Braniff, 30 August 1909, RG 75, CCF, Keshena, Accession #71728; R. G. Valentine to Braniff, 16 October 1909, RG 75, CCF,

Keshena, Accession #46003-09; Braniff to CIA, 26 October 1909, RG 75, CCF, Keshena, Accession #46009-09; "Report of Thomas J. King, Jr., on Menominee Logging Operation and Mills, 15 March 1910, RG 75, CCF, Keshena, Accession #21100-10.

31. Nicholson also secured a waiver of the 20-million-foot annual production limit in order to manufacture into lumber the burned timber as quickly as possible. A. S. Nicholson to Ayer, 26 January 1914, Ayer Papers; Barrow, Wade, Guthrie and Co., "Menominee Indian Mills, Report on Operations for the Period April 1, 1908 to June 30, 1934," Section II, 1935; NA-GLB, RG 75; Kinney, *Indian Forest and Range,* 122–23.

32. E. A. Braniff to CIA, 28 August 1909, RG 75, CCF, Keshena, Accession #93992; *ARCIA,* 1909, 7, 56; A. S. Nicholson, "Annual Report of the Menominee Lumbering Operations, July 1, 1910 to June 30, 1911," RG 75, CCF, Keshena (no accession number); A. S. Nicholson, "Annual Report . . . July 1, 1911 to June 30, 1912," RG 75, CCF, Keshena (no accession number); A. S. Nicholson, "Annual Report . . . July 1, 1912 to June 30, 1913," RG 75, CCF, Keshena, Accession #84373; A. S. Nicholson, "Account of the Menominee Indian Mills with a brief statement from the Superintendent's last report," 1913, Ayer Papers. For an interesting narrative account, see especially Nicholson, "Menominee Indians Working Their Way," 19.

33. A. S. Nicholson, "Annual Report . . . July 1, 1911 to June 30, 1912," RG 75, CCF, Keshena (no accession number); A. S. Nicholson, "Annual Report . . . July 1, 1912 to June 30, 1913," RG 75, CCF, Keshena, Accession #84373. "Annual Report Fiscal Year Ending June 30, 1914," Ayer Papers. For Reginald Oshkosh and the "reimbursable fund," see "Minutes of a Council Meeting Held and Convened by the Menominee Tribe of Indians, on the Green, Near the Keshena Indian Agency Office, in Keshena, Wisconsin, on the Fourteenth Day of September, 1912," RG 75, CCF, Keshena, Accession #110042-12-054.

34. "Memorandum from Mr. Nicholson," Ayer papers; Nicholson, "Menominee Indians Working Their Way," 19–23; "Annual Report Fiscal Year Ending June 30, 1914," Ayer Papers.

35. Mitchell Oshkenaniew to Braniff, 30 August 1909, RG 75, CCF, Keshena, Accession #71728; August A. Brueninger to Secretary Richard A. Ballinger, 20 August 1909, RG 75, CCF, Keshena, Accession #93992-09.

36. E. A. Braniff to CIA, 28 August 1909, RG 75, CCF, Keshena, Accession #93992-09; Thomas LaBelle to Senator R. M. La Follette, 29 June 1910, RG 75, CCF, Keshena, Accession #56015-10; R. M. La Follette to R. G. Valentine, 8 July 1910; Acting Commissioner C. F. Hauke to La Follette, 15 July 1910; both RG 75, CCF, Keshena, Accession #56015-10; Assistant Commissioner F. H. Abbott to John Kaquatosh, 8 February 1911, RG 75, CCF, Keshena, Accession #2829-11.

37. James A. Carroll to T. B. Wilson, Superintendent, Keshena Indian Boarding School, 29 October 1909, RG 75, CCF, Keshena, Accession #90666-09; Carroll to CIA, 9 November 1909, RG 75, CCF, Keshena, Accession #91339-09; A. M. Riley to CIA, 21 March 1910, RG 75, CCF, Keshena, Accession #24214-10. "Report of Thomas J. King, Jr., on Menominee Logging and Mills, 15 March 1910," RG 75, CCF, Keshena, Accession #21100-10.

38. Carroll to T. B. Wilson, 29 October 1909, RG75, CCF, Keshena, Accession #90666-09; "Report of Thomas J. King, Jr., on Menominee Logging and Mills, 15 March 1910," RG 75, CCF, Keshena, Accession #21100-10; Oshkenaniew to Braniff, 30 August 1909, RG 75, CCF, Keshena, Accession #71728-09.

39. Oshkenaniew to Braniff, 30 August 1909, RG 75, CCF, Keshena, Accession #71728-09; "Minutes of a Council Meeting held by the Menominee Tribe of

Indians at Council House, Keshena, Wisconsin, on August 29th, 1910," RG 75, CCF, Keshena (no accession number).

40. Seventeen Members of GAR Post No. 261 to President Woodrow Wilson, 27 June 1913, RG 75, CCF, Keshena, Accession #82040-13. Indian Commissioner Cato Sells drafted a reply to this letter and in it condescendingly told the old men, "It has been the view of the Office that the making of generous per capita payments to Indians was not conducive to their best interests." Rather, it was "believed that an opportunity for regular employment such as is afforded by the Menominee Mills is of infinitely greater value to the majority of the Menominees than per capita payments would be." One would guess that this would be of little solace to elderly men who had slim hopes of ever landing a job in the mill—or of standing up to the physical requirements of such a job. Cato Sells to Joseph Ledergerber, GAR Post No. 261, 1 August 1913, RG 75, CCF, Keshena, Accession #82040-13.

41. Petition, signed by twenty-four Menominees, to A. S. Nicholson, 21 February 1912. *Hearings*, 1914, 779.

42. Reginald Oshkosh to A.S. Nicholson, 21 February 1912, *Hearings*, 1914, 779.

43. Ibid., 780.

44. "Hearing, Menominee Indian Delegation, Before Commissioner of Indian Affairs," 26 February 1912; Mose Tucker, George McCall, and Weiskesit to Commissioner of Indian Affairs, 4 March 1912; "Hearing, Menominee Indian Delegation, Before Chief of the Land Division, Office of Indian Affairs," 9 March 1913; "Statement of Reginald Oshkosh"; all in *Hearings*, 1914, 781–93.

45. "Minutes of the Council. Proceedings of a Council Meeting Held and Convened by the Menomonee Tribe of Indians . . . on March 12, 1912," RG 75, CCF, Keshena, Accession #25083-12-054; "Minutes of a Council Meeting Held and Convened by the Menominee Tribe of Indians . . . on the Fourteenth Day of September, 1912," RG 75, CCF, Keshena, Accession #110042-12-054; "Minutes of the Council Meeting Held by the Menominee Indians . . . on March 15, 1913," RG 75, CCF, Keshena, Accession # 38320-13-054.

46. Minutes of a Council Meeting Held and Convened by the Menominee Tribe of Indians . . . on the Twenty-first Day of May, 1913"; "Supplementary to proceedings of Council Meeting held by the Menominee Tribe . . . on May 21st, 1913, and concluded on May 22, 1913," RG 75, CCF, Keshena, Accession #79638-13-054.

47. Mitchell Oshkenaniew to Webster Ballinger, 6 September 1913; Ballinger to Oshkenaniew, 11 September 1913; both in Ayer Papers.

Webster Ballinger's uncle was Richard Ballinger, Taft's embattled secretary of the interior, and this led to charges that he was chosen for his supposed influence in Washington. See "Report of Edward E. Ayer's correspondence with Mr. A. S. Nicholson," 3–15 December 1913," in *Hearings*, 1914, 895. Melissa Meyer demonstrates that Ballinger later played a role in the massive White Earth timber fraud. See Meyer, *White Earth Tragedy*, 196.

On Louis LaFrambois, see, for instance, "Report of Mr. Edward E. Ayer's interview with Mr. Louis LaFrambois, at the Menomonee Indian Reservation, Neopit, Wisconsin, December 1, 1913"; "Minutes of a Conference Held at Keshena, Wisconsin, on the Menominee Indian Reservation on Friday, September 10, 1915, in the Assembly Hall at the School House, there Being Present 263 Adult Male Indians of the Menominee Tribe of Indians"; Louis LaFrambois to D. F. Tyrrell, December 1913; all in Ayer Papers. On Prickett, some salient sources are "Minutes of a Council Meeting Held and Convened by the Menominee Tribe of

Indians . . . on the Twenty-first Day of May, 1913"; "Supplementary to proceedings of Council Meeting held by the Menominee Tribe . . . on May 21st, 1913, and concluded on May 22, 1913," RG 75, CCF, Keshena, Accession #79638-13-054; "Report of Mr. Edward E. Ayer's interview with Mr. Thomas Prickett, one of the Committee appointed by the tribe, at Menominee Indian Reservation, Neopit, Wisconsin, December 1, 1913," Ayer Papers; "Hearing, Menominee Indian Delegation, Before Chief of the Land Division, Office of Indian Affairs," 9 March 1912, in *Hearings, 1914*, 773, 894–95. For the department's repeated attempts to revoke his membership in the tribe and remove him from the reservation, see T. B. Wilson to CIA, 7 June 1910; Acting Commissioner C. F. Hauke to Secretary of the Interior, 20 August 1910; Acting Commissioner C. F. Hauke to A. S. Nicholson, 1 September 1910, all in RG 75, CCF, Keshena, Accession #47175-10.

48. Ballinger to Oshkenaniew, 11 September 1913; D. F. Tyrrell to Cato Sells, 20 November 1913; both in Ayer Papers.

49. Lawrence W. Towner, *An Uncommon Collection of Uncommon Collections: The Newberry Library* (Chicago: the Newberry Library, 1985), 20–21; F. H. Abbott to Edward E. Ayer, 3 November 1913, Ayer Papers; "Report of Mr. Edward E. Ayer on the Menominee Indian Reservation, January 1914," pp. 7–8, 10, 18, Ayer Papers.

50. D. F. Tyrrell, "In re Administration of A. S. Nicholson, United States Superintendent, Menominee Indian Reservation, Wisconsin," petition placed before the Commissioner of Indian Affairs, 16 December 1913, pp. 1–5, Ayer Papers.

51. "Report of Mr. Edward E. Ayer on the Menominee Indian Reservation," January 1914, Ayer Papers; "Copy of Report of L. P. Holland, woodsman in the employ of Ayer & Lord Tie Company, Chicago." Ayer Papers. "Report of Mr. Edward E. Ayer," Ayer Papers; J. P. Kinney, "Memorandum regarding the charges filed against Superintendent A. S. Nicholson of the Keshena Indian School by Mr. D. F. Tyrrell under date of December 16, 1913," RG 75, CCF, Keshena, Accession #23284-14. See also J. P. Kinney, Ayer Report, p. 18, Ayer Papers.

52. "Report of Mr. Edward E. Ayer's interview with Mr. Peter Lookaround," storekeeper, at Menominee Indian Reservation, Neopit, Wisconsin, November 29, 1913"; "Report of Mr. Edward E. Ayer's interview with Mr. Joe Gristo, policeman, at Menominee Indian Reservation, Neopit, Wisconsin, November 29, 1913"; both in Ayer Papers.

53. "Report of Mr. Edward E. Ayer's interview with Mr. Thomas Prickett, one of the Committee appointed by the tribe, at Menominee Indian Reservation, Neopit, Wisconsin, December 1, 1913"; "Hon. Edward E. Ayer, of the Indian Commissioners, interrogating Thomas Prickett," 17 December 1913; "Report of Mr. Edward E. Ayer's interview with Mr. Louis LaFrambois, at the Menominee Indian Reservation, Neopit, Wisconsin, 1 December 1913"; all in Ayer Papers.

54. Louis LaFrambois to Ayer, 17 December 1913; Ayer Report, pp. 13–14, 19, Ayer Papers.

55. Mitchell Oshkenaniew to Edward E. Ayer, 3 December 1913; Edward E. Ayer to Mitchell Oshkenaniew, 6 December 1913; both in Ayer Papers.

56. "Report of Mr. Edward E. Ayer," p. 15; Reginald Oshkosh to Edward E. Ayer, 10 January 1914; both in Ayer Papers.

57. Frank S. Gauthier to D. F. Tyrrell, 16 December 1913; Louis LaFrambois to D. F. Tyrrell, 16, 17 December 1913; both in RG 75, CCF, Keshena, Accession #151837-13; Reverend Simon Schwarz to E. E. Ayer, 18 December 1913, Ayer Papers; Webster Ballinger to CIA, 31 December 1913, RG 75, CCF, Keshena, Accession #2109-14.

58. Barrow, Wade, Guthrie and Co., "Menominee Indian Mills, Report on Operations for the Period April 1, 1908 to June 3, 1934." Exhibit XXXIV, "Condensed Profit and Loss Account of the Menominee Indian Mills"; Tyrrell to Ayer, 13 December 1913; Tyrrell to Ayer, 27 January 1914; all in Ayer Papers. See also *Hearings*, 1914, 894–95, 902.

59. "Minutes of a Conference Held at Keshena, Wisconsin, on the Menominee Indian Reservation on Friday, September 10, 1915, in the Assembly Hall at the School House, there Being Present 263 Adult Male Indians of the Menominee Tribe of Indians," Ayer Papers. See also "Minutes of the Council Meeting Held by the Menominee Indians in the Council Room, Agency Building, Keshena, Wisconsin, January 16, 1915," RG 75, CCF, Keshena, Accession #16691-15-054.

60. "Minutes of a Conference Held at Keshena, Wisconsin, on the Menominee Indian Reservation on Friday, September 10, 1915."

61. Ibid.

62. Nicholson to CIA, 4 June 1915, RG 75, CCF, Keshena, Accession #264301-15-054. For annuity request, see, for instance, "Minutes of the Council Meeting Held by the Menominee Indians in the Council Room, Agency Building, Keshena, Wisconsin, January 16, 1915," RG 75, CCF, Keshena, Accession #16691-15-054; Antoine Stick, John Dick, Mose Kitson, 14 other Menominees to A. S. Nicholson, 9 June 1915, NA RG 75, CCF, Keshena, Accession #64301-15-054; "Minutes of the proceedings of a General Council of the Menominee tribe of Indians held at Keshena, Wisconsin, on the 24th day of February, 1917," RG 75, CCF, Keshena, Accession #51826-17-054.

63. "Minutes of a Conference Held at Keshena, Wisconsin, on the Menominee Indian Reservation on Friday, September 10, 1915, in the Assembly Hall at the School House, there Being Present 263 Adult Male Indians of the Menominee Tribe of Indians," Ayer Papers; "Minutes of the Council Meeting Held by the Menominee Indians, in the Council Room, Agency Building, Keshena, Wisconsin," 16 January 1915, RG 75, CCF, Keshena, Accession #16691-15-054.

64. Lewis, "Reservation Leadership," 124–48; Foster, *Being Comanche*, 13–19; Fowler, *Shared Symbols*, 5–12. See also Hosmer, "Reflections on Indian Cultural 'Brokers,'" 493–509.

65. Meyer, *White Earth Tragedy*; Miner, *The Corporation and the Indian*.

5. THE TSIMSHIANS OF BRITISH COLUMBIA

1. Peter Kolchin, *Unfree Labor: American Slavery and Russian Serfdom* (Cambridge, Mass.: Belknap Press of Harvard University Press, 1987), ix.

2. The literature on world-systems theories is vast, and growing still, and I have discussed some of the salient points in the introductory chapter. For a recent discussion, see Chase-Dunn and Hall, "World Systems in North America," 23–72.

3. While Temlaxham refers specifically to Coast Tsimshian myth and history, all Tsimshian peoples seemingly have similar stories, hence my decision to offer this as a "generalized" history. Texts of various "stories" of Temlaxham can be found in many places. My very abbreviated version is influenced by several tales related in Jay Miller's *Tsimshian Culture: A Light Through the Ages* (Lincoln: University of Nebraska Press, 1997), 57–73. Probably the most famous version was recorded by anthropologist Marius Barbeau in *The Downfall of Temlaham* (Toronto: Macmillan, 1928). See also "Migration Down the Skeena River," in *Tsimshian Narratives, I: Tricksters, Shamans and Heroes*, ed. John J. Cove and George

F. MacDonald, Canadian Museum of Civilization, Mercury Series, Paper No. 3 (Ottawa: Canadian Museum of History, 1987), 257–78; and, "Temlaham," in "Tsimshian Texts," ed. Franz Boas, Bureau of American Ethnology, *Bulletin No. 27* (Washington, D.C.: Bureau of American Ethnology, 1902), 221–25.

4. For my discussion of traditional Tsimshian culture and society, I am indebted to several important sources. Jay Miller's *Tsimshian Culture* is a creative construction that emphasizes integrative components over a discussion of discrete cultural elements. I also have relied on his spellings of tribal names and territories. Miller's work draws upon a vast scholarship in Tsimshian studies, salient titles including Viola E. Garfield, *Tsimshian Clan and Society*, University of Washington Publications in Anthropology 7, 3 (Seattle: University of Washington Press, 1939), 167–340; Margaret Seguin, ed., *The Tsimshian: Images of the Past; Views for the Present* (Vancouver: University of British Columbia Press, 1984); Jay Miller and Carol Eastman, eds., *The Tsimshian and Their Neighbors of the North Pacific Coast* (Seattle: University of Washington Press, 1984); and Franz Boas, "Tsimshian Mythology," in *Thirty-first Annual Report of the Bureau of American Ethnology for the Years 1909–1910* (Washington, D.C.: Bureau of American Ethnology, 1916). I have relied as well on other sources, including Jonathan Dean's important dissertation, "'Rich Men,' 'Big Powers,' and Wastelands: The Tlingit-Tsimshian Border of the Northern Pacific Littoral, 1799 to 1867" (Ph.D. diss., University of Chicago, 1993); Philip Drucker's classic book *Indians of the Northwest Coast* (New York: American Museum of Natural History Press, 1963); and several entries in volume 7 of the Smithsonian Institution's *Handbook of North American Indians*. See Marjorie M. Halpin and Margaret Seguin, "Tsimshian Peoples: Southern Tsimshian, Coast Tsimshian, Nishga, and Gitksan," in *Northwest Coast*, ed. Wayne Suttles, vol. 7 of *Handbook of North American Indians*, ed. William C. Sturtevant (Washington, D.C.: Smithsonian Institution Press, 1990), 267–84.. For the preceding discussion, see Miller, *Tsimshian Culture*, 16–20; Garfield, *Tsimshian Clan and Society*, 173; Halpin and Seguin, "Tsimshian Peoples," 267; and Seguin, *The Tsimshian*, ix–x.

5. Miller, *Tsimshian Culture*, 21–29; Halpin and Seguin, "Tsimshian Peoples," 269–71; Seguin, *The Tsimshian*, x–xiii; Drucker, *Indians of the Northwest Coast*, 35–55; Wayne Suttles, "Coping with Abundance: Subsistence on the Northwest Coast," in *Man the Hunter*, ed. Richard B. Lee and Irven DeVore (New York: Aldine, 1987), 56.

6. For a particularly cogent recapitulation of Tsimshian cultural forms, see Miller, *Tsimshian Culture*, 15–29.

7. For the distinction between *adawx* and *ma'lesk*, see Susan Marsden and Robert Galois, "The Tsimshian, the Hudson's Bay Company, and the Geopolitics of the Northwest Coast Fur Trade, 1787–1840," *The Canadian Geographer/Le Geographie canadien* 39 (1995): 169–70.

8. Miller, *Tsimshian Culture*, 30–44, offers precisely this argument.

9. Boas recorded this *ma'lesk* as "The Prince Who Was Taken Away by the Spring Salmon." See Boas, *Tsimshian Mythology*, 192–206. For another version, see Cove and MacDonald, *Tsimshian Narratives, I*, 220–26.

10. Gitxsan substitute Fireweed for Blackfish and Frog/Raven for Raven; Nisga'a substitute Frog/Raven for Raven. Garfield, *Tsimshian Clan and Society*, 173–74; Seguin, *The Tsimshian*, x–xx; Halpin and Seguin, "Tsimshian Peoples," 274–75.

11. Miller, *Tsimshian Culture*, 44–55, offers a complete description of the concept of "house." See also Garfield, *Tsimshian Clan and Society*, 174; Halpin and Seguin, "Tsimshian Peoples," 275.

12. Miller, *Tsimshian Culture*, 2, 55, summarizes the case for a moiety structure, as do John A. Dunn in "International Matri-moieties in Personal Property Inheritance," in Miller and Eastman, *The Tsimshian and Their Neighbors of the North Pacific Coast*, 36–57; and Alice Bee Kasakoff in "Gitksan Term Usage," in Miller and Eastman, *The Tsimshian and Their Neighbors of the North Pacific Coast*, 69–108, among others.

13. Garfield, *Tsimshian Clan and Society*, 175; Seguin, *The Tsimshians*, xii–xiii; Halpin and Seguin, "Tsimshian Peoples," 274–75.

14. Garfield, *Tsimshian Clan and Society*, 178; Halpin and Seguin, "Tsimshian Peoples," 276; Philip Drucker, "Rank, Wealth, and Kinship in Northwest Coast Society," *American Anthropologist* 41 (January–March 1939): 58–62.

15. Miller, *Tsimshian Culture*, 18–19, 118–21; Seguin, *The Tsimshian*, xiii; Drucker, "Rank, Wealth, and Kinship," 58–62, 64; Garfield, *Tsimshian Clan and Society*, 177; Halpin and Seguin, "Tsimshian Peoples," 275; Michael E. Harkin, *The Heiltsuks: Dialogues of Culture and History on the Northwest Coast* (Lincoln: University of Nebraska Press, 1997).

16. Drucker, "Rank, Wealth, and Kinship," 56–57.

17. Miller, *Tsimshian Culture*, 17–19; Dean, "'Rich Men,'" 31–34; Garfield, *Tsimshian Clan and Society*, 178; Seguin and Halpin, "Tsimshian Peoples," 275–76; Suttles, "Coping with Abundance," 65–66.

18. Garfield, *Tsimshian Clan and Society*, 177–78; 271–72; Halpin and Seguin, "Tsimshian Peoples," 276; Drucker, "Rank, Wealth, and Kinship," 56–57.

19. Garfield, *Tsimshian Clan and Society*, 271; Drucker, *Indians of the Northwest Coast*, 130–31. For more on the debate regarding the economic value of slaves, see Viola Garfield, "A Research Problem in Northwest Indian Economics," *American Anthropologist*, n.s., 47 (1945): 628; Suttles "Coping with Abundance," 65–66; and two recent book-length studies of slavery on the Northwest Coast: Leland Donald, *Aboriginal Slavery on the Northwest Coast of North America* (Berkeley, University of California Press, 1997); and Robert H. Ruby and John A. Brown, *Indian Slavery in the Pacific Northwest* (Spokane, Wash.: A. H. Clark, 1993).

20. Carol Cooper, "Native Women of the Northern Pacific Coast: An Historical Perspective," *Revue d'etudes canadiennes/Journal of Canadian Studies* 27 (Winter 1992–93): 44–75, provides a well-written, cogent discussion of this issue. See also Jo-Anne Fiske, "Colonization and the Decline of Women's Status: The Tsimshian Case," *Feminist Studies* 17 (Fall 1991): 509–35; Halpin and Seguin, "Tsimshian Peoples," 269–81.

21. I have been influenced as well by several studies on Indian gender issues. See, among many others, Eleanor Leacock, "Montagnais Women and the Jesuit Program for Colonization," in *Women and Colonization: Anthropological Perspectives*, ed. Mona Etienne and Eleanor Leacock (New York: Praeger, 1980), 25–42; and Shoemaker, *Negotiators of Change*.

22. "Potlatch" derives from the Nootka *patshatl*, meaning "gift" or "giving," and made its way into general use through the Chinook trade jargon. See Drucker, *Indians of the Northwest Coast*, 131–43, for a general description. For Tsimshian potlatching see, Miller, *Tsimshian Culture*, 81–86; Jay Miller, "Feasting with the Southern Tsimshian," in Seguin, *The Tsimshian*, 27–30; Halpin and Seguin, "Tsimshian Peoples," 278–79; and Garfield, *Tsimshian Clan and Society*, 192–93, 217–19. Margaret Seguin, in "Understanding the Tsimshian 'Potlatch,'" in *Native Peoples: The Canadian Experience*, ed. R. Bruce Morrison and C. Roderick Wilson (Toronto: McClelland and Stewart, 1986), 473–500, argues that the feast complex was a symbolic "discourse" with supernatural powers who took human

form as invited guests. In this connection, the process of distributing gifts was a purifying ritual that established the feast-giver's relationship with his ancestors, "chiefs" from the animal kingdom, and supernatural forces in general.

23. Miller, *Tsimshian Culture*, 81–86; Drucker, "Rank, Wealth, and Kinship," 62–64; Garfield, *Tsimshian Clan and Society*, 192–97, 216–17; Marjorie Halpin, "The Structure of Tsimshian Totemism," in Miller and Eastman, *The Tsimshian and Their Neighbors*, 16–35.

24. Suttles, "Coping with Abundance," 66–68, makes the case for an economic dimension to potlatching. See also Garfield, *Tsimshian Clan and Society*, 216–19; Halpin and Seguin, "Tsimshian Peoples," 278–81. I will not rehash the formalist-substantivist debate here, but Stuart Plattner, *Economic Anthropology* (Stanford, Calif.: Stanford University Press, 1989) and Richard White, *The Middle Ground*, offer concise descriptions of the parameters of that discussion.

25. The most complete discussion of Russian-Tlingit relations during the period is Jonathan Dean's massive dissertation, "'Rich Men.'" For brief recapitulations, see pages 134–36, 156–58, and 188–90. I have relied as well on Robin A. Fisher, *Contact and Conflict: Indian-European Relations in British Columbia, 1774–1890* (Vancouver: University of British Columbia Press, 1977), 2–23; Wilson Duff, *The Indian History of British Columbia*, vol. 1, *The Impact of the White Man*, Anthropology in British Columbia, Memoirs, No. 5 (Victoria Provincial Museum, 1964), and several entries in volume 8 of the Smithsonian Institution's *Handbook of North American Indians*. These are: Frederica de Laguna, "Tlingit," esp. pp. 223–25; and Douglas Cole and David Darling, "History of the Early Period," pp. 119–34.

26. Dean, "'Rich Men,'" 127–48; Fisher, *Contact and Conflict*, 2–23; Cole and Darling, "History of the Early Period," 119–34; Drucker, *Indians of the Northwest Coast*, 28–33.

27. Dean, "'Rich Men,'" 127–48; Fisher, *Contact and Conflict*, 4–23; Cole and Darling, "History of the Early Period," 124–28; Ken Campbell, "Hartley Bay, British Columbia: A History," in Seguin, *The Tsimshian*, 5–6. Quotations are from Albert P. Niblack, *The Coast Indians of Southern Alaska and Northern British Columbia* (1890; New York: Johnson Reprint Corporation, 1970), 337.

28. Entitled "The Origin of the Name Hale," recorded by Tsimshian anthropologist William Beynon in 1916, this version of a particularly well-known *adawx* is from John J. Cove and George F. MacDonald, eds., *Tsimshian Narratives, II: Trade and Warfare*, Canadian Museum of Civilization, Mercury Series, Paper No. 3 (Ottawa: Canadian Museum of History, 1987), 158–59.

29. Philip Drucker is most closely associated with this "enrichment thesis." See Drucker, *Indians of the Northwest Coast*, 27–28, for a brief recapitulation of the general argument. Fisher, in *Contact and Conflict*, 20–22, agrees with Drucker, but more recent analyses suggest a more complex picture. See Dean, "'Rich Men,'" 127–30, 139–48; Robert Steven Grumet, "Changes in Coast Tsimshian Redistributive Activities in the Fort Simpson Region of British Columbia, 1788–1862," *Ethnohistory* 22 (Fall 1975): 295–318. Marsden and Galois, "The Tsimshian," offer an interpretation that focuses much more sharply on the Tsimshian side of the equation, suggesting both enrichment and continuity.

30. This is the thesis advanced by Robert Grumet in his "Changes in Coast Tsimshian Redistributive Activities." Dean, "'Rich Men,'" 139–48, elaborates on the point that contact was not an "epitomizing event" but rather the beginning of evolving relationships. For Neshake, see Cooper, "Native Women of the Northern Pacific Coast," 53–55. For broader conclusions on women as intermediaries, see Jennifer S. H. Brown, *Strangers in Blood*; and Devens, *Countering Colonialism*.

31. See particularly "The Supremacy of Legaix," *adawx* recorded by William Beynon in 1947, and in *Tsimshian Narratives, II,* 106–7. Also, Dean, "'Rich Men,'" 43–50, 244–55; Grumet, "Changes in Coast Tsimshian Redistributive Activities," 304–12; Marsden and Galois, "The Tsimshian," 170–72.

32. The *adawx* "Legaix's Triumph," related by Matthew Johnson (Gispaxlo'ots), was recorded by William Beynon in 1926. See *Tsimshian Narratives, II,* 120–23. See also Miller, *Tsimshian Culture,* 134–36; Boas, *Tsimshian Mythology,* 510; Garfield, *Tsimshian Clan and Society,* 182–91.

33. "The Supremacy of Legaix," *Tsimshian Narratives, II,* 106. Marsden and Galois, "The Tsimshian," 171–74, offer a detailed account of Ligeex's maneuvers in this respect, the best produced to date. See also Miller, *Tsimshian Culture,* 131–36.

34. Marsden and Galois, "The Tsimshian," 171–74; Grumet, "Changes in Coast Tsimshian Redistributive Activities," 304–8; Dean, "'Rich Men,'" 244–50; Garfield, *Tsimshian Clan and Society,* 184–91.

35. Marsden and Galois, "The Tsimshian," 175–76; Garfield, *Tsimshian Clan and Society,* 186–91; Grumet, "Changes in Coast Redistributive Activities," 304–8.

36. Marsden and Galois, "The Tsimshian," 177–79; Cooper, "Native Women of the Northern Pacific Coast," 55.

37. Dean, "'Rich Men,'" 265, 376–77; Marsden and Galois, "The Tsimshian," 177–79; Fisher, *Contact and Conflict,* 25–40; Grumet, "Changes in Coast Tsimshian Redistributive Activities," 303–9; Cole and Darling, "History of the Early Period," 125; Garfield, *Tsimshian Clan and Society,* 339. For the Kwagiul parallel, see Helen Codere, *Fighting with Property: A Study of Kwakiutl Potlatching and Warfare, 1792–1930,* Monographs of the American Ethnological Society, 18 (New York: J. J. Augustin, 1950).

38. Niblack, *Coast Indians,* 337; Fisher, *Contact and Conflict,* 31, 46–48; Grumet, "Coast Tsimshian Redistributive Activities," 305–11; Drucker, *Indians of the Northwest Coast,* 199; Cole and Darling, "History of the Early Period," 129–30; Garfield, *Tsimshian Clan and Society,* 208–9; Miller, "Feasting with the Southern Tsimshian," 27–30. Helen Codere, in *Fighting with Property,* notes a similar process among Kwaguls at Fort Rupert.

39. Robert T. Boyd, "Demographic History, 1774–1874," in *Northwest Coast,* ed. Wayne Suttles, vol. 7 of *Handbook of North American Indians,* ed. William C. Sturtevant (Washington, D.C.: Smithsonian Institution Press, 1990), 135–48; Grumet, "Changes in Coast Tsimshian Redistributive Activities," 309–11; Miller, "Feasting with the Southern Tsimshian," 28–31; Garfield, *Tsimshian Clan and Society,* 208–9; Drucker, *Indians of the Northwest Coast,* 137–40.

40. Fisher, *Contact and Conflict,* 45–48. The quotation is from Grumet, "Changes in Coast Tsimshian Redistributive Activities," 306.

41. J. E. Michael Kew, "History of Coastal British Columbia Since 1846," in *Northwest Coast,* ed. Wayne Suttles, vol. 7 of *Handbook of North American Indians,* ed. William C. Sturtevant (Washington, D.C.: Smithsonian Institution Press, 1990), 159–62; Fisher, *Contact and Conflict,* 49–52; 70–72. Much has been written about James Douglas's Indian policies with most scholars praising him for his just and foresighted practice of creating "reserves" on Vancouver Island—a policy that subsequent governors largely repudiated. For more on Douglas, see Paul Tennant, *Aboriginal Peoples and Politics: The Indian Land Question in British Columbia, 1849–1989* (Vancouver: University of British Columbia Press, 1991), 17–39; Miller, *Skyscrapers Hide the Heavens,* 145–47; Fisher, *Contact and Conflict,* 50–72, 95–97, 102–6; and Knight, *Indians at Work,* 28–32, 233–43.

42. Duncan George Forbes Macdonald, C.E., *British Columbia and Vancouver's Island. Comprising a Description of These Dependencies: Their Physical Character, Climate, Capabilities, Population, Trade, Natural History, Geology, Ethnology, Gold-Fields, and Future Prospects. Also, an Account of the Manners and Customs of the Native Indians* (London: Longman, 1862), 125.

43. For more on racial attitudes, see Fisher, *Contact and Conflict*, 73–94; Knight, *Indians at Work*, 237–40; Christine Bolt, *Victorian Attitudes Toward Race* (London: Routledge and Kegan Paul, 1971).

44. Miller, "Feasting with the Southern Tsimshian," 31; Halpin and Seguin, "Tsimshian Peoples," 280–81; Knight, *Indians at Work*, 239–42; Fisher, *Contact and Conflict*, 109–15; Boyd, "Demographic History, 1774–1874," 140–43; Fisher, *Contact and Conflict*, 115; Kew, "History of Coastal British Columbia," 159–60; Fisher, *Contact and Conflict*, 168–70. The single best study of the British navy and its impact on native groups of British Columbia is Barry Gough, *Gunboat Frontier: British Maritime Authority and Northwest Coast Indians, 1846–1890* (Vancouver: University of British Columbia Press, 1984).

45. Jean Usher's *William Duncan of Metlakatla: A Victorian Missionary in British Columbia*, National Museums of Canada, Publications in History, No. 5 (Ottawa: National Museum of Canada, 1974), remains the most probing single study of William Duncan's life and work.

6. WILLIAM DUNCAN AND THE GENESIS OF METLAKATLA

1. "Metlakahtla Village Song," English version, William Duncan Papers, Notebook [n.d.], National Archives of Canada Record Group MG 29, D 55, microfilm reel M-2331, p. 18100 [henceforth, WD/reel number, series, and page]. The primary source for work on William Duncan remains his voluminous papers, the originals of which are housed at New Metlakatla, Alaska. For this work, I have relied on microfilm copies made available by the National Archives of Canada, Manuscript Division, Ottawa, Canada. Other sets reside with the United States National Archives, Anchorage, Alaska Branch, and the University of British Columbia Library, Vancouver, British Columbia.

2. For this biographical sketch of William Duncan, I am indebted to Jean Usher's *William Duncan of Metlakatla*, esp. 2–8; and Murray, *The Devil and Mr. Duncan*, esp. 17–23. For Duncan's library, see particularly WD/M-2326, 9355. For more on the Victorian philosophy of self-help, see Usher, *William Duncan of Metlakatla*, 4–7; J. F. C. Harrison, "The Victorian Gospel of Success," *Victorian Studies* 1 (December 1957): 155–64; W. E. Houghton, *The Victorian Frame of Mind* (New Haven, Conn.: Yale University Press, 1957).

3. Usher, *William Duncan of Metlakatla*, 8–16. For more on the Church Missionary Society, see Eugene Stock, *The History of the Church Missionary Society, Its Environment, Its Men and Its Work*, vols. 1–3 (London: Church Missionary Society, 1899); for Victorian attitudes toward native peoples, see John Webster Grant, *Moon over Wintertime: Missionaries and the Indians of Canada in Encounter Since 1534* (Toronto: University of Toronto Press, 1984); and Bolt, *Victorian Attitudes Toward Race*. A concise work on Henry Venn's missionary philosophy is J. F. A. Ajayi's, "Henry Venn and the Policy of Development," *Journal of the Historical Society of Nigeria* 6 (December 1959): 331–42. Frederick Hoxie, in *A Final Promise*, discusses similar attitudes among United States missionaries and philanthropists.

4. Usher, *William Duncan of Metlakatla*, 15–17. See also H. A. C. Cairns, *The*

Clash of Cultures: Early Race Relations in Central Africa (New York: Praeger, 1965), 222–35; Roland Oliver, *The Missionary Factor in East Africa* (London: Longmans, 1952), 7–13, 288–89.

5. Ajayi, "Henry Venn and the Policy of Development," 331–39; S. M. Johnstone, *Samuel Marsden, a Pioneer of Civilization in the South Seas* (Sydney: Angus and Robertson, 1932), 60–69; Stock, *History of the Church Missionary Society*, vol. 2: 85–98, 419–20; Usher, *William Duncan of Metlakatla*, 16–20, 23–24; Henry Venn, "Minutes upon the Employment and Ordination of Native Teachers," 1851, quoted in Stock, *History of the Church Missionary Society*, 2:415.

6. Venn, "Instructions of the Parent Committee to those about to join the Yoruba Mission," 21 October 1856, as cited in Usher, *William Duncan of Metlakatla*, 25; Ajayi, "Henry Venn and the Policy of Development," 335–39; Stock, *History of the Church Missionary Society*, 2:415–18; Usher, 21–23, 26–27. For more on the drive to encourage "legitimate trade" in Africa, see J. D. Fage, *A History of Africa* (New York: Knopf, 1978), 325–42. For more on similar philosophies supporting United States policies, see Hoxie, *A Final Promise*.

7. This incident is related in the *adawx* "When Legaix Tried to Murder Mr. Duncan," recorded by William Beynon in 1950, in *Tsimshian Narratives, II*, 206. Usher, *William Duncan of Metlakatla*, 27–30, 40–41; Prevost's letter, 1856, quoted in Stock, *History of the Church Missionary Society*, 2:612–14; Murray, *The Devil and Mr. Duncan*, 24–31.

8. Jonathan Dean explores the question of violence in some detail, concluding that while claims supporting escalating violence may be overstated, on the eve of Duncan's visit Fort Simpson Tsimshians had engaged in "one of the largest bouts of drinking yet recorded, which would make a predictable spectacle on the young missionary's mind." See Dean, "'Rich Men'", 535–39. Also Miller, *Skyscrapers Hide the Heavens*, 145–47; Fisher, *Contact and Conflict*, 58–72.

9. Journal, 14 January 1858, WD/M2329, 14853–54; Stock, *History of the Church Missionary Society*, 2:615; Dean, "'Rich Men,'" 538–39. Duncan apparently submitted copies, probably revised, to the Church Missionary Society, and these entries appeared in CMS bulletins and elsewhere. The preceding statements appear in *The Church Missionary Intelligencer* (London: Seeley, Jackson, and Halliday, 1858), 246–51; R. C. Mayne, *Four Years in British Columbia and Vancouver Island: An Account of Their Forests, Rivers, Coasts, Gold Fields, and Resources for Colonisation* (London: John Murray, 1862), 263–64, 284–88; and most likely in other publications. This edition of *The Church Missionary Intelligencer* was included in the Sir Henry Wellcome Collection, NA-Alaska, RG 200, A-L File, Box 98, File # 176.

10. Clah diaries, 2 March 1861–24, Tsimshian Tribal Council photocopy [henceforth, TTC photocopy], pp. 5695–98. The originals of the Clah diaries are held by the Henry Wellcome Institute, London, England. Microfilm copies are available through the National Archives of Canada. I consulted photocopies held by the Tsimshian Tribal Council, Prince Rupert, British Columbia, and graciously made available to me. The citation form, including page numbers, refers to that collection only.

11. Ibid. Duncan, letter to the Church Missionary Society, ca. 1858, quoted in Stock, *History of the Church Missionary Society*, 2:615; "Goods received of the Hudson's Bay Company, 1857–60," in Finances, 1853–1888, WD/M-2334, 22123–30; R. M. Galois, "Colonial Encounters: The Worlds of Arthur Wellington Clah, 1855–1881," *BC Studies* 115/116 (Autumn/Winter 1997/98): 134. For Duncan's account of his first sermon, see letter to the Church Missionary Society, ca. 1858, quoted in Stock, *History of the Church Missionary Society*, 2:615.

12. "How Tamks Saved William Duncan's Life," story told by Wellington Clah (Tamks), recorded by William Beynon, 1950, in, *Tsimshian Narratives, II*, 210–12; Galois, "Colonial Encounters," 135–36. For another version, see "When Legaix Tried to Murder Mr. Duncan," story told by John Tate (Salaben) Gispaxloats, recorded by William Beynon, 1950, in, *Tsimshian Narratives, II*, 206–8.

13. Robert Galois, in "Colonial Encounters," 135–36, offers this argument. He relies on Michael E. Harkin, "Power and Progress: The Evangelic Dialogue Among Heiltsuk," *Ethnohistory* 40 (1993): 1–33; and John Comaroff and Jean Comaroff, *Ethnography and the Historical Imagination* (Boulder, Colo.: Westview Press, 192), 187–94.

14. Duncan, diary, 17, 25 November 1859, in Mayne, *Four Years in British Columbia*, 315–19; "School Enrollment, 1859," WD/M-2330, 15039–42, 15049–50; Diary of Shooquanahts, 27 April, 1858, in Mayne, *Four Years in British Columbia*, 338; Usher, *William Duncan of Metlakatla*, 46–50; Murray, *The Devil and Mr. Duncan*, 47–49; Journal [n.d.], WD/M-2329, 14858–59.

15. "When Legaix Tried to Murder Mr. Duncan" in, *Tsimshian Narratives, II*, 206–7. See also "How Tamks Saved William Duncan's Life," in *Tsimshian Narratives, II*, 211

16. Homer G. Barnett, in "Applied Anthropology in 1860," *Applied Anthropology* 1 (April–June 1942): 20–21, offers this story regarding Clah's past, and it is supported by Galois, "Colonial Encounters," 134, and Dean, "'Rich Men,'" 535, who find evidence in William McNeill's diary entry for 13 September 1857.

17. Clah diaries, 24 March 1861, TTC photocopy, p. 5698.

18. Mission Papers, 1861–80, WD/M-2331, 17598–99; "Names of Boarders, Mission School, Metlakahtla, B.C., 1862–72," WD/M-2329, 13847; Duncan to CMS, ca. 1858, quoted in Stock, *History of the Church Missionary Society*, 2:617. For Duncan's evaluation of the Fort Simpson physical environment, see Journal, 7 October 1857, WD/M-2326, 9544. See also "Goods received of the Hudson's Bay Company, 1857–60," in Finances, 1853–1888, WD/M-2334, 22123–30; Galois, "Colonial Encounters," 133; Murray, *The Devil and Mr. Duncan*, 72; Dean, "'Rich Men,'" 600–602; Henry Wellcome, *The Story of Metlakahtla* (New York: Saxon and Co., 1887), 18.

19. Miller, *Skyscrapers Hide the Heavens*, 145–47; Fisher, *Contact and Conflict*, 58–72, 98–99, 114–15. For Duncan's perspectives on Victoria, and his proposal for reorganizing refugee communities, see Duncan, Journal, 14 May 1861, WD/M-2327, 10023–24, and, "Memoirs," [n.d.], WD/M-2329, 13876–77; Usher, *William Duncan of Metlakatla*, 55–56; Murray, *The Devil and Mr. Duncan*, 57–60. For Clah's commentary on conditions in Victoria, see Clah diaries, 12 March 1862, TTC photocopy, pp. 5734–35.

20. William Duncan, "Memoirs," [n.d.], WD/M-2329, 13874, and 13877–78; "Memoirs," [n.d.], WD/M-2330, 14863; Mission Papers, 1861–1880, WD/M-2331, 17598–99; Duncan to CMS, ca. 1862, quoted in Stock, *History of the Church Missionary Society*, 2:617. See also William Benyon, "The Tsimshians of Metlakatla, Alaska," *American Anthropologist*, n.s., 43 (1941): 83; Dean, "'Rich Men,'" 600; Murray, *The Devil and Mr. Duncan*, 50; Wellcome, *Story of Metlakahtla*, 19–20.

21. Barnett, "Applied Anthropology in 1860," 19–33; Benyon, "The Tsimshians of Metlakatla, Alaska," 38–88. Jay Miller, in Miller and Eastman, *The Tsimshians and Their Neighbors*, 138–39, supports this conclusion.

22. Mission Papers, 1861–1880, WD/M-2331, 17598–603.

23. Ibid., 17598–99; Community Registers, WD/M-2330, 15191. Homer G.

Barnett, "Personal Conflicts and Cultural Change," *Social Forces* 20 (March 1941): 106–11; Galois, "Colonial Encounters," 137–38.

24. Brian Hosmer, interview with Arnold Booth, Metlakatla, Alaska, 28 July 1995; Hosmer, interview with Russell Hayward, Metlakatla, Alaska, 28 July 1995, 9 August 1995; Hosmer, interview with Joyce and Alvin Leask, Metlakatla, British Columbia, 2 August 1995. Original audiotapes in the possession of the author.

25. Clah Diaries, 2 March 1861 to 24 March 1861, TTC photocopy, pp. 5695–98; 12 March 1862, TTC photocopy, pp. 5731–35; 14 May 1862, TTC photocopy, pp. 5748–49; 20 May 1862, TTC photocopy pp. 5750–15. For more on the smallpox epidemic of 1862–63, see Boyd, "Demographic History, 143–44. In a diary entry for 1 January 1863, Clah reported deaths from smallpox as exceeding 400 persons. Clah Diaries, 1 January 1863, TTC photocopy, p. 5801. See also Dean, "'Rich Men,'" 598–602; Galois, "Colonial Encounters," 137–39.

26. Clah Diaries, 21 June 1862, TTC photocopy, pp. 5759–60.

27. Mission Papers, 1861–1880, WD/M-2331, 17598–99; Clah Diaries, 4 June 1862, TTC photocopy, p. 5756; 19 June, 1862, TTC photocopy, p. 5767; 25 July 1862, TTC photocopy, pp. 5765–67; "Moses A. Hewson's Record Book," pp. 1–2, NA, RG 200, A-L File, I4-1877-J 1898, folder 314.

28. Elizabeth Furniss, in "Resistance, Coercion, and Revitalization: The Shuswap Encounter with Roman Catholic Missionaries, 1860–1900," *Ethnohistory* 42 (Spring 1995): 231–63, offers a clearly written discussion of this issue.

29. See William Simmons, "Culture Theory in Contemporary Ethnohistory," *Ethnohistory* 35 (Winter 1988): 1–14; Michael Harkin, "Engendering Discipline: Discourse and Counterdiscourse in the Methodist-Heiltsuk Dialogue," *Ethnohistory* 43 (Fall 1996): 643–66.

30. Clah Diaries 19 January 1865, TTC photocopy, p. 6057; Galois, "Colonial Encounters," 137–40.

31. Metlakatla Account Ledgers, 1863–64, WD/M-2333, 20324–25, 20370–71, 20388–89; Clah Diaries, 11 September 1863, TTC photocopy, pp. 5191–92; 19 March 1864, TTC photocopy, pp. 5937–38; 20 April 1864, TTC photocopy, p. 5950; 14 June 1864, TTC photocopy, p. 5988.

32. Metlakatla Account Ledgers, 1863–64, WD/M-2333, 20008–9, 20426–27, 20324–25, 20327–71, 20388–89, 20396–97, 20398–99.

33. "Goods received of the Hudson's Bay Company, 1857–60," in Finances, 1853–1862, WD/M-2334, 22123–30; Metlakatla Account Ledgers, 1863–64, WD/M-2333, 20008–9; William Duncan, J.P., in account with the Government of British Columbia, 1862–71," WD/M-2332, 19259–70; "Government of British Columbia in Account with W. Duncan, J.P., 1871–80," WD/M-2334, 22175–78, 22230–37, 22250–53, 22264–65, 22282–87, 23415–16.

34. Miller, *Tsimshian Culture,* 138–39; Dean, "'Rich Men,'" 600–602. I am indebted as well to the late Russell Hayward of Metlakatla, Alaska, who suggested to me that Metlakatla was, in reality, "Duncan's tribe." Brian Hosmer, interview with Russell Hayward, Metlakatla, Alaska, 28 July 1995. Original audiotapes in the possession of the author.

35. "Register of Male Settlers at Metlakahtla and the payment of their Yearly Tax, 1863–66," WD/M-2330, 15192–201; "General Receipts and Expenditures," 1863–80, WD/M-2333, 20153–89, 20195–206, 20219–20; "New Settlers, 1867–70," WD/M-2330, 15203–4; "List of Settlers who have taken vows and joined the community, January 1873–January 1, 1879," WD/M-2329, 14712–19; Letter signed by Weenahks, Liggy oo cheeost, Weash yahkahs, Tum coush, Shim will chee oost, Tum dee naych, Yeh lam, Queesh, Tlith ron, Hahwah, Shoget, Wah eeast kin haydah,

"members of the Kitkaht of Tsimshean Nation," 25 February 1873, WD/M-2330, 15657, quoted in Ken Campbell, "Hartley Bay, B.C.: A History," in Seguin, *The Tsimshians*, 8; Duncan to the Executive Committee of the Church Missionary Society, 7 March 1876, Letterbook Number 2, WD/M-2321, 8882, pp. 557–62; Duncan to CMS, 7 March 1879, Letterbook Number 2, WD/M-2321, 8883, pp. 309–12.

7. METLAKATLA AND THE MARKET

1. "Summary of Estimates, 1867–68," WD/M-2332, 19316–19; James G. Swan to Commissioner Ezra A. Hayt, October 19, 1878, in *Report upon the Customs District, Public Service, and Resources of Alaska Territory, by William Gouverneur Morris, Special Agent of the Treasury Department*, 45th Cong., 3d sess., 1879, Sen. Ex. Doc. 59, 71–73. Crosby's career is fascinating in its own right. While often at odds with Duncan, Crosby acknowledged his debt to his Anglican contemporary, and the two remained in close contact right up to 1887, when Duncan departed for Alaska. For more on Crosby, see Clarence Bolt, *Thomas Crosby and the Tsimshian: Small Shoes for Feet Too Large* (Vancouver: University of British Columbia Press, 1993); Grant, *Moon over Wintertime*, 133–36; Robin Fisher, *Contact and Conflict*, 138–41; and Crosby's own writings: *Among the An-ko-me-mums* (Toronto: William Briggs, 1907); and *Up and Down the North Pacific Coast by Canoe and Mission Ship* (Toronto: Missionary Society of the Methodist Church, 1914). For the Durieu "system," see Grant, *Moon over Wintertime*, 125–27; Fisher, *Contact and Conflict*, 138–39; and Edwin Lemert, "The Life and Death of an Indian State," *Human Organization* 13, no. 3 (1954): 23–27.

2. "Rules of Metlakahtla, October 15, 1862," WD/M-2330, 15190; Murray, *The Devil and Mr. Duncan*, 75–76; Usher, *William Duncan of Metlakatla*, 63–64.

3. "General Plan," 1871, WD/M-2325, 14667–78. For sample rolls, see "Metlakahtla Council, ca. 1865," WD/M-2330, 15191; "Metlakahtla Council, 1 January 1869," WD/M-2329, 14651–52; "Metlakahtla Council, 1 February 1870," WD/M-2329, 14653–54; "Metlakahtla Council, 1 January 1872," WD/M-2329, 14670; "Metlakahtla Council, 1 January 1874," WD/M-2329, 14659–60; "Metlakahtla Office Holders, 1 January 1881," WD/M-2329, 14720–32. Quotation is from Usher, *William Duncan of Metlakatla*, 78.

4. Duncan to Israel Wood Powell, 13 August 1881, Letterbook Number 2, WD/M-2321, 8883, pp. 448–53; Henry Ridley and James P. O'Reilly (natives), agreement to "watch over" Alfred Auclaire, 6 January 1880, WD/M-2330, 15663; George Usher and Oliver Scott (natives), promise to enforce "moral conduct" of A. Aisfore, 6 January 1880, WD/M-2330, 15667. Bond signed by Paul Sebassoh, Samuel Pelham, John Tait, Robert Allen, Robert Hewson, Philip Barnard, Thomas Eaton, Christopher Gibson, Sydney Campbell, and Solomon Burton, who promise to watch over Alfred Atkinson, Frank Allen, Matthew Eaton, Charles Venn, and Cowdeknay, 6 January 1880, WD/M-2330, 15668. Quotation is from "Minutes of the Council Meeting," 29 May 1871, WD/M-2329, 14657. See also "Some of the Indians who had committed fault against the village during 1870 and addressed by W. Duncan," Council Meeting, 27 May 1871, WD/M-2329, 14656; "Restitution of property to Nakepahman and John," ca. February, 1865, WD/M-2331, 17505–6.

5. Clah diaries, 10/30/70, TTC photocopy, pp. 6538–39. Jo-Anne Fiske, in "Colonization and the Decline of Women's Status," 524–31, offers this interpretation. On the other hand, Carol Cooper, in "Native Women of the Northern

Pacific Coast," 44–75, offers a more nuanced account. See also Devens, *Countering Colonization*.

6. Clah diaries, 3/12/71, TTC photocopy, p. 6572; Cooper, "Native Women of the Northern Pacific Coast"; Harkin, "Engendering Discipline," 657.

7. Clah's diaries include several references to feasting at Ligeex's house and evidence that the former chief continued to exploit hunting and fishing territories. Among others see Clah Diary, 1/19/75, TTC photocopy, p. 6057; 4/30/66, p. 6248; 10/20/70, pp. 6452–54.

8. "Outlay of Profits of Trade, 1866–68," WD/M-2333, 20111–14; "Testimony of Kahlp, aged 35," in Wellcome, *Story of Metlakahtla*, 55–56.

9. "Public Works to be carried out from the Village Tax," [n.d], WD/M-2330, 15191; "Outlay of Profits from Trade," 1863–71," WD/M-20111-19; "Minutes of the Council Meeting," 12 January 1875," WD/M-2325, 14665; "Minutes of the Council Meeting, 31 March 1870," WD/M-2329, 14655–56; "Minutes of the Council Meeting, 3 January 1881," WD/M-2329, 14730; Usher, *William Duncan of Metlakatla*, 85–86.

10. "Report of Rev. R. J. Dundas, Columbia Mission," *Annual Report* (London: Rivingtons, 1870), 54; Usher, *William Duncan of Metlakatla*, 81–83.

11. District of Metlakahtla, British Columbia, case against Robert Cunningham of Fort Simpson, WD/M-2330, 15760–69, 15773–82; Drake, Jackson, and Aikman [attorneys] to Duncan, 13 October 1868, WD/M-2330, 15785; William Duncan to Messrs. Drake, Jackson, and Aikman, 28 October 1868, WD/M-2330, 15783–84; Drake, Jackson, and Aikman, 9 November 1868, WD/M-2330, 15787–90; "Statement of Clah, witness, in case against John Collins," [n.d.], 1870, WD/M-2330, 15791, 15806. Cases in which Metlakatlans acted as witnesses and where Metlakatla constables arrested suspected violators are numerous. For a few examples, see "Statement of Eli Hamblet, Metlakatla constable, witness in case against Peter Cargotish," WD/M-2330, 15808–9; "Deposition of Alfred Aucland, an Indian of Metlakahtla," in case against Peter Cargotish, WD/M-2330, 15815–16; "Deposition of Clah, an Indian from Fort Simpson," WD/M-2330, 15818. For financial benefits accruing from law enforcement duties, see "William Duncan, J.P., in account with the Government of British Columbia, 1862–71," WD/M-2332, 19259–70; "Government of British Columbia in Account with W. Duncan, J.P., 1871–80," WD/M-2334, 22175–78, 22230–37, 22250–53, 22264–65, 22282–87, 23415–16; Duncan to A. C. Elliot, Provincial Secretary, 26 July 1876, Letterbook Number 3, WD/M-2321, 8883, pp. 637–38; Duncan to J. Englehardt, 6 August 1878, Letterbook Number 2, WD/M-2321, 8883, pp. 185–88; Usher, *William Duncan of Metlakatla,* 80–81; Government of British Columbia, in Account with William Duncan, J.P., 1862–71, WD/M-2333, 19259–70; 1871–80, WD/M-2334, 22175–78, 22230–37, 22250–53, 22264–65, 22282–87, 23415–16.

12. "Statement of Yakahdates, Chief of a tribe of Kitaklan Indians, Skeena river," 23 May 1872, WD/M-2330, 15885; Case of Neashyakahnaht versus five defendants accused of destroying a ceremonial pole, decided 20 July 1874, WD/M-2330, 16013–25; Duncan to W. A. G. Young, 14 April 1868, quoted in Usher, *William Duncan of Metlakatla*, 81; Gough, *Gunboat Frontier,* 181–82; Duncan to Joseph W. Trutch, Governor of British Columbia, 30 March 1876, Letterbook Number 1, WD/M-2321, 8882, p. 583; Duncan to Trutch, 11 May 1876, Letterbook Number 1, WD/M-2321, 8882, pp. 598–601.

13. For the Melumkaupa case, see Duncan to the Honorable A. C. Elliot, Attorney General of British Columbia, 24 September 1877. Letterbook Number 2, WD/M-2321, 8883, p. 66; "Bill of Complaint Between Mel-um-coi-pui

[Melumkaupa] (plaintiff) and William Duncan (defendant). Before the Supreme Court of British Columbia in Chancery," 30 August 1877. WD/M-2330, 15678–83. For the Oliver Scott case, see WD/M-2330, 16098–72.

14. Clah diaries, 3/17/74, TTC photocopy, pp. 6826–27; "Bill of Complaint Against William Duncan," [ca. 1875], WD/M-2330, 15687–93; Duncan to D. W. Higgins, Victoria, 4 March 1875, Letterbook Number 1, WD/M-2321, 8882, pp. 462–65; Duncan to John McAlister, Port Essington, 3 July 1876, Letterbook Number 1, WD/M-2321, 8882, pp. 632–34; Duncan to Dr. Ash, 27 January 1875, Letterbook Number 1, WD/M-2321, 8882, pp. 431–33; Duncan to Ash, 15 July 1875, Letterbook Number 1, WD/M-2321, 8882, p. 474.

15. For the tendency for constables to "advance" to seats on the village council, see Metlakahtla Council, 1867–68, WD/M-2330, 15191; Metlakahtla Council, 1 January 1869, WD/M-2329, 14651–52; Metlakathla Council, 1 February 1870, WD/M-2329, 14653–54; Metlakahtla Council, 1 January 1872, WD/M-2329, 14670; Metlakahtla Constables, 1 January 1868, WD/M-2330, 15191; Metlakahtla Constables, 1869–70, WD/M-2329, 14552; Metlakahtla Constables, 1 January 1872, WD/M-2329, 14670; Metlakahtla Council and Constables, 1 January 1874, WD/M-2329, 14659–60; Metlakahtla Office Holders, 1 January 1881, WD/M-2329, 14720–32.

16. Metlakahtla Store Account, 1863–64, WD/M-2333, 20008–9; Duncan, "Memoirs," [n.d], WD/M-2330, 14863–65; Wellcome, *Story of Metlakahtla*, 29–32; Usher, *William Duncan of Metlakatla*, 67; Murray, *The Devil and Mr. Duncan*, 77; Hamilton Moffatt to the Board of Management, the Honourable Hudson's Bay Company at Victoria, 31 December 1863, quoted in Usher, *William Duncan of Metlakatla*, 68; Duncan, "Memoirs," [n.d], WD/M-2330, 14863–65; "William Duncan in Account with the Government of British Columbia," WD/M-2333, 19261–62; Wellcome, *Story of Metlakahtla*, 29; Usher, *William Duncan of Metlakatla*, 68; "Schooner Carolena in Account with Shareholders, Metlakahtla," 1863–66, WD/M-2333, 19982–85; Wellcome, *Story of Metlakahtla*, 29; Usher, *William Duncan of Metlakatla*, 68.

17. "Indian Village, Metlakahtla, in Account with the Government of British Columbia, 1862–69," WD/M-2333, 19259; "Outlay of Profits of Trade, 1868," WD/M-2333, 20111–12; Murray, *The Devil and Mr. Duncan*, 90–91. Quotation is from Wellcome, *Story of Metlakahtla*, 32.

18. "Register, Schooner *Carolena*," 17 September 1863, WD/M-2329, 14628–30.

19. For a representative sample of purchases during the space of one year, see "Register of Metlakahtla, 10 February 1875," Letterbook Number 1, WD/M-2321, 8882, pp. 439–40; "Requisition for Metlakahtla, 11 February 1875," Letterbook Number 1, WD/M-2321, 8882, pp. 449–50; "Requisition for Metlakahtla," 15 July 1875, Letterbook Number 1, WD/M-2321, 8882, pp. 472–73; "Requisition for Goods for Metlakahtla sent to Messrs. Dickeson & Stewart, London," 10 November 1875, Letterbook Number 1, WD/M-2321, 8882, pp. 529–32; "List of Medicines for Metlakahtla," 7 March 1876, Letterbook Number 1, WD/M-2321, 8882, p. 556. For export figures, see "William Duncan, Metlakahtla, B.C., in account with the Church Missionary Society, 1863–64," Church Accounts, WD/M-2333, 19986–87; "Metlakahtla, B.C., Trade Account, 1863," Exports, WD/M-2329, 14631–38; "Exports by the Schooner Carolena," February 1864, Exports, WD/M-2329, 14644; Metlakahtla Exports, 1864–65, WD/M-2333, 20008–11, 20398–99, 20426–27. See also "Fur Account," 1871, WD/M-2334, 22210–11; Metlakahtla Store in Account with J. Englehardt, Victoria, 1870–75, WD/M-2334, 22811–14, 22187–90; "From Metlakahtla 9

Nov. 1875 to Messrs. Dickeson & Stewart, London. A Case of Furs," 9 November 1875, Letterbook Number 1, WD/M-2321, 8882, p. 528; William Duncan to Dickeson and Stewart, London, 10 November 1875, Letterbook Number 1, WD/M-2321, 8882, pp. 533–35; William Duncan to Dickeson and Stewart, 8 June 1876, Letterbook Number 1, WD/M-2321, 8882, pp. 608–11; Metlakahtla Store in Account with Dickeson & Stewart, London, 1870–75, WD/M-2334, 22171–72, 22268–69.

20. "Stock Taking Yearly, Metlakahtla Store," 1870–March 1871, Letterbook Number 1, WD/M-2321, 8882, p. 469; "Metlakahtla, Misc. Account, 1863–66," WD/M-2333, 20008–13; "Sundry Persons, in Account with the Metlakahtla Store," 1873–77, WD/M-2333, 20531–40; "Indian Deposits at 5%, with Metlakahtla store," 1873–78, WD/M-2334, 22228–29, 22289–90; "Outlay of Profits of Trade," 1863–71, WD/M-2333, 20111–19.

21. "Account of William Rudland, Storekeeper," 1866–67, WD/M-2333, 20034–37; 1869–71, WD/M-2334, 22165–68; "Account of James Rudland, Storekeeper," 1876, WD/M-2334, 22170–71; 1877–78, WD/M-2333, 20547–48, 20595–96, 20633–34; Duncan to Mr. Gray, 21 October 1876, Letterbook Number 1, WD/M-2321, 8882, pp., 686–87; Duncan to J. Englehardt, 8 March 1879, Letterbook Number 2, WD/M-2321, 8883, pp. 314–17. For the link between Duncan's activities and "applied anthropology," see Usher, *William Duncan of Metlakatla*, 67–69; Morris Zaslow, "The Missionary as Social Reformer: The Case of William Duncan," *Journal of the Canadian Church Historical Society* 8 (September 1966): 60–62; Barnett, "Applied Anthropology in 1860," 23–26.

22. Duncan to Dickeson & Stewart, London, 10 February 1875, Letterbook Number 1, WD/M-2321, 8882, pp. 437–38; Duncan to J. Englehardt, 26 July 1876, Letterbook Number 1, WD/M-2321, 8882, p. 640.

23. Duncan to J. Englehardt, 16 March 1876, Letterbook Number 1, WD/M-2321, 8882, pp. 549–51; Duncan to Dickeson & Stewart, 8 June 1876, Letterbook Number 1, WD/M-2321, 8882, pp. 608–11.

24. Duncan to Mr. G. Fair, Portland, Or., 10 February 1875, Letterbook Number 1, WD/M-2321, 8882, pp. 442–44; Duncan to Megrew & Fair, San Francisco, 8 June 1876, Letterbook Number 1, WD/M-2321, 8882, pp. 616–19; Duncan to Gray, 21 October 1876, Letterbook Number 1, WD/M-2321, 8882, pp. 686–91.

25. Duncan to Gray, 21 October 1876, Letterbook Number 1, WD/M-2321, 8882, pp. 692–93.

26. Metlakatla Exports, September 1863," WD/M-2329, 14631–38; "Outlay of Profits of Trade," 1866–67, WD/M-2333, 20111–13.

27. "Register, Schooner *Carolena*, 17 September 1863," WD/M-2329, 14630; "William Duncan, Mess. Account," 1863–65, WD/M-2333, 19886–89; Duncan to Dr. Ash, Victoria, B.C., 11 October 1875, Letterbook Number 1, WD/M-2321, 8882, p. 515; "Indian Curiosities Sold to Dr. I. W. Powell, 1878–79," WD/M-2333, 20621–22; Metlakahtla Store Account with Paul Sebassoh, 1878, WD/M-2334, 20553–54; Metlakahtla Store Account with Israel Powell, Indian Superintendent, 1879, WD/M-2334, 20688–89.

28. Outlay of Profits of Trade," 1866–68, WD/M-2333, 20111–12; William Duncan, in Account with the Church Missionary Society, 1866–67, WD/M-2333, 20024–25; Metlakahtla, Receipts and Expenditures, 1867, WD/M-2333, 20196; Usher, *William Duncan of Metlakatla*, 68; Wellcome, *Story of Metlakahtla*, 35.

29. Bishop Edward Cridge, ca. 1875, quoted in Wellcome, *Story of Metlakahtla*, 84.

30. Saw Mill Account, 1869–70, WD/M-2334, 22198–99, 1873–75, WD/M-2333, 19090; William Duncan, in Account with the Government of British Colum-

bia, 1862–69, WD/M-2333, 19261; "Outlay of Profits of Trade," 1868. WD/M-2333, 20112–13; Usher, *William Duncan of Metlakatla*, 68–69.

31. "New Church Building," in Receipts and Expenditures, 1870–77, WD/M-2333, 20152–72; Usher, *William Duncan of Metlakatla*, 69–70.

32. "New Church Building," in Receipts and Expenditures, 1870–77, WD/M-2333, 20152–72; Usher, *William Duncan of Metlakatla*, 69–70; Murray, *The Devil and Mr. Duncan*, 110–12; Wellcome, *Story of Metlakahtla*, 122. Quotation is attributed to Charles Halleck, ca. 1875, quoted in Wellcome, *Story of Metlakahtla*, 129.

33. Miller, *Tsimshian Culture*, 141–42; Usher, *William Duncan of Metlakatla*, 69–70; Duncan to the Executive Committee of the Church Missionary Society, 7 March 1876, Letterbook Number 1, WD/M-2321, 8882, pp. 557–62; Superintendent General of Indian Affairs, Ottawa, in Account with William Duncan, 1875, WD/M-2334, 22236–37; Duncan to Dr. Israel W. Powell, 13 August 1881, Letterbook Number 2, WD/M-2321, 8883, pp. 448–53.

34. Duncan to Dr. Israel W. Powell, 22 March 1880, Letterbook Number 2, WD/M-2321, 8883, pp. 362–64; Superintendent General of Indian Affairs, Ottawa, in Account with William Duncan, 1875–78, WD/M-2333, 20541–46, 20615–16, 20646–47; William Duncan to the Executive Committee of the Church Missionary Society, 7 March 1879, Letterbook Number 2, WD/M-2321, 8883, pp. 309–12; Duncan to Powell, 22 March 1880, Letterbook Number 2, WD/M-2321, 8883, pp. 362–64; Usher, *William Duncan of Metlakatla*, 69; Miller, *Tsimshian Culture*, 144. Description offered by Charles Halleck, ca. 1881, in Wellcome, *Story of Metlakahtla*, 129.

35. "Plant of the New Saw Mill," in Receipts and Expenditures, 1876–80, WD/M-2333, 20202; Requisition for saw mill supplies, 1878, Letterbook Number 2, WD/M-2321, 8883, p. 132; Sawmill, Disbursements and Receipts, 1876–82, WD/M-2334, 21890–91, 21908–9, 21920–21, 21934–35, 21986–87, 22014–17, 22034, 22042; Duncan to the Executive Committee of the Church Missionary Society, 7 March 1879, Letterbook Number 2, WD/M-2321, 8883, pp. 309–12; "Sundry Persons in Account with the Sawmill," 1876–77, WD/M-2333, 20617–20; "Summary of Receipts from Builders at the Village of Metlakahtla showing what each received from the Government Grant of $1000 made in the year 1875 to William Duncan," WD/M-2333, 19468; "Summary of Receipts, Continued, from Indians of Metlakahtla, B. Columbia showing what each received of W. Duncan from the Grant in Aid of building new Village made by Indian Department June 1875 and June 1881, total $2000," WD/M-2333, 19469.

36. Sawmill, Disbursements and Receipts, 1876–82, WD/M-2334, 21890–91, 21908–9, 21920–21, 21934–35, 21986–87, 22014–17, 22034, 22042; Duncan to Northwestern Commercial Company, Inverness, B.C., 20 August 1878, Letterbook Number 2, WD/M-2321, 8883, pp. 201–2; Metlakahtla Sawmill, 1882, WD/M-2333, 20738–39.

37. Duncan to Englehardt, 13 June 1878, Letterbook Number 2, WD/M-2321, 8883, pp. 147–50; Duncan to J. C. Bales, Victoria, 16 May 1878, Letterbook Number 2, WD/M-2321, 8883, pp. 139–42; Duncan to Englehardt, 13 June 1878, Letterbook Number 2, WD/M-2321, 8883, pp. 147–50; Duncan to Englehardt, 6 August 1878, Letterbook Number 2, WD/M-2321, 8883, pp. 185–88; Duncan to J. C. Bales, Victoria, 16 May 1878, Letterbook Number 2, WD/M-2321, 8883, pp. 139–42; Duncan to Englehardt, 6 August 1878, Letterbook Number 2, WD/M-2321, 8883, pp. 185–88; Government Grants to Metlakahtla, 1876, WD/M-2334, 22282; Receipts and Expenditures, 1872–78, WD/M-2333, 20197–200.

38. Receipts and Expenditures, 1870–71, WD/M-2333, 20197–98; William Duncan in Account with the Church Missionary Society, 1869–70, WD/M-2334, 22149–50; Usher, *William Duncan of Metlakatla*, 70–72; Wellcome, *Story of Metlakahtla*, 36.

39. Wellcome, *Story of Metlakahtla*, 37–39.

40. Fur Accounts with the Metlakahtla Trade Shop, 1871–72, WD/M-2334, 22210–11; Sea Otter Hunters Account, 1875, WD/M-2334, 22256–57; Shingle Makers Account, 1877–78, WD/M-2333, 20601–2; Coopers Company, 1877–78, WD/M-2333, 20603–4; Weaving Company, 1877–78, WD/M-2333, 20607, 20625–26, 20637; Hunters' Company Account, 1879–80, WD/M-2333, 20676–84; Loggers Account with the Saw Mill, 1880, WD/M-2334, 22544–45, 22638, 22644; Brickyard Account, 1881–82, WD/M-2334, 22711; Sash Shop Account, 1881–83, WD/M-2334, 22687–88; Metlakahtla Saw Mill Account, 1882, WD/M-2333, 20738–39.

41. William Duncan, "Finances," 1870–79, WD/M-22334, 20153–73, 20541–46, 20615–16, 20646–47, 22147–63, 22179–88, 22328–46. Given William Duncan's unusual accounting methods, the above figures are estimates only.

42. William Duncan, in Account with the Church Missionary Society, 1865–66, WD/M-2333, 20666–67; 1866–67, WD/M-2333, 20024–25; 1869–80, WD/M-2334, 22147–64, 22328–29, 22346–47, 22356–57, 22368–70, 22390–91; Duncan, in account with J. Englehardt, 1872, WD/M-2334, 22185–88; Duncan, in account with J. Englehardt, 1872, WD/M-2334, 22185–88; Duncan, in account with J. Englehardt, 1877, WD/M-2334, 22279–81, 22298–301; Government of British Columbia, in Account with William Duncan, J.P., 1871–76, 1880, WD/M-2334, 22175–78, 22230–37, 22250–53, 22264–65, 22283–87, 22416–17.

43. Duncan to Englehardt, 14 July 1875, Letterbook Number 1, WD/M-2321, 8882, pp. 468–71; Duncan to Englehardt, 11 October 1875, Letterbook Number 1, WD/M-2321, 8882, pp. 504–11; Marble Company Account, 1877–78, WD/M-2333, 20605–6; Duncan to Englehardt, 6 March 1876, Letterbook Number 1, WD/M-2321, 8882, pp. 549–51; Duncan to Englehardt, 9 November 1878, Letterbook Number 2, WE/M-2321, 8883, pp. 262–67.

44. Duncan to Dickeson and Stewart, 3 March 1875, Letterbook Number 1, WD/M-2321, 8882, pp. 452–55; Duncan to Englehardt, 26 July 1876, Letterbook Number 1, WD/M-2321, 8882, pp. 640–46; Duncan to Israel Powell, 22 March 1880, Letterbook Number 2, WD/M-2321, 8883, 362–64; Receipts and Expenditures, 1877–78, WD/M-2330, 20197–98; Coopers Company, general account, 1877–79, WD/M-2333, 20603–4, 20625–26, 20637–38; Duncan, in Account with J. Englehardt, 1877–78, WD/M-2334, 22276–81; Duncan to J. C. Bales, Victoria, 16 May, 1878, Letterbook Number 2, WD/M-2321, 8883, pp. 139–42; Duncan to Englehardt, 13 June 1878, Letterbook Number 2, WD/M-2321, 8883, pp. 147–50; Duncan to Englehardt, 6 August 1878, Letterbook Number 2, WD/M-2321, 8883, pp. 185–88. Duncan's interest in Australian markets stems, at least in part, from his dissatisfaction with low prices prevailing in Victoria. See Duncan to Englehardt, 9 November 1878, Letterbook Number 2, WD/M-2321, 8883, pp. 262–67; Duncan to Englehardt, 10 December 1878, Letterbook Number 2, WD/M-2321, 8883, pp. 279–85; Duncan to Israel Powell, 22 March 1880, Letterbook Number 2, WD/M-2321, 8883, pp. 362–64.; Duncan to Northwestern Commercial Company, Inverness, B.C., 19 July 1878, Letterbook Number 2, WD/M-2321, 8883, p. 163.

45. Duncan to Englehardt, 15 September 1875, Letterbook Number 1, WD/M-2321, 8882, pp. 497–99; Duncan to Englehardt, 11 October 1875, Letterbook Number 1, WD/M-2321, 8882, pp. 504–11; Duncan to Englehardt, 6 March

1876, Letterbook Number 1, WD/M-2321, 8882, pp. 549–51; Duncan to Engle-hardt, 13 June 1878, Letterbook Number 2, WD/M-2321, 8883, pp. 147–50; Dun-can to Englehardt, 10 December 1878, Letterbook Number 2, WD/M-2321, 8883, pp. 279–84.

46. Receipts and Expenditures, 1876–82, WD/M-2333, 20198–202; Met-lakahtla, in account with Sea Otter Hunters, 1876, WD/M-2333, 22256–57; Met-lakahtla, in account with Shingle Makers, 1877–78, WD/M-2333, 20601–2; Metlakahtla, in account with the Weaving Company, 1877–78, WD/M-2333, 20607; Metlakahtla, in account with the Hunters' Companies, 1879, WD/M-2333, 20676–84; Loggers Account with the Saw Mill, 1880, WD/M-2334, 22544–45, 22638–44; Metlakahtla, in account with the Brickyard, 1881–82, WD/M-2334, 22711; Sash Shop Account, 1881–83, WD/M-2334, 22687–88; Metlakahtla, Eco-nomic and Community Activities, 1883, WD/M-2330, 15205–58; "Sundry Per-sons, in Account with the Metlakahtla Store," 1873–77, WD/M-2333, 20531–40; 1882, WD/M-2333, 20782–83, 20857. 20866; 1883, WD/M-2333, 209136, 21002–3; William Duncan, Business Account, 1884, WD/M-2333, 21355–60, 1885, WD/M-2333, 21440–41, 21474–75, 21548–49, 21586–87; Metlakahtla Cooperative Store, Ledgerbook, 1884, WD/M-2333, 21311–14, 1885, 21568–69, 21600–601, 21712–19.

47. Duncan to W. M. Neil, Inverness, B.C., 28 August 1878, Letterbook Num-ber 2, WD/M-2321, 8883, p. 202.

48. Ibid.; Duncan to Englehardt, 8 March 1879, Letterbook Number 2, WD/M-2321, 8883, pp. 314–17.

49. Duncan to W. M. Neil, Inverness, B.C., 28 August 1878, Letterbook Num-ber 2, WD/M-2321, 8883, p. 202; Duncan to Englehardt, 8 March 1879, Letterbook Number 2, WD/M-2321, 8883, pp. 314–17; Duncan to Englehardt, 5 May 1879, Letterbook Number 2, WD/M-2321, 8883, pp. 330–31; Duncan to J. Boscowitz, Victoria, 14 June 1880, Letterbook Number 2, WD/M-2321, 8883, pp. 375–78.

50. Account with Sea Otter Hunters, 1875, WD/M-2334, 22256–57; Account with Shingle Makers, 1877–78, WD/M-2333, 20601–2; Loggers Account with the Saw Mill, 1880–81, WD/M-2334, 22544–45, 22638–44; Sash Shop Account, 1877, WD/M-2334, 22687–88; Account with Fred Ridley, Shingle Maker, 1878–79, WD/M-2333, 20559–60, 20668–69; Account with Hunters Companies, 1879, WD/M-2333, 20576–84; Account with Henry Ridley, trader and hunter, 1876–77, WD/M-2333, 20527–28; 1882, WD/M-2333, 20751; 1884, WD/M-2333, 20888; Account with James Rudland, Storekeeper, 1876–78, WD/M-2333, 20547–48, 20595–96, 20633–34, WD/M–2334, 22169–70, 1883, WD/M-2333, 21317–18, 21342, 21379–80.

51. "Report of A. Milletich, Acting Deputy Collector and Inspector," Sitka, Alaska, May 28, 1876, in William Guouverneur Morris, Special Agent of the Trea-sury Department, *Report upon the Customs District, Public Service, and Resources of Alaska Territory*, 45th Cong., 3d sess., Sen. Ex. Doc. 59, 1879, p. 38–39.

52. Ibid.

53. Ibid.

54. For more on the creation of these associated missions, see, Murray, *The Devil and Mr. Duncan*, 94–95, 102–3, 122, 126, 129–35, 144, 150–53; Usher, *William Duncan of Metlakatla*, 95–97. See also Daniel Raunet, *Without Honor, Without Sur-render: A History of the Nishga Land Claims* (Vancouver: Douglas and McIntyre, 1984); Fisher, *Contact and Conflict*, 127, 136–37, 205; W. H. Collison, *In the Wake of the War Canoe* (London: Longmans, Green, 1915); William Henry Pierce, *From Pot-latch to Pulpit, Being the Autobiography of the Rev. William Henry Pierce, Native Mis-sionary to the Indian Tribes of the Northwest Coast of British Columbia* (Vancouver:

Vancouver Bindery, 1933); Duncan, in Account with the Church Missionary Society, 1865–66, WD/M-2333, 20603–4, 20666–67; 1866–67, 20024–25; 1878, WD/M-2334, 22328–29; 1879, 22346–47, 22356–57; 1880, 22368–69, 22390–91; Register of Goods, Nass Mission, 1866, WD/M-2332, 19208–9; Metlakahtla Store, account with Kincolith Mission, 1871–74, WD/M-2334, 22202–7, 22246–47; 1875–76, WD/M-2334, 22260–61; Reverend W. H. Collison, Nass River Mission, Account with Metlakahtla Store, 1874–76, WD/M-2334, 22258–59; Rev. W. H. Collison, Queen Charlotte Island, Account with Metlakahtla Store, 1876–78, WD/M-2333, 20051–52; Metlakahtla Store, Account with Henry Schutt, Kincolith Mission, 1876–77, WD/M-2333, 20495–96; Reverend Robert Tomlinson, Kincolith, Account with Metlakahtla Store, 1877–78, WD/M-2333, 20505–6; Rev. A. J. Hall, Fort Rupert Mission, Account with Metlakahtla, 1877–78, WD/M-2333, 20525–26; 1879–81, WD/M-2334, 22371–72; Fort Rupert Mission, Expenses incurred during the year 1880, WD/M-2332, 19219–24; George Sneath, Massett, Q.C. Island, Account with Metlakahtla, 1880, WD/M-2334, 22400–401; Rev. Robert Tomlinson, Skeena River, Account with Metlakahtla, 1881–82, WD/M-2334, 22449–50.

55. Government of British Columbia, in account with William Duncan, J.P, 1875–76, 1878, WD/M-2334, 22252, 22264; Duncan, in account with the Church Missionary Society, 1878, WD/M-2334, 22328–29; Metlakahtla Council and Constables, 1 January 1874, WD/M-2329, 14659–60; Metlakahtla Office Holders, 1 January 1881, WD/M-2329, 14720–32; Metlakahtla Council, 1883, WD/M-2330, 15210–14.

56. William Duncan, in Account with the Church Missionary Society, 1876, WD/M-2334, 22163; Coopers' Company Account, 1877–78, WD/M-2333, 20603–4; Metlakahtla Store, in Account with John Tait, trader, teacher, 1873–78, WD/M-2334, 22244–45, 1878–79, 20629–30; Murray, *The Devil and Mr. Duncan*, 122.

57. Marble Company Account, 1877–78, WD/M-2333, 20605; Coopers and Fishing Company Account, 1878, WD/M-2333, 20637; Metlakahtla Store, in Account with David Leask, 1873–75, WD/M-2334, 22240–41, 1878–79, 22290–91; 1880, 22382–83; "Subscriptions for building a new town hall, collected by D. Leask," 1883, WD/M-2330, 15225–30; Metlakahtla Council, 1 January 1874, WD/M-2329, 14659–60; Metlakahtla Office Holders, 1 January 1881, WD/M-2329, 14720–32; Murray, *The Devil and Mr. Duncan*, 135; Usher, *William Duncan of Metlakatla*, 119–20.

58. William Duncan, in Account with the Church Missionary Society, 1880, WD/M-2334, 22390–91; David Leask to Duncan, 15 March 1879, NA, RG 200, A-L File, File I-4, Box 111, folder 314.

59. Leask to Duncan, 29 March 1879, NA, RG 200, A-L File, File I-4, Box 111, folder 314; "Requisition for David Leask, Massett, Q.I. [Queen Charlotte Island], 29 March 1879, NA, RG 200, A-L File, File I-4, Box 111, folder 314; Duncan to the Secretary of the Church Missionary Society, 30 September 1878, Letterbook Number 2, WD/M-2321, 8883, pp. 231–37; Duncan to the Executive Committee of the Church Missionary Society, 7 March 1879, Letterbook Number 2, WD/M-2321, 8883, pp. 309–12; David Leask, Private Account, 1883–84, WD/M-2333, 21341.

60. Leask to Duncan, 25 September 1879, 12 April 1880, 28 August 1880, 18 September 1880, NA, RG 200, A-L File, File I-4, Box 111, folder 314.

61. Duncan to C. L. Windsor, Inverness, B.C., 5 June 1877, Letterbook Number 2, WD/M-2321, 8883, p. 34; Duncan to Mr. White, Inverness, B.C., 1 June 1880, Letterbook Number 2, WD/M-2321, 8883, pp. 367–69; Duncan to Edward Hutchinson, Financial Secretary of the Church Missionary Society, Letterbook

Number 2, WD/M-2321, 8883, pp. 428–31. For a discussion of the Inverness Cannery and other Skeena River operations, see Dianne Newell, *Tangled Webs of History: Indians and the Law in Canada's Pacific Coast Fisheries* (Toronto: University of Toronto Press, 1993), 46–65.

62. Leask to Duncan, 18 September 1880, NA, RG 200, A-L File, File I-4, Box 111, folder 314; Duncan to Israel Powell, 1 October 1877, Letterbook Number 2, WD/M-2321, 8883, pp. 79–81.

8. OUTLINES OF A METLAKATLA IDENTITY

A segment of this chapter appeared previously as "'White Men Are Putting Their Hands Into Our Pockets': Metlakatla and the Struggle for Resource Rights in British Columbia, 1862–1887," *Alaska History* 8 (Fall 1993): 1–20.

1. David Leask to George C. Thomas, Philadelphia, 26 October 1887, National Archives–Alaska Pacific Region, Record Group 200 [henceforth, NA-APR, RG 200], A-L File, Box 116, File #381.

2. "Cash Account with Inverness Cannery, 1880–81," WD/M-2334, 22671. For lumber sales, see Duncan to British American Packing Company, Victoria, 3 March 1883, Letterbook Number 2, WD/M-2321, 8883, p. 474; Duncan to Inverness Cannery, 21 April 1883, Letterbook Number 3, WD/M-2321, 8883, p. 521. Newell, *Tangled Webs of History*, 52–55, 75–87. In Rolfe Knight's *Indians at Work*, of the 2,710 employees at the seventeen British Columbia canneries in 1884, roughly half were natives, and most of them were women. Native males typically worked as fishermen, evidence of a persistence of the aboriginal division of labor. In 1898 the fifty-one canneries employed 936 natives out of a total workforce of 3,666 (2,340 were Chinese, and 390 were whites); in 1900, 1,056 natives, 2,640 Chinese, and 440 whites worked for the sixty-four canneries; and in 1905, there were 1,176 natives, 2,940 Chinese, and 490 whites working in the industry. See Knight, *Indians at Work*, 29–36, 78–112; the statistics quoted above are from p. 88.

3. Duncan to Israel W. Powell, 1 October 1881, Letterbook Number 2, WD/M-23321, 8883, pp. 79–81; *Report of the Superintendent General of Indian Affairs, British Columbia*, 1881 (Ottawa: Department of Indian Affairs), 16636.

4. William Duncan, in account with W. J. Macdonald, 1880–82, "General Finances, 1853–1886," WD/M-2334, 22404–6; William Duncan, in account with Captain Orlebar, R.N., 1881–82, "General Finances, 1853–86," WD/M-2334, 22460–61; Duncan to Israel W. Powell, 28 April 1883, Letterbook Number 2, WD/M-2321, 8883, pp. 526–29; Notation of sale of fifty shares in cannery, 30 January 1882, in "Notebooks, unbound," WD/M-2329, 14507; "Testimony of William Duncan," in British Columbia, *Metlakatlah Inquiry, 1884, Report of the Commissioners Together with the Evidence* (Victoria: Government Printer, 1885), xxx [henceforth, *Metlakatlah Inquiry, 1884*]; Murray, *The Devil and Mr. Duncan*, 138; Usher, *William Duncan*, 74.
There seems to be some discrepancy in the interest held by natives in the cannery. Duncan's ledger books indicate that fifty natives purchased $100 shares on the terms noted above, but in the course of an 1884 investigation into conditions at Metlakahtla, Duncan testified, "There is really only one Indian that has an interest in the cannery. I have offered others a chance to come in. More are, in a sense, interested. Should the profits permit it, there will be several Indians that will partake of the profits." It may be that in suggesting that "more are, in a sense, interested," Duncan was referring to the system of loans and shares. For this testimony, see *Metlakatlah Inquiry, 1884*, xxx. "Memorandum of Association, Met-

lakahtla Cooperative Store," 1883, WD/M-2331, 17490; Duncan to W. Heathorne, Victoria, B.C., 24 February 1883, Letterbook Number 2, WD/M-2321, 8883, p. 466; "Shares in the Metlakahtla Cooperative Store, 1882–83," WD/M-2334, 22778–79; "Testimony of William Duncan," *Metlakatlah Inquiry, 1884,* xxxi.

5. "List of Shareholders, Co-operative Store, Metlakahtla, 19 November 1884," in *Metlakatlah Inquiry, 1884,* lxxx; Duncan to Turner, Beeton Co., Victoria, 14 April 1884, Letterbook Number 2, WD/M-2321, 8883, pp. 44–47.

6. "Cannery Corps," Metlakahtla, 30 January 1882, WD/M-2331, 16600; Duncan to Israel W. Powell, 28 April 1883, Letterbook Number 2, WD/M-2321, 8883, pp. 526–29; Cannery, General Expenses, 1881–82, WD/M-2329, 14317–21. Wages quoted for Henrietta Allen and Marcia Booth seem about average for female laborers; WD/M-2324, 20827, 20833. For others, see Accounts with: Lucy Atkinson, Eliza Barnes, Sarah Blyth, Lucy Calvert, Rebecca Keith, Rhoda Pearson, Barbara Reese, and Ada Stanley; all in WD/M-2324, 20937, 20819, 20820, 20947, 20831, 20830, 20925, 20837.

7. Duncan to Powell, 28 April 1883, Letterbook Number 2, WD/M-2321, 8883, pp. 526–29.

8. Duncan to Englehardt, 22 February 1883, Letterbook Number 2, WD/M-2321, 8883, pp. 458–61; Duncan to J. E. White, Manager, Inverness Cannery, Letterbook Number 2, WD/M-2321, 8883, p. 522; Duncan to Turner, Beeton Company, Victoria, 11 October 1883, Letterbook Number 2, WD/M-2321, 8883, pp. 570–71; Duncan to Turner, Beeton Company, Victoria, 20 November 1883, Letterbook Number 2, WD/M-2321, 8883, pp. 603–4.

9. Accounts—General, Cannery, and Store Accounts, 1883–84, WD/M-2332, 19173–78, 19181, 19195–201; Duncan to Turner, Beeton Company, 19 July 1884, Letterbook Number 2, 8883, 113–15; Duncan to Turner, Beeton Company, 14 August 1884, Letterbook Number 2, WD/M-2321, 8883, pp. 138–39; Duncan to Turner, Beeton Company, 16 September 1884, Letterbook Number 2, WD/M-2321, 8883, p. 161; Duncan to Turner, Beeton Company, 11 August 1884, Letterbook Number 2, WD/M-2321, 8883, pp. 123–24; Duncan to Turner, Beeton Company, 5 January 1885, Letterbook Number 3, WD/M-2321, 8884, p. 109; William M. Ross, "Salmon Cannery Distribution on the Nass and Skeena Rivers of British Columbia, 1877–1926," manuscript, University of British Columbia Library Special Collection, pp. 38–39, cited in Knight, *Indians at Work,* 55.

10. "Wage Account," 1883–85, WD/M-2334, 21062–68; Metlakahtla Cannery Account, 1883–84, WD/M-2334, 21452–53.

11. See Accounts with Archie Ridley & Co., Henry Ridley & Co., William Alford, Alfred Aucland, Jacob Bolton, Andrew Campbell, Theodore Dundas, Paul Legaic, Matthias Simpson & Co., and Peter Spaulding, all in WD/M-2324, 21024, 20888, 20751, 21060–61, 21014, 20840, 21027, 20765, 21015, 21084, 20827, 20742, 21526–27, 21023, 20901. Note: all accounts are for the years 1883–85, and page numbers are listed in the same order as the names given above.

12. For examples of wages paid for cannery work, see Accounts with Frank Allen, Jr., Alfred Atkinson, Timothy Buxton, Arthur Dundas, Simon Keith, Nathan Lawson, Ed Mather, and Matthew Usher, all in WD/M-2324, 21343–44, 21387–88, 21488–89, 21317–18, 20750, 20802, 21399–400, 20887, 20878, 20840. Notations given in same sequence as above.

13. "Testimony of William Duncan," in *Metlakatlah Inquiry, 1884,* xxxvii.

14. See, again, Accounts with Archie Ridley & Co., Henry Ridley & Co., William Alford, Alfred Aucland, Jacob Bolton, Andrew Campbell, Theodore Dundas, Matthias Simpson & Co., and Peter Spaulding, all in WD/M-2324, 21024,

20888, 20751, 21060–61, 21014, 20840, 21027, 20765, 21015, 21084, 20827, 21526–27, 21023, 20901. For Lucy and Rebecca Auriol, see Solomon Auriol's account, WD/M-2324, 21403–4.

15. Account with Timothy Buxton, 1882, WD/M-2324, 20750; Account with Will Morgan (Shay), 1885–86, WD/M-2324, 21428–29; Account with Edward Achtseay, 1885, WD/M-2324, 21423–24; Account with Robert Hewson, 1884–86, WD/M-2324, 21021, 21423–24. Metlakatla continued to export large quantities of furs throughout the early 1880s. See "List of furs for sale, Victoria, 22 June 1883, Letterbook Number 2, WD/M-2321, 8883, p. 541; Duncan to H. J. Hartnall, Victoria, 14 July 1883, Letterbook Number 2, WD/M-2321, 8883, p. 547; Duncan to H. J. Hartnall, 20 November 1883, Letterbook Number 2, WD/M-2321, 8883, p. 602; Duncan to Turner, Beeton and Company, 14 April 1884, Letterbook Number 3, WD/M-2321, 8884, pp. 44–47; Duncan to Hartnall, 21 May 1884, Letterbook Number 3, WD/M-2321, 8884, p. 64; Duncan to Leeks & Co., San Francisco, 23 May 1884, Letterbook Number 3, WD/M-2321, 8884, pp. 68–69.

16. Account with David Leask, 1883–85, WD/M-2324, 21018, 21341, 21486–87.

17. Account with Paul Leegaic [Legaic], 1882–83, WD/M-2324, 20742, 21010.

18. Rev. William Ridley to CMS, 1 November 1879; quoted in Eugene Stock, *A History of the Church Missionary Society*, vol. 3 (London: Church Missionary Society, 1899), 251–52. See also Ridley to CMS, 28 February 1880, quoted in Usher, *William Duncan of Metlakatla*, 111.

19. For earlier suggestions of a Duncan "autocracy," see H. B. Owen to CMS, 9 October 1867, quoted in Usher, *William Duncan of Metlakatla*, 109; Report of Israel Wood Powell, British Columbia Indian Superintendent, 26 August 1879, Canada, Department of the Interior, *Annual Report, 1879*, 16698. Jean Usher provides a detailed analysis of the Tractarian dispute, its impact on the CMS, and the break between Cridge and Hills. See Usher, *William Duncan of Metlakatla*, 97–101. For more on the Tractarian dispute, see A. O. J. Cockshut, *Anglican Attitudes: A Study of Victorian Religious Controversies* (London: Collins, 1959). On Bompass's visit and Duncan's reaction, see Usher, *William Duncan of Metlakatla*, 104–5; Stock, *History of the Church Missionary Society*, 3:250; Duncan to CMS, 4 March 1878, Letterbook Number 2, WD/M-2321, 8883, pp. 101–8; Usher, *William Duncan of Metlakatla*, 105–6. On Duncan withholding the sacraments, see Duncan to CMS, 29 March 1876, Letterbook Number 1, WD/M-2321, 8882, pp. 563–74; Usher, *William Duncan of Metlakatla*, 91–93. On Tomlinson, see Duncan to CMS, 29 March 1876, Letterbook Number 1, WD/M-2321, 8882, pp. 563–74

20. Duncan to CMS, 29 March 1876, Letterbook Number 1, WD/M-2321, 8882, pp. 563–74.

21. Duncan to CMS, 4 March 1878, Letterbook Number 2, WD/M-2321, 8883, pp. 101–8.

22. Ibid.

23. Ibid. A. J. Hall was removed from Metlakatla and transferred to Fort Rupert. Murray, *The Devil and Mr. Duncan*, 131; Usher, *William Duncan of Metlakatla*, 115.

24. The details surrounding the circumstances of Duncan's separation from the CMS are well known and need not be repeated here. See *William Duncan of Metlakatla*, Usher, 112–17; Murray, *The Devil and Mr. Duncan*, 139–47, and Wellcome, *Story of Metlakahtla*, 195–210. For official notice of dismissal, see Fred E. Wigram and W. Gray, Secretaries, Church Missionary Society, to Duncan, 29 September 1881, NA-APR, RG 200, A-L File, Box 116, File #381.

25. *Metlakatlah Inquiry, 1884*, xlv–xlvi.

26. Ibid., xviii–xix.

27. Ibid., xix, xxvii; Murray, *The Devil and Mr. Duncan*, 149; Usher, *William Duncan of Metlakatla*, 122–23.

28. *Metlakatlah Inquiry, 1884*, xix.

29. Ibid., lvi–lvii.

30. Ibid., ix, xix; Report of Israel W. Powell, British Columbia Indian Superintendent, in Canada, *Annual Report of the Department of Indian Affairs* [henceforth, *ARDIA*], 1883, 106; Usher, *William Duncan of Metlakatla*, 122; Wellcome, *Story of Metlakahtla*, 217.

31. *Metlakatla Inquiry*, x.

32. Duncan to Ridley, 29 November 1882, in ibid., xx.

33. *ARDIA*, 1883, 106–7; Usher, *William Duncan of Metlakatla*, 122–23; Murray, *The Devil and Mr. Duncan*, 165–76; Wellcome, *Story of Metlakahtla*, 220–21.

34. *ARDIA*, 1884, 16647–48; Wellcome, *Story of Metlakahtla*, 235; *Metlakatlah Inquiry, 1884*, x, lvii.

35. *ARDIA*, 1884, 16648; *Metlakatlah Inquiry, 1884*, vii, xxi, lxiv.

36. Metlakahtla Council to Bishop Ridley, 22 October 1884, quoted in *Metlakatlah Inquiry, 1884*, xiii.

37. Robin Fisher argues that the "consolidation of settlement," in other words, the influx of white immigrants into British Columbia and the efforts of provincial politicians to accede to the demands of the new arrivals, accounts for the rapid decline in the fortunes of native peoples during the 1870s and 1880s. See Fisher, *Contact and Conflict*, 176–211. Census figures indicate that whereas natives accounted for between 65 and 85 percent of the province's total population of 45,000 to 50,000 in 1870, by 1885 the native population had shrunk to 28,000, which was roughly 50 percent of the total of 49,500. By 1891, natives constituted less than one-third of the total of 98,200. Figures quoted in Knight, *Indians at War*, 29; Ficher, *Contact and Conflict*, 201.

For a more detailed discussion of British Columbia and Dominion Indian policies, see chapter 2. See also Miller, *Skyscrapers Hide the Heavens*, 17–52.

38. Blank certificate for title to land in Metlakahtla, [n.d.], WD/M–2329, n.p.

39. David Laird, Memo, 2 November 1874, British Columbia, *Papers Connected with the Indian Land Question, 1850–1875* (Victoria: Government Printer 1875; repr., Victoria: Queens Printer, 1987), 150–51; Duncan to Powell, 4 February 1875, WD/M–2329, 14287–88.

40. Duncan to Laird, May, 1875, *Papers Connected with the Indian Land Question, 1850–1875*, 13–15; Duncan CMS, 11 October 1875, Letterbook 2, WD/M–2321, 8883, pp. 518–21; Fisher, *Contact and Conflict*, 182–88; Usher, *William Duncan of Metlakatla*, 121–22; Murray, *The Devil and Mr. Duncan*, 116–18. For a more detailed discussion of Duncan's role in proposing ideas for Indian policy reform, see Tennant, *Aboriginal Peoples and Politics*, 39–50. Fisher, *Contact and Conflict*, 178–98, provides a detailed account of the impact of settler influence on efforts to reform Indian policy in British Columbia, as well as the counterproposals offered by individuals like William Duncan and Israel Wood Powell.

41. Duncan to Windsor Canning Co., 4 July 1878, Letterbook Number 2, WD/M–2321, 8883, p. 157.

42. Duncan to W. N. Neil, General Manager, North Western Commercial Company, Inverness, 27 July 1878, Letterbook Number 2, WD/M–2321, 8883, pp. 167–70.

43. Ibid.

44. "Speeches by the Indians to Admiral Prevost," 22 January 1878, Letter-book Number 2, WD/M-2321, 8883, pp. 171–79.

45. Ibid.

46. Ibid.

47. Address of Governor-General Earl Dufferin, 20 September 1876, quoted in Wellcome, *Story of Metlakahtla,* 293–95; William Duncan, "Memoirs," [n.d.], WD/M-2329, 13880–88; Tennant, *Aboriginal Peoples and Politics,* 49–50.

48. Fisher, *Contact and Conflict,* 188; Tennant, *Aboriginal Peoples and Politics,* 50. For more on the dispute over completion of the trans-Canada railroad and threats of secession, see Margaret A. Ormsby, *British Columbia: A History* (Vancouver: Macmillan of Canada, 1958), 259–92; and Martin Robbin, *The Rush for Spoils: The Company Province, 1871–1933* (Toronto: McClelland and Stewart, 1972), 12–49; *Metlakatlah Inquiry, 1884,* ii; Duncan to Hale, 20 January 1880, Letterbook Number 2, WD/M-2321, 8883, pp. 352–55

49. *Metlakatlah Inquiry, 1884,* lxxvi–lxxvii. O'Reilly replaced Gilbert Sproat as reserve commissioner, but, according to Fisher, his mission was not to negotiate the creation of large reserves. Rather, like his brother-in-law, Lieutenant Governor Joseph Trutch, O'Reilly was committed to reducing, not preserving, native landholdings. See Fisher, *Contact and Conflict,* 198–200.

50. Usher, *William Duncan of Metlakatla,* 125–26; Murray, *The Devil and Mr. Duncan,* 167–69; *ARDIA,* 1884, 16648; *Metlakatlah Inquiry, 1884,* ii–vii, xii, lxxvii; A. C. Anderson to Hon. J. W. McLellan, Minister of Marines and Fisheries, 20 December 1883, quoted in Usher, *William Duncan of Metlakatla,* 123.

51. Duncan to A. C. Elliot, 27 October 1884, Letterbook Number 2, WD/M-2321, 8883, pp. 170–71.

52. *Metlakatlah Inquiry, 1884,* iii.

53. Ibid., vi.

54. Ibid., v, li–lii, xlv, lvi, lx, xii.

55. For these and other addresses by natives, see ibid., xxvi–xxvii, lx–lxi, lxvii–lxix.

56. Ibid., 134–36.

57. William Duncan, "Memoirs," [n.d.], WD/M-2329, 13881–83; Usher, *William Duncan of Metlakatla,* 131–33.

58. *ARDIA,* 1886, 16651; Usher, *William Duncan of Metlakatla,* 134; Wellcome, *Story of Metlakahtla,* 320–21; Gough, *Gunboat Frontier,* 184–86; John W. Arctander, *The Apostle of Alaska: The Story of William Duncan of Metlakahtla* (New York: Fleming H. Revell, 1909), 283.

59. Paul Legaic, Alfred Dudoward, Matthias Haldane, Daniel Auriol, and Albert Shakes, "For the People of Metlakahtla and Fort Simpson," to Commander J. E. T. Nicholls, 17 November 1886, quoted in Wellcome, *Story of Metlakahtla,* 428–29. See also Gough, *Gunboat Frontier,* 185–86.

60. "Belligerent Indians," letter by David Leask in the *Daily Colonist,* Victoria, B.C., 30 October 1886; cited in Wellcome, *Story of Metlakahtla,* 442–46. "Ephah" is a unit of dry measure used by biblical Hebrews; "him," is a unit of liquid measure used by biblical Hebrews.

61. "The Metlakahtlans," letter by Dr. J. S. Helmcken in the *Daily Colonist,* Victoria, B.C., 2 November 1886; cited in Wellcome, *Story of Metlakahtla,* 449–52; Arctander, *Apostle of Alaska,* 283–84.

62. *Metlakatlah Inquiry, 1884,* xx.

63. Wellcome, *Story of Metlakahtla,* 347; Usher, *William Duncan of Metlakatla,* 133; Murray, *The Devil and Mr. Duncan,* 187–91; Governor A. P. Swineford to Sec-

retary of the Treasury, 9 February 1887; Sheldon Jackson to Secretary of the Treasury, 9 February 1887; Duncan to United States Secretary of the Treasury, 9 February 1887; all three quoted in Wellcome, *Story of Metlakahtla*, 347–49.

64. Henry Wellcome was a colorful, indeed controversial, character who made a considerable fortune selling patent medicines. For more on his career, see Murray, *The Devil and Mr. Duncan*, 188–92, 195–98, 213–14.

65. Wellcome, *Story of Metlakahtla*, 376–77; Usher, *William Duncan of Metlakatla*, 133; Murray, *The Devil and Mr. Duncan*, 190; "Notes for Address, New York," February 1887, WD/M-2329, 13281–92; "Notes for Address," [n.d.], WD/M-2329, 13214; "Notes for Address, Portland," 30 June 1887, WD/M-2329, 13274–75; "Notes for Address," [n.d.], WD/M-2329, 13113–17; "Notes for Address, [n.d.], WD/M-2329, 13118–24; "Notes for Address," [n.d.], WD/M-2329, 13132–47; "Notes for Address at the Congregational Church, Chicago," 19 June 1887, WD/M-2329, 13223–24; Usher, *William Duncan of Metlakatla*, 133; Murray, *The Devil and Mr. Duncan*, 191–92.

66. Mr. Duncan's address before the Board of Indian Commissioners, and the Conference of Missionary Boards, and the Indian Rights Association, 6 January 1887; cited in Wellcome, Appendix, 384–94.

67. New York *World*, 30 June 1887. Similar sentiments were expressed in newspapers all across the nation. For an exhaustive list, see "Survey of Conditions of the Indians in the United States," 74th Cong., 2d sess, 1939, Part 35, Metlakahtla Indians, Alaska (Washington, D.C.: GPO, 1939), 18545–46; Murray, *The Devil and Mr. Duncan*, 193–95, 220–21; Usher, *William Duncan of Metlakatla*, 133–34; Metlakahtla Native Council, "Notification of Claim to Annette Island," 17 September 1887, WD/M-2330, 15273–78; Act of Congress, 3 March 1891 (26 Stat. 1101).

68. Murray, *The Devil and Mr. Duncan*, 195; Metlakahtla, B.C., Account with David Leask, January–May 1887, WD/M-2334, 21732–33; Metlakahtla, B.C., Account with John Tait, January–December 1887, WD/M-2334, 21706–7; Port Chester, Annette Island, General Account, April–August 1887, WD/M-2334, 21740–41.

69. *ARDIA*, 1887, 16661; Usher, *William Duncan of Metlakatla*, 134; Murray, *The Devil and Mr. Duncan*, 200–205; Speech of Samuel Pelham, [1887?], quoted in Wellcome, *Story of Metlakahtla*, 422.

70. Duncan to S. Horton, Magistrate of Fort Simpson and Metlakahtla, 17 October 1887, WD/M-2330, 15287–92; Duncan to Governor Swineford, 27 October 1887, WD/M-2330, 15293–97.

71. WD/M-2322, 320. An 1888 census lists the population at 725, and in 1895 the population also stood at 823, with the breakdown as follows: "Tsimpshian," 717, "Tlinkits," 94, "Hydahs," 7, "Englishmen," 3, "Canadians," 1, "Japanee," 1. WD/M-2329, 13577–608; WD/M-2329, 13392–422. For a list of outside contributors, including "friends in England," see Duncan to Mr. Agnes, 15 May 1891, WD/M-2322, 335–38, and Duncan to Fischer and Macdonald, Seattle, 13 May 1891, WD/M-2322, 322–24. In connection with the settlement of Duncan's estate in 1919, the Interior Department commissioned an audit of his personal finances. The result is reams of data that can be found in the Henry Wellcome collection (RG 200) housed at the National Archives, Alaska Pacific Branch. See "William Duncan Accounting Ledgers, 1887–1916," NA-APR, RG 200, A-L File, "unfiled material." Future studies probably will require a more comprehensive analysis of those data than I have provided here.

72. For a sampling of lumber sales, see Duncan to Alaska Salmon Packing and Fur Company, 1 May 1888 WD/M-2322, 312–13; Duncan to Alaska Salmon

Packing and Fur Company, 11 May 1888, WD/M-2322, pp. 315–16; Duncan to Alaska Salmon Packing and Fur Company, 3 June 1891, WD/M-2322, p. 353; Duncan to Alaska Salmon Packing and Fur Company, 13 August 1891, WD/M-2322, p. 415; Duncan to Charles E. Ingersoll, Ketchikan, 26 March 1900, WD/M-2324, p. 104; Duncan to R. L. Dunn, 8 May 1900, WD/M-2324, p. 168; "Timber Bought by the Metlakahtla Industrial Co. in 1904 of the Metlakahtla Indians," WD/M-2325, 255.

73. "Account Showing Numbers of Cases of Salmon packed each Day during Salmon Season, 1891–1912," WD/M-2329, 14592–608; "William Duncan Accounting Ledgers, 1887–1916," and "Fire Relief Fund," 7 February 1893; both in NA-APR, RG 200, A-L File, Box 162, "unfiled material." For Duncan's accounting of wages earned between 1887 and 1900, see Duncan to John Brady, Governor of Alaska, 3 January 1900, WD/M-2324, 8890, 24–36. Duncan also filed annual reports with shareholders of the Metlakahtla Industrial Company, and these reports typically included descriptions of MIC business (including the cannery), as well as community affairs. For a sampling, see Duncan to Strong, 22 February 1894, WD/M-2322, 8886, pp. 417–21; Duncan to Strong, 18 October 1894, WD/M-2322, 8887, pp. 126–31; Duncan to Strong, 19 January 1895, WD/M-2323, 8887, pp. 253–56; Duncan to Strong, 15 April 1895, WD/M-2323, 8887, pp. 362–64; Duncan to A. B. Alexander, Agent, U.S. Fish Commission, 1 May 1903, WD/M-2325, 8891, pp. 407–12; Duncan to Strong, 29 August 1904, WD/M-2325, 8892, pp. 263–67; Duncan to Kelley-Clarke, 13 December 1904, WD/M-2325, 8892, p. 293.

74. For a sampling of correspondence having to do with the formation, and functioning, of the Metlakahtla Industrial Company, see Duncan to Ladd and Tilton, Portland, Oregon, 10 June 1891, WD/M-2322, 8884, p. 355; A. Young, Astoria, Oregon, to Duncan, 20 May 1891, WD/M-2322, 8884, p. 371; Duncan to Thomas Strong, 11 June 1891, WD/M-2322, 8884, p. 372; Duncan to Ladd and Tilton, 25 June 1891, WD/M-2322, 8884, p. 377; Duncan to Strong, 19 December 1894, WD/M-2322, 8884, pp. 220–24; Duncan to Strong, 16 March 1895, WD/M-2323, 8884, p. 320. In 1904, John Tait, Catherine Marsden, Abel Faber, Edward Benson, and Solomon Dundas were the only native shareholders in the MIC. See Duncan to Strong, 25 July 1904, WD/M-2325, 8892, p. 237.

75. By no means an exhaustive accounting of native commercial activities, a sampling can be found in the following. Fur exports: Duncan to Fischer and Macdonald, 13 May 1891, WD/M-2322, 8884, pp. 322–24; Duncan to Fischer and Macdonald, Seattle, 13 July 1891, WD/M-2322, 8884, pp. 393–94; Duncan to H. F. Norton Co., Seattle, 7 March 1902, WD/M-2324, 8890, p. 70; Duncan to J. W. Archtander, 23 April 1906, WD/M-2325, 8895, p. 61. Native stores: Duncan to Thomas M. Green, 29 March 1895, WD/M-2323, 8888, p. 328; Duncan to Mutual Mercantile Agency, Tacoma, 22 June 1900, WD/M-2324, 8890, p. 232; Duncan to Levi Strauss and Co., San Francisco, 22 October 1900, WD/M-2324, 8890, p. 353; Duncan to F. Paige, 16 January 1899, WD/M-2324, 8890, p. 465; Duncan to James A. Snoddy, Seattle, 2 April 1906, WD/M-2325, 8894, p. 46. For work around the community, see in particular, Duncan to Mr. Agnes, 15 May 1891, WD/M-2322, 8884, pp. 335–38. For John Tait and David Leask, see Fischer and Macdonald to Duncan, 5 December 1891, NA/APB, RG 200, Box 116, File 382; Duncan to Dittenhoefer, Hass and Co., Portland, 29 July 1891, WD/M-2322, 8884, p. 326; Duncan to Strong, 17 September 1901, WD/M-2324, 8890, pp. 656–57; Duncan to Strong, 2 December 1901, WD/M-2324, 8891, pp. 10–12; Duncan to Strong, 3 February 1905, WD/M-2325, 8894, p. 316; Duncan to Fischer Brothers, Seattle, 5 May 1894, WD/M-2322, 8884, n.p.; Duncan to Fischer Brothers, 21 June 1894, WD/M-2322,

8890, p. 498; Duncan to Fischer Brothers, 30 March 1895, WD/M-2322, 8887, p. 328; Duncan to Seattle Hardware Co., 17 June 1895, WD/M-2323, 8888, p. 418; Duncan to Fischer Brothers, 27 September 1895, WD/M-2323, 8888, n.p.

76. For fishing on the Skeena and Nass, see Duncan to Fischer and Macdonald, 27 June 1893, WD/M-2322, 8886, pp. 238–39; Duncan to Fischer and Macdonald, 12 July 1893, WD/M-2322, 8886, p. 250; Duncan to John Brady, 3 January 1900, WD/M-2324, 8890, pp. 24–36; Duncan to Wannuck Packing Co., Wansborough, B.C., 24 May, 1902, WD/M-2324, 8891, p. 161. For one conflict between Metlakatlans and Nisga'a over *oolichan* fisheries, see, Duncan to Macdonald, 28 March 1902, WD/M-2325, 8891, pp. 101–2.

77. *Papers Relating to the Commission Appointed to Enquire into the Condition of the Indians of the North-West Coast, 1887* (Victoria: Government Printing Office, 1888), 16–18, 20, 22, 34.

78. Ibid., 41–44.

79. Duncan to Strong, 20 June 1894, WD/M-2322, 8886, pp. 494–96; Duncan to Dexter, Horton and Co., 19 August 1901, James H. Woodman, WD/M-2324, 8890, p. 624. For correspondence with, or about, the Rudlands, see Duncan to Mary Rudland, 24 February 1900, WD/M-2324, 8890, p. 71; Duncan to James H. Woodman, 6 January 1893, WD/M-2322, 8886, p. 388. Beynon, "The Tsimshians of Metlakatla," 83–88; Barnett, "Personal Conflicts and Cultural Change," Viola Garfield, *The Tsimshian and Their Neighbors* (Seattle: University of Washington Press, 1951). Interview with Russell Hayward, Metlakatla, Alaska, 28 July 1995, 9 August 1995; Interview with Arnold Booth, Metlakatla, Alaska, 28 July 1995; Interview with Joyce and Elvin Leask, Metlakatla, B.C., 2 August 1995; originals in possession of the author; duplicate copies in Metlakatla, Alaska, and Metlakatla, British Columbia.

80. For fishing stations in Alaska and conflicts associated with this, see Duncan to Strong, 10 July 1891, WD/M-2322, 8884, p. 391; Duncan to Strong, 22 February 1894, WD/M-2322, 8886, pp. 417–21; Duncan to Armsby, Co., 11 January 1896, WD/M-2323, 8888, pp. 116–17; Duncan to Governor John G. Brady, 8 January 1900, NA-APR, RG 200, Box 112, File# 326–1. Beginning in 1917, native Thomas Hanbury began providing detailed annual fishing reports to Henry Wellcome. His report for 1917 is a representative sample and provides evidence that Metlakatlans still fished both Alaskan and British Columbian streams. See Thomas Hanbury to Henry Wellcome, 20 October 1917, NA-APR, RG 200, Box 110, File #303.

81. For a standard description of the Alaska Organic Act of 1884, see Ernest Gruening, *The State of Alaska: A Definitive History of America's Northernmost Frontier* (New York: Random House, 1968), 47–52. See, as well, Rosita Worl, "History of Southeastern Alaska Since 1867," in *Northwest Coast*, ed. Wayne Suttles, vol. 7 of *Handbook of North American Indians*, ed. William C. Sturtevant (Washington, D.C.: Smithsonian Institution Press, 1990), 151–53. For Duncan and the Organic Act, see Duncan to John J. Brice, 2 December 1896, WD/M-2323, 8888, pp. 408–28.

82. Census of 1895, WD/M-2329, 13392–422; Duncan to Strong, 18 October 1894, WD/M-2322, 8887, pp. 126–31; Duncan to Governor Swineford, 10 February 1902, WD/M-2324, 8891, pp. 53–54. For more details on relations with neighboring Tlingits, including Metlakatla's efforts to gain access to fishing stations, see Duncan to Lyman E. Knapp, Governor of Alaska, 9 October 1890, WD/M-2322, 8884, pp. 488–89; Duncan to Strong, 22 February 1894, WD/M-2322, 8886, pp. 417–21; Duncan to Lieut. D. Peacock, U.S.N., 21 October 1893, WD/M-2323, 8884, p. 325.

83. For an outline of the Alaska Packers Association, see Gruening, *State of Alaska*, 166–72, 252–65, 577–89.

84. Duncan to J. K. Armsby, San Francisco, 2 March 1895, WD/M-2323, 8887, pp. 298–300; Duncan to Joseph Murray, Fort Collins, Colorado, 11 January 1896, WD/M-2323, 8888, pp. 111–12; Duncan to Strong, 11 January 1896, WD/M-2323, 8888, pp. 113–15; Duncan to James Sheakley, Governor of Alaska, 17 July 1896, WD/M-2323, 8888, pp. 305–6; Duncan to John J. Brice, U.S. Fish Commissioner, 2 December 1896, WD/M-2323, 8888, pp. 408–28. For further detail on Duncan's complaints regarding the APA, see Duncan to Armsby, 6 June 1892, WD/M-2322, 8886, p. 60; Duncan to Armsby, 12 September 1893, WD/M-2322, 8886, pp. 284–85; Duncan to Joseph Murray, 15 October 1895, WD/M-2323, 8888, pp. 23–27; Duncan to Strong, 10 April 1896, WD/M-2323, 8888, p. 199.

85. For complaints against Loring, see Duncan to John J. Brice, U.S. Fish Commissioner, 2 December 1896, WD/M-2323, 8888, pp. 408–28; Duncan to James Skeakley, 17 May 1897, WD/M-2323, 8889, pp. 53–54. For Duncan's negotiations with Loring, see Duncan to Robert Hechman, 12 May 1896, WD/M-2323, 8888, pp. 240–41; Duncan to W. H. Pratt, 11 June 1901, WD/M-2324, 8890, p. 556; Duncan to Pratt, 7 June 1901, WD/M-2324, 8890, p. 554; Duncan to George Rounsfell, 12 June 1906, WD/M-2325, 8891, p. 80. On Ed Benson's mission to Loring, see Duncan to Hechman, 11 July 1903, WD/M-2325, 8890, p. 470. For a representative indication of Duncan's claims regarding the superiority of "hand pack" salmon, see Duncan to J. K. Armsby, San Francisco, 12 September 1893, WD/M-2322, 8886, pp. 284–85.

86. Duncan to H. Pratt, Ketchikan, 2 July 1901, WD/M-2324, 8890, p. 588; Duncan to J. R. Hechtman, 9 July 1901, WD/M-2324, 8890, p. 600; Duncan to Alaska Packers Association, San Francisco, 30 January 1899, WD/M-2324, 8889, pp. 466–68.

87. Duncan to Fischer Brothers, 30 March 1895, WD/M-2323, 8887, p. 328; Duncan to Standard Canning Company, 5 November 1896, WD/M-2323, 8888, p. 386 (female cannery workers); Duncan to B. W. Booth, Benjamin Dundas, Roderic Merchison, Geoffrey Parker, Moses Hewson, Mark Milne, Jr., Eli Tait, Samuel Eaton, Stephen Ridley, Jonah Hudson (native Metlakatlans), 8 April 1903, WD/M-2325, 8891, p. 378; Duncan to Charles H. Cosgrove, Ketchikan, 11 April 1903, WD/M-2325, 8891, p. 382.

88. For labor shortages as Metlakatlans contracted with commercial canneries, see Duncan to Charles H. Isham, Census Agent, 4 August 1891, WD/M-2322, 8884, p. 413; Duncan to Wannuck Packing Co., Wansborough, B.C., 24 May 1902, WD/M-2324, 8891, p. 161; Duncan to Fischer Brothers, 6 July 1897, WD/M-2323, 8889, p. 106; Duncan to Strong, 8 May 1903, WD/M-2325, 8891, pp. 417–20. For Asian laborers, see Duncan to Bohlman, 27 January 1893, WD/M-2322, 8886, pp. 85–86; Duncan to Fisher and Macdonald, Seattle, 27 June 1893, WD/M-2322, 8886, pp. 238–43; Duncan to Fischer and Macdonald, 12 July 1893, WD/M-2322, 8886, p. 250.

89. Duncan to Strong, 22 February 1894, WD/M-2322, 8886, pp. 417–21; Duncan to H. M. Kutchink Special Agent, Treasury Dept., 20 November 1899, WD/M-2324, 8889, p. 700; Duncan to W. F. Shedd, 14 July 1900, WD/M-2324, 8890, n.p.; Duncan to J. R. Hechman, Loring, 16 July 1901,WD/M-2324, 8890, pp. 604–5; Duncan to George Clark, Wrangell, 3 October 1902, WD/M-2325, 8891, p. 266; Duncan to Charles H. Cosgrove, 11 April 1903, WD/M-2325, 8891, p. 382; Duncan to Louis Sumner and Henry Webster, Loggers, 18 April 1903, WD/M-2325, 8891, p. 396; Duncan to H. K. Love, Juneau, 30 October 1905, WD/M-2325,

8892, p. 457; Peter Simpson to William Duncan, February 1914, NA-APR, RG 200, Box 110, File #301. For a listing of occupations for those natives from southeastern Alaska (including Metlakatlans) who had attended Sitka Indian Industrial School, see William A. Kelly to Sheldon Jackson, 25 December 1899, in "Report of the Commissioner of Education, 1898–99," NA-APR, RG 200, Box 110, File #326-1.

90. For correspondence regarding Peter Simpson's cannery proposal, see Duncan to Peter Simpson, 15 January 1891, WD/M-2324, 8890, p. 424; Duncan to Simpson, 11 June 1900, WD/M-2324, 8890, p. 220. On the Verney brothers' sawmill, see Duncan to Mrs. Mary Rudland, Metlakatla, B.C., 25 May 1900, WD/M-2324, 8890, p. 196; Duncan to Dexter, Horton and Co., 4 May 1901, WD/M-2324, 8890, p. 509; E. A. Verney to William Duncan, 8 April 1901, 3 May 1901, 30 October 1902, 11 June 1904, 25 September 1905; all in NA-APR, RG 200, Box 110, File #312. See Edmund Verney to Henry S. Wellcome, 24 February 1917, NA-APR, RG 200, Box 110, File #303; "Report of the Council Meetings at Metlakatla, December 14 and 15 [1916], which Mr. Wellcome Attended," NA-APR, RG 200, Box 112, File #343; and Edward Marsden to Henry Wellcome, 15 December 1916, NA-APR, RG 200, Box 112, File #344, for conflicts between Verney and Duncan, including accusations, from both sides, of financial malfeasance. I also relied on Russell Hayward's interesting discussion of this matter; interview with Russell Hayward, Metlakatla Alaska, 9 August 1995..

91. Duncan to Strong, 2 December 1901, WD/M-2321, 8884, pp. 10–12; Duncan to Mr. Weaver, Seattle, 17 September 1900, WD/M-2324, 8890, p. 315. Duncan apparently expended some effort trying to clear David Leask's debts. For a sampling of communications with Leask's creditors, see Duncan to Strong, 9 January 1900, WD/M-2324, 8890, pp. 39–40; Duncan to Fischer Brothers, 5 March 1900, WD/M-2324, 8890, p. 81; Duncan to Fischer Brothers, 26 March 1900, WD/M-2324, 8889, p. 110; Duncan to Fischer Brothers, 27 August 1900, WD/M-2324, 8890, p. 288.

92. On leasing the mill, see Duncan to Strong, 2 December 1901, WD/M-2321, 8884, pp. 10–12; Duncan to Strong, 27 June 1904, WD/M-2325, 8890, pp. 222–24. For the abortive effort to transfer management to the United States government, see W. R. Logan, Inspector, Department of the Interior, Bureau of Education, Alaska Division, to C. S. Ucker, Chief Clerk, Interior Department, 6 March 1911; Strong to Duncan, 28 June 1911; Strong to Duncan, 19 March 1912; Governor W. E. Clark to Secretary of the Interior, 28 May 1912; all in NA-APR, RG 200, A-L File, Box 112, File #333.

93. Petition signed by fifty-two "workingmen and residents of Metlakatla," 1 March 1915, NA-APR, RG 200, Box 110, File #302; Robert Tomlinson to Duncan, 17 July 1912, NA-APR, RG 200, A-L File, Box 112, File #332. For a more favorable evaluation of Duncan's decision to close the cannery and sawmill, see "Report of G. M. Fripp on conditions at Metlakahtla in 1916. Conducted and consolidated with a letter of Mr. Fripp (Aug 8, 1917)," NA-APR, RG 200, A-L File, Box 112, File #341.

94. Tomlinson to Duncan, 17 July 1912, NA-APR, RG 200, A-L File, Box 112, File #332.

CONCLUSION

1. Governor J. F. A. Strong to Secretary of the Interior, 20 October 1913, National Archives, Record Group 75, Series 806, Alaska Division, General Correspondence [henceforth, NA, RG 75, Series 806], Box 63, Metlakahtla, 1913–14.

2. To this date, Peter Murray's book *The Devil and Mr. Duncan* remains the most complete history of Duncan's New Metlakatla. Much of this discussion is based on Murray's work, which, while lacking footnotes, is generally true to both the documentary evidence and other, less complete works. For a taste of the discussion among Metlakatlans regarding the education issue, see Thomas Hanbury to Moses Hewson, 17 July 1916; Edward Benson to Dr. B. L. Myers, 9 December 1916; Moses Hewson to Dr. B. L. Myers, 9 December 1916; Soloman Dundas to Myers, 9 December 1916; all in NA-APR, RG 200, A-L File, Box 110, File #302. For more on New Metlakahtla, see John A. Dunn and Arnold Booth, "Tsimshian of Metlakatla, Alaska," *Northwest Coast,* ed. Wayne Suttles, vol. 7 of *Handbook of North American Indians,* ed. William C. Sturtevant (Washington, D.C.: Smithsonian Institution Press, 1990), 294–97; and Beynon, "The Tsimshians of Metlakatla, Alaska," 83–88; Glenn Smith, "Education for the Natives of Alaska: The Work of the United States Bureau of Education, 1884–1931,"*Journal of the West* 6 (July 1967): 440–50.

3. For more on Duncan's continuing relationship with Henry Wellcome, see Murray, *The Devil and Mr. Duncan,* 213–14, 237, 257, 271, 292–97, 301–5, 322–27.

4. Harold French, "Duncan of Metlakahtla Deserted," *Overland Monthly* 62 (October 1913): 327–35.

5. J. F. A. Strong to Secretary of the Interior, 20 October 1913, NA, RG 75, Series 806, Box 63, Metlakahtla, 1913–14.

6. That suit proved unsuccessful. See *Alfred Baines, Ellen Handbury, Edward Benson, Jacob Scott, Adolphus Calvert and Catherine Marsden v. Metlakatla Industrial Company, W.S. Ladd, Henry Failing, Thomas N. Strong, William Duncan, Stockholders of Metlakatla Industrial Company,* suit filed 12 January 1916, NA, RG 75, Series 806, Box 75, Metlakatla, 1915–16. See also, Murray, *The Devil and Mr. Duncan,* 247–49.

7. Alfred Atkinson, Dan Reece, Theo. Dundas, Simon Dalton, Benj. Haldane, Adolphus Calvert, Sydney Campbell, and Frank Allen to Charles L. Thompson, 16 January 1914, NA-APR, RG 200, A-L File, File #301. For a listing of some members of the pro- and anti-Duncan "factions," see Moses Hewson to Robert Tomlinson, 6 April 1914, NA-APR, RG 200, A-L File, File #301; and, Murray, *The Devil and Mr. Duncan,* 272–79.

8. Edward Marsden, Secretary, Metlakahtla Native Council, to Henry S. Wellcome, 15 December 1916, NA, RG 75, Series 806, Box 75, Metlakatla, 1915–16.

9. While Peter Murray's work remains the best source on Edward Marsden, he deserves a full-length biography. Marsden reportedly was the first Indian in Alaska to receive a license to preach and in his lifetime was a well-known figure to "Friends of the Indian" and was instrumental in the founding of the Alaska Native Brotherhood. For more on Marsden, see Murray, *The Devil and Mr. Duncan,* 222–30, 265–69, 275–81, 285–86, 298–304, 310–12, 318–30; and Philip Drucker, "The Native Brotherhoods: Modern Intertribal Organizations on the Northwest Coast, *Smithsonian Institution, Bureau of American Ethnology, Bulletin No. 168* (Washington, D.C.: GPO, 1958), 17, 21, 34, 38, 74. Dunn and Booth, in "Tsimshian of Metlakatla, Alaska," 294–97, provide a brief sketch, as does H. David Brumble III, although he mistakenly claims that Marsden attended Carlisle. See Brumble, *American Indian Autobiography* (Berkeley: University of California Press, 1988), 143, 240–41.

10. Duncan to Edward Marsden, 4 March 1895, Letterbook Number 5, WD/M-2323, 8887, pp. 306–11.

11. Murray, *The Devil and Mr. Duncan,* 229–30.

12. For more on Edward Marsden, his efforts in Saxman, and the federal government's role in supplanting William Duncan, see Murray, *The Devil and Mr.*

Duncan, passim; Dunn and Booth, "Tsimshian of Metlakatla, Alaska," 295–97. For one native view of the situation, see Thomas Hanbury to Henry S. Wellcome, 27 March 1918, NA-APR, RG 200, A-L File, Box 116, File #386.

13. Evidence of a Marsden–federal government "conspiracy" derives primarily from efforts by Henry Wellcome and Reverend Mark Allison Matthews, who, beginning shortly after Duncan was stripped of his control over Metlakatla, began assembling documents to support this contention. Their motives were partly to salvage Duncan's reputation and partly to gain control over Duncan's estate, then in the hands of administrators chosen by the federal government. In 1939 Matthews presented a lengthy report to the United States Senate, which, although overwritten, offers a compelling case. See "Survey of Conditions of the Indians in the United States," 74th Cong., 2d sess., 1939; part 35, "Metlakahtla Indians, Alaska" (Washington, D.C.: GPO, 1939) [henceforth, "Survey . . . 1939"]. For a more organized account, see Murray, *The Devil and Mr. Duncan*, 315–26; Dunn and Booth, "Tsimshian of Metlakatla, Alaska," 294–95.

14. Marsden to Duncan 18 April 1895, "Survey . . . 1939," 18676.

15. Edward Marsden, "Father Duncan and His Converts. The Future of Metlakahtla," Ketchikan *Progressive*, 27 March 1915.

16. Marsden to Duncan 19 February 1916, "Survey . . . 1939," 18686.

17. Marsden to W. T. Lopp, 17 September 1913, "Survey . . . 1939," 18676.

18. Marsden to Richard Henry Pratt, 8 January 1918, "Survey . . . 1939," 18688.

19. Marsden to Secretary of the Interior, 18 February 1927, "Survey. . .1939," 18690.

20. White, *The Roots of Dependency*, 321. In *Arapahoe Politics* and *Shared Symbols*, Loretta Fowler offers a detailed examination of similar "revolutions in values," or what she calls "reinterpretation of symbols of culture." For a similar argument but in a non-Indian context, see Jean Comaroff, *Body of Power, Spirit of Resistance: The Culture and History of a South African People* (Chicago: University of Chicago Press, 1985).

21. Hewson to Tomlinson, 6 April 1914, NA-APR, RG 200, A-L File, Box 110, File #301; Hewson to Wellcome, 6 April 1918, NA-APR, RG 200, A-L File, Box 110, File #304; Salina Leask Gamble to Edward Marsden, October 1915; Salina Leask Gamble to Duncan, 25 May 1916; both in NA-APR, RG 200, A-L File, Box 116, File #384.

22. Arthur Wellington Clah to William Duncan, 30 June 1914, NA-APR, RG 200, A-L File, Box 110, File 301.

23. Edward Marsden to Reverend J. H. Condit, 6 December 1916, NA-APR, RG 200, A-L, Box 116, File #384.

24. Leonard Carlson, *Indians, Bureaucrats, and Land: The Dawes Act and the Decline of Indian Farming* (Westport, Conn.: Greenwood Press, 1981); Sarah Carter, *Lost Harvests: Prairie Indian Reserve Farmers and Government Policy* (Montreal: McGill-Queen's University Press, 1990).

25. For another view of the link between the economics of the potlatch and its social functions, see James Andrew McDonald, "The Marginalization of the Tsimshian Cultural Ecology: The Seasonal Cycle," in *Native People, Native Lands: Canadian Indians, Inuit and Metis*, ed. Bruce Alden Cox, Carleton Library Series, No. 142 (Ottawa: Carleton University Press, 1991), 189–218.

Bibliography

MANUSCRIPT COLLECTIONS

The Newberry Library, Chicago, Illinois

Ayer, Edward Everett. "Papers concerning the United States Board of Indian Commissioners collected by Mr. Ayer, 1913–1919."

National Archives—Alaska Pacific Branch, Anchorage, Alaska

Sir Henry Wellcome Papers. Record Group 200
Records of the Alaska Division of the Bureau of Indian Affairs Concerning Metlakatla, 1887–1933. Record Group 75.

National Archives—Great Lakes Branch, Chicago, Illinois

Barrow, Wade Guthrie, and Company. "Menominee Indian Mills. Report on Operations for the Period April 1, 1908 to June 30, 1934." Section II, 1935.
Keshena Agency and Menominee Indian Mills. "Correspondence of the Superintendent with the Commissioner of Indian Affairs, 1909–1926." National Archives. Record Group 75. Bureau of Indian Affairs.
———. "Correspondence of the Superintendent with the Commissioner of Indian Affairs, Re: Lumber Prices, 1911–1924." National Archives. Record Group 75. Bureau of Indian Affairs.
Menominee Mills. "Copies of Letters Received by the Superintendent, February 1903–November 1906." Record Group 75. Bureau of Indian Affairs.
———. "Records of the Forest Supervisor, 1905–35." Record Group 75. Bureau of Indian Affairs.

National Archives, Washington, D.C.

Alaska Division. General Correspondence, Southeastern District, Metlakatla. Record Group 75, Series 806.
Green Bay Agency. Letters Received, Office of Indian Affairs, 1881–1907. Record Group 75.
Keshena Agency. Letters Received, Office of Indian Affairs, 1907–1939. Record Group 75, Central Classified Files.

Public Archives of Canada, Manuscript Division, Ottawa, Canada

William Duncan Collection. Correspondence, Diaries, Notebooks, Entry-Books, Mission Records, 1853–1916. MG 29, D 55 (microfilmed).

Tsimshian Tribal Council, Prince Rupert, British Columbia, Canada
Arthur Wellington Clah Papers (photocopies).

THESES AND DISSERTATIONS

Beck, David Robert Martin. "Siege and Survival: Menominee Responses to an Encroaching World." Ph.D. diss., University of Illinois, 1994.
Darling, John D. "The Effects of Culture Contact on the Tsimshian System of Land Tenure During the Nineteenth Century." M.A. thesis, University of British Columbia, 1955.
Dean, Jonathan R. "'Rich Men,' 'Big Powers,' and Wastelands: The Tlingit-Tsimshian Border of the Northern Pacific Littoral, 1799 to 1867." Ph.D. diss., University of Chicago, 1993.
MacKay, Katherine L. "Warrior into Welder: A History of Federal Employment Programs for American Indians, 1878–1972." Ph.D. diss., University of Utah, 1987.
Orfield, Gary C. "Ideology and the Indian: A Study of the Termination Policy." M.A. thesis, University of Chicago, 1965.
Ross, William M. "Salmon Cannery Distribution on the Nass and Skeena Rivers, 1877–1926." M.S. thesis, University of British Columbia, 1967.

GOVERNMENT PUBLICATIONS

"An act to authorize the sale of timber on certain lands reserved for the use of the Menominee tribe of Indians, in the State of Wisconsin." *Public Law* 153 (26 Stats., p. 146), 1889.
Board of Indian Commissioners. *Annual Reports of the Board of Indian Commissioners.* Washington, D.C.: Government Printing Office, 1877–1910.
Bridgeman, S. E. "Rev. William Duncan, the Alaskan Pearl Seeker." S. Doc. 275. 55th Cong., 2d sess.
British Columbia. *Metlakatlah Inquiry, 1884. Report of the Commissioners' Together with the Evidence.* Victoria: Government Printer, 1885.
———. *Papers Connected with the Indian Land Question, 1850–1875.* Victoria: Government Printer, 1875. Reprint, Victoria: Queens Printer, 1987.
British Columbia. Commission Appointed into the Conditions of the Indians of the North-west Coast. *Papers Relating to the Commission Appointed into the Conditions of the Indians of the North-west Coast, 1887.* Victoria: Government Printer, 1887.
Canada. "An Act to encourage the gradual Civilization of this Province, and to amend the laws respective Indians." *20 Vic. cap. 26, 1857.*
Canada. Department of Indian Affairs. *Annual Reports of the Department of Indian Affairs, 1871–88.*
———. *Report of the Superintendent General of Indian Affairs, British Columbia,* 1881.
Collins, J. W. "Report on the Fisheries of the Pacific Coast of the United States." In *United States Commission on Fish and Fisheries, Report for 1888.* Washington, D.C.: GPO, 1892.
Congressional Record. 52d Cong., 1st sess., 1893, Vol. 23, pp. 3405, 4805.
La Follette, Senator Robert M. "Cutting and Sale of Timber on Menominee Indian Reservation, Wis." Sen. Rpt. 6669, 59th Cong., 2d sess. February 14, 1907.

——. "Cutting Timber on Indian Reservations in Wisconsin." 60th Cong., 1st sess., 23 January 1908. Sen. Rpt. 110.

LeMay et al. v. United States, 52 C. Cls. 521 (1917).

Menominee Tribe v. United States, 101 C. Cls. 22, 25 (1944).

Menominee Tribe v. United States, 118 C. Cls. 290, 316, 327 (1951).

Menominee Tribe v. United States, 388, F. 2d 998, 1001 (Ct. Cl. 1967) aff'd 391 U.S. 404 (1968).

Op. Atty. Gen. 194, 195 (1888).

Public Law 36. (1882).

Public Law 74. [La Follette Act]. 35 Stat. 51–52 (1908).

Public Law 327. 34 Stat. 547 (1906).

Rathburn, Richard. "A Review of the Fisheries in the Contiguous Waters of the State of Washington and British Columbia." In *Report of the U.S. Commissioner of Fisheries for 1899*, pp. 253–350. Washington, D.C., 1900.

United States Congress. "Creation of the Annette Island Reserve Alaska." Act of Congress. 26 Stat. 1101, 1891.

United States Congress. House. 20th Cong., 2d sess., 1829, H. Doc. 117.

——. "Cutting of Timber on Indian Reservations in Wisconsin." 59th Cong., 1st sess., 1906, H. Rpt. 287.

——. 59th Cong., 2d sess., 1907, H. Rpt. 7280.

——. "Sale of Certain Timber of the Menominee Indian Reservation, Wisconsin," 59th Cong., 1st sess., 1907, H. Doc. 490.

——. "Cutting of Timber, etc., on Indian Reservations in Wisconsin." 60th Cong., 1st sess., 1908, H. Rpt. 1086.

——. "U.S. Joint Commission to Investigate Indian Affairs." 63d Cong., 3d sess., 1915, H. Doc. 1669.

——. *The Indian Problem*. Resolution of the Committee of One Hundred appointed by the Secretary of the Interior and a review of the Indian Problem. 68th Cong., 1st sess., 1924, H. Doc. 149.

United States Congress. House Debate. "Cutting Timber on the Menominee Indian Reservation." March 16, 1907. *Congressional Record* 48, pp. 3410–14.

United States Congress. Joint Commission on Indian Affairs. *Hearing Before the Joint Commission of the United States to Investigate Indian Affairs*. Part 8, Menominee Indian Reservation. 63d Cong., 2d sess. Washington, D.C.: GPO, 1914.

——. *Hearing Before the Joint Commission of the United States to Investigate Indian Affairs*. Part 8A, Menominee Indian Reservation. 63d Cong., 2d sess. Washington, D.C.: GPO, 1914.

United States Congress, Senate. *Report upon the Customs District, Public Service, and Resources of Alaska Territory, by William Gouverneur Morris, Special Agent of the Treasury Department*. 45th Cong., 3d sess., 1879, S. Ex. Doc. 59.

——. "Proposed Amendment to Senate Bill 2929." 52d Cong., 1st sess., 1892.

——. *Letter from the Secretary of the Interior, Transmitting, in Response to the Resolution of the Senate of May 23, 1898, Copy of a Report Touching the Colony of Natives on Annette Island, Alaska, Prepared by Dr. William Duncan, Together with Copies of the Files and Records of the Department Relating to Annette Island and Its Occupancy by the Metlakahtla Indians and Alaskan Natives*. 55th Cong., 2d sess., 1898, S. Doc. 275.

——. "Cutting and Sale of Timber on Menominee Indian Reservation, Wisconsin." 59th Cong., 2d sess., 1907, S. Rpt. 6669.

——. *Condition of Indian Affairs in Wisconsin*. Hearings Before the Committee on Indian Affairs, United States Senate, on Senate Resolution No. 263, 60th Cong., 2d sess. Washington, D.C.: GPO, 1910.

————. Committee on Indian Affairs. *Survey of Conditions of the Indians of the United States.* Part 33. Hearings June 29 and July 2, 1934. Washington, D.C.: GPO, 1934.

————. Subcommittee on Indian Affairs. "Survey of Conditions of the Indians in the United States." *Part 35, Metlakahtla Indians.* 74th Cong., 2d sess. Washington, D.C.: GPO, 1939.

United States Department of the Interior. *Rules and Regulations for Annette Island Reserve, Alaska. For Metlakahtla Indians and Other Alaskan Natives.* Washington, D.C.: GPO, 1915.

United States Department of the Interior, Bureau of Indian Affairs. *Annual Reports of the Comissioner of Indian Affairs.* Washington, D.C.: GPO, 1870–1930.

United States v. Cook, 19 Wallace, 591 (1874).

Wallace P. Cook and Charles W. Chickeney, et al. v. Menominee Tribe of Indians and the United States of America 54 C. Cls. 208–211 (1919).

INTERVIEWS CONDUCTED BY THE AUTHOR

Booth, Arnold. Interview with author. Metlakatla, Alaska. 28 July 1995. Tape in possession of the author. Duplicate copy in possession of the Metlakatla Indian Community, Metlakatla, Alaska.

Hayward, Russell. Interview with author. Metlakatla, Alaska, 28 July 1995, 9 August 1995. Tape in possession of the author. Duplicate copy in possession of the Metlakatla Indian Community, Metlakatla, Alaska.

Leask, Joyce, and Elvin Leask. Interview with author. Metlakatla, British Columbia, 2 August 1995. Tape in possession of the author. Duplicate copy in possession of the Metlakatla Indian Reserve, Metlakatla, British Columbia.

Waukau, Lawrence. Telephone interview with author. 20 March 1998. Tape in possession of the author.

PUBLISHED PRIMARY SOURCES

Abbott, Frederick H. *The Administration of Indian Affairs in Canada.* Washington, D.C.: GPO, 1915.

Arctander, John W. *The Apostle of Alaska: The Story of William Duncan of Metlakahtla.* New York: Fleming H. Revell, 1909.

Ayer, Edward E. *Report on Menominee Indian Reservation.* Washington, D.C.: Board of Indian Commissioners, 1914.

Begg, Alexander. *A Sketch of the Successful Missionary Work of William Duncan, 1858–1901.* Victoria: by the author, 1910.

British Columbia. *Guide to the Province of British Columbia for 1877–78.* Victoria: T. N. Hibben and Co., 1878.

Carlisle Indian School. *The Red Man.* Vols. 1–9 (February 1907–19). New York: Johnson Reprint Co., 1971.

Church Missionary Intelligencer. London: Seeley, Jackson, and Halliday, 1858.

Cockshut, A. O. J. *Anglican Attitudes: A Study of Victorian Religious Controversies.* London: Collins, 1959.

Collison, William H. *In the Wake of the War Canoe.* London: Longmans, Green, 1915.

Crosby, Thomas. *Among the An-ko-me-mums.* Toronto: William Briggs, 1907.

————. *Up and Down the North Pacific Coast by Canoe and Mission Ship.* Toronto: Missionary Society of the Methodist Church, 1914.

Davis, George T. B. *Metlakahtla, A True Narrative of the Red Man*. Chicago: Ram's Horn, 1904.

Duncan, William, ed. *The Metlakahtlan*. Vol. 1, nos. 1–6. March 1888–March 1890.

French, Harold. "Duncan of Metlakahtla Deserted." *Overland Monthly* 62 (October 1913): 327–35.

Gatchet, Anthony Marie. "Five Years in America (Cinq Ans en Amerique): Journal of a Missionary Among Redskins, 1859." Translated by Joseph Schafer. *Wisconsin Magazine of History* 18 (1834–35): 66–76, 191–204, 345–59.

Helmcken, Dr. J. S. "The Metlakahtlans." *Daily Colonist* [Victoria], 2 November 1886.

Indian Rights Association. *Annual Reports of the Indian Rights Association*. Philadelphia: Indian Rights Association, 1890–1920.

———. *Indian Truth*. Edited by Matthiew K. Sniffen. Vols. 1–2 (1924–25); 3–4 (1926–27); 5–6 (1928–29); 7–8 (1930–31). Philadelphia: Indian Rights Association.

Leask, David. "Belligerent Indians." *Daily Colonist* [Victoria], 30 October 1886.

Macdonald, Duncan George Forbes, C.E. *British Columbia and Vancouver's Island. Comprising a Description of These Dependencies: Their Physical Character, Climate, Capabilities, Population, Trade, Natural History, Geology, Ethnology, Gold-Fields, and Future Prospects. Also, an Account of the Manners and Customs of the Native Indians*. London: Longman, 1862.

Marsden, Edward. "Father Duncan and His Converts. The Future of Metlakahtla." Ketchikan *Progressive*, 27 March 1915.

Mayne, R. C. *Four Years in British Columbia and Vancouver Island: An Account of Their Forests, Rivers, Coasts, Gold Fields, and Resources for Colonisation*. London: John Murray, 1862.

Moorehead, Warren K. *The American Indian in the United States, 1850–1914*. Andover, Mass.: Andover Press, 1914.

Morgan, Lewis Henry. "Factory System for Indian Reservations." *Nation*, 27 July 1876, 58–59.

Niblack, Albert P. *The Coast Indians of Southern Alaska and Northern British Columbia*. 1890. Reprint, New York: Johnson Reprint Corp., 1970.

Nicholson, A. S. "The Menominee Indians Working Their Way." *The Red Man* 5, no. 1 (September 1912): 17–23.

Pierce, William Henry. *From Potlatch to Pulpit, Being the Autobiography of the Rev. William Henry Pierce, Native Missionary to the Indian Tribes of the Northwest Coast of British Columbia*. Vancouver: Vancouver Bindery, 1933.

Proceedings of the Annual Meetings of the Lake Mohonk Conference of Friends of the Indian. Philadelphia: Lake Mohonk Conference on the Indian, 1883–1916.

Scidmore, E. Ruhamah. *Alaska: Its Southern Coast and the Sitkan Archipelago*. Boston: D. Lothrup and Co., 1885.

Scott, Duncan Campbell. "Indian Affairs, 1867–1912." In *Canada and Its Provinces: A History of the Canadian People and their Institutions by One Hundred Associates*, edited by Adam Shortt and Arthur G. Doughty, 7:591–626. Toronto: Glasgow, Brook and Co., 1914.

Sessions, Francis C. *From Yellowstone Park to Alaska*. New York: Welch, Fracker Co., 1890.

Shawano County Advocate, 16 April 1882.

Society of American Indians. *Quarterly Journal of the Society of American Indians* 1, no. 1, 15 April 1913.

Stock, Eugene. *The History of the Church Missionary Society, Its Environment, Its Men and Its Work*. Vols. 1–3. London: Church Missionary Society, 1899.

Thwaits, Reuben G., ed. *The Jesuit Relations and Allied Documents: Travel and Explorations of the Jesuit Missionaries in New France, 1610–1791.* 73 vols. Cleveland: Burrows Brothers, 1896–1901.
Vaux, George, J. "The Menominee Indian Reservation." Report of Mr. George Vaux Jr., Chairman of the Board of Indian Commissioners, 1922. Washington, D.C.: Board of Indian Commissioners, 1922.
Walker, Francis A. *The Indian Question.* Boston: J. R. Osgood and Co., 1874.
Wellcome, Henry S. *The Story of Metlakahtla.* New York: Saxon and Co., 1887.
"With Words of Fire: How the Indians at Keshena Defended Their Property." Milwaukee *Daily Sentinal,* 2 July 1890.

SECONDARY SOURCES

Articles

Ajayi, J. F. A. "Henry Venn and the Policy of Development." *Journal of the Historical Society of Nigeria* 6 (December 1959): 331–42.
Anders, Gary C. "Theories of Underdevelopment and the American Indian." *Journal of Economic Issues* 14 (September 1980): 681–701.
———. "The Reduction of a Self-Sufficient People to Poverty and Welfare Dependence: An Analysis of the Causes of Cherokee Indian Underdevelopment." *American Journal of Economics and Sociology* 40 (July 1981): 225–37.
Baird, W. David. "Are the Five Tribes of Oklahoma 'Real Indians'?" *Western Historical Quarterly* 21 (February 1990): 5–20.
Barbeau, Marius C. "Tsimshian Myths." In *National Museum of Canada, Bulletin No. 174.* Ottawa: National Museum of Canada, 1961.
Barnett, Homer G. "Personal Conflicts and Cultural Change." *Social Forces* 20 (March 1941): 160–71.
———. "Applied Anthropology in 1860." *Applied Anthropology* 1 (April–June 1942): 19–32.
Barrett, S. A. "The Dream Dance of the Chippewa and Menominee Indians of Northern Wisconsin." In *Bulletin of the Public Museum of the City of Milwaukee,* vol. 1, article 4, pp. 253–406. Milwaukee: Milwaukee Public Museum, 1911.
Barsh, Russell Lawrence. "Contemporary Marxist Theory and Native American Reality. *American Indian Quarterly* 12 (Summer 1988): 187–212.
Bee, Robert, and Ronald Ginerich. "Colonialism, Classes, and Ethnic Identity: Native Americans and the National Political Economy." *Studies in Comparative International Developement* 12 (Summer 1977): 70–93.
Bendix, Reinhard. "Tradition and Modernity Reconsidered." *Comparative Studies in Society and History* 9 (1967): 292–346.
Beynon, William. "The Tshimshians of Metlakatla, Alaska." *American Anthropologist,* n.s., 43 (1941): 83–88.
Boos, Franz. "Tsimshian Texts." In *Bureau of American Ethnology, Bulletin No. 27,* 1–244. Washington, D.C.: Bureau of American Ethnology, 1902.
———. "Tsimshian Mythology." In *Thirty-first Annual Report of the Bureau of American Ethnology.* Washington, D.C.: Bureau of American Ethnology, 1916.
Boxberger, Daniel L. "In and Out of the Labor Force: The Lummi Indians and the Development of the Commercial Salmon Fishery of North Puget Sound, 1880–1900." *Ethnohistory* 35 (Spring 1988): 99–130.

——. "The Lummi Indians and the Canadian/American Pacific Salmon Treaty." *American Indian Quarterly* 12 (Fall 1988): 299–311.

Boyd, Robert T. "Demographic History, 1774–1874." In *Northwest Coast*, edited by Wayne Suttles, 135–48. Vol. 7 of *Handbook of North American Indians*, edited by William C. Sturtevant. Washington, D.C.: Smithsonian Institution Press, 1990.

Brass, E. "The File Hills Colony." *Saskatchewan History* 6 (Spring 1953): 45–59.

Braund, Kathryn Holland. "Guardians of Tradition and Handmaidens to Change: Women's Roles in Creek Economic and Social Life in the Eighteenth Century." *American Indian Quarterly* 14 (1990): 239–58.

Brockman, C. Thomas. "Reciprocity and Market Exchange on the Flathead Reservation." *Northwest Anthropological Research Notes* 5 (Spring 1971): 77–96.

Brown, R. Gordon. "Missions and Cultural Diffusion." *American Journal of Sociology* 50 (November 1944): 214–20.

Buffalohead, Priscilla K. "Farmers, Warriors, Traders: A French Look at Ojibway Women." *Minnesota History* 48 (1983): 236–44.

Carporaso, James A. "Dependence, Dependency, and Power in the Global System: A Structural and Behavioral Analysis." *International Organization* 32 (Winter 1978): 13–43.

Champagne, Duane. "Social Structure, Revitalization Movements and State Building: Social Change in Four Native American Societies." *American Sociological Review* 48 (December 1983): 754–63.

——. *Strategies and Conditions of Political and Cultural Survival in American Indian Societies.* Cultural Survival, Occasional Papers, No. 21. Boston: Cultural Survival, 1985.

Chase-Dunn, Christopher, and Thomas D. Hall. "World Systems in North America: Networks, Rise and Fall and Pulsations of Trade in Stateless Systems." *American Indian Culture and Research Journal* 22 (1998): 23–72.

Cole, Douglas, and David Darling. "History of the Early Period." In *Northwest Coast*, edited by Wayne Suttles, 119–34. Vol. 7 of *Handbook of North American Indians*, edited by William C. Sturtevant. Washington, D.C.: Smithsonian Institution Press, 1990.

Cooper, Carol. "Native Women of the Northern Pacific Coast: An Historical Perspective." *Revue d'etudes canadiennes/Journal of Canadian Studies* 27 (Winter 1992–93): 44–75.

Drucker, Philip. "Rank, Wealth, and Kinship in Northwest Coast Society." *American Anthropologist* 41 (January–March 1939): 55–64.

——. "The Native Brotherhoods: Modern Intertribal Organizations on the Northwest Coast." *Smithsonian Institution, Bureau of American Ethnology, Bulletin No. 168.* Washington, D.C.: GPO, 1958.

Dunn, John A., and Arnold Booth. "Tsimshian of Metlakatla, Alaska." In *Northwest Coast*, edited by Wayne Suttles, 294–97. Vol. 7 of *Handbook of North American Indians*, edited by William C. Sturtevant. Washington, D.C.: Smithsonian Institution Press, 1990.

Edmunds, Newton. "Economic Development of Indian Reserves." *Human Organization* 20 (Winter 1961–62): 197–202.

Fisher, Robin. "The Impact of European Settlement on the Indigenous Peoples of Australia, New Zealand, and British Columbia: Some Comparative Dimensions." *Canadian Ethnic Studies* 12 (1980): 1–14.

Fiske, Jo-Anne. "Colonization and the Decline of Women's Status: The Tsimshian Case." *Feminist Studies* 17 (Fall 1991): 509–35.

Fowler, Verna. "Menominee." In *Encyclopedia of North American Indians,* edited by Frederick E. Hoxie, 371–73. Boston: Houghton Mifflin, 1996.

Furniss, Elizabeth. "Resistance, Coercion, and Revitalization: The Shuswap Encounter with Roman Catholic Missionaries, 1860–1900." *Ethnohistory* 42, (Spring 1995): 231–63.

Galois, R. M. "Colonial Encounters: The Worlds of Arthur Wellington Clah, 1855–1881." *BC Studies* 115/116 (Autumn/Winter 1997/98): 105–47.

Garfield, Viola. "A Research Problem in Northwest Indian Economics." *American Anthropologist* 47 (1945): 627–30.

Goldman, Irving. "Evolution and Anthropology." *Victorian Studies* 3 (September 1959): 55–75.

Gresko, Jacqueline. "White 'Rites' and Indian 'Rites': Indian Education and Native Responses in the West, 1870–1910." In *Western Canada: Past and Present,* edited by Anthony W. Rasporich, 163–81. Calgary: McClelland and Stewart West, 1975.

Grumet, Robert Steven. "Changes in Coast Tsimshian Redistributive Activities in the Fort Simpson Region of British Columbia, 1788–1862." *Ethnohistory* 22 (Fall 1975): 294–318.

Gudeman, Stephen. "A View of the North from the South." In *Overcoming Economic Dependency.* The Newberry Library, D'Arcy McNickle Center for the History of the American Indian, Occasional Papers in Curriculum Series, Occasional Paper No. 9, 8–24. Chicago: The Newberry Library, 1988.

Hagan, William T. "Private Property, the Indian's Door to Civilization." *Ethnohistory* 3 (Spring 1956): 126–37.

———. "United States Indian Policies, 1860–1900." In *History of Indian-White Relations,* edited by Wilcomb E. Washburn, 51–65. Vol. 4 of *Handbook of North American Indians,* edited by William C. Sturtevant. Washington, D.C.: Smithsonian Institution Press, 1988.

Hall, Thomas D. "Peripheries, Regions of Refuge, and Nonstate Societies: Toward a Theory of Reactive Social Change." *Social Science Quarterly* 64 (1983): 582–95.

———. "Incorporation into the World System: Toward a Critique." *American Sociological Review* 51 (June 1986): 390–402.

———. "Native Americans and Incorporation: Patterns and Problems." *American Indian Culture and Research Journal* 11 (1987): 1–30.

———. "Historical Sociology and Native Americans: Methodological Problems." *American Indian Quarterly* 13 (Summer 1989): 223–38.

Halpin, Marjorie M., and Margaret Seguin. "Tsimshian Peoples: Southern Tsimshian, Coast Tsimshian, Nishga, and Gitksan." In *Northwest Coast,* edited by Wayne Suttles, 267–84. Vol. 7 of *Handbook of North American Indians,* edited by William C. Sturtevant. Washington, D.C.: Smithsonian Institution Press, 1990.

Harkin, Michael E. "Power and Progress: The Evangelic Dialogue Among the Heiltsuk." *Ethnohistory* 40 (1993): 1–33.

———. "Engendering Discipline: Discourse and Counterdiscourse in the Methodist-Heiltsuk Dialogue." *Ethnohistory* 43 (Fall 1996): 643–66.

Harrison, J. F. C. "The Victorian Gospel of Success." *Victorian Studies* 1 (December 1957): 155–64.

Heritage, William. "Forestry, Past and Future, on Indian Reservations in Minnesota." *Journal of Forestry* 34 (July 1936): 648–52.

———. "Forestry Accomplishments in the Indian Service in the United States." *Journal of Forestry* 37 (September 1939): 717–18.

Hertzberg, Hazel Whitman. "Indian Rights Movement, 1887–1973." In *History of Indian-White Relations*, edited by Wilcomb E. Washburn, 66–80. Vol. 4 of *Handbook of North American Indians*, edited by William C. Sturtevant. Washington, D.C.: Smithsonian Institution Press, 1988.

Hertzberg, Stephen J. "The Menominee Indians: From Treaty to Trusteeship." *Wisconsin Magazine of History* 60 (Summer 1977): 267–329.

Hilger, M. Inez. "Some Early Customs of the Menomini Indians." *Journal de la Société des Americanistes de Paris*, n.s., 49 (1960): 45–68.

Hoffman, Walter James. "The Menomini Indians." In *Fourteenth Annual Report of the Bureau of Ethnology, for the Years 1892–93*, 11–315. Washington, D.C.: GPO, 1896.

Hosmer, Brian C. "Creating Indian Entrepreneurs: The Menominees, Neopit Mills, and Timber Exploitation, 1890–1915." *American Indian Culture and Research Journal* 15 (1991): 1–28.

———. "'White Men Are Putting Their Hands into Our Pockets': Metlakatla and the Struggle for Resource Rights in British Columbia, 1862–1887." *Alaska History* 8 (Fall 1993): 1–20.

———. "Reflections on Indian Cultural 'Brokers': Reginald Oshkosh, Mitchell Oshkenaniew, and the Politics of Menominee Lumbering." *Ethnohistory* 44 (Summer 1997): 493–509.

Hoxie, Frederick E. "The End of the Savage: Indian Policy in the United States Senate, 1880–1900." *Chronicles of Oklahoma* 45 (Summer 1977): 157–79.

Jacobson, Cardell. "Internal Colonialism and Native Americans: Indian Labor in the United States from 1871 to World War II." *Social Science Quarterly* 65 (1984): 158–71.

Jamieson, Stuart. "Native Indians and the Trade Union Movement in British Columbia." *Human Organization* 20 (Winter 1961–62): 219–25.

Jenks, Albert E. "The Wild Rice Gatherers of the Upper Lakes: A Study in American Primitive Economics." In *Nineteenth Annual Report of the Bureau of American Ethnology for the Years 1897–98*, 1013–1137. Washington, D.C.: GPO, 1900.

Jorgensen, Joseph. "A Century of Political Economic Effects on American Indian Society, 1880–1980." *Journal of Ethnic Studies* 6 (1978): 1–82.

Kay, Jeanne. "Wisconsin Indian Hunting Patterns, 1634–1836." *Annals of the Association of American Geographers* 69 (1979): 403–15.

Keller, Robert H. "America's Native Sweet: Chippewa Treaties and the Right to Harvest Maple Sugar." *American Indian Quarterly* 13 (Spring 1989): 117–36.

Kelly, Lawrence C. "United States Indian Policies, 1900–1980." In *History of Indian-White Relations*, edited by Wilcomb E. Washburn, 66–80. Vol. 4 of *Handbook of North American Indians*, edited by William C. Sturtevant. Washington, D.C.: Smithsonian Institution Press, 1988.

Kew, J. E. Michael. "History of Coastal British Columbia Since 1846." In *Northwest Coast*, edited by Wayne Suttles, 159–68. Vol. 7 of *Handbook of North American Indians*, edited by William C. Sturtevant. Washington, D.C.: Smithsonian Institution Press, 1990.

Kinney, J. P., with Elwood R. Mander and George Morgan Jr. "Beginning Indian Land Forestry: An Oral History Interview." *Forest History* 15 (July 1971): 6–15.

Leacock, Eleanor. "Montagnais Women and the Jesuit Program for Colonization." In *Women and Colonization: Anthropological Perspectives*, edited by Mona Etienne and Eleanor Leacock. New York: Prager, 1980.

Lemert, Edwin. "The Life and Death of an Indian State." *Human Organization* 13 no. 3 (1954): 23–27.

Lewis, David Rich. "Reservation Leadership and the Progressive-Traditional Dichotomy: William Wash and the Northern Utes, 1865–1928." *Ethnohistory* 38 (1991): 124–42.

Lurie, Nancy Oestreich. "Menominee Termination: From Reservation to Colony." *Human Organization* 31 (Fall 1972): 257–70.

———. "Relations Between Indians and Anthropologists." In *History of Indian-White Relations*, edited by Wilcomb E. Washburn, 549–61. Vol. 4 of *Handbook of North American Indians*, edited by William C. Sturtevant. Washington, D.C.: Smithsonian Institution Press, 1988.

McDonald, James Andrew. "The Marginalization of the Tsimshian Cultural Ecology: The Seasonal Cycle." In *Native People, Native Lands: Canadian Indians, Inuit and Metis*, edited by Bruce Alden Cox, 189–218. Ottawa: Carleton University Press, 1991.

Marsden, Susan, and Robert Galois. "The Tsimshian, the Hudson's Bay Company, and the Geopolitics of Northwest Coast Fur Trade, 1787–1840." *The Canadian Geographer/Le Geographie canadien* 39 (1995): 169–83.

Mathes, Valerie Sherer. "Nineteenth-Century Women and Reform: The Women's National Indian Association." *American Indian Quarterly* 14 (Winter 1990): 1–18.

Mooney, James, "The Ghost Dance Religion and the Sioux Outbreak of 1890," *Bureau of American Ethnology, Annual Report for 1892–93*. Vol. 14, no. 2. Washington, D.C.: GPO, 1896.

Moore, Joan W. "American Minorities and 'New Nation' Perspectives." *Pacific Sociological Review* 19 (October 1976): 447–67.

Murphy, Nancy Eldersveld. "Autonomy and the Economic Roles of Indian Women of the Fox-Winnebago River Region, 1763–1832." In *Negotiators of Change: Historical Perspectives on Native American Women*, edited by Nancy Shoemaker, 72–89. New York: Routledge, 1994.

Nathan, Judith. "An Analysis of an Industrial Boarding School, 1847–1860: A Phase in Maori Education." *New Zealand Journal of History* 7, no. 1 (April 1973): 47–59.

Orfield, Gary. "The War on Menominee Poverty." *Wisconsin State Indians Research Institute Journal* 1 (March 1965): 54–63.

Page, Vicki. "Reservation Development in the United States: Periphery to the Core." *American Indian Culture and Research Journal* 9 (1985): 21–35.

Peroff, Nicholas C. "Menominee." In *Native America in the Twentieth Century, An Encyclopedia*, edited by Mary B. Davis, 329–30. New York: Garland, 1994.

Pottinger, Richard. "Indian Reservation Labor Markets: A Navajo Assessment and Challenge." *American Indian Culture and Research Journal* 9 (1985): 1–20.

Provinse, John. "The American Indian in Transition." *American Anthropologist*, n.s., 56 (1954): 386–94.

Redfield, Robert, Ralph Linton, and Melvin J. Herskovits, eds. "A Memorandum on the Study of Acculturation." *American Anthropologist*, n.s., 38 (1936): 149–52.

Redford, James. "Attendance at Indian Residential Schools in British Columbia, 1890–1912." *BC Studies* 44 (Winter 1979–80): 41–56.

Ritzenthaler, Robert E. "The Menominee Indian Sawmill: A Successful Community Project." *Wisconsin Archaeologist*, n.s., 32 (June 1951): 39–44.

Robertson, Melvin L. "A Brief History of the Menominee Indians." *Wisconsin State Indian Research Institute Journal* 1 (March 1965): 4–19.

Sady, Rachel Reese. "The Menominee: Transition from Trusteeship." *Applied Anthropology* 6, no. 2 (Spring 1947): 1–14.

Satterlee, John V. "Folklore of the Menomini Indians." In *Anthropological Papers of the American Museum of Natural History.* Vol. 12, pt. III. New York: American Museum of Natural History, 1915.

Shoemaker, Nancy. "The Rise or Fall of Iroquois Women." *Journal of Women's History* 2 (1991): 39–57.

Simmons, William. "Culture Theory in Contemporary Ethnohistory." *Ethnohistory* 35 (Winter 1988): 1–14.

Skinner, Alanson B. "Social Life and Ceremonial Bundles of the Menomini Indians." In *Anthropological Papers of the American Museum of Natural History.* Vol. 13, pt. I, pp. 1–165. New York: American Museum of Natural History, 1913.

———. "Associations and Ceremonies of the Menomini Indians." In *Anthropological Papers of the American Museum of Natural History.* Vol. 12, pt. II. New York: American Museum of Natural History, 1915.

———. "Menominee Sketches." *Wisconsin Archaeologist* 20 (1921): 41–74.

Skinner, Alanson B., and John V. Satterlee. "Folklore of the Menomini Indians." In *Anthropological Papers of the American Museum of Natural History.* Vol. 13, pt. III. New York: American Museum of Natural History, 1915.

Smith, Glenn. "Education for the Natives of Alaska: The Work of the United States Bureau of Education, 1884–1931." *Journal of the West* 6 (July 1967): 440–50.

Snipp, C. Matthew. "The Changing Political and Economic Status of the American Indians: From Captive Nations to Internal Colonies." *American Journal of Economics and Sociology* 45 (April 1986): 145–57.

———. "American Indians and Natural Resource Development: Indigenous Peoples' Land, Now Sought After, Has Produced New Indian–White Problems." *American Journal of Economics and Sociology* 45 (October 1986): 457–74.

Spindler, Louise D. "Menominee." In *Northeast,* edited by Bruce G. Trigger, 708–24. Vol. 15 of *Handbook of North American Indians,* edited by William C. Sturtevant. Washington, D.C.: Smithsonian Institution Press, 1988.

Spindler, Louise S. "Male and Female Adaptations in Culture Change." *American Anthropologist* 60 (1958): 217–33.

Surtees, Robert J. "Canadian Indian Policies." In *History of Indian-White Relations,* edited by Wilcomb E. Washburn, 202–10. Vol. 4 of *Handbook of North American Indians,* edited by William C. Sturtevant. Washington, D.C.: Smithsonian Institution Press, 1988.

Suttles, Wayne. "Coping with Abundance: Subsistence on the Northwest Coast." In *Man the Hunter: The First Intensive Survey of a Single, Crucial Stage of Human Development—Man's Once Universal Hunting Way of Life,* edited by Richard B. Lee and Irven DeVore, 56–68. 2d ed. New York: Aldine, 1987.

Szasz, Margaret Connell, and Carmelita S. Ryan. "American Indian Education." In *History of Indian-White Relations,* edited by Wilcomb E. Washburn, 284–300. Vol. 4 of *Handbook of North American Indians,* edited by William C. Sturtevant. Washington, D.C.: Smithsonian Institution Press, 1988.

Tollefson, Kenneth D. "From Localized Clans to Regional Corporations: The Acculturation of the Tlingit." *Western Canadian Journal of Anthropology* 8 (1975): 1–20.

Twining, Charles E. "Plunder and Progress: The Lumbering Industry in Historical Perspective." *Wisconsin Magazine of History* 47 (Winter 1963–64): 116–24.

Usher, Jean. "Apostles and Aborigines: The Social Theory of the Church Missionary Society." *Histoire Sociale-Social History* 7 (April 1971): 50–70.

Vogt, Evan Z. "The Acculturation of American Indians." *Annals of the American Academy of Political and Social Science* 311 (1957): 137–46.

Woehlke, Walter V. "Success Story: Menominee Forest." *American Indian* 2 (Spring 1944): 13–17.

Wyatt, Victoria. "Alaskan Indian Wage Earners in the Nineteenth Century." *Pacific Northwest Quarterly* 78 (January–April 1987): 43–49.

Zaslow, Morris. "The Missionary as Social Reformer: The Case of William Duncan." *Journal of the Canadian Church Historical Society* 8 (September 1966): 52–68.

Books

Adams, John W. *The Gitksan Potlatch: Population Flux, Resource Ownership, and Reciprocity.* Toronto: Holt, Rinehart and Winston of Canada, 1973.

Adams, William Y. *Shonto: A Study of the Role of the Trader in a Modern Navajo Community.* Bulletin No. 188. Washington, D.C.: Bureau of American Ethnology, 1963.

Ajayi, J. F. A. *Church Missions in Nigeria, 1841–1891: The Making of a New Elite.* Evanston, Ill.: Northwestern University Press, 1965.

Ambler, Marjane. *Breaking the Iron Bonds: Indian Control of Energy Development.* Lawrence: University Press of Kansas, 1990.

Anderson, Gary Clayton. *Kinsmen of Another Kind: Dakota-White Relations in the Upper Mississippi Valley, 1650–1862.* Lincoln: University of Nebraska Press, 1984.

Baran, Paul. *The Political Economy of Growth.* New York: Monthly Review Press, 1957.

Barbeau, Marius C. *The Downfall of Temlaham.* Toronto: Macmillan, 1928.

Barnett, Homer G. *The Coast Salish of British Columbia.* Westport, Conn.: Greenwood Press, 1975.

Barrera, Mario. *Race and Culture in the Southwest: A Theory of Racial Inequality.* Notre Dame, Ind.: University of Notre Dame Press, 1979.

Bee, Robert L. *The Politics of American Indian Policy.* Cambridge, Mass.: Stenkman, 1982.

Berkhofer, Robert F., Jr. *The White Man's Indian: Images of the American Indian from Columbus to the Present.* New York: Vintage Books, 1978.

Bieder, Robert E. *Science Encounters the Indian: The Early Years of American Ethnology.* Norman: University of Oklahoma Press, 1986.

Bishop, Charles A. *The Northern Ojibwa and the Fur Trade: An Historical and Ecological Study.* Toronto: Holt, Rinehart and Winston of Canada, 1974.

Blair, Emma Helen, ed. *The Indian Tribes of the Upper Mississippi Valley and Region of the Great Lakes.* Vol. 2. Cleveland: Arthur H. Clark, 1911.

Bloomfield, L. *Menomini Texts.* Publications of the American Ethnological Society, vol. 12. New York: American Ethnological Society, 1928.

Boas, Franz. *The Indians of British Columbia: Tlingit, Haida, Tsimshian, Kotmaqa.* Report of the British Association for the Advancement of Science, 1889. Fifth Report on the Northwestern Tribes of Canada. London: British Association for the Advancement of Science, 1890.

Bolt, Christine. *Victorian Attitudes Toward Race.* London: Routledge and Kegan Paul, 1971.

Bolt, Clarence. *Thomas Crosby and the Tsimshian: Small Shoes for Feet Too Large.* Vancouver: University of British Columbia Press, 1993.

Boxberger, Daniel L. *To Fish in Common: The Ethnohistory of Lummi Indian Salmon Fishing.* Lincoln: University of Nebraska Press, 1989.

Brown, Jennifer S. H. *Strangers in Blood: Fur Trade Company Families in Indian Country.* Vancouver: University of British Columbia Press, 1980.

Brumble, H. David, III. *American Indian Autobiography.* Berkeley: University of California Press, 1988.

Burt, Larry W. *Tribalism in Crisis: Federal Indian Policy, 1953–61*. Albuquerque: University of New Mexico Press, 1982.

Cail, R. E. *Land, Men and the Law: The Disposal of Crown Land in British Columbia, 1871–1913*. Vancouver: University of British Columbia Press, 1974.

Cairns, H. A. C. *The Clash of Cultures: Early Race Relations in Central Africa*. New York: Praeger, 1965.

Callender, Charles. *Social Organization of the Central Algonkian Indians*. Milwaukee Public Museum, Publications in Anthropology, No. 7. Milwaukee: Milwaukee Public Museum, 1962.

Carlson, Leonard. *Indians, Bureaucrats, and Land: The Dawes Act and the Decline of Indian Farming*. Westport, Conn.: Greenwood Press, 1981.

Carter, Sarah. *Lost Harvests: Prairie Indian Reserve Farmers and Government Policy*. Montreal: McGill-Queen's University Press, 1990.

Chapman, H. H. *The Menominee Indian Timber Case History: Proposals for Settlement*. New Haven, Conn.: Yale University School of Law, 1957.

Chase-Dunn, Christopher, and Thomas D. Hall. *Rise and Demise: Comparing World Systems*. Boulder, Colo.: Westview Press, 1997.

Chilicote, Ronald H., and Dale L. Johnston, eds. *Theories of Development*. Beverly Hills, Calif.: Sage, 1983.

Codere, Helen. *Fighting with Property: A Study of Kwakiutl Potlatching and Warfare, 1792–1930*. Monographs of the American Ethnological Society, 18. New York: J. J. Augustin, 1950.

Cole, Douglas, and Ira Chaikin. *An Iron Hand upon the People: The Law Against the Potlatch on the Northwest Coast*. Seattle: University of Washington Press, 1990.

Comaroff, Jean. *Body of Power, Spirit of Resistance: The Culture and History of a South African People*. Chicago: University of Chicago Press, 1985.

Comaroff, John, and Jean Comaroff. *Ethnography and the Historical Imagination*. Boulder, Colo.: Westview Press, 1992.

Congressional Quarterly. *Congressional Quarterly's Guide to U.S. Elections*. 2d ed. Washington, D.C.: Congressional Quarterly, 1985.

Cooley, Richard A. *Politics and Conservation: The Decline of the Alaska Salmon*. New York: Harper and Row, 1963.

Cornell, Stephen, *The Return of the Native: American Indian Political Resurgence*. New York: Oxford University Press, 1988.

Cove, John J., and George F. MacDonald, eds. *Tsimshian Narratives, I: Tricksters, Shamans and Heroes*. Canadian Museum of Civilization, Mercury Series, Paper No. 3. Ottawa: Canadian Museum of History, 1987.

———. *Tsimshian Narratives, II: Trade and Warfare*. Canadian Museum of Civilization, Mercury Series, Paper No. 3. Ottawa: Canadian Museum of History, 1987.

Cronon, William. *Changes in the Land: Indians, Colonists, and the Ecology of New England*. New York: Hill and Wang, 1983.

Crutchfield, James A., and Giulio Pontecorvo. *The Pacific Salmon Fisheries: A Study of Irrational Conservation*. Baltimore: Johns Hopkins University Press, 1969.

Danziger, Edmund Jefferson. *The Chippewas of Lake Superior*. Norman: University of Oklahoma Press, 1979.

Deloria, Vine, Jr. *American Indian Policy in the Twentieth Century*. Norman: University of Oklahoma Press, 1985.

Deloria, Vine, Jr., and Clifford M. Lytle. *American Indians, American Justice*. Austin: University of Texas Press, 1983.

Devens, Carol. *Countering Colonization: Native American Women and Great Lakes Missions, 1630–1900*. Berkeley: University of California Press, 1992.

Donald, Leland. *Aboriginal Slavery on the Northwest Coast of North America*. Berkeley: University of California Press, 1997.

Dowd, Gregory. *A Spirited Resistance: The North American Indian Struggle for Unity, 1745–1815*. Baltimore: Johns Hopkins University Press, 1992.

Drucker, Philip. *Indians of the Northwest Coast*. New York: American Museum of Natural History Press, 1963.

Duff, Wilson. *The Indian History of British Columbia*. Vol. 1, *The Impact of the White Man*. Anthropology in British Columbia, Memoirs, No. 5. Victoria: Provincial Museum, 1964.

Edmunds, R. David. *The Shawnee Prophet*. Lincoln: University of Nebraska Press, 1983.

Eggan, Fred, ed. *Social Anthropology of North American Tribes*. Enlarged edition. Chicago: University of Chicago Press, 1955.

Fage, J. D. *A History of Africa*. New York: Knopf, 1978.

Fisher, Anthony C. *Resource and Environmental Economics*. New York: Cambridge University Press, 1981.

Fisher, Robin A. *Contact and Conflict: Indian-European Relations in British Columbia, 1774–1890*. Vancouver: University of British Columbia Press, 1977.

Foster, Morris W. *Being Comanche: A Social History of an American Indian Community*. Tucson: University of Arizona Press, 1991.

Fowler, Loretta. *Arapahoe Politics, 1851–1978: Symbols in Crises of Authority*. Lincoln: University of Nebraska Press, 1982.

——. *Shared Symbols, Contested Meanings: Gros Ventre Culture and History, 1778–1984*. Ithaca, N.Y.: Cornell University Press, 1987.

Frank, André Gunder. *Capitalism and Underdevelopment in Latin America: Historical Studies of Chile and Brazil*. New York: Monthly Review Press, 1967.

Fries, Robert F. *Empire in Pine: The Story of Logging in Wisconsin, 1830–1900*. Madison: State Historical Society of Wisconsin, 1951.

Fritz, Henry E. *The Movement for Indian Assimilation, 1860–1900*. Philadelphia: University of Pennsylvania Press, 1966.

Furtado, Celso. *Accumulation and Development*. New York: St. Martin's Press, 1983.

Gallagher, John, and Ronald Robinson. *Africa and the Victorians*. New York: Anchor Books, 1968.

Garfield, Viola E. *Tsimshian Clan and Society*. University of Washington Publications in Anthropology, 7, 3. Seattle: University of Washington Press, 1939.

——. *The Tsimshian and Their Neighbors*. Seattle: University of Washington Press, 1951.

Geertz, Clifford. *The Interpretation of Cultures*. New York: Basic Books, 1973.

Gough, Barry. *Gunboat Frontier: British Maritime Authority and Northwest Coast Indians, 1846–1890*. Vancouver: University of British Columbia Press, 1984.

Grant, John Webster. *Moon over Wintertime: Missionaries and the Indians of Canada in Encounter Since 1534*. Toronto: University of Toronto Press, 1984.

Gruening, Ernest. *The State of Alaska: A Definitive History of America's Northernmost Frontier*. New York: Random House, 1968.

Hagan, William T. *Indian Police and Judges: Experiments in Acculturation and Control*. New Haven, Conn.: Yale University Press, 1966.

——. *The Indian Rights Association: The Herbert Welsh Years, 1882–1904*. Tucson: University of Arizona Press, 1985.

Haller, John S., Jr. *Outcasts from Evolution: Scientific Attitudes of Racial Inferiority, 1859–1900*. Urbana: University of Illinois Press, 1971.

Harkin, Michael E. *The Heiltsuks: Dialogues of Culture and History on the Northwest Coast*. Lincoln: University of Nebraska Press, 1997.

Haviland, William A. *Cultural Anthropology*. 3d ed. New York: Holt, Rinehart and Winston, 1981.

Hawthorn, H. B., C. S. Belshaw, and S. M. Jamieson. *The Indians of British Columbia: A Study of Contemporary Social Adjustment*. Victoria: University of British Columbia Press, 1958.

Hays, Samuel P. *Conservation and the Gospel of Efficiency: The Progressive Conservation Movement, 1890–1920*. Cambridge, Mass.: Harvard University Press, 1959.

Hechter, Michael. *Internal Colonialism: The Celtic Fringe in British National Development, 1536–1966*. Berkeley: University of California Press, 1975.

Henriksson, Markku. *The Indian on Capital Hill: Indian Legislation and the United States Congress, 1862–1907*. Studia Historica 25. Helsinki: Finnish Historical Society, 1988.

Hertzberg, Hazel Whitman. *The Search for an American Indian Identity: Modern Pan-Indian Movements*. Syracuse, N.Y.: Syracuse University Press, 1971.

Hickerson, Harold. *The Chippewas and Their Neighbors*. New York: Holt, Rinehart and Winston, 1970.

Houghton, W. E. *The Victorian Frame of Mind*. New Haven, Conn.: Yale University Press, 1957.

Hoxie, Frederick E. *A Final Promise: The Campaign to Assimilate the Indians, 1880–1920*. Lincoln: University of Nebraska Press, 1984.

————. *Parading Through History: The Making of the Crow Nation in America, 1805–1935*. New York: Cambridge University Press, 1995.

Hurt, R. Douglas. *Indian Agriculture in America: Prehistory to the Present*. Lawrence: University Press of Kansas, 1987.

Iverson, Peter. *The Navajo Nation*. Westport, Conn.: Greenwood Press, 1981.

————. *Carlos Montezuma and the Changing World of Indians*. Albuquerque: University of New Mexico Press, 1982.

————. *When Indians Became Cowboys: Native Peoples and Cattle Ranching in the American West*. Norman: University of Oklahoma Press, 1994.

Jennings, Francis. *The Invasion of America: Indians, Colonialism and the Cant of Conquest*. Chapel Hill: University of North Carolina Press, 1975.

Johnstone, S. M. *Samuel Marsden, a Pioneer of Civilisation in the South Seas*. Sydney: Angus and Robertson, 1932.

Jorgensen, Joseph G. *The Sun Dance Religion: Power for the Powerless*. Chicago: University of Chicago Press, 1972.

Keesing, Felix. *The Menominee Indians of Wisconsin: A Study of Three Centuries of Cultural Contact and Change*. 2d ed. Madison: University of Wisconsin Press, 1987.

Keller, Robert H., Jr. *American Protestantism and United States Indian Policy, 1869–82*. Lincoln: University of Nebraska Press, 1976.

Kinney, J. P. *A Continent Lost—A Civilization Won: Indian Land Tenure in America*. Baltimore: Johns Hopkins University Press, 1937.

————. *Indian Forest and Range: A History of the Administration and Conservation of the Redman's Heritage*. Washington, D.C.: Forestry Enterprises, 1950.

Knight, Rolf. *Indians at Work: An Informal History of Native Indian Labour in British Columbia, 1858–1930*. Vancouver: New Star Books, 1978.

Kolchin, Peter. *Unfree Labor: American Slavery and Russian Serfdom*. Cambridge, Mass.: Belknap Press of Harvard University Press, 1987.

Kvasnicka, Robert M., and Herman J. Viola, eds. *The Commissioners of Indian Affairs, 1824–1977*. Lincoln: University of Nebraska Press, 1979.

Landes, Ruth. *Ojibwa Religion and the Midewiwin*. Madison: University of Wisconsin Press, 1969.

LaViolette, Forrest. *The Struggle for Survival: Indian Cultures and the Protestant Ethic in British Columbia*. Toronto: University of Toronto Press, 1973.

Lee, Richard B., and Irven DeVore, eds. *Man the Hunter: The First Intensive Survey of a Single, Crucial Stage of Human Development—Man's Once Universal Hunting Way of Life*. 2d ed. New York: Aldine de Gruyter, 1987.

Lewis, David Rich. *Neither Wolf nor Dog: American Indians, Environment and Agrarian Change*. New York: Oxford University Press, 1994.

Linton, Ralph, ed. *Acculturation in Seven American Indian Tribes*. New York: Appleton-Century, 1940.

Littlefield, Alice, and Martha C. Knack, eds. *Native Americans and Wage Labor: Ethnohistorical Perspectives*. Norman: University of Oklahoma Press, 1996.

Macgregor, Gordon. *Warriors Without Weapons: A Study of the Society and Personality Development of the Pine Ridge Sioux*. Chicago: University of Chicago Press, 1946.

McEvoy, Arthur. *The Fisherman's Problem: Ecology and Law in the California Fisheries, 1850–1980*. New York: Cambridge University Press, 1987.

Mead, Margaret. *The Changing Culture of an Indian Tribe*. New York: Columbia University Press, 1932.

Meek, Ronald L. *Social Science and the Ignoble Savage*. Cambridge: Cambridge University Press, 1976.

Merriam, Lewis, et al. *The Problems of Indian Administration*. Baltimore: Johns Hopkins University Press, 1928.

Meyer, Melissa L. *The White Earth Tragedy: Ethnicity and Dispossession at a Minnesota Anishinaabe Reservation, 1889–1920*. Lincoln: University of Nebraska Press, 1994.

Miller, James R. *Skyscrapers Hide the Heavens: A History of Indian-White Relations in Canada*. Toronto: University of Toronto Press, 1989.

Miller, Jay. *Tsimshian Culture: A Light Through the Ages*. Lincoln: University of Nebraska Press, 1997.

Miller, Jay, and Carol M. Eastman, eds. *The Tsimshian and Their Neighbors of the North Pacific Coast*. Seattle: University of Washington Press, 1984.

Miner, H. Craig. *The Corporation and the Indian: Tribal Sovereignty and Industrial Civilization in Indian Territory, 1865–1907*. 2d ed. Norman: University of Oklahoma Press, 1988.

Moore, John H. *The Cheyenne Nation: A Social and Demographic History*. Lincoln: University of Nebraska Press, 1987.

Morgan, Lewis Henry. *Ancient Society; or, Researches in the Lines of Human Progress from Savagery Through Barbarism to Civilization*. New York: Henry Holt, 1877.

Morrison, R. Bruce, and C. Roderick Wilson, eds. *Native Peoples: The Canadian Experience*. Toronto: McClelland and Stewart, 1986.

Mowry, George E. *The Era of Theodore Roosevelt and the Birth of Modern America, 1900–1912*. New York: Harper and Brothers, 1958.

Murray, Peter. *The Devil and Mr. Duncan: A History of the Two Metlakatlas*. Vancouver: Sono Nis Press, 1985.

Newell, Dianne. *Tangled Webs of History: Indians and the Law in Canada's Pacific Coast Fisheries*. Toronto: University of Toronto Press, 1993.

Nock, David A. *A Victorian Missionary and Canadian Indian Policy: Cultural Synthesis vs. Cultural Replacement*. Waterloo: Wilfred Laurier University Press, 1987.

Oliver, Roland. *The Missionary Factor in East Africa*. London: Longmans, 1952.

Ormsby, Margaret A. *British Columbia: A History*. Vancouver: Macmillan of Canada, 1958.

Ortiz, Roxanne Dunbar, ed. *Economic Development in American Indian Reservations.* Albuquerque: University of New Mexico Press, 1979.

Ourada, Patricia K. *The Menominee Indians: A History.* Norman: University of Oklahoma Press, 1979.

Pearce, Roy Harvey. *Savagism and Civilization: A Study of the Indian and the American Mind.* Rev. ed. Baltimore: Johns Hopkins University Press, 1971.

Peroff, Nicholas, *Menominee Drums: Tribal Termination and Restoration, 1954–1974.* Norman: University of Oklahoma Press, 1982.

Pinkett, Harold T. *Gifford Pinchot, Private and Public Forester.* Champaign: University of Illinois Press, 1970.

Plattner, Stuart. *Economic Anthropology.* Stanford, Calif.: Stanford University Press, 1989.

Porter, Frank W., III, ed. *Strategies for Survival: American Indians in the Eastern United States.* Westport Conn.: Greenwood Press, 1986.

Priest, Loring Benson. *Uncle Sam's Stepchildren: The Reformation of United States Indian Policy, 1865–1887.* New York: Octagon Books, 1969.

Prucha, Francis Paul. *American Indian Policy in Crisis: Christian Reformers and the Indian, 1865–1900.* Norman: University of Oklahoma Press, 1976.

———. *The Great White Father.* Abridged edition. Lincoln: University of Nebraska Press, 1984.

Rasparich, A. W., ed. *Western Canada: Past and Present.* Calgary: McClelland and Stewart West, 1975.

Raunet, Daniel. *Without Honor, Without Surrender: A History of the Nishga Land Claims.* Vancouver: Douglas and McIntyre, 1984.

Richter, Daniel K. *The Ordeal of the Longhouse: The Peoples of the Iroquois League in the Era of European Colonization.* Chapel Hill: University of North Carolina Press, 1992.

Robbin, Martin. *The Rush for Spoils: The Company Province, 1871–1933.* Toronto: McClelland and Stewart, 1972.

Robbins, William G. *Lumberjacks and Legislators: Political Economy of the U.S. Lumber Industry, 1890–1941.* College Station: Texas A&M University Press, 1984.

———. *American Forestry: A History of National, State, and Private Cooperation.* Lincoln: University of Nebraska Press, 1985.

Rostow, Walt W. *The Stages of Economic Growth.* Cambridge: Cambridge University Press, 1960.

Ruby, Robert H., and John A. Brown. *Indians of the Pacific Northwest: A History.* Norman: University of Oklahoma Press, 1981.

———. *Indian Slavery in the Pacific Northwest.* Spokane, Wash.: A. H. Clark, 1993.

Sahlins, Marshall D. *Islands of History.* Chicago: University of Chicago Press, 1985.

Samek, Hana. *The Blackfoot Confederacy, 1880–1920: A Comparative Study of Canadian and United States Indian Policy.* Albuquerque: University of New Mexico Press, 1987.

Seguin, Margaret, ed. *The Tsimshian: Images of the Past; Views for the Present.* Vancouver: University of British Columbia Press, 1984.

Shoemaker, Nancy, ed. *Negotiators of Change: Historical Perspectives on Native American Women.* New York: Routledge, 1995.

Slotkin, James S. *The Menomini Powwow: A Study in Cultural Decay.* Milwaukee Public Museum Publications in Anthropology, no. 4. Milwaukee, Wis.: Public Museum, 1957.

Spicer, Edward H., ed. *Perspectives in American Indian Culture Change.* Chicago: University of Chicago Press, 1961.

Spindler, George D. *Sociocultural and Psychological Processes in Menominee Acculturation*. University of California Publications in Culture and Society, 5. Berkeley: University of California Press, 1955.

Spindler, George D., and Louise S. Spindler. *Dreamers with Power: The Menominee*. 2d ed. Prospect Heights, Ill.: Waveland Press, 1984.

Stocking, George W., Jr. *Race, Culture and Evolution: Essays in the History of Anthropology*. Rev. ed. Chicago: University of Chicago Press, 1982.

Sunder, John E. *The Fur Trade on the Upper Missouri, 1840–1865*. Norman: University of Oklahoma Press, 1965.

Suttles, Wayne. *Coast Salish Essays*. Seattle: University of Washington Press, 1987.

Szaz, Margaret Connell. *Education and the American Indian: The Road to Self-Determination Since 1928*. Albuquerque: University of New Mexico Press, 1977.

Tennant, Paul. *Aboriginal Peoples and Politics: The Indian Land Question in British Columbia, 1849–1989*. Vancouver: University of British Columbia Press, 1991.

Titley, E. Brian. *A Narrow Vision: Duncan Campbell Scott and the Administration of Indian Affairs in Canada*. Vancouver: University of British Columbia Press, 1986.

Trautmann, Thomas R. *Lewis Henry Morgan and the Invention of Kinship*. Berkeley: University of California Press, 1987.

Usher, Jean. *William Duncan of Metlakatla: A Victorian Missionary in British Columbia*. National Museum of Canada, Publications in History, No. 5. Ottawa: National Museum of Man, 1974.

Utley, Robert M. *Battlefield and Classroom: Four Decades with the American Indian*. New Haven, Conn.: Yale University Press, 1964.

———. *The Indian Frontier of the American West, 1846–1890*. Albuquerque: University of New Mexico Press, 1984.

Van Kirk, Sylvia. *Many Tender Ties: Women in Fur Trade Society, 1676–1870*. Norman: University of Oklahoma Press, 1980.

Vennum, Thomas, Jr. *Wild Rice and the Ojibway People*. St. Paul: Minnesota Historical Society Press, 1988.

Waddell, Jack O., and O. Michael Watson, eds. *The American Indian in Urban Society*. Boston: Little, Brown, 1971.

Wallace, Anthony F. C. *Culture and Personality*. 2d ed. New York: Random House, 1970.

———. *The Death and Rebirth of the Seneca*. New York: Vintage Books, 1972.

Wallerstein, Immanuel. *The Modern World-System: Capitalist Agriculture and the Origins of European World Economy in the Sixteenth Century*. New York: Academic Press, 1974.

Washburn, Wilcomb E. *The Assault on Indian Tribalism: The General Allotment Law (Dawes Act) of 1887*. Philadelphia: Lippincott, 1975.

White, Richard. *The Roots of Dependency: Subsistence, Environment, and Social Change Among the Choctaws, Pawnees, and Navajos*. Lincoln: University of Nebraska Press, 1983.

———. *The Middle Ground: Indians, Empires, and Republics in the Great Lakes Region, 1650–1815*. New York: Cambridge University Press, 1991.

White, Robert H. *Tribal Assets: The Rebirth of Native America*. New York: Henry Holt, 1990.

Wilson, Terry P. *The Underground Reservation: Osage Oil*. Lincoln: University of Nebraska Press, 1985.

Wolf, Eric R. *Europe and the People Without History*. Berkeley: University of California Press, 1982.

Index